The 'Made in Germany' Champion Brands

To my wife, Mercy

The 'Made in Germany' Champion Brands

Nation Branding, Innovation and World Export Leadership

UGESH A. JOSEPH

LONDON AND NEW YORK

First published in paperback 2024

First published 2013 by Gower Publishing

Published 2016 by Routledge
4 Park Square, Milton Park, Abingdon, Oxon OX14 4RN

and by Routledge
605 Third Avenue, New York, NY 10158

Routledge is an imprint of the Taylor & Francis Group, an informa business

Gower Applied Business Research
Our programme provides leaders, practitioners, scholars and researchers with thought provoking, cutting edge books that combine conceptual insights, interdisciplinary rigour and practical relevance in key areas of business and management.

British Library Cataloguing in Publication Data
A catalogue record for this book is available from the British Library.

The Library of Congress has cataloged the printed edition as follows:
Joseph, Ugesh A.
 The 'Made in Germany' champion brands: nation branding, innovation and world export leadership / by Ugesh A. Joseph.
   pages cm
 Includes bibliographical references and index.
  ISBN 978-1-4094-6646-8 (hardback: alk. paper)—ISBN 978-1-4094-6647-5 (ebook)—ISBN 978-1-4094-6648-2 (epub)
  1. Branding (Marketing)—Germany. 2. Export marketing—Germany. I. Title.

HF5415.1255.J678 2013
382.0943—dc23

2013020029

ISBN: 978-1-4094-6646-8 (hbk)
ISBN: 978-1-03-283753-6 (pbk)
ISBN: 978-1-315-55590-4 (ebk)

DOI: 10.4324/9781315555904

Contents

Foreword

As Europe and the world struggle with the aftermath of the financial crisis, Germany as a nation stands resolute in its growth and export sales to the world. Germany, Europe's strongest economy, is seen as a pillar of strength and hope for not only the recession afflicted nations of Europe but also for the global economy.

While the 1989 reunification rejoined East with West Germany, the two sides could not have been more different economically. Germany has since overcome many challenges on its road to becoming the success story that it is today.

The effort the author makes to unravel the apparent mystique of Germany's success to a global audience is truly commendable. From a multi-dimensional, extensively researched perspective, Ugesh Joseph insightfully gives the reader a sense of the nation and its complex character – from its immediate past to its present-day 'Champion Brands' and the nations 'Facilitators and Influencers'.

His studied look at the 'Made in Germany' image and how this affects a nation's positive image, especially its quality image for its products and services, is truly noteworthy. Added to this discussion is his important inclusion of what he calls the 'Facilitators and Influencers' to the 'Made in Germany' image – a significant, holistic element in the nation-branding discussion.

Mr. Joseph professionally selects and classifies around 200 of the best champion brands into relevant and appropriate categories. He then analyses the nation's strongest products and services in terms of size, reputation and importance. Mr. Joseph illustrates how innovation and a pragmatic business sense have helped these champion brand companies to become some of the world's leading exporters today.

This work is essential reading for all those entrepreneurs, managers, academics, students and researchers, the media, government officials and anyone who is connected with Germany or has an interest in knowing more about the country, its prominent products and services and its influential socio-cultural elements.

This book will certainly help the reader to better understand Germany, especially from economic and business perspectives, while giving a sense of its character from a holistic point of view. The author shares useful and insightful information about a nation that has so much to contribute to the world. I wish the book and the author great success that is truly well deserved.

Hermann Simon
Chairman
Simon-Kucher & Partners

1 Branding and the 'Made in Germany' Brand: A Perspective

The image and reputation of countries, like cities and regions of the world, have a process similar to that of companies, products and services. All places have what might be called their brand images. But the process of branding them is still subject to academic and practitioner debate.

Today, with the state of globalisation, the world is one huge, diversified market. What this means to each of those countries/places and regions is that they need to compete for their share of consumers, industrial or other, for their products and services. They must compete to attract tourists, investors, entrepreneurs, skilled labour and students. They must vie for their share of international, sporting and cultural events and, finally, they need to get positive attention and respect from the international media, people of other countries and their governments.

Before we dwell on the specific case of Germany, it would be worthwhile to go through a couple of definitions with relation to a 'brand' and a 'nation brand'. According to P. Doyle in *The Marketing Book*, '... a successful Brand is a name, symbol, design, or some combination, which identifies the 'product' of a particular organisation as having a sustainable differential advantage'. (Doyle)

On the other hand, Lynch and Chernatony define brands, '... as clusters of functional and emotional values that promise a unique and welcome experience between a buyer and a seller'. (Lynch)

While Keith Dinnie, in his book, 'Nation Branding: Concepts, Issues, Practice', states that, 'The Nation Brand is defined as the unique, multi-dimensional blend of elements that provide the nation with culturally grounded differentiation and relevance for all of its target audiences'. (Dinnie)

According to O'Shaughnessy and Jackson, 'The image of a nation is so complex and fluid as to deny the clarity implicit in a term such as brand image; different parts of a nation's identity come into focus on the international stage at different times, affected by current political events and even the latest movie or news bulletin'. (O'Shaughnessy)

Illustrative of this is the case of Germany. After the 2006 Football World Cup celebrations, the internal and external image had markedly changed for the better – in terms of perception by a general audience – to a place that was open to visitors, celebration and enjoyment.

The Football World Cup brought out the best in the German psyche and Germans emerged as a fun-loving, friendly people in contrast to the previous stereotype of being serious and humourless. In fact, the event was a pleasant revelation to the Germans themselves, as they embraced the positive vibe. The degree of enthusiasm, tolerance, warmth and openness during the four-week-long football carnival was a surprise to all. Old clichés and stereotypes were dropped and Germany earned a better, more upbeat and fairer image. Even without these events, Germany needs to maintain this positive energy to help maintain its brand equity in the long run, because it is important to remember that a nation is also perceived from the sum of its individuals.

Germans, generally, tend to be rational and direct in their communication style and punctual and orderly in their home and work life. For the most part, they are meticulous and long-term planners who value reliability in their business relations.

In an annually conducted global survey known as the Nation Brand Index (NBI), Germany scored significantly and was repeatedly ranked higher after the football tournament. Around 20,000 adults in 20 different countries were asked to assess the country's image and reputation in terms of culture, exports, politics, its people and its attractiveness to tourists, immigrants and investments. Germany was named the world's 'Best Overall Brand' among 50 countries measured in 2008.

The NBI founder, Simon Anholt is reported to have said, 'The NBI is a report card for countries, measuring the world's perception of each nation as if it were a public brand. Within the top 10 most positively perceived countries, the ranking reveals a strong correlation between a nation's overall brand and its economic status'. (www.gfk.com/ group/press) This explanation underscores the fact that a nation's products, services, corporate brands and their cumulative success are an integral part of a nation's brand.

In a similar tone, Senior Vice-President and Director of the NBI study at Gfk Roper Public Affairs & Media, Xiaoyan Zhao, states, 'Much as a commercial brand relies on a favourable public opinion to sell products, countries depend on their reputation and image to bring in tourists, business, investment and other facets important to a nation's financial strength and it's international standing'. (www.gfk.com/group/press)

The parallels between the process of corporate branding and nation branding lie in the complexity and multifaceted nature of the two entities, given the multiple target audiences that need to be catered to.

According to Ludlow Schmidt, co-founder of Chris-Ludlow Consultancy, 'Corporate Brands make a nation, but I'm not convinced nations themselves can be brands'.

While Simon Anholt states, '... But national branding is difficult because countries are "complex and contradictory"'. (Booth)

Nevertheless, there are an increasing number of countries around the world believing and practising nation-branding in order to differentiate themselves from other nations and improve their economic performance, especially in relation to tourism, exports and investments.

Accordingly, Simon Anholt, while contributing with a practitioner's insight in Dinnie's book 'Nation Branding', has said, '... Yet, what really seems to make a difference to the images of countries is when they become dedicated to developing new ideas, policies, laws, products, services, companies, buildings, art and science. When those innovations prove a few simple truths about the country they come from, reputation starts to move; the, place produces a buzz, people pay attention and prepare to change their minds'. (Anholt)

The German government had initiated just such a campaign in 2004 on innovation with an Internet portal for information and various events, presentations, lectures, etc., with the slogan 'Partner for Innovation', the objective being to establish cooperation between all relevant institutions in business, politics, science and culture to initiate innovation processes. This is essentially targeting experts, decision-makers, young scientists, creative people and members of the 'Mittelstand' or the small and medium-sized enterprises in Germany.

A similar campaign, started earlier and still in existence, touted Germany as 'The Land of Ideas' and helped to strengthen and maintain Germany's reputation both within the country and abroad. This campaign focuses on its past and present achievements in science and culture, and as a land of poets, thinkers, musicians and scientists with a track record of innovative products to show for it, under the 'Made in Germany' label. The effort was also to build and encourage a network of people and institutions so as to support a range of creative, innovative ideas and initiatives, especially in the area of new business ventures. A multimedia campaign was utilised to target people in Germany and abroad, especially decision-makers, creative people and potential investors into the country. The underlying message is that of a country with a world-class quality reputation thanks to its innovativeness and entrepreneurial spirit.

Wally Olins, Saffron Brand Consultant's Chairman, who led the Wolff-Olins in-depth study of the German 'brand' in 2000, had said, '… a growing emphasis on national stereotypes is leading to "grotesque distortions" of the reality of countries, which must be addressed'. (Booth)

It is a matter of image and identity in which image would refer to how someone, something or some place is perceived, whereas identity refers to what someone, a thing or a place really or truly is.

The gap between the two leads to stereotypes and distortions of the reality of products, services, people and places. Applying branding strategies to nation brands is subject to error, unless all of the multi-dimensional aspects of a country are taken into consideration to reflect its true reality. Sub-systems or their parts cater to individual target groups, for there are many facets to a nation brand identity. The commercial brands of products and services that a nation offers its customers, both domestic and external, represent a major facet of the nation brand identity. Another aspect that embodies the soul or true essence of a nation is its culture, specifically its people, the language, their literature, music, sports and sporting achievements, architecture and design and food and drink habits and so on. Culture is a multi-dimensional whole that distinguishes a people and a nation, a tangible element that makes a people and a nation unique.

According to Philip Glouchevitch in his book, *Juggernaut*, 'The good side of the German character, however, is thoroughness, which Germans more often than not put to good advantage. Take the excellent reputation for quality enjoyed by German products everywhere. As consumers, Germans have been raised to demand the highest quality; as manufacturers, they organise their businesses to satisfy that demand'. (Glouchevitch)

German business is organised to maintain this high quality of manufacturing and precision engineering. Supported by a network of research organisations and with exacting technical standards that are enforced by various technical standards organisations, primarily the TÜV, they regularly inspect for the highest in safety and quality standards.

To most German entrepreneurs, wealth comes from producing quality goods and services and not from speculation, and it is wealth that is shared, in the sense of keeping their workers happy and motivated and engaged in other socially responsible activities.

For centuries, in fact since the Middle Ages, Germany has had a strong history and tradition of stressing quality, as seen in the existence of various craft guilds that trained and mentored a huge reservoir of skilled labour, ingraining the values of quality and hard work. Over the years, these core values of skill, quality, hard work, innovation and efficiency have become a major component of the actual nation brand identity of Germany. This identity has manifested itself in various popular, global brands like the Volkswagen Beetle, Mercedes-Benz luxury coupes, BMW cars, the Porsche sports car, Lufthansa, SAP, Adidas, Puma and so on.

Jaworski and Fosher (2003), in their paper, 'National Brand Identity & Its Effect on Corporate Brands: The Nation Brand Effect (NBE)' state, 'This Nation Brand Identity had a big boost from the Nation Brand Effect (NBE), which in turn, is sustained by the core values that gives rise to the German Brand Identity. In essence, a nation's people, beliefs and history give rise to a Nation's Brand Identity (core values) which gives rise to a Nation's Brand Effect (NBE), which in turn sustains and reinforces both a literal full cycle of Brand building'.

They go on to further state that, 'There is no doubt that the rise & success of German Companies globally (often setting standards for quality and innovation) was and is assisted by the NBE. The NBE flowing back into Germany and reinforcing the ingredients (people, culture & history) and core values that give rise to it in the first place, makes them stronger, which in turn, further reinforces the German NBE … and so on. This is literally one big reinforcement cycle'. (Jaworski)

So, in the case of Germany, the development of its national brand identity is an integral part of the growth and development of its exports, the 'Made in Germany' label that has a world-class reputation.

Among the many elements believed to influence consumer perceptions of products and services, i.e. brands, in an age of globalisation and increased competition is the concept of country of origin (COO) effects. This is generally defined as the country of manufacture or assembly as given by the 'Made in' label. The COO effect of a product or service has been found to influence a consumer's attitude and behaviour towards that product or service. It effects how consumers evaluate those product and services in terms of quality and value to them.

Other elements, like a nation's culture, are used by consumers to arrive at extrinsic and intrinsic cues about the products and services that are offered to them in the marketplace by the nation. However, research evidence states that this is not always the case, as in certain examples where specific product features were decisive in the choice for the given product/service category. Like price, guarantee period, brand reputation, etc., choice also depends on whether or not there is a match between the country image and the brand's desired features.

Al Ries, the famous marketing strategist and co-author with his daughter, Laura Ries, of the book, *The 22 Immutable Laws of Branding*, has this to say, 'Since value lies in the mind of the consumer, the perception of where the brand came from can add or subtract value. … The perception of a country is important. … To be successful as a worldwide brand, you need to do two things: 1. You need to be first. 2. Your product needs to fit the perceptions of its country of origin'. (Ries) It is a strategy which Germany and its brands have adopted for quite a while with great success.

Some of the other significant academic research that has been conducted in this area over the years, especially with regard to the 'Made in' label or the COO, is summarised below.

According to Han (1989), 'A distinction is proposed between country image as a Halo effect, where the general image of a country's products is transferred to the specific product category and country image as a summary construct, where the specific product images are the building blocks of the general image'. (Han)

In a research paper written by, Papadopoulos and Heslop (1993), it was proposed that the term product–country image (PCI) be used to account for the multi-dimensional character of products/brands as also the multiple places involved in a global production process. (Papadopoulos)

Furthermore, Askegaard and Ger (1998) argued that the analyses of images attached to a product and its place(s) of origin must use a richer set of connotations than those used in standard approaches. They acknowledged the cultural context in consumer product evaluations by proposing the contextualised product–place image or the CPPI. (Askegaard)

Although some other studies do not give primary importance to country-of-origin effects, most studies have indicated its importance.

O'Shaughnessy and Jackson (2000), in their paper, 'Treating the Nation as a Brand: Some neglected Issues', have said that 'One conclusion is that the reputational capital of a nation with respect to a product category will influence choice more than a nation's overall attractiveness, though fragments of a nation's imagery may nonetheless be successfully exploited'. (O'Shaughnessy)

Now, most academics, researchers and practitioners agree that a country's image results from a broad, multi-dimensional mix of factors that includes its geography, history, various cultural elements, famous citizens, ongoing events and proclamations and its products and services – all of these together make each nation unique and give each nation its unique identity.

My intention here is to showcase the best of German brands, the champion brands that are made in Germany – a diverse and broad range of products, services and corporate brands.

I start with the 'Superstars' or the truly world-class brands, the brands that feature in the top 100 brands of the world and several more that deserve to be in this category. Next are the 'Star brands' of the German industrial firmament. Following this, we come to one of the main sections of the champion German brands that constitute the 'Mittelstand', or the small and medium-sized enterprises, what I would like to call, the 'less known champions' who together constitute a major part of the German economy. The last section consists of select, innovative and emergent stars, most of which are fairly new, driven by an entrepreneurial spirit and have made a mark on the German industrial establishment.

The book's middle section also consists of important elements in this discussion of country image and identity, what I would call the facilitators and influencers of German brands to the 'Made in Germany' label. These are comprised of the important institutions, governmental, economic and social; the research and testing institutions; and the trade fairs and exhibitions. And of course a brief description of the political system and political parties is included, as well as social and cultural elements that contribute and influence the whole, such as the arts, music and musicians, architecture and design, the media, sports and sportsmen, food and drink, etc.

As all of these elements facilitate and influence the production of quality goods and services and contribute to the positive image of the 'Made in Germany' brands, their reputation is not only one of quality but also of reliability, innovation and cutting-edge technology. These facilitators and influencers have especially helped the 'less-known' or 'hidden champions' and have helped to create a new line of innovative entrepreneurs and emergent stars.

So, here's to the champion German brands.

Before we look at the companies themselves, we will first look at a bit of post-war German history, and subsequently how they rose from the rubble to become world export leaders, as well as the major contributing factors for their resurgence and resounding success.

2 *From Rubble to an Economic Miracle to a World Export Leader*

To better understand a nation and its brands, it is necessary to know a little about its modern economic history, the factors that led to its development and to its present state. In the case of Germany, it was in the year 1945 after the end of the ruinous Second World War that Germany entered what was called the time of 'Zero Hour' or (Null Stunde). During this period, most of Germany lay in ruins and was in a state of utter poverty. German society had to be rebuilt from the aftermath of World War II. From this abject state, the re-birth and recovery of this country began.

To understand the makings of German business today, it is crucial to understand what the Germans went through immediately after the war, in a time of rubble and misery. Despite these conditions, they set themselves to the task of rebuilding a nation from scratch. Everybody was determined, worked hard and with a purpose, helping others who needed help, and in the process moved forward together. This collaboration formed the basis for a strong sense of social responsibility, a strong work ethic and a commitment to rebuild the nation. The businessmen of the time had to improvise and optimise with what they had and believe in the future, for they had survived the terrible war. They were optimistic about the future and believed in themselves and their hard work. In hard times or during common misfortune, people come together to make the best of little to benefit all and cater to each individual's needs.

This core feeling helped give birth to the 'Social Market Economy', which led the government of the time to adopt this system as part of a social and human dimension to their policies, a government that favoured free competition and made the environment conducive for such a market economy, while at the same time providing health and other social benefits for workers and less-fortunate sections of the populace. It took around 20 years for the then West German economy to turn itself around and perform what the media termed an 'economic miracle'. In large measure, the reasons for this turnaround were the economic policies put in place by the successive governments of the time and the social ethic practised by the entire population, from the novice apprentice to seasoned employees, unions, executives, businessmen and other entrepreneurs. Loyalty to the organisation and commitment to one's job also were factors. The company or organisation was viewed as part of the community, an important social component, which believed in the greater good of all.

In the early days, the German system of financial disclosure, in which the company assets are written down regularly so as to increase the company's hidden reserves, helped buffer the early economic system from sudden financial fluctuations. There was also an attitude of showing discretion while presenting one's profits and a marked distaste for ostentation and unnecessary publicity or display of wealth.

According to the late founder of Otto Versand, Werner Otto, who began the successful, Hamburg-based mail-order house, 'Germans work more intensively. They don't regard hard work as just a job, but as a task or duty'. While discussing success in a business, he said that, 'Success comes down to making and selling a product that people want to buy and having the common sense to know it when you have got it. The rest is secondary'. (Glouchevitch)

Those early days of improvisation and common sense were necessary to survive and rebuild a nation from the post-war chaos and ruin. Over the years, German industry has transformed itself into a model of order and structure that works together and with determination.

A large part of the early and continuing success is also due to the excellent relations between management and the trade unions, in which the policy on both sides has been one of consensus rather than conflict. The German worker is treated with respect and is of concern to management, as are the improvements in job quality, productivity, wages and non-wage benefits paid to the employees. The unions have indeed played a major role in a positive, fruitful and stabilizing direction for German industry. They were responsible to a great extent for keeping the 'social market economy' smoothly running with the miracle of German productivity to show. In fact, unions helped raise the standard of living for employees in Germany without losing out on competitive advantage or productivity in any way.

Unions have been fairly apolitical and progressive in their outlook, knowing the cost of strikes to all concerned. Management, in turn, appreciates the value of human capital and the importance of keeping employees satisfied in their jobs as a key to productivity. All of this has resulted in increased productivity and production, expanding exports while enjoying a continued rise in the standard of living of the general populace.

IG Metall (IGM) is the largest, most powerful union in the country with around 2.4 million members and headquarters in Frankfurt am Main. It covers workers in the steel, automobile, textile, wood, plastics and other such industries, representing both blue collar and white collar workers. They are a major player when it comes to bargaining for better working conditions, wages, benefits and other work-related regulations. IGM is a member of the German Confederation of Trade Unions and is also a member of some international union organisations. Their slogan is 'Together for a good living'.

The other large and important German trade union is Ver.di, an abbreviation for 'Vereinte Dienstleistungsgewerkschaft', which translates as United Services Union. This union has around 2.3 million members with headquarters in Berlin. As a multi-service, free trade union, it includes people employed in over 1,000 different trades and professions. They have a powerful position in collective bargaining with regard to many areas and even bring their influence to bear on political decision-making.

In later years, the social welfare system became fairly extensive and has grown to be one of the largest areas of spending. Nevertheless, German philosophy and policy in this regard has supported a state role, combining the virtues of a social welfare system with the benefits of a market system.

The term 'Wirtschaftswunder', meaning 'economic miracle', was first used by the Western media to describe the rapid reconstruction and development of the then West

German economy. It started with the replacement of the ReichsMark with the creation of a new currency, the Deutsche Mark, as legal tender.

This move was initiated in 1948 by the government of Chancellor Konrad Adenauer and his finance minister, Ludwig Erhard (who later became Chancellor), and is considered the 'Father' of the German economic miracle. This period saw Germany's rapid industrial growth with a long-lasting period of low inflation. Among other measures that facilitated this growth was the dismantling of old rules and regulations in order to facilitate a free economy so as to establish a strong foundation for the new state of West Germany.

Ludwig Erhard pushed through further reforms that, along with the Marshall Plan aid, helped facilitate the German economic miracle. Rationing and price controls came to an end, duties on imports lowered and tax on overtime work was abolished. Erhard encouraged production of consumer goods to stimulate employment and economic revival. The boom lasted into the 1990s and the wealth spread downward to lower-paid workers. In fact, German incomes tripled between 1950 and 1965.

One significant world event that led to the acceptance of German products in the Western world was the Korean War (1950–1953). Due to an increase in demand for goods worldwide, especially in the west, that could not be met by existing producers, German production more than doubled its exports during and after this war.

Some of the other factors which contributed to the rejuvenation of the German economy were the quality of hard work, long hours and working at full capacity. The period from the 1950s to the early 1970s saw Germany develop into one of the world's most developed economies. Aided and supported by the thousands of 'Gastarbeiter' (guest workers) who mainly arrived from Greece, Italy, Turkey, Portugal and Poland, they helped sustain the country's economic upswing during this period.

The industrial boom truly began in 1950 with a growth rate of industrial production that was a staggering 25 per cent. The growth slowed a bit in the 1960s and then improved again. Since then it has maintained a mature growth with significant gains in exports. By 1991, the German economy had become the largest European exporter in absolute terms, almost on par with the US and a little ahead of Japan, the world export leader at the time.

Prior to 1990, Germany was divided into East and West Germany. Today, unified Germany is a federal, parliamentary republic of 16 states with a current population of around 81 million. The capital and largest city is Berlin. Germany is the world's fourth largest economy by nominal GDP and the fifth largest by purchasing-power parity, whereas with regard to exports, it is the second largest in the world and the third largest importer of goods.

Germany's central geographical location gives it a strategic position in the middle of Europe. It has one of the best infrastructure systems in Europe. With an exemplary and legendary Autobahn (highway) system, a high-speed rail system, domestic and international, connected waterways, a thriving port in Hamburg, second only to Rotterdam and excellent airports that connect with direct flights to all parts of the world, travel is fast and convenient and contributes significantly to Germany's economic strength and efficiency.

In German, the word 'Messe' or trade fair is a German institution, the oldest being the Consumer Trade Fair in Frankfurt, which is said to have a 750-year history. Frankfurt also hosts a popular book fair and several others, both smaller and larger. It now has several permanent halls and buildings specially designed for holding these fairs spread over several acres of land in the very centre of the city. These fairs are truly international in scope, drawing visitors and businesses from all over the world. They are seen as essential to business-building and networking events that showcase the latest developments in the relevant industry and product categories. Other cities that host popular fairs are Hannover, Berlin, Düsseldorf, Cologne, Munich and Leipzig.

Frankfurt is also the headquarters for the European Union's Central Bank, the ECB, and is Germany's financial centre, with the country's principal stock market, the Frankfurt DAX exchange.

In Germany, industry and trade associations play a significant role in the economy as compared to other countries. These associations are democratically elected and help in lobbying for the interests of the concerned industry.

Among the largest of the umbrella groups are the Bundesverband der Deutschen Industries (BDI) and the Deutscher Industrie und Handelstag or Kammer, now known as the (DIHK). They now have an extended role of supporting and promoting various industry groups, promoting new entrepreneurs, venture capital funding and so on, apart from their main role of consulting with government over industrial policies and norms, export controls, tariff regimes and so forth.

Here, mention must also be made of the Technischer Uberwachungs Verein (Technical Supervisory Association) or TÜV, which is pronounced similar to the word 'toof'. This organisation is the primary technical organisation that oversees the task of inspecting products for quality and safety. The TÜV seal of approval is a stamp of quality and standardisation, ensuring that products from automobiles to taps comply with all of the necessary safety, environmental, quality and other governmental and industry regulations.

Concern for the environment and meeting environmental regulations is a major concern for German business because community pressures to maintain a clean environment with minimal waste and to use recycling technology are a social imperative.

German business culture is a shining example of competing fiercely in a tough and open market while simultaneously supporting and nourishing society at large in many ways, from the many benefits to workers and the immediate community, to the famed German corporate apprenticeship system, where on-the-job training is available for teenagers in a wide variety of professions and skills. This apprenticeship covers the entire gamut from blue collar to white collar professions and it is reputed to be exhaustive and fairly demanding of the apprentice. It is true training, and successful completion is subject to passing numerous written and on-the-job examinations and tests. The continued success of this apprenticeship system is reflected in corporate Germany's commitment to it and the fair amount of financial and other resources as well as time invested in it.

The German apprenticeship system has been in existence since the fourteenth century when guilds were created for various professions, such as jewellers, wood workers, shoe-makers and so on. Over the years, this system has transformed into two- to three-year apprenticeship training for new employees joining German industry. At present, it is a comprehensive system and includes every new young entrant into the German job market who has completed the requisite school exams. This system has become the single largest source of skilled labour for German companies.

Several famous German managers and heads of corporations started their careers as apprentices. The key philosophy is that however small the job, the apprentice is taught the value of their role in the larger picture. The benefits of this system are huge, as youth unemployment is kept to a minimum, there is a steady supply of skilled labour and the cost for training is undertaken by private entrepreneurs. This is one major reason why German industry is able to maintain the quality of their products as Germany's labour force is perhaps one of the most skilled and well trained in the world.

Also worth noting is the large number of research and innovation centres like the Fraunhofer Institutes and The Max-Planck and Robert Bosch centres. Germany's system of universities and research and innovation centres is the largest in Europe. In fact, Germany leads Europe in annual patent registrations.

Although Germany is home to some of the largest global corporations and brands – of the international Fortune Global 500, 37 have their corporate headquarters in Germany – the true strength of the German economy lies in its 'Mittelstand', that is its small and medium-sized enterprises (SMEs).

According to Harvard Business School professor Michael Porter, who in 1990 in his famous book, *The Competitive Advantage of Nations*, stated, 'No country in the world, including Japan, exhibits the breadth and depth of industries with strong international positions'. (Porter) German industries at that time made up about 30 per cent of the world export market and this number was increasing, from pumps to packaging machines to a wide range of products. In fact, the list keeps growing with the introduction of new technologies such as the fields of nano, bio and alternative energies. Many of these companies are now among the top three worldwide in terms of market share and revenues, reaching several billion Euros annually.

The Mittelstand companies are usually individual or family-owned businesses (80 per cent are personally-held enterprises), with their hometown and the immediate community as base for their enterprise and operations. Their contribution to the country's economy is immense as they contribute to a substantial percentage of all exports and employ over two-thirds of the working populace.

Among the many characteristics of Mittelstand companies is the fact that they operate in a niche market for various product categories. Their preference for privacy, tight controls, social commitment and keeping a low profile are other hallmarks.

Their characteristics and reasons for success are many and have been widely discussed by Hermann Simon in his illuminating book, *Hidden Champions: Lessons from 500 of the World's Best Unknown Companies*. They practice a leadership style that is both authoritarian in the fundamentals and participative in the details. Although their values can seem conservative, they work hard and have low employee absenteeism and high employee loyalty.

Designing unique products, which undergo constant innovation, they earn market leadership through quality, performance and reliability. Exporting most of their products, they remain close to their customers. These and other drivers, like paying equal attention to internal resources and competencies in the face of external opportunities, pay off in the long term. These traits, combined with a narrow market focus with a global orientation, and only outsourcing certain management tasks such as legal and financial services, lead to staying focused and delivering on customer needs and technology.

Hermann Simon has also remarked that these companies teach others through their work that good management means doing small things better than their competitors, relying on simplicity in processes and organizational structures. (Simon)

The participation of the leading Mittelstand owners and their top executives gives most German trade associations the respect and influence not seen elsewhere. In fact, this atmosphere of trust means that many Mittelstand companies choose to do all their production in Germany, catering only to the export market. Needless to say, the work ethic propounded by the Mittelstand is ingrained deeply into the German business and social psyche.

As Europe's largest economy and the fourth largest in the world in terms of nominal GDP, Germany is the world's third largest exporter, with a value of $1.408 trillion being exported in 2011. Exports account for more than a third of the country's national output. Since the early nineties, Germany has maintained a pre-eminent position in the world in terms of exports, always being in the top three worldwide in value. A large part goes to Western European countries, the US and now Eastern Europe, although exports to Asia and other parts of the world are also growing and constitute a fair share of the total. Germany enjoys a trade surplus with most of its trade partners.

According to the World Trade Organization (WTO), Germany was the world's top exporter in 2005, leading all other countries with a trade surplus of $197 billion. Germany is the world leader in mechanical engineering products, holding about 20 per cent of the global market. The core German exports include products such as vehicles, machinery, chemical goods, electronics and optics. German companies are also among the world's largest and technologically advanced producers of iron, steel, cement, food and beverages. It is among the leading producers and exporters of wind turbines and solar power technology in the world, being a leading proponent and driver for the clean, green industrial makeover.

Sustaining this leading position as a top exporter in the world are not only Germany's top global brands but also the several hundred brands of the Mittelstand, the SMEs that have successfully maintained their sterling performance and give ample proof to the quality of the 'Made in Germany' label.

CHAPTER **3** *The Superstars*

The Superstars are the global brands that have been hugely successful in world markets. For the initial list, I have chosen to use Interbrand's annual study of the 100 Best Global Brands. In 2009, 11 German brands managed to make it to the top 100. They are Mercedes-Benz, SAP, BMW, Siemens, Volkswagen, Adidas, Audi, Allianz, Porsche, NIVEA and PUMA in that order. Most of them retained their positions in the 2011 and 2012 top 100 lists as well.

What, then, are the basic criteria that Interbrand uses to arrive at this list? Essentially, a brand must have publicly available marketing and financial data, be recognisable beyond its base of customers and must derive at least a third of its earnings from outside its home country. They only study individual brands and not portfolios of brands. Also excluded are airlines and pharmaceutical companies, for reasons of difficulty in computing and attributing brand values to products as per their given criteria.

The methodology followed by Interbrand is to rate the brand by its net earnings after deducting for operating costs, taxes and capital costs from its total sales and arriving at what they call 'economic earnings', from this they assign 'brand earnings', i.e. the revenue that the brand alone generates. They then calculate a 'brand strength score' by assessing the brand's performance against a set of seven measures of important factors: leadership, market, trend, stability, protection, diversification and brand support. The 'business earnings' are then adjusted, based on future risk to the strength of the brand, to arrive at a net-present-value (NPV) of the brand. This 'brand value' becomes a key performance indicator for brand strategy and a measure for branding decisions. (www.interbrand.com)

All financial analysis is based on publicly available company information and from a range of analyst's reports. They use in-house research to establish individual brand scores to arrive at the 'brand earnings' for each of the brands studied. Their own qualitative and quantitative analysis to arrive at a NPV for the brand is based on data collected from July to June of each year. Essentially, this is similar to the way corporate assets are valued, based on its NPV or future earnings of the asset or brand.

The Interbrand survey in partnership with *Business Week* is considered to be one of the most influential benchmark studies by business leaders on the world's most valuable brands. Their valuation techniques have long been recognised by businesses, academics and regulatory bodies as valuable strategic tools. Among the 11 brands from the Interbrand list are five automotive brands, two sporting goods manufacturers, a diversified corporation, a computer software company, a financial services brand and a personal care brand. They are global brands with a presence worldwide and are known to consumers almost everywhere.

To this distinguished list of brands, I wish to include nine other very popular and global German brands. In my view they, too, deserve to be in this list as the 'Superstar' German brands. Over the years they have matured and grown into deserving and popular global brands. They have been selected not only for their size and performance but also for their renown and reputation as fine examples of successful German entrepreneurship at the highest level in their respective areas of operation – brands that are among the flagship brands of the country that add premium value to the 'Made in Germany' label.

The first in this selection is the Otto Group, one of the world's largest mail-order companies and one of the pioneering success stories of post-war Germany.

The next is BASF, which is one of the world's largest chemical companies founded in 1865.

Bayer AG is another mega, global pharmaceutical and chemical giant founded in 1863, which celebrates 150 years of its successful existence in 2013.

The Bosch group is another corporate giant, established in 1886 and now a leading global supplier of technology and services, represented in around 150 countries.

Lufthansa is the well-recognised German brand, flying high on its worldwide success not only in aviation but also in logistics, maintenance and catering.

Another interesting inclusion is the Deutsche Post DHL brand that brings two powerful brands to the marketplace. Today, the group is among the top 10 of the largest employers of the world, employing around 470,000 employees in over 200 countries and territories, forming a global network of postal and logistics services.

The Deutsche Telekom AG is one of the world's leading telecom companies, with over 200 million customers and representation in around 50 countries.

Deutsche Bank has grown in size, performance and influence over the years to become a truly global player.

Two other company brands that were suggested for inclusion in this section but declined are Aldi, the retail giant, and Munich Re, the reinsurance company.

Finally, I have included a media conglomerate, the Bertelsmann Group, which celebrated 175 years of its existence in 2010. They produce, serve and market media in over 50 countries, with successful and popular brands such as the RTL group, the number one European television and radio broadcaster, Random House, the world's largest book publishing group, and Gruner+Jahr, Europe's biggest magazine publisher. It is a privately-held media giant.

In my view and that of several practitioners and academics, these global brands constitute the 'Superstars' of the German industrial landscape.

Mercedes-Benz

Daimler AG, the world-famous German manufacturer of premium cars has its origins in Benz & Co, founded in 1881 in Mannheim, and Daimler-Motoren-Gesellschaft, founded in 1890 in Stuttgart. Daimler AG and its brand Mercedes-Benz represent the invention of the automobile and formed each phase of its development significantly. At present, they also manufacture trucks, buses, coaches and internal combustion engines.

The founding fathers of the company were Carl Benz and Gottlieb Daimler. Carl Benz created the first petrol-powered car, called the Benz Patent-Motorwagen, while Gottlieb Daimler and his engineer Wilhelm Maybach developed the first fast-running petrol engine and equipped a carriage with it, thus creating the first four-wheeled automobile in 1886. After Daimler's death in 1900, chief engineer Wilhelm Maybach developed the first modern automobile, the 35 hp Mercedes. In 1926, the companies founded by Daimler and Benz merged into Daimler-Benz AG and the first Mercedes-Benz brand named automobiles came onto the market. Their official three-pointed star with wreaths and circular bands was up and running. Their logo is considered simple and very effective and easily recognised by most people. The year 2011 was a jubilee year for Daimler AG, celebrating '125 years of the Inventor of the Automobile'.

The company has its present headquarters in Stuttgart, with Dieter Zetsche as the chairman of the Board of Management of Daimler AG and head of Mercedes-Benz Cars. Manfred Bischoff is the chairman of the Supervisory Board. For fiscal year 2011, The Daimler Group achieved total group revenues of €106.540 billion while employing over 271,000 people worldwide. Of this, Mercedes-Benz Cars achieved revenues of €57.420 billion worldwide.

Mercedes-Benz vehicles are manufactured and distributed in all the continents of the world. They have a full range of passenger, light commercial and heavy commercial vehicles and equipment. They are the world's largest manufacturer of trucks and several models of buses and vans are also produced mainly for the European and Asian markets. Mercedes-Benz also has gained a unique series of motor sports victories, from the early beginnings until the present.

In a McLaren Mercedes Formula One racing car, Mika Häkkinen won the Driver's championship in 1998 and 1999, followed by Lewis Hamilton in 2008. In 2009, the Brawn GP Formula One team used Mercedes engines to help it win the Constructor's championship with Jenson Button who became the F1 Driver's champion. In 2010, after the team was taken over by Daimler AG, it was renamed Mercedes GP.

Over the years, Mercedes-Benz has been credited with several firsts and innovations that have added to its brand value. Starting with the first internal combustion engine vehicles which were developed independently by the founders Carl Benz and Gottlieb Daimler to the first diesel-engine production car, it also pioneered the safety body with crumple zones, ABS anti-lock braking system and airbags, seven-speed automatic transmission, the Electronic Stability Programme, Active Brake Assist and highly efficient BlueTEC Diesel and BlueDIRECT petrol engines. Several years of vehicle safety innovation helped win it the European Commercial Vehicle Safety Award, presented in Klettwitz in 2007. The ADAC 'Yellow Angel 2007' for the Mercedes-Benz 'Active Brake Assist', which also received the 'Safety Award 2007' from the Belgian Commercial Vehicle journalists in Brussels. These awards have been followed by many more over the years for safety and innovation.

For decades Mercedes-Benz has been involved in extensive research and development (R&D) in alternative drive systems which lead to several models of electric vehicles, fuel-cell vehicles and hybrid vehicles, using a lithium ion battery for the first time. The whole package of fuel-saving technologies developed by Mercedes-Benz is summarised under the 'BlueEfficiency' label.

From cutting-edge design to technical innovation, each Mercedes-Benz vehicle is created with passion, quality and immaculate attention to detail. It is said, that Mercedes built the market for expensive cars by using the concept of 'prestige' as its strategy. It was used with finesse and subtlety to build its brand image over the years. Its pricing strategy was up-market with product engineering to back it up; using the promotional language, 'Engineered like no other car in the world', in one of its earlier US campaigns. Thus, with the name, reputation and history, Mercedes-Benz became the car of choice for the wealthy. Mercedes-Benz has reinvented the motor car over the years, pushing the boundaries of automotive engineering to new heights and creating a succession of iconic vehicles.

Today, the brand evolution continues under the guidance of Gordon Wagener, Mercedes-Benz Head of Design, who says, '... a Mercedes needs to have surfaces that reflect emotion, intellect and execution. The Mercedes should be premium, in every segment'.

Traditionally, the flagship model, the S-Class Saloon determines any new design philosophy for the rest of the range. As Wagener explains, 'We create individual characters and families all under one philosophy'.

As vehicle segments become less clearly defined, opportunities arise with respect to alternative fuels and environmental concerns. This has helped Mercedes-Benz design a new range of concept cars like the 'Blue Zero' range of highly efficient and practical passenger cars, which provide fuel efficient solutions suitable for a wide range of driving situations.

In a fairly recent J.D. Power and Associates study of motor vehicle models, Mercedes-Benz ranked third in overall satisfaction and fourth in service satisfaction. Besides, they have also won the sports model category for their CLK class and came in second in the executive/luxury class within the E-Class. Mercedes-Benz has also scooped the Safety Award for their innovative 'Attention Assist System', at the prestigious annual Car of the Year awards. A Mercedes-Benz S-Class has caught the judge's eye in the luxury car category, in their words 'Built to the most exacting standards using gorgeous materials'. The S350 CDI Blue Efficiency was crowned the best luxury car for 2010. It comes as no surprise since the S-Class range of models is the worldwide market leader in the premium segment.

Mercedes-Benz develops new models with passion, detail, and responsibility.

The basis of Mercedes-Benz's market success is an exciting range of models including elegant sedans, comfortable station wagons, sporty Cabriolets or powerful off-roaders, to round off the portfolio. From A to S Class, from the volume models like the new E-C introduced in 2009 to the new Mercedes-Benz SLS AMG (for hand-crafted precision and top flight performance), the Mercedes-Benz models are leaders in their respective market segments. (www.mercedes-benz.com) / (www.daimler.com)

SAP

SAP AG is the leading German software development and consulting corporation. It provides enterprise-wide software applications and support services to businesses of all shapes and sizes. Their objective is to help companies make their business processes more efficient, agile and to create sustainable new value.

SAP AG was founded in 1972 by five former IBM employees – Dietmar Hoop, Hans-Werner Hector, Hasso Plattner, Klaus Tschira and Claus Wellenreuther. They launched a company called SAP, the acronym in German stands for 'Systemanalyse und Programmentwicklung' (System Analysis and Program Development), in the city of Mannheim. Their vision was to develop standard application software for real-time business processing. In 1976, it moved to its present headquarters in Walldorf. SAP currently has sales and developmental locations in more than 130 countries worldwide and is listed on several exchanges, including the Frankfurt stock exchange, NYSE and others.

Present co-CEOs are Bill McDermott, and Jim Hagemann Snabe. They have more than 55,000 employees in over 130 countries serving more than 183,000 customers worldwide with total sales revenues of €14.23 billion as of fiscal year 2011. While typically seen as a company serving mainly large-enterprise customers, currently 79 per cent of SAP's customers are small- to mid-size businesses.

SAP is the world's largest business software company and the third largest independent software provider in terms of revenue as of 2007. More than three-quarters of the Forbes 500, 80 per cent of the Dow Jones Sustainability Index and 85 per cent of the top 100 most valued brands in the world are powered by SAP software. In 2012, SAP celebrated 40 years of innovative existence.

The company's best-known product is its SAP Enterprise Resource Planning Software, popularly known as (SAP ERP). This software targets the business software requirements of mid-size and large organisations in various types of industries and sectors. The software allows for open communication within and between the various company functions. SAP's ERP solution includes several modules that support key functional areas, namely SAP ERP Financials, SAP ERP Logistics (SCM and SRM), SAP ERP Human Resource Management Systems, SAP CRM (Customer Relationship Management) and SAP PLM (Product Life-Cycle Management).

Other major product offerings include the Net Weaver platform, Governance, Risk and Compliance (GRC) solutions and several others like Duet, Enterprise SOA and Performance Management Solutions. SAP Business One and SAP Business All-in-One for small and medium-sized enterprises. The SAP Business by Design is a software-as-a-service offering and provides a fully integrated ERP solution. SAP also has an expanded, product suite of Business Intelligence (BI) solutions.

In its quest for growth, central to SAP's strategy are partnerships. It has the industry's largest network of software solution providers, value-added resellers, distributors and technology and service partners, totalling around 2,400 certified partners. SAP partners include global services partners with cross-industry, multinational consulting capabilities, which provide integrated products that complement SAP Business Suite solutions.

R&D is at the heart of SAP's customer-focused innovation strategy. Led by SAP Research and SAP Labs, SAP's R&D efforts investigate new technology and develop new applications for delivering business value to current and future SAP customers. The R&D investment is an astounding €1.939 billion, representing 13.6% of total revenue. SAP Research is the global technology research and innovation unit of SAP. It explores emerging IT trends and drives applied research and the incubation of promising projects while focusing on the business impact and contribution to the SAP portfolio. The business model of SAP Research is based on co-innovation with customers, partners and other third parties; activities range from large-scale collaborative research projects with academic and industrial partners to specific innovation projects with individual customers. The best-validated results and technologies are further developed into prototypes and potential business opportunities within SAP. SAP's global research network consists of 19 locations worldwide and involves more than 800 partners from industry, academia and governments as well as SAP customers.

The SAP Labs network includes locations in high-tech centres across the globe that deliver local market-oriented solutions optimised for customer value. Each SAP Labs location has the flexibility of a small company as an integral part of the global network and each has a clear focus topic and area of responsibility. SAP Labs engage closely with universities, offering leadership talks, engineering courses and exchange programs.

In 2005, SAP entered the world of B2B and B2C social media when it introduced the SAP Developer Network (SDN), now called the SAP Community Network (SCN), which is a community of more than two million developers, consultants, integrators and business analysts. The idea was to open the company's content, strategy and technical information to a global audience. This offered control of both product and promotion because the developers promote what they have made, using SAP source code, across the SAP Community Network and beyond. This is an excellent example of a brand's engagement with their communities through social media, that is, blogs, social networking sites like Facebook and Twitter.

SAP AG primarily uses its worldwide network of subsidiaries to market and distribute SAP products and services locally. In certain countries they have established distribution agreements with independent resellers rather than with subsidiaries. SAP has also developed an independent sales and support force through value-added resellers who assume responsibility for the licensing, implementation and support of SAP solutions, particularly in the SAP Business One application and qualified SAP Business All-In-One partner solutions. The SAP strategy for growth is primarily through organic growth, co-innovation and focussed acquisitions.

They have a social investment strategy that consists of leveraging their strengths to create social change, like providing their software to non-profits worldwide to enable them to better serve their mission. SAP invests their capital in innovative approaches to strengthening education, expanding economic opportunity and creating long-term change in all the continents. They also help emerging entrepreneurs succeed by fostering innovation and economic growth. (www.sap.com)

BMW

The famed German automobile, motorcycle and engine manufacturing company was founded in 1916 by Franz Josep Popp. The name BMW stands for 'Bayerische Motoren Werke' in German, in English Bavarian Motor Works (BMW).

Its headquarters are in Munich, the Bavarian capital. The present CEO and chairman of the board of management is Norbert Reithofer, and Joachim Milberg is the chairman of the supervisory board. Sales revenue as of fiscal year 2011 was €68.821 billion. They have plants, small and large, worldwide, employing over 100,000 employees. The Rolls-Royce range of cars is a subsidiary brand of BMW. It also owns and produces the MINI brand of automobiles.

The circular blue and white BMW logo is supposedly to have evolved from the circular Rapp Motoren Werke company logo, from which the BMW company logo grew to combine with the white and blue colours of the flag of the state of Bavaria, which was reversed to produce the BMW roundel.

During the Second World War, the company produced aircraft engines and other arms and ammunition, however these activities were discontinued at the end of the war. In 1992, BMW acquired a large stake in the California-based, industrial design studio, 'Design Works' USA, which they fully acquired in 1995. BMW has also created a range of high-end bicycles, which are sold online and through dealerships.

With its three brands – BMW, MINI and Rolls-Royce motor cars – the BMW Group has set its sights set firmly on the premium sector of the international automobile market. To achieve its objectives, the company knows how to deploy its strength with an efficiency that is unmatched in the automotive industry. The strategic objective is clearly defined: The BMW Group is the leading provider of premium products and premium services for individual mobility, defined as, automobiles, motorcycles and bicycles.

Since its inception, the BMW brand has stood for one thing: 'sheer driving pleasure'. Sporting and dynamic performance combined with peerless design and exclusive quality, resulting in the unique appeal of BMW cars.

Agility and economy are the most important considerations in the BMW Group's worldwide production network. They manufacture their products at 29 plants in 14 countries on five continents (Asia, Africa, Europe, North America and South America). BMW cars are produced in 14 locations. The MINI and Rolls-Royce production are in Great Britain, while BMW motorcycles are manufactured in Berlin and Husqvarna motorcycles in Italy. The same consistent standards of quality, safety and processes at all locations guarantee worldwide premium products, made by the BMW Group.

BMW started to produce cars in 1928 with the BMW 3/15 PS. This was a technically redone Austin Seven produced under license. The 'New Class', produced from 1962 onwards, established a new era for BMW. This was a line of compact sedans and coupes, starting with the 1926, 1500 model and continuing through to the last 2002s in 1977. The current models starts with the 1 series, launched in 2004, BMW's smallest car and available in coupé/convertible variations. Then they have the 3 series, a compact executive car, the 5 series and a mid-size executive car available in sedan and station wagon forms. BMW's full-size flagship, the Executive Sedan, is the 7 series. Additional vehicles are the compact crossover SUV/sports activity vehicle (SAV) – the BMW X1, X3, X5, the X6 Sports Activity Coupé and the Z4 Sports Roadster. They also offer the BMW 6 series as a Coupé, Gran Coupé and as a Convertible.

Based on the 3 series, the M3 defined an entirely new market for BMW; that of a race-ready production vehicle, popularly acclaimed by enthusiasts in large part due to its unique design and award-winning engines. Currently 30 BMW Group models emit less than 120 grams CO_2 per kilometre while 73 models emit 140 grams of CO_2 or less.

BMW has been an engine supplier to Formula 1 racing teams like Williams, Benetton, Brabham and Arrows. From 2000 until 2006 they were engine suppliers for the BMW Williams F1 Team. From 1982 until 1987 they were engine suppliers for Brabham, 1985–1986 for Benetton, 1984–1986 for Arrows and from 1983 to1984 for ATS. In 1983, Nelson Piquet became Formula 1 World Champion in a Brabham with a BMW engine.

According to executives responsible for marketing innovation at BMW, addressing emotions is equally important because a car is not only valuable for its technology. This is why they look for trends and opportunities to transmit the character of their brand and awaken feelings. In their marketing communications, they combine technological innovation with emotion, which lets them create new impulses that strengthen their brand.

According to Al Ries, leading American marketing strategist and best-selling author, who in his book, *The 22 Immutable Laws of Branding*, says, 'What comes to mind when you think about owning a BMW? A car that's fun to drive. The ultimate driving machine. BMW owns the word "driving" in the mind. And, as a result, BMW has become the second largest-selling European luxury car in America'. He continues, that, 'BMW has been the ultimate driving machine for twenty-five years'. His remarks were in reference to the fact that BMW retains its strategy, even though the brand went through three separate advertising agencies.

Annette Baumeister, head of material and colour design of a BMW automobile project, said, 'No innovation is possible without risk! We also create designs which go far beyond classical lines. At the BMW Group, we want individuality and innovativeness to catch people's eyes immediately. An automobile's design should draw attention to itself – in a graceful, pleasing manner. We remain true to ourselves but are bold enough to develop distinctive features which we are convinced about'. (BMW-2010) The company's goal is to create lasting value.

Among BMW's ambitious plans is the one for a Mega City Vehicle, set to launch in 2013. The Mega City Vehicle will be a zero emission urban car for the world's metropolitan regions. To be marketed under a sub-brand of BMW called BMW i, the ultra-light yet high-strength composite CFRP (carbon fibre reinforced plastic) will make it significantly lighter than all other conventional cars, and in terms of sustainability, it will set new standards across the entire value-added chain. The Mega City Vehicle has already been shown as the BMW i3 Concept. Furthermore, a modern sports car with plug-in-hybrid-drive was presented to the public as the BMW i8 Concept.

For almost 100 years, design has been created at BMW by people for people. With the design of their corporate headquarters, the 'Four Cylinders' by Karl Schwanzer in 1972, the company placed a deliberate emphasis on an innovative, dynamic design, which was to continue later with the emergence of several trend-setting buildings in Germany and abroad. Perfection and innovation in technology and design are the identity-defining characteristics of all BMW Group products. (www.bmw.com)

Siemens

Siemens AG, the engineering conglomerate, was founded by Werner von Siemens in 1847 in Berlin. In 1848, Siemens built the first long-distance telegraph line in Europe, from Berlin to Frankfurt am Main. This was followed by a line between Finland and Crimea in 1855 and a link to North America from Europe in 1874.

In 1881, a Siemens AC alternator driven by a watermill was used to power the world's first electric street lighting in a town in the UK. They later went on to manufacture light bulbs as a joint venture under the OSRAM brand name. From light bulbs to radios, television sets and electron microscopes, these were the company's pre-war manufacturing products.

Today their businesses cover a diverse range of products, from communication systems, power generation, automation, lighting, medical technology, transportation and automotive to railway vehicles, building technologies, home appliances, fire alarms, IT services and the Siemens PLM Software. They even offer services for business, financing and construction. Technological excellence, innovation, quality, reliability and international focus have been their hallmarks for 165 years, making them strong and linking them to their shareholders, employees and customers as a partner of trust.

In effect, Siemens is Europe's largest engineering conglomerate. They are active in 190 regions of the world occupying leading market and technological positions worldwide. The company has four main business sectors: energy, healthcare, industry and infrastructure and cities. The new President and CEOof the Management Board is Joe Kaeser, and Gerhard Cromme is the Chairman of the Supervisory Board. They have three international headquarters at Erlangen, Berlin and Munich.

In fiscal 2012, their roughly 370,000 employees generated revenue from continuing operations of about €78 billion and income from continuing operations of €5.2 billion. In addition to over 285 manufacturing locations they also have office buildings, warehouses, R&D facilities and sales offices in nearly every country of the globe.

Responsible, excellent and innovative – these are their values that define Siemens and what it does. Sustainability in the broad sense – support for long-term environmental, economic and social progress – is the guiding principle of all their actions. They provide the world with the solutions it needs to master the challenges of demographic change, urbanisation, climate change and globalisation.

In the Energy sector they are a world-leading supplier of a wide array of products, solutions and services in the field of energy technology. In the drive to create a sustainable energy system based on the more efficient use of fossil resources and renewable energies, electrical power will play a key role. The energy chain from multiple sources and end-uses is rapidly becoming the power system or matrix as they call it. Their innovative and efficient products are enabling customers to succeed in an increasingly complex, technological and economic environment – particularly in the areas of power generation, power transmission and oil and gas production. With their know-how, products and core components, they already cover key areas of the power matrix.

In the Healthcare sector, they are a major single-source supplier of technology to the industry worldwide and a trend-setter in medical imaging, laboratory diagnostics, healthcare IT and hearing instruments. They offer products and solutions for the entire healthcare continuum – from prevention and early detection to diagnosis, treatment and follow-up care. By improving clinical workflows and tailoring them to specific diseases, they are making healthcare faster, better and more cost effective.

In the Industry sector, they are one of the world's leading suppliers of innovative and environmentally friendly products and solutions for industrial customers. With their end-to-end automation solutions, drive technologies, industrial IT and industry software, in-depth industry expertise and closely integrated services, they are increasing their customers' productivity, efficiency and flexibility– while strengthening their own competitiveness.

Finally, in their Infrastructure and Cities sector or division, they offer an extensive portfolio of sustainable technologies in the areas of transportation and logistics, power grid solutions and products, and building technologies. Bundling Siemens's unique infrastructure know-how, they supply customers around the world with products, solutions and services from a single source while benefiting from the dynamic growth of cities and infrastructure markets. Their cross-division offerings enable them to serve particularly attractive markets like data centres and airports. They are making their customers more competitive, enhancing the quality of urban life and providing Siemens with opportunities for profitable growth.

Siemens power of innovation and their pioneering spirit have always been the key pillars of their success. In fiscal 2012, they maintained their high level of R&D expenditure, investing some €4.2 billion to develop new technologies and bring them to market readiness in all their business areas. Their innovations impact many areas of everyday life. In fiscal 2012, they had roughly 29,500 R&D employees, of whom 12,900 were in Germany. To remain at the cutting edge of innovation, they participate in over 1,000 research partnerships a year with universities, research institutes and other partners around the world.

Their patent portfolio is comprised of some 57,300 patents worldwide. In patent applications, they are as of 2012 in first place in Europe. In patents granted, they are at tenth place in the US. In fiscal 2012, Siemens employees submitted around 8,900 invention reports – or an average of about 40 per workday.

The task of Siemens Corporate Technology (CT) is to create innovations that will shape the technologies of today and tomorrow and help them exploit more fully the potential of their integrated technology company. As a reliable strategic partner for their business units, CT makes important contributions along the entire value chain – from R&D to production technologies, manufacturing processes and product and solutions testing. Maintaining a global network of experts, the organisation works hand-in-hand with their operating units to define their technology and innovation strategy. Its more than 7,000 employees contribute in-depth knowledge of fundamental technologies, models and trends as well as a wealth of software and process know-how. Networked with universities and research centres worldwide, CT has major research facilities in Germany, the US, China, Russia, India and Austria.

Product responsibility at Siemens goes beyond 'cradle-to-grave' to encompass the entire product life-cycle. With well over 100,000 different products and solutions, it is of essence to Siemens that they work to maintain unified design and development standards and they correctly implement legal regulations and requirements, while continuing to improve energy and resource efficiency. For Siemens, sustainability means acting in the best interests of coming generations, with respect to the economy, environment and society. Their key achievements in this important area are 317 million tons of less CO_2 emissions by their customers, €29.9 billion in revenue with their environmental portfolio, 20% reduction in their CO_2 emissions and 20 per cent increase in their energy efficiency. (www.siemens.com)

Volkswagen (VW)

Volkswagen or VW in short means 'people's car' in German. The Beetle car has been made famous the world over in movies, books and popular culture as the 'Love Car' or the 'Love Bug' as made famous in the Hollywood picture of the same name. In fact, previous headlines in German and other languages was, 'Out Of Love for the Car' and 'Think Small'. The present slogan of VW is, 'Das Auto' which means, 'The Car'.

VW is a public limited company, manufacturing automobiles and other vehicles in the town of Wolfsburg, which is in the state of Lower Saxony. Volkswagen was originally founded in 1937 by the German Labour Front, the trade union of the time, the objective being to have an affordable, 'peoples car' for the general public. The Beetle was the first to be developed and produced by them.

The Volkswagen Group, with its headquarters in Wolfsburg, is one of the world's leading automobile manufacturers and the largest car maker in Europe. In 2011, the group increased the number of vehicles delivered to customers to 8.265 million (2010: 7.203 million), corresponding to a 12.3 per cent share of the world passenger car market.

In Western Europe over one in five new cars (23.0 per cent) comes from the Volkswagen Group. Group sales revenue in 2011 totaled €159 billion (2010: €126.9 billion). Profit after tax in the 2011 financial year amounted to €15.8 billion (2010: €7.2 billion).

Today, the Volkswagen Group is made up of 12 brands from seven European countries: Volkswagen, Audi, SEAT, ŠKODA, Bentley, Bugatti, Lamborghini, Porsche, Ducati, Volkswagen Commercial Vehicles, Scania and MAN.

Each brand has its own character and operates as an independent entity on the market. The product spectrum extends from low-consumption small cars to luxury class vehicles. In the commercial vehicle sector, the product offering ranges from pick-ups to buses and heavy trucks.

The Volkswagen Group is also active in other fields of business, manufacturing large-bore diesel engines for marine and stationary applications (turnkey power plants), turbochargers, turbomachinery (steam and gas turbines), compressors and chemical reactors, and also producing vehicle transmissions, special gear units for wind turbines, slide bearings and couplings as well as testing systems for the mobility sector.

The group operates 99 production plants in 18 European countries and a further nine countries in the Americas, Asia and Africa. Each working day, 501,956 employees worldwide produce some 34,500 vehicles, are involved in vehicle-related services or work in the other fields of business. The Volkswagen Group sells its vehicles in 153 countries. (These figures are as of December 31, 2011 and exclude Ducati and Porsche.)

It is the goal of the group to offer attractive, safe and environmentally sound vehicles which are competitive in an increasingly tough market and which set world standards in their respective classes.

The present Chairman of the Board of Management of Volkswagen AG is Martin Winterkorn. Ferdinand K. Piëch is the Chairman of the Supervisory Board of VW AG, responsible for monitoring management and approving important corporate decisions.

The VW passenger car brand has a total of 24 models, and sub-models. They are, the up!, the Polo, the Golf, the Jetta, the Passat, the VW CC, the Phaeton, the Golf Estate, the Passat Estate, the Golf Cabriolet, the EOS, the Golf GTI, the Beetle, the Scirocco, the Tiguan, the Touareg, the Touareg Hybrid, the Touran, the Sharan, the R-Models, the Blue Motion Models, the Caddy, the Multivan and the California. Each of these models is available as per their region and their availability. The Gol is an exclusive model for Brazil, while in China they have two exclusive models – the New Lavida and the Santana. They also have a collection of other exclusive models.

Think Blue embodies Volkswagen's goal of creating environmentally friendly products and solutions, encouraging more eco-conscious behaviour and contributing to a sustainable future. It's about being more responsible on the road and more environmentally conscious – not just in their cars, but everywhere, every day. It is an attitude at Volkswagen, and it is something that goes way beyond marketing, something which today already covers product features, sustainable production and logistics, etc.

In the 'Think Blue' campaign, the colour blue has been used predominantly to match with the Volkswagen brand logo and the 'Blue Motion' environmental label. According to a senior executive of Marketing for the Volkswagen Group and the Volkswagen brand, 'Our goal is to establish "Think Blue" as an expression of our corporate mindset and a firm feature of the Volkswagen brand's ecologically sustainable activities'. Explaining, he says, 'We have deliberately chosen an international slogan because environmental protection, knows no national boundaries. The campaign is in line with the Volkswagen brand values: innovative, valuable and responsible'.

Their latest advertising campaign maintains continuity with the past campaigns. It takes up the thread of the 'Think Small' campaign that accompanied the triumphant international success of the Beetle as the People's Car in the 1960s. The 'Think Small' slogan symbolised the Volkswagen brand's achievement in democratising mobility, the world over. The challenge of the future lies in achieving efficient and sustainable mobility for everyone. Volkswagen intends to lead the way, by the 'Think Blue' campaign and attitude.

Volkswagen has had a long chequered history in motorsports, starting in 1966 with Formula Vee – for circuit racing cars, the Formula Super Vee. They have also produced a stable of famous Formula One drivers, to victories in Formula Three. Since 2001, they have concentrated their efforts on developing its circuit racing championship, the Volkswagen Racing Cup and in competing in the Paris to Dakar Cross-Country Rally.

The company has won several awards over the years for its cars. The latest being, the, Sustainovation Award 2012, that, Volkswagen Passenger Cars brand received for its 'Think Blue Factory' environmental program. According to independent consultants Interbrand, Volkswagen is the number one German carmaker in the field of environmental conservation and sustainability – and the number four worldwide as per their 2012 ratings. Their new Golf has received a top five-star rating by the European consumer protection organisation Euro NCAP. It also won the award for innovations in the area of integral safety at the highly esteemed Euro NCAP Advanced Awards in November 2012.

Their advertising has received special accolades in 2012 after winning, a total of 23 Lions – more than any other automobile brand – at the 59th International Festival of Creativity in the French city of Cannes. Volkswagen is known to set advertising trends over the years and produce legendary motifs like the 'Beetle' and the 'Think Small' campaigns. (www.volkswagen.com)

adidas

adidas AG is the world famous German sports goods manufacturer that was founded in 1924 by the brothers Adolf and Rudi Dassler in a town called Herzogenaurach in the southern German state of Bayern. The brothers split in 1947, and Rudolph or Rudi Dassler formed a new company, which he later called PUMA. The brand name adidas is actually a blend from the founder's name, namely, 'Adi' (which is a nickname for Adolf) and 'das' from Dassler, his surname. This name was officially registered by him in 1949.

In addition to sports footwear, the company also produces sportswear or apparel such as shirts, shorts, pants, skirts, etc.; sports equipment including racquets, bats, balls, etc.; and accessories such as sandals, watches, eye-wear, bags, caps and socks. A recent addition is the adidas range of deodorants, perfumes, after-shaves and lotions for both men and women.

The company gained worldwide fame during and after the 1936 Summer Olympics in Berlin, when Adi Dassler persuaded the legendary US athlete Jesse Owens to use their running shoes, which he did with resounding success; winning four golds and, in the process, making the Dassler shoes famous! The three stripes on the shoes were first used in 1949. After a period spanning almost 70 years, the Dassler family withdrew from the company in 1989 and the enterprise was transformed into a corporation.

The adidas Group has well over 46,000 employees worldwide, with more than 3,500 working in the company's headquarters in Herzogenaurach, southern Germany. A team of designers, product developers and experts in bio-mechanics and material technology carry out research in Portland, USA and at the centre in Scheinfeld near Nuremberg. The adidas Group strives to be the global leader in the sporting goods industry with brands built on a passion for sports and a sporting lifestyle. With brands such as adidas, Reebok, TaylorMade, CCM Hockey and Rockport in its portfolio, the adidas Group offers a broad range of products. As a global player, the adidas Group is represented in major markets all over the world. The group is comprised of around 170 subsidiaries with headquarters in Herzogenaurach. Herbert Hainer is the present CEO of the adidas Group, and Igor Landau is the Chairman of the Supervisory Board. The sales revenue for financial year 2011 was €13.344 billion.

Their strategy, put simply, is one of continuously strengthening their brands and products to improve their competitive position and financial performance. Essentially, they strive to be the global leader in the sporting goods industry with a passion for sports and the sporting lifestyle. They seek to continuously improve the quality, look, feel and image of their products to exceed consumer expectations, so as to provide them with the highest value. adidas are innovation and design leaders who seek to help athletes and sportsmen and women of all skill levels to achieve peak performance with every product they bring to the market.

The adidas Group has also reorganised itself to provide a solid platform for growth. In 2009, they took the strategic decision to move from a vertically integrated brand structure into a functional multi-brand structure for the, adidas and Reebok brands. This approach helps them to tackle opportunities from several angles, as both a mass and a niche player, providing distinct and relevant products to a wide spectrum of customers. This enables each brand to keep a unique identity and focus on its core competencies while simultaneously providing the group with a product offering, so as to increase their leverage in the marketplace. In 2010, the adidas group announced Route 2015, the most comprehensive strategic business plan the company has ever introduced. Until 2015, the adidas Group wants to achieve €17 billion in net sales and an operating margin of 11 per cent.

Their distribution strategy follows a distinctive approach to provide tailored solutions for all types of business models, from wholesale and retail to performance and style-oriented businesses. In doing so, they provide their customers with superior service to secure prime shelf space for their brands. They have also committed themselves to building strategic competencies in their own retail outlets and in e-commerce.

In May 2011, their current campaign 'adidas is all in' was launched, leveraging the adidas Sport Performance, adidas Originals and adidas Sport Style sub-brands, ensuring that it is the most diverse and all-encompassing glimpse into the brand ever. The campaign showcases adidas's distinctive presence across and into different sports, cultures and lifestyles, fusing the worlds of sport, music and fashion.

The guiding principle of adidas Sport Performance is 'Play to Win'. Inspired by the motivation of founder Adi Dassler, Sport Performance brings passion for great products to athletes in all sports, allowing them to be faster, stronger, smarter, cooler and natural. The main focus of adidas Sport Performance is on five key categories: football, basketball, running, training and outdoor.

adidas Sport Style houses two groups. The Originals Group is the authentic, iconic sportswear label for the street and its message is 'Celebrate Originality'. The Fashion Group is defined as the future of Sportswear and includes the labels Y-3, Porsche Design Sport, adidas SLVR and adidas NEO. Through these four labels, adidas brings authentic sportswear to the full spectrum of lifestyle consumers.

Top English fashion designer, Stella McCartney, the daughter of ex-Beatle band member Paul McCartney, has been designing collections since 2004 called 'adidas by Stella McCartney'; she also designed the performance collection for Team GB for the London 2012 Olympic Games.

In 2005, adidas introduced the first-ever shoe to utilise a microprocessor. They called it, 'The Worlds First Intelligent Shoe'.

adidas was the official FIFA World Cup 2010 football manufacturer. The ball was named 'Jabulani', which in Bantu, a language of South Africa, means to celebrate.

In May 2010, adidas presented the lightest and fastest football boot ever produced, the F50 adizero; it is a revolutionary new boot that weighs only an astonishing 165 grams! Lionel Messi, the famed Argentinian football player was the first player to wear the distinctive chameleon purple, white and electricity colour during the FIFA 2010 World Cup.

Over the years adidas has maintained the tradition of sponsoring sportspersons and sports teams in various sports, globally as part of their strategy in marketing communications. They also partly sponsor major sporting events like the Summer and Winter Olympics, major league soccer and events such as the London Marathon.

adidas strives to be a sustainable company, one that recognises its responsibilities towards the environment, their employees and the people who make their products. They are currently re-engineering their approach to the environment. (www.adidas.com)

Audi

Audi AG is the German manufacturer of automobiles which are marketed and sold under the Audi brand name. It was founded in 1909 by August Horch in the town of Zwickau, in the eastern state of Saxony. The brand name AUDI is based on the founder's surname 'Horch' which in German means 'to listen', similar to the English word 'hark' which in Latin is 'Audi'. The English word audible is derived from this Latin root word.

In 1932, Audi merged with Horch, DKW and Wanderer automobile manufacturers to form the Auto Union. This was when the famous logo of the four inter-linked rings was first used to symbolise these four brands that joined together as one.

After the Second World War, the company moved to Ingolstadt in Bavaria. In 1958, Daimler-Benz took an 87 per cent holding in the Auto Union Company and subsequently in 1964, the Volkswagen Group bought complete control of the Ingolstadt plant and operations. The newly merged company was known as the Audi NSU Auto Union AG and saw the emergence of Audi as a distinct brand, when it was introduced to other parts of the world. In 1985, the company's official name was shortened to Audi AG, a wholly-owned subsidiary of the Volkswagen group.

Audi AG produces several models of automobiles and engines for the same. The present headquarters are in Ingolstadt, Bavaria in southern Germany, with production locations in Germany, Hungary, Belgium, China and India. Rupert Stadler is the present Chairman of the Board of Management of Audi AG, and Martin Winterkorn is the Chairman of the Supervisory Board. The Audi Group increased its revenue in 2011 to a record new level of €44.096 billion while employing over 62,000 people worldwide.

Audi can look back on a long tradition and a rich history in the manufacture of luxury cars in the premium or luxury segment, starting with large cars which had eight-cylinder engines, built in the late 20s, like Audi Type R, also known as the Imperator. In 1988, Audi undertook a new and successful project to establish itself in the luxury class segment, the large sedan with the name V8. It was equipped with an eight-cylinder engine. In the second version, the 'quattro' permanent all-wheel drive, a first in the premium segment was already standard. The first generation A8 produced in 1994 marked the first use of the aluminium Audi space-frame (ASF) body, a technological breakthrough in the series produced car. The second generation A8 followed in 2002 with the adaptive air suspension and the innovative MMI control system. In 2003, the single-frame radiator grille became the new face of the brand.

Audi has maintained its primary slogan, 'Vorsprung durch Technik', which in English means 'leading through technique' (or 'technology'). This phrase was developed in the 1970s and has since been maintained in Audi advertising campaigns all over the world. The Audi brand embodies progressive design, ground-breaking technology and enhanced driving pleasure.

The new A8 is a concentrated high-tech package that confirms the Audi claim to technical leadership. This is the top version of its flagship model. The A8 LW12 quattro, with a long wheelbase and a 12-cylinder engine, sets new standards of luxury, dynamics and efficiency in the top automobile manufacturing league. It has a powerful presence, with a design clearly derived from the brand's genes. This design has undergone further refinement with taut lines, which makes it athletic and elegant to the eye. It has an elegant interior with a craftsman's fit and finish. According, to Rupert Sadler, Chairman of the Board of Management of Audi AG, 'The new Audi A8 is the sportiest sedan in the segment. It combines numerous functions in a new and intelligent way. And it is unmatched in the stylistic elements and impression of the interior.'

Among the other notable models are the Audi A3, the A3 Sportback, the A3 Cabriolet and the S3, which are sporty models in the compact segment. A refined style, agile driving fun and elaborate technology with new attentive details on both the exterior and interior, are their other significant attributes.

The Audi R8 Spyder 5.2 FSI quattro combines breathtaking performance with the experience of open-top driving. In a recent design competition the readers of a German auto magazine chose Audi as 'The brand with the most beautiful cars', with the R8 Spyder finishing on the podium in the category for, 'Most Beautiful Car Model'!

Then of course, there is the Audi e-tron, which is a compact sports car with an all-electric drive. Two electric motors with a combined output of 150 kW accelerates the coupé with an ASF-design aluminium body, from 0 to 200 km/h in just 5.9 seconds.

The new e-tron model series from Audi will gain another member, the Audi A1 e-tron which is a Mega City Vehicle (MCV) with an innovative drive technology. It comes equipped with a powerful electric motor for zero-emission driving in the city. There is also an internal combustion engine on-board that recharges the battery in cases of emergency or otherwise, a compact electric car in the premium class.

Audi is the worldwide leader in the field of lightweight design. For over 15 years, Audi has been producing aluminium bodies based on the Audi Space Frame (ASF) technology. Numerous patents and awards have documented the innovative power of this technology, including, European Inventor of the Year 2008. Lightweight design is one of their greatest strengths and is also typical of the brand because it combines dynamics with efficiency. The Audi engineers are working on many new ideas for making the car even lighter and thus even more efficient. For Audi, lightweight design is a fundamental technology for the sustainable mobility of the future.

At the 2010 Michelin Challenge Bibendum, which is one of the world's most important forums in the domain of sustainable mobility, Audi emerged as the overall winner for its lightweight ASF and Design Award for the Audi e-tron electronic sports car.

Another innovative project undertaken by the development teams at Audi is The Travolution Project, which is a working concept for a dialogue between cars and traffic signals. It reduces the amount of time spent at standstill or during acceleration and in this way significantly reduces the vehicle's fuel consumption. Journalists and traffic planners, who tested Travolution during demonstration runs, in the Ingolstadt, Audi headquarters, obtained immediate and dramatic results. Reduced waiting times at traffic signals cut fuel consumption by 17 per cent! In a full year that would save on average as much as 700,000 litres or 184,920 gallons of fuel! (www.audi.com)

Allianz

Allianz SE is one of the largest financial services providers in the world. It was founded in 1890 in Munich and was based in Berlin. After World War II, they moved to Munich and have been headquartered there since. They provide financial products in the areas of insurance, banking and asset management. Allianz is the second largest international insurance and financial services company in the world.

With approximately 142,000 employees worldwide as of December 2011, the Allianz Group serves approximately 78 million customers in around 70 countries. In financial year 2011, the Allianz Group achieved total revenues of €103.560 billion. They are also one of the world's largest asset managers, with third-party assets of €1.281 trillion under management as of 2011.

In 2006, Allianz AG (AktienGesellschaft) became Allianz SE. SE stands for Societas Europaea, which is a new European legal form for stock corporations in the EU. It became the first company in the Euro Stoxx 50 Index to adopt the legal form of an SE or Societas Europaea.

As part of Allianz AG's conversion to Allianz SE, the existing two-tier system consisting of a board of management and a supervisory board has been retained. The board of management is made up 11 members. The Chairman of the Board of Management is Michael Diekmann, the *de facto* CEO. The supervisory board of Allianz SE consists of 12 members divided into six shareholder and six employee representatives. As per SE regulations, the chairman of the supervisory board must be a shareholder representative. Helmut Perlet has been the elected Chairman of the Supervisory Board.

The stated goal of the company is, 'To build the strongest financial community'. To achieve this, they have set forth certain fundamental principles and management priorities. The fundamental principles help them earn the trust of their customers and partners by offering the highest level of expertise, integrity and sustainability. Their management priorities consist of maintaining a clear focus on operating profitability, financial strength, reducing complexity for efficient global best practice transfer and sustainable improvement of their competitive position. The aim is nothing less than, 'Delivering the Best of Allianz'.

The Leadership Values set forth by the Allianz management to drive their strategic objectives, essentially consists of Aligning Strategy and communicating this to all the stakeholders, promoting a high performance culture, focusing on their customers, developing their employees and building on mutual trust and feedback.

Allianz is one of the leading insurance groups in the world and ranks number one in the German property–casualty and life insurance markets based on gross, written and statutory premiums. Their product portfolio includes a wide array of property–casualty, life/health insurance products for both private and corporate customers. Among the products for their private customers are ones that cover accidents abroad, emergency services for your home, old-age provision and car insurance for all situations. Products for business customers include products like, agro-insurance, employee benefits and green insurance for large infrastructure projects where they can offset the local environmental degradation, so as to minimise the project's environmental impact. Other products consist of insurance coverage for buildings and facilities, loss of earnings, liability and workers compensation, claims management, risk consulting and alternative risk transfer. Allianz also mitigates risk of mega projects, like the one in South Korea, Incheon Bay, where one of the world's largest bridges is being built. The insurance line of business is conducted worldwide – mainly in Europe, the US and in the Asia-Pacific region.

Allianz is one of the five largest asset managers in the world. They serve a comprehensive range of retail and institutional asset management clients. Their institutional customers include corporate and public pension funds, insurance and other financial services companies, governments, charities and financial advisors.

As of January 1, 2012, Allianz runs the asset management business out of two distinct investment management businesses, PIMCO and AGI. Both units operate under Allianz Asset Management (AAM), focusing solely on financial and overarching governance matters. This change is driven by the significant growth in asset management in recent years. In this domain, primary regions are the US, Germany, France, Italy and the Asia-Pacific region.

In banking, the core market, Germany, is served by the brand name Allianz Bank. The main thrust of their activities lies in addressing the financial needs of their agency's customers.

According to, Christian Deuringer, Senior Vice-President Global Brand Management at Allianz SE, 'We have entered a new era in our global brand positioning, which comes with corresponding challenges. Allianz's recently created worldwide Market Management function enables us to link the brand and execution strategy more strongly to our business. It was particularly important to us to pursue these goals with our colleagues in the operating companies'. They hope to use worldwide synergies to strengthen the Allianz brand and sales in the future.

Among their many corporate sponsorships, the most well known is being the global safety partner of Formula One. They also provided naming rights for the Allianz Arena, a well-known football stadium in the north of Munich, the Allianz Stadium in Sydney and both the Allianz Riviera in Nice and the Allianz Park in London, which is scheduled to open in 2013. In addition, Allianz actively supports the Paralympic movement and athletes around the world.

To date, the Allianz Group has developed over 80 products and services that help mitigate climate change and take its environmental impact into account. The products range from asset management to insurance and assistance. On the asset management site, sustainable development is supported through socially responsible and environmentally sound investments.

They also help their customers benefit from business opportunities of evolving markets such as carbon emissions trading and clean and environmental technologies, so that customers can cope with the changing environment and benefit from the opportunities of a low-carbon economy. (www.allianz.com)

Porsche

Porsche AG is the well-known German manufacturer of luxury, high-end performance automobiles. The company was founded in 1931 by Ferdinand Porsche, an Austro-Hungarian engineer born in 1875 in Maffersdorf, a Bohemian town. He set up offices in the city district of Zuffenhausen in Stuttgart, in the present state of Baden-Württemberg. They have plants in Stuttgart and in Leipzig.

Porsche's well-known corporate logo of a Black Horse is based on the coat of arms of the then Free People's State of Württemberg of former Weimar Germany. Stuttgart was the capital, and after the political consolidation of West Germany in 1949, the state of Baden-Württemberg was formed.

In August 2009, Porsche Automobil Holding SE, the holding company of Porsche AG and the Volkswagen Group, reached an agreement to merge the two companies in 2011 to form an Integrated Automotive Group. As of now, the company is officially called the Porsche Automobil Holding SE. This goal was achieved in August 2012, such that Porsche AG is now effectively a 100 per cent subsidiary of Volkswagen.

The CEO of Porsche SE is Martin Winterkorn, and the current President of the Executive BoardCEO of Porsche AG is Matthias Müller. Wolfgang Porsche is the Chairman of the Supervisory Board of both Porsche SE and Porsche AG as well. The manufacturing company Porsche AG, as of 30 September 2012, employed over 17,000 employees worldwide, while total revenue for the fiscal year of 2011 was €10.928 billion.

Porsche's main focus is the manufacture of luxury automobiles, although they have an additional business of automotive financial services. In the early days of the company, tractors were manufactured. The current stable of brands or models is the, Boxster, Cayman, 911, Panamera and the Cayenne. Each of these models has several additional variations or sub-models.

The basis of the Porsche principle is a set of values and philosophies that together have created or added value along with the 'Made in Germany' stamp and because of it, with responsibility to the customer and to their own heritage. They concentrate on what they do best: building sports cars. The engineering or technical principle of the company is to develop technical evolutions that give their sports cars a soul. The proof that such high standards of quality are upheld is the fact that two-thirds of all Porsche vehicles ever built are still on the road, which is attributable to the cars' 'genes', built in at the factory.

Porsche has built cars to win races, and their cars have won the Le Mans 24-hour race 16 times, the Targa Florio and the Paris-Dakar Cross-Country races several times and with Porsche engines, the Formula One world Championship three times; different Porsche vehicles have been developed for different generations. The accumulated experience and know-how accumulated over the years has helped Porsche develop a singular sports car concept that has laid the foundation for their present model range. They equip every generation produced with state-of-the-art technology, with a design that is characterised by sensitivity and restraint, which is the reason why the Porsche Brand enjoys unsurpassed prestige in the US.

A representative survey was carried out in 2006 by the Luxury Institute in New York, which questioned more than 500 households with a gross annual income over $200,000 and a net worth of at least $750,000. The results show Porsche as the best of the luxury automobile brands. According to the institute, the reasons for the success of the Porsche brand are its uniqueness and its exclusivity. The survey also found that the brand is most frequently driven by people who are admired and respected by others.

Peter Schwarzenbauer, the then President and CEO of Porsche North America, responded by saying, 'We are delighted to be crowned as the most prestigious premium brand for the second time in a row.... This goes to show that our product strategy is absolutely on the money'.

Today, Porsche is available in more than 100 countries, through their regional offices and distribution companies. Their presence around the globe is that of a lean, powerful and flexible company that is export-driven. To make a Porsche an absolute one-of-a-kind, Porsche Exclusive offers a broad array of ex-factory options. Here a Porsche may be extensively personalised and retrofitted with technical accessories, leaving nothing to be desired.

Porsche stands for dynamism, agility, flexibility, as well as speed, elegance, safety and of course quality. The present Porsche model range has sports cars like the Boxster and its Spyder version to their most famous model, the 911. The Cayman is a hard top car, similar in design to the Boxster, but with a higher price range. The high-performance, luxury saloon/sedan is the Panamera, whereas the Cayenne is Porsche's mid-size luxury sport utility vehicle or SUV. One other model that had a limited run was the Carrera GT which stopped being produced in 2006.

Porsche's latest introduction is the 918 Spyder, the concept car for the twenty-first century, symbolising the future of sports car design. The mid-engine, two-seater combines the driving performance of a super sports car with the emissions of a sub-compact. Its plug-in hybrid design achieves a CO^2 emission of only 70 grams to the kilometre! (113 grams/mile) and a fuel consumption of 3.0 litres per 100 kilometres! Porsche combines a V8 engine with a power output of more than 500 horse power with three electric motors delivering a total of 160 KW. It is able to reach top speeds of over 320 kilometres per hour – what is called Porsche Intelligent Performance. This eco-super Porsche was unveiled at the Geneva Motor Show to rave reviews the world over.

At the previous New York International Auto Show, the Porsche 911 was declared the '2012 World Performance Car'.

Their R&D centre in Weissach, Germany, is the nucleus of their know-how, which was first developed by Ferdinand Porsche in 1931. Here 5,800 valid patents worldwide are administered, with another 250 being added each year. The Weissach R&D centre is the think-tank of Porsche. They have workshops, test benches, laboratories, measuring centres, a wind tunnel, crash test facilities, etc., and it is where Porsche models are designed, developed and improved upon.

Marking the three world premieres of the Cayenne S Hybrid, the GTR 3 R Hybrid racing car with electrical front-axle drive and fly-wheel, mass power storage, as well as the 918 Spyder concept car with plug-in hybrid technology, the in-house publishing division of the Porsche Museum in Stuttgart recently published the new volume on Ferdinand Porsche-the Pioneer of Hybrid Drive, showing previously unpublished photos and drawings from their Archives, of the first, fully-functional, full hybrid, the Semper Vivus as it was then called, around a century ago. (www.porsche.com)

NIVEA

NIVEA is a personal skin care brand, which is owned by the German company Beiersdorf AG. Paul C. Beiersdorf was the man who gave his name to the company. In 1880, he took over a chemist's shop in Hamburg. Putting his skills and knowledge of physics to use, he soon built a laboratory and offered his services to doctors. Working, in close cooperation with Paul Gerson Unna, the leading dermatologist of the time, he developed a process in their laboratory in Hamburg to manufacture medical plasters, which was later patented in 1882. The date of this patent specification – 28 March 1882 – is considered to be the company's founding date. In 1890, a pharmacist by the name of Oscar Troplowitz acquired the laboratory from Paul C. Beiersdorf and quickly expanded it into a leading branded goods company. In 1892, he built a new factory in Eimsbüttel in Hamburg. To this day, it remains the site of the company's headquarters.

Troplowitz was a true entrepreneur who thought both in customer and market terms, ensuring the further development of its manufacturing on a sound scientific footing. He continued Paul C. Beiersdorf's cooperation with P. Gerson Unna and recruited the chemist Isaac Lifschütz, who was the inventor of the emulsifier Eucerit the basic ingredient and key to the unique properties of NIVEA cream. In 1906, Troplowitz's brother-in-law, Hannes Mankiewicz became a partner in the company.

Driven by innovation, Troplowitz and Mankiewicz created branded goods of consistently reliable quality to benefit a broad range of customers. Troplowitz was convinced that this would be a successful concept for the future. He saw great opportunities for cosmetic care products in particular. This laid the foundations for the company's orientation. After becoming a public limited company in 1922, the company saw its steady development into an international enterprise and at the same time of its establishment and expansion as a leading manufacturer of branded skin and beauty care products.

The present CEO of the Beiersdorf AG is Stefan F. Heidenreich who is also Chairman of the Executive Board of Beiersdorf AG; Reinhard Pöllath is the Chairman of the Supervisory Board. For fiscal year 2011, Beiersdorf generated group sales of €5.633 billion.

The group is comprised of three global brands, with NIVEA in the mass-market, Eucerin for dermo- cosmetics and La Prairie in the luxury segment. In 2011, the NIVEA brand celebrated its 100th anniversary – 'A Century of Skin Care'.

Beiersdorf has a global presence with 150 affiliates and currently employs more than 17,000 people worldwide. They have been listed in the DAX since December 2008. Its flagship brand NIVEA is the world's number one skin care brand. Other brands in its internationally, successful brand portfolio include Eucerin, Labello, La Prairie, 8x4, Florena and Hansaplast/Elastoplast. Their affiliate company Tesa SE is one of the world's leading manufacturers of self-adhesive products and system solutions for industry, trade and consumers.

The name NIVEA alluded to the crème's pure white appearance, which is derived from the Latin word for snow. In addition to Eucerit to bind the oils with water, it also contains glycerine, a little citric acid and, to give it a delicate scent, oil of rose and lily of the valley. Although NIVEA Crème has been continually updated in line with the latest scientific developments, the essence of the recipe has changed little in over 100 years.

The blue tin with the brand name NIVEA in white celebrated its debut in 1925. In the 1950s NIVEA Crème had long since achieved classical brand status and a large number of skincare products were launched under the NIVEA umbrella. The supermarket boom, the abolition of recommended retail prices and new market players led to increased competition in the 1970s. Beiersdorf responded with a challenging advertising campaign that underlined NIVEA's historical leadership claim. The campaign centred on NIVEA Crème and differentiated it from the competition by emphasising its unique quality, unrivalled effectiveness and honesty.

In the 1980s, the Beiersdorf Management recognised the growth potential offered by the NIVEA brand. In fact, European studies had revealed that the NIVEA brand enjoyed a high level of trust and that consumers would accept new products under the umbrella of the NIVEA brand. In line with these consumer expectations, NIVEA introduced a large number of products, offering their customers a high level of quality. This, expansion strategy in the 1980s was systematically continued into the 1990s with the launch of sub-brands, such as NIVEA Hair Care and NIVEA Bath Care. With increased globalisation, NIVEA's focused brand management allowed it to develop into the largest skin care brand in the world. At present, consumers in more than 170 countries worldwide use the NIVEA brand. (www.nivea.com)/www.beiersdorf.com)

PUMA

PUMA SE is another major German sport/lifestyle company that was founded in 1948 by Rudolf Dassler, the elder of the two Dassler brothers. The younger brother Adolf or Adi had founded adidas. The elder brother Rudi started his own company in the same town of Herzogenaurach, in the present state of Bavaria in southern Germany. He chose to set up shop on the other side of the Aurach River in Herzogenaurach, which used to be the company's headquarters before it moved into its new office building PUMAVision Headquarters in 2009. PUMA became a public company in 1986.

The long-time CEO of the company was Jochen Zeitz. He was appointed chairman and CEO in 1993 at the age of 30, becoming the youngest chairman in German industrial history to lead a public company. He managed to transform PUMA, from a low-priced brand into a premium sport/lifestyle company and one of the top three brands in the sporting goods industry worldwide by sticking to a long-term development plan that he introduced in 1993.

The present range of products extends from sport performance and sport/lifestyle footwear, apparel and accessories. French luxury goods company PPR (Pinault-Printemp-Redoute), renamed Kering on June 2013 now holds 82.99 per cent of PUMA shares and is represented by Francois-Henri Pinault who is the present Deputy Chairman of the Administrative Board and the Chairman Jean-François Palus. The CEO of Managing Directors is Björn Gulden.

The consolidation is set to strengthen PUMA's position as the leading sport/lifestyle company in the long run and is set to create the perfect platform for the further global expansion of the company and the ongoing implementation of its strategy. Although Kering is the parent company with majority stock holding, PUMA is set to remain an individual company.

PUMA has the long-term mission of becoming the most desirable and sustainable, sport/lifestyle company. PUMA's position is to be strengthened, through the opportunities offered by the sport/lifestyle market in all categories and regions. PUMA is positioned as a sport/lifestyle brand that takes pleasure in skilfully combining influences from both sports and lifestyle trends and which strives to contribute to a better world.

PUMA's sustainability concept, PUMAVision, states that the company is committed to work in ways that contribute to the world by supporting creativity, sustainability and peace, and by staying true to the values of being fair, honest, positive and creative in decisions made and actions taken.

PUMA starts in sports and ends in fashion. Its sport performance and lifestyle labels focus on sports such as football, running, golf, sailing, cricket and motorsport (for driving shoes and racing suits). The Black Label also features collaborations with renowned designers such as Yasuhiro Mihara, Sergio Rossi, Philipe Starck and the late Alexander McQueen.

The PUMA Group also owns brands like Cobra Golf and Tretorn. At present, the group distributes products in more than 120 countries employing over 11,000 people worldwide. PUMA's consolidated sales for the financial year of 2011 was €3.009 billion.

Over the years, PUMA has used the services of some of the best sports persons in the world, to promote and endorse the PUMA brand, from the likes of Pele, the Williams sisters, to Usain Bolt. They also include teams such as the 2006 Football World Cup champions, Italy. They have continued to strengthen their sport/lifestyle brand through unique events and marketing campaigns, like the Puma City in Boston and during the Volvo Ocean Race.

They recently refined their brand manual '10', so as to incorporate the PUMAVision into it among other brand innovations. Their new brand promise is to joyfully mix the influences of sport and lifestyle with a desire to contribute to a better world. 'Joy' is what they will try to bring to their customers and what they think will differentiate them from their competition, by talking about the moments of joy inherent in both sport and life. The brand that remembers what it is like to play the game; to play it with joy. They feel it is time to bring the joy back again. PUMA's brand strategy intends to bring the feeling of joy while being the best at doing it. In doing so, they intend to become a stronger, more confident brand and continue their tradition of fun-infused products and campaigns.

To this end, the company has initiated the programs of PUMA.Safe, a program that focuses on environmental and social issues, PUMA.Peace a program supporting global peace and PUMA.Creative, a program supporting artists and creative organisations. The goal is to provide real and practical expressions of this vision to build, among other things, a more sustainable future for themselves and their stakeholders.

According to Reiner Hengstamm, Global Director of PUMA.Safe, 'Supply chain sustainability is a key part of PUMA's overall sustainability strategy. Without sustainable suppliers, we will not be able to produce sustainable products or credibly report about PUMA's own sustainability initiatives. The Global Action Network for Transparency in the Supply Chain (GANTSch) project helps to ensure that our suppliers fully embrace the concept of sustainability and introduce respective programs in their companies'.

PUMA has already started the next pivotal phase of the long-term 360° Sustainability Program by implementing the eco-friendly packaging system 'Clever Little Bag'. This new innovative solution will significantly reduce the amount of waste and CO_2 emissions that traditional product packaging, such as shoe boxes and apparel polyethylene bags, generates and underpins PUMA's target of reducing carbon, energy, water and waste by 25 per cent and developing 50 per cent of its international product collections in footwear, apparel and accessories according to best practice sustainability standards by 2015.

They will also completely offset their own global CO_2 emissions to become the first carbon neutral company within the sport/lifestyle industry. PUMA compensates its direct and indirect CO_2 emissions through offsetting projects in Africa that also take the needs of local communities and conservation of biodiversity into account. The company has deeply embedded its long-term sustainability program into its operations and product cycle, making it an integral part of PUMA's DNA.

PUMA has developed many product and process innovations over the years, including the introduction of the revolutionary S.P.A technology. The first manufacturer to offer sport shoes with Velcro fasteners, the TRINOMIC sports shoe system, INSPECTOR, a growth control system for children's shoes, and the DISC SYSTEM sports shoe. The CELLERATOR, introduction of the CELL technology for the first foam-free mid-sole and production of fire-proof footwear in partnership with Porsche and Sparco are some of the other, well-known, successful innovations. (www.puma.com)

The Otto Group

The Otto Group is considered the world's largest mail-order company with subsidiaries and affiliates in Europe, Asia, South America and the United States. It was founded in 1949 by Werner Otto in Hamburg, as Otto Versand GmbH & Co. Under the stewardship of the founder's eldest son, Michael, the company became the world's leading catalogue mail-order company in the world by the year 1987. The privately held company is very much a family concern, being owned and operated by the Otto family. With headquarters in Hamburg, the Otto Group's numerous catalogue businesses in 20 countries include Grattan and Freemans in the UK, 3 Suisses in France and Heine, Schwab and the flagship brand of OTTO in Germany. The development of this company is today seen as one of the most impressive stories of post-war Germany.

Werner Otto started the company with delivering shoes and then came textiles and hardware. In the 1970s, the company grew through mergers, acquisitions, joint ventures and founding new companies. Hans-Otto Schrader has been the Otto Group Chairman and CEO since 2007, and Michael Otto is the Chairman of the Supervisory Board. For financial year 2011, the Otto Group increased its consolidated revenues to €11.597 billion.

At present, the Otto Group is a holding company, a leading retail and services company whose 123 major companies and 53,000 employees in 20 countries help conduct business in a worldwide network. The combination of retail, financial, logistics, travel and other services allows the group to serve its customers as a reliable partner. It is said to be the world's biggest online retailer for fashion and lifestyle products, and the world's second largest web retailer overall, 480 stores worldwide and more than 60 online shops, group-wide.

The Otto Group companies are divided into three segments or divisions: Multi-Channel Retail, Financial Services with the Hanseatic Bank and EOS and other services with the Hermes Group GmbH coordinating all the activities of their logistics companies in Germany, the UK, Austria and Italy. The Otto Group encompasses a large number of companies operating in the major economic zones of the world. All these companies are linked by the common activity of trading and related services, in different product lines, target groups and distribution channels.

The Otto Group mission is embraced in the motto, the power of responsibility. It represents the values to which the group and all its companies are firmly committed: profitability, innovation, diversity and sustainability.

For the Otto Group, leading through a passion for their customers, means seeking to not only advise and support their customers but to serve them in every possible way by offering their customer's quality goods and services at fair prices. Although the Otto Group has long since expanded its operations to include practically all distribution channels, the mail-order business and its fundamentals are still the main characteristics of their business. They believe the key to long-term business success lies in continuously reinforcing and building on that element of trust between the retailer and the customer. Today, the group has gone forth into international trading, financing and services. The high standards of the Otto Group are also reflected in the pre-sales and after-sales services they offer.

The Otto Group is known to be an innovator from its early days, offering its customers the best products and services at all times. Otto was the first player in the German market to introduce buying on account in 1952 and in 1990, the first player to offer 24-hour service. They began selling on the Internet in the mid-1990s, much before many other retailers. The multi-channel strategy it started at that time has helped give rise to substantial synergistic benefits from the interaction of their mail-order business, the retail store business and e-commerce.

OTTO, the core company of the group or the flagship brand of the Otto Group, has two main catalogues and some 60 specialist catalogues appearing every year, OTTO gives its customers access to up-to-the-minute trends, specifically geared towards its particular target groups. Orders can be placed in the Otto shops, by phone, mail or fax, on the Internet or via TV shopping.

OTTO is much more than a substantial mail-order sales company, it is also a dynamic established and resilient brand . The recipe for success is a combination of the strong OTTO umbrella brand, licensed and third-party brands and its own brands. The OTTO brand is likeable, credible, dynamic, innovative and self-confident.

Working with well-known personalities since 1985, such as supermodels Giselle Bundchen and Heidi Klum as well as fashion designer Jette Joop, these endorsements and partnerships have contributed to the positive image of the OTTO brand and have increased its sales substantially.

Today, the main catalogue is published three times a year, and extends to some 1,000 pages. The print run totals 20 million and the catalogue offers over 100,000 articles per season, covering areas as diverse as fashion and clothing, homes and furnishings and modern technical appliances and products. It provides an extensive and optimised range of goods.

The Otto Group believes in social responsibility, environmental protection and fair cooperation as guiding principles in all their activities. They also undertake various charitable and socially responsible projects in several underdeveloped regions of the world. (www.ottogroup.com)

BASF

BASF SE is amongst the world's largest chemical companies. It was founded in 1865 by Friedrich Engelhorn, in Mannheim. He then started a stock corporation under the name Badische Anilin & Soda Factory. The company name BASF is derived from this original name of the company. The first manufacturing facility was built on the opposite side of the Rhine River in Ludwigshafen, in the present state of Rhineland-Palatinate. The original headquarters are still located here, as is its largest integrated production site, employing around 33,000 people. This site was completely destroyed during the Second World War and was later rebuilt. In 1952, BASF was re-founded under its own name.

To date, the company has six large integrated production sites, or what the company calls Verbund sites. These sites are about interlinking production plants, energy flows, logistics and infrastructure. On these sites, chemical processes consume less energy, produce higher product yields and conserve resources. In addition to these sites, the company also has around 370 smaller production plants worldwide, which serve customers and partners in almost all the countries of the world.

The BASF portfolio is comprised of chemicals (inorganics, petrochemicals and intermediates), plastics (performance polymers and polyurethanes), performance products (dispersions and pigments, care chemicals, paper chemicals and performance chemicals), functional solutions (catalysts, construction chemicals and coatings), agricultural solutions (crop protection) and oil and gas. Their 15 divisions develop strategy for BASF's 76 strategic business units and are organised according to sectors and products.

In financial year 2011, BASF posted total sales of €73.5 billion while employing over 111,000 people worldwide. Kurt Bock is the new Chairman of the Board of Executive Directors, while H.C. Eggert Voscherau is the Chairman of the Supervisory Board of BASF SE. The board of executive directors concerns itself with corporate governance, the management and supervision of company activities.

To gain a good understanding of the depth and range of BASF's products, one needs to really look at the customer industries they cater to. Across all industries, the customers expect solutions that help improve quality, increase comfort and reduce energy consumption. At BASF, they offer their customers, tailor-made solutions that create value for them.

In the packaging industry, BASF supplies raw materials for different applications such as rigid and flexible plastics, foams, paper, cardboard, cartons as well as labels and closures. BASF's new development in material and auxiliary materials enables their customers to develop and implement innovative packaging solutions. BASF is fulfilling requirements in the areas of environmental protection and business through innovative, biodegradable plastics. Ecovio® is the first BASF plastic based on the renewable raw material, corn. The other component is the biodegradable plastic Ecoflex®. This plastic can be used to produce flexible filaments, manufacturing carrier bags or other applications, including cling films, laminates for packaging and breathable films for the hygiene sector, etc.

In the construction industry, whether it is a new building, a renovation or interior work, raw materials and products from BASF play a major role, with energy efficient, economical and ecologically sound products. Besides classic raw materials, BASF also offers a number of ready-to-use construction products such as tile adhesives, industry and sports flooring and many more.

For the pharmaceutical industry, BASF provides generic, active ingredients for many therapeutic fields of application, making it the market leader for ibuprofen, pseudoephedrine, caffeine and theophylline. BASF has a comprehensive portfolio and unparalleled skills at every stage of the pharmaceutical value chain from drug discovery, pre-clinical studies, clinical phases I–III, API manufacturing, drug formulation and packaging. They support and deliver in terms of innovation, speed-to-market and cost effectiveness.

As one of the world's largest suppliers of plastics, BASF has one of the most comprehensive lines in this realm, ranging from automotive engineering, the electrical and electronics sectors, in household appliances, precision technology to medical technology.

In the personal care industry, BASF has a portfolio that includes products for hair, oral care, skin and sun care as well as decorative cosmetics. The high-quality range includes actives, polymers, effect pigments, UV absorbers and surfactants. Their comprehensive portfolio for the personal care industry is completed by BASF Beauty Care Solutions and Aroma Chemicals. Their detergents, cleaners and formulators line includes all major products needed in the detergent and cleaner industry for household, industrial and institutional applications, for chemical–technical applications and in the formulation and personal care industries.

Finally, BASF's solutions and products for the automotive industry include power trains and chassis, interiors, electronics, exteriors, safety, environmental and specials like powder injection moulding and hybrid components. All of these are meant to enhance comfort, increase performance, reduce fuel consumption, improve safety and decrease emissions, helping carmakers and suppliers to produce more efficiently.

BASF's stated objective is to remain the world's leading chemical company. They describe how they intend to achieve this in the, 'We Create Chemistry' strategy, which was presented in November 2011. This strategy builds on BASF's success in recent years and defines ambitious goals for the future. The company sees that sustainability is becoming increasingly important as a key factor for growth and value creation. For BASF, sustainable development means the combination of long-term oriented economic success with environmental protection and social responsibility. Customers want sustainable products and system solutions, and the company's employees expect BASF to integrate sustainability firmly into its day-to-day activities. That is why the company is integrating sustainability much more closely into its business. For example, the Eco-Efficiency Analysis developed by BASF is a strategic tool to optimise products, processes or whole system solutions regarding both the cost and the environmental impact over the entire life cycle.

Another of their understandings is that diversity plus inclusion is a strategic factor for their business success, where they regard their employee's uniqueness and diversity as enrichment, given that every employee counts for a good corporate culture and lasting success.

According to Andreas Kreimeyer, Research Executive Director at BASF, 'BASF has a solid track record of innovations beginning over 140 years ago that continuously contribute to improve people's lives'. In the BASF network, they have organised their research to combine marketing impulses with scientific insights into innovative products. BASF has more than 10,100 employees in R&D in 70 locations worldwide. BASF Future Business and BASF Venture Capital are also active in this research network as they develop new business areas for BASF through their access to new technologies and as per customer demands.

For the second time in succession, BASF heads the, 'Good Company Ranking'. The ranking is carried out every two years by *manager magazin*, Germany's top business magazine and Kirchoff Consulting. In this study, the 19 largest European corporations listed on the DAX and STOXX were evaluated for their sustainability in the following categories: environment, human resources, social responsibility and economic performance. In all four categories, the independent expert groups gave BASF, 83, out of a total of hundred points, well ahead of the other companies. (www.basf.com)

Bayer

Bayer AG is the German pharmaceutical and chemical company which was founded in 1863 by Friedrich Bayer and his partner Johann Friedrich Weskott in Barmen, a town in the state of North-Rhine Westphalia, close to the German city of Wuppertal. Bayer celebrates 150 years of its existence in 2013.

Bayer became famous for first introducing aspirin to the world. However, Bayer lost its trademark status for aspirin in the US, UK and France during World War I. It is now widely used to describe all brands of the compound in those countries as a generic name, whereas in over 80 other countries, it is still registered as a trademark of Bayer.

Today, Bayer is a global enterprise with core competencies in the fields of healthcare, agriculture and high-tech materials. The company's products and services are designed to benefit people and improve their quality of life. In fiscal year 2011, Bayer employed 112,000 people worldwide and had sales revenues of €36.5 billion. The R&D investment during this period was €2.9 billion.

The present headquarters are situated in Leverkusen, in the state of North-Rhine Westphalia. Marijn Dekkers is the present CEO and Chairman of the Board of Management of Bayer AG since October 2010, while Manfred Schneider is the Chairman of the Supervisory Board. Bayer AG defines common values, goals and strategies for the entire group. The three subgroups, namely Bayer HealthCare, Bayer CropScience and Bayer MaterialScience and the three service companies operate independently, led by the strategic management holding company. The Corporate Centre supports the Group Management Board in its task of strategic leadership.

The Bayer HealthCare Group, with headquarters in Leverkusen, researches, develops, manufactures and markets innovative products for the prevention, diagnosis and treatment of diseases. The company plays an important part in improving the health of both people and animals. This subgroup is comprised of four global divisions, namely consumer care, medical care (diabetes care and Medrad, over-the-counter medicines and dietary supplements), animal health (veterinary products and grooming products) and pharmaceuticals (prescription medicines). The best-selling products in this group are the following: Adalat® for hypertension treatment; Advantage®, a flea control product for dogs and cats; Contour®, an umbrella brand for blood glucose monitoring systems and services; Aspirin®, the pain reliever, based on acetylsalicylic acid; Avelox®, a drugmeans to treat respiratory infections; Betaferon® and Betaseron®, speciality drugs to treat multiple sclerosis; Ciprobay® and Cipro®, medicines to treat infectious diseases; Kogenate®, for hemophilia treatment; Nexavar®, a medicine to treat kidney and liver cancer; Ultravist® and Yaz® (oral contraceptive), among many others. And, of course, there is Alka-Seltzer, the popular antacid and pain-reliever in the US.

The Bayer CropScience Group is one of the world's leading innovative crop science companies in the areas of seeds, crop protection and non-agricultural pest control. The company offers a wide range of products including high value seeds, innovative crop protection solutions based on chemical and biological modes of action as well as an extensive service backup for modern, sustainable agriculture. In the area of non-agricultural applications, Bayer CropScience has a broad portfolio of products and services to control pests at home in the garden and in forestry applications.

The company pledges its full support for the aims of the Convention on Biological Diversity, which has three main goals: 1) conservation of biological diversity, 2) sustainable use of its components, and 3) fair and equitable sharing of benefits arising from genetic resources. This was adopted at the United Nations Conference on Environment and Development (UNCED), also known as the Earth Summit, in Rio de Janeiro in 1992. Although it is clear that high-quality and affordable food products are urgently required worldwide, a stable and healthy basis for production is equally necessary. To this end, both the conservation of biodiversity and well-functioning ecosystems play a central role in this pursuit. They form the foundation for sustainable agriculture, which is one of the firmly established goals of Bayer CropScience.

The Bayer MaterialScience Group is one of the world's largest producers of polymers and high-performance plastics. Its innovative advances in coatings, adhesives, insulating materials and sealants, polycarbonates and polyurethanes significantly enhance the quality of lives. Products holding leading positions on the world market account for a large proportion of the company's sales. The subgroup's portfolio is divided into three business units, namely, 1) polyurethanes, 2) polycarbonates, and 3) coatings, adhesives and specialities.

They also have an industrial operations area in this sub-group. One comes across intelligent solutions involving Bayer Material Science products in an enormous variety of applications, such as in the automotive, electrical and electronic industries, in construction, packaging, medical engineering, footwear, sports and leisure, textiles and clothing, health, wood and furniture, home, garden and sanitation, cosmetics, mechanical and plant engineering and many others.

The materials and products of tomorrow are being researched and designed today in many of Bayer's laboratories in various locations and with various external partners worldwide. The current areas of interest include bio-based materials and processes, opto-electronics, high-performance polymers, nano-composites, functional surfaces and coatings and in catalysis.

The wealth of knowledge that Bayer researchers have gained about people, animals, plants, materials and inter-disciplinary technologies provides the basis for long-term sustained growth. Researchers and scientists are responsible for pioneering inventions that revolutionised medicine, chemistry and materials development with products like Aspirin®, Germanin®, Resochin®, Makrolon®, Adalat®, sulfoanimides, polyurethanes and many more.

Bayer's latest sustainability development report won top ranking at the 2011 CR Reporting Awards from the online service provider coporateregister.com. Their past two reports, documents the progress made in projects focusing on global healthcare, nutrition for a growing world population and climate protection. This report is aligned to the guidelines of the Global Reporting Initiative (GRI), the internationally recognised standard for sustainable development reporting, and received an A+ from the GRI – the highest possible rating. It has also held firm to its objective of investing €1 billion in climate relevant R&D.

As part of the Eco-Commercial Building (ECB) program – a central element of the Bayer Climate Program – the company established a partnership network with suppliers, construction firms and architects to generate tailored solutions for energy-efficient commercial and public buildings. As a result of their efforts, their overall water consumption and greenhouse gas emissions fell by 13.3 per cent and 4.1 per cent respectively in the year ending 2011. Bayer considers workforce diversity to be an important value and resource for creative solutions and a key factor in facilitating successful operations in an international context. (www.bayer.com)

Bosch

In 1886, Robert Bosch founded the Workshop for Precision Mechanics and Electrical Engineering in Stuttgart. This was the birth of today's globally active enterprise, the Robert Bosch GmbH otherwise known simply as Bosch.

The company's over 125-year history has been one of innovative drive and social commitment. The Bosch trademark, an armature in a circle, is symbolic of one of its first innovations – the spark plug used in internal combustion engines. Bosch's first high-voltage magneto was developed in 1902; this invention set out to conquer the whole world, then, came the production of batteries for both four- and two-wheelers in 1922.

Today, the Bosch Group is a leading global supplier of technology and services, in the areas of automotive and industrial technology, consumer goods and building technology. Some 300,000 associates (or employees) generated sales of €51.494 billion in fiscal year 2011. They have around 112 production locations in Germany and around 164 sites outside Germany.

The Bosch Group is comprised of the Robert Bosch GmbH and its more than 350 subsidiaries and regional companies in over 60 countries. If its sales and service partners are included, then Bosch is represented in roughly 150 countries. This worldwide development, manufacturing and sales network is the foundation for growth. In 2011, the Bosch group spent some €4.2 billion for R&D and applied for over 4,100 patents worldwide. Given all its products and services, Bosch enhances the quality of life by providing solutions which are both innovative and beneficial; their present corporate slogan is 'Invented for Life'.

Since 1964, Bosch's majority shareholder has been the Robert Bosch Stiftung GmbH, a charitable foundation. This foundation carries on the charitable and social endeavours of the company's founder in contemporary form, having spent in total €1.2 billion for various causes since its founding. Today, the foundation holds a 92 per cent stake in the share capital of Robert Bosch GmbH. The share dividend received by the foundation is also used exclusively for charitable purposes, that is, to support general medical care, international understanding, social work, training and education. The Bosch family holds only 7 per cent of the total share capital.

Volkmar Denner is the Chairman of the Board of Management of the Robert Bosch GmbH, and Franz Fehrenbach is the Chairman of the Supervisory Council.

The three major business sectors for the Bosch group are the automotive, industrial, consumer goods and building technology. From January 2013, Bosch will have four business sectors: automotive technology, industrial technology, consumer goods and energy and building technology.

For the automotive sector, Bosch provides for the ever-more-demanding requirements in respect to economical fuel consumption, lower emissions and driving fun. The areas of their expertise extend from gasoline and diesel systems, chassis systems, brakes and control, electrical drives, starter motors and generators to car multimedia, automotive electronics, automotive aftermarket and steering systems. The company also spends some €400 million each year in the promising field of electromobility.

Bosch Rexroth AG a subsidiary of the Bosch Group is one of the leading specialists worldwide in drive and control technology. This company is the supplier of choice for more than 500,000 customers for high-quality electrical, hydraulic, pneumatic and mechatronic components and systems, for application in industrial automation, mobile equipment in commercial vehicles and also in renewable energy.

While Bosch Packaging Technology, is one of the leading suppliers for holistic systems for packaging and process technology. They develop, produce and distribute modules and systems for the pharmaceutical, confectionery and cosmetic industries, as well as for other food and non-food industries.

The solar energy division is a new business that develops, manufactures and markets mono- and poly-crystalline silicon solar cells. The company also produces thin-film solar modules, based on amorphous and micro-morphous technology. They are the leading providers of silicon-based photovoltaic products.

In their consumer goods and building technology segment, they produce power tools for both DIY and for professionals, being the world market leader for portable electric power tools and power tool accessories. They also have innovative gardening tools with brands such as Bosch, Skil and Dremel.

In the household appliances segment, the range of reliable, long-serving products has made Bosch, one of Europe's leading manufacturers of household appliances. Household appliances from Bosch have an accomplished design and include innovative, intelligent functions. Whether it is cooking, freezing, dishwashing, laundry washing or drying, the household appliances are intelligent, enjoyable and stylish to look at.

Bosch Thermotechnik has a wide portfolio of energy-efficient and environmentally friendly solutions from floor-standing and wall-hung heating boilers to heat pumps and co-generation plants to solar systems and water heaters. This division includes several international and regional brands like Buderus and Junkers as well. In the UK, the Worcester Bosch Group is the brand for heating and hot water solutions.

Bosch Security Systems is another subsidiary in this segment, which is a global supplier of security, safety and various communication products, solutions and services, from video surveillance systems to conference systems and care solutions. The Bosch Communication Centre is also an international provider of business process outsourcing services.

With more than 15,000 Bosch Service Workshops in more than 140 countries, they are part of the largest independent workshop organisation in the world, the Bosch Service Worldwide. They are also the world's largest, independent supplier of original equipment for automotive manufacturers. Bosch diagnostics offer services for utilising state-of-the-art diagnostics technologies for vehicle manufacturers and their service organisations.

The ground work for innovation at the Bosch Group is done by Corporate Sector Research and Advanced Engineering, where 1,300 employees are performing seminal work on the technologies that will shape our lives in the future, from future systems for automotive and software intensive to future systems for industrial, consumer goods and building technology. They also work on advanced functional materials and micro-systems technologies, metal and plastics technology, production automation and principles and designs for energy conversion. A total of 38,500 researchers and developers are involved in all of Bosch's R&D activities.

Among the many values at Bosch are the ones that encompass change and continuity,. where the future is result focused, taking responsibility for the company's actions in keeping with the interests of society. This is driven by initiative and determination, openness and trust, fairness, being reliable and credible in a culturally diverse state as a precondition for their global success.

Finally, to put it in the words of founder, Robert Bosch, as regards quality standards, he said in 1919, 'It has always been an unbearable thought to me that someone could inspect one of my products and find it inferior in any way. For that reason, I have constantly tried to deliver only products which withstand the closest scrutiny – products which prove themselves superior in every respect'. (www.bosch.com)

Lufthansa

The Deutsche Lufthansa AG was initially founded in 1926, after a merger between two smaller airlines of the time called Deutscher Aero Lloyd and Junkers Luftverkehr. After the Second World War, Lufthansa was reborn as a new entity in 1953 as Deutsche Lufthansa Aktiengesellschaft.

Today, Lufthansa AG is the flagship German carrier and the largest European airline in terms of total passengers carried. The word 'Lufthansa' is derived from two German words, 'Luft' meaning air in German and 'Hansa' after the Hanseatic League, which was a powerful medieval trading group active along the coast of northern Europe during the thirteenth to seventeenth centuries. The Lufthansa logo, an encircled Crane in flight was first created in 1918.

Although Lufthansa's registered office and corporate headquarters are located in Deutz, in Cologne, the main operations base and primary traffic hub is at Frankfurt airport in Frankfurt am Main. It has another hub in Munich. Frankfurt International airport houses the Lufthansa Aviation Centre with several important Lufthansa departments.

Deutsche Lufthansa AG is a global aviation group operating in five business segments: the passenger airline business, logistics, maintenance, repair and overhaul (MRO), catering and IT services. The Lufthansa Group includes a total of more than 400 subsidiaries and associated companies.

Lufthansa AG acts as the parent company with an executive board consisting of four members. The executive board is responsible for managing the group, determining strategy and ensuring a sustainable increase in its value. The supervisory board appoints and advises the executive board and monitors its activities. The group attaches overriding importance to quality, innovation, safety and reliability. Corporate governance at Lufthansa is reflected by responsible, corporate leadership and control, which targets sustainable value creation in accordance with high international standards.

The Lufthansa Group employed some 120,000 personnel at the end of 2011 and achieved total operating revenue of €28.7 billion for the year. Christoph Franz is the Chairman of the Executive Board and CEO of Lufthansa AG, Wolfgang Röller is the Honorary Chairman and Jürgen Weber the Chairman of the Supervisory Board of Lufthansa AG.

According to the magazine, *Flight International*, the airline is the world's fifth largest, in terms of overall passengers carried, operating services to 216 international destinations in around 83 countries across Europe, Asia, Africa and the Americas. Together with its partners it covers around 410 destinations. As of 2012, the Lufthansa Group has around 696 different aircraft in its fleet. It is said that it has the third-largest airline fleet in the world when combined with its subsidiaries. Lufthansa is also a founding member of Star Alliance, the world's largest airlines alliance, which was formed in 1997, together with Thai Airways, United Airlines, Air Canada and Scandinavian Airlines System (SAS). Today, this alliance groups together 27 leading airlines, which offer flights to almost any point on the globe.

Under the Lufthansa regional brand, carriers of the likes of Air Dolomiti, Augsburg Airways, Lufthansa City Line, Contact Air and Eurowings operate point-to-point flights across Europe, as well as connecting flights to onward international destinations on Lufthansa's behalf. They also have bilateral cooperation accords with a host of quality airlines like Aegean Airlines, Air India, Air Malta, Cirrus Airlines, Ethiopian Airlines, Lux Air, Mexicana, Qatar Airways and TACA.

As of 2011, more than 100 million passengers flew with the Lufthansa Group that in 2011 included Lufthansa Regional and Lufthansa Italia, Austrian Airlines, British Midland, SWISS, Germanwings as well as Brussels Airlines, Jet Blue and Sun Express.

Lufthansa actively participates in the ongoing consolidation of the airline businesses in Europe by acquiring stakes in Brussels Airlines, for example, or taking over other carriers like Austrian Airlines. They do this whenever it makes economic and strategic sense. The group is accordingly evolving into a multi-hub and multi-brand airline system.

Lufthansa Cargo AG is the logistics services provider in the Lufthansa Group. Based in Kelsterbach, Germany, the company ranks among the world's biggest cargo carriers, offering customers, time-definite transport services coupled with superior quality and security standards. In general, express and special segments, it covers around 300 destinations worldwide with its own fleet of freight carriers as well as the belly capacity of Lufthansa's passenger aircraft and road services. The bulk of the cargo is trans-shipped through the Frankfurt air-cargo hub. In 2011, there was a transport volume of around 1.8 million tonnes of cargo and mail.

The third important segment is Lufthansa Technik AG, which is one of the world's leading independent providers of aircraft related maintenance, repair, overhaul, modification and conversion, engines and components for commercial passenger aircraft. More than 2,000 aircraft are serviced by Lufthansa Technik in a year, on the basis of exclusive contracts.

The LSG Sky Chefs Group or the LSG Lufthansa Service Holding AG is the world's leading provider in airline catering and in all upstream and downstream in-flight service processes. This group consists of 148 companies with more than 200 facilities in 50 countries. Its products and services include airline catering, in-flight equipment and logistics, the management of on-board service, in-flight retail as well as related airport services. They produce around 492 million airline meals a year.

Finally, the last business segment comes under the aegis of Lufthansa Systems AG, a leading provider of IT Services for the airlines and aviation industry. It is equipped with a unique product portfolio of superior IT solutions designed to increase the efficiency and cost-efficacy of customer operations. Other activities include Lufthansa Flight Training, Lufthansa Air Plus, a global leader in business travel management solutions, and the Lufthansa Commercial Holding, which handles the financial stakes, held by Lufthansa in other companies.

The year 2010 saw Lufthansa incorporate the first Airbus A380 in its fleet. This super-jumbo carries 40 per cent more passengers than a Boeing 747. The highly efficient engines from Rolls-Royce Trent 900 type, not only leads in lower fuel consumption, but also in lower noise emissions. Further, the latest composite materials make for less weight and reduced fuel consumption, one of the many reasons why it was only one of three airlines officially recognised in the renowned Dow Jones Sustainability Index (DJSI). (www.lufthansa.com)

Deutsche Post DHL

Deutsche Post DHL is the world's leading mail and logistics group. With headquarters in Bonn, the group employs about 470,000 employees in more than 200 countries and territories, forming a global network of postal and logistics services focused on service, quality and sustainability. The Deutsche Post brand caters to postal and communication services, while the DHL brand caters to provide products and services in the areas of express, forwarding, freight, supply chain and mail.

The history of the group goes way back to the year 1491, when Franz Von Taxis founded the modern postal system. He sets up a courier network in Germany that would eventually grow to cover all of western Europe by the mid sixteenth century. It was on 18 March 1924, that pursuant to the Reichspost Finance Act, Deutsche Reichspost comes under the administration of the Reich Ministry of Posts, an independent enterprise. Deutsche Reichspost is succeeded by Deutsche Bundespost a government agency, which in 1995, was officially privatised. DHL was founded in 1969 by Adrian Dalsy, Larry Hillblom and Robert Lynn in San Francisco. The name DHL is derived from the first letters of their respective last names. DHL became a wholly-owned subsidiary of Deutsche Post AG in 2002.

Deutsche Post DHL brings two powerful brands to the marketplace – the Deutsche Post brand stands for personal proximity, reliable quality and ground-breaking services. Its success is built on the unique infrastructure it has in Germany. While the DHL brand stands for personal commitment, pro-active solutions and local strength in the parcel business as well as in the international express and logistics operations. Today, the group is among the top 10 of the largest employers in the world. They manage more than 1 million customer contacts per hour. For fiscal year 2011, the group had total revenues of €52.829 billion. Frank Appel is the present CEO of Deutsche Post AG, while Wulf von Schimmelmann is the Chairman of the Supervisory Board. KfW Bankengruppe holds 30.5 per cent of the share capital and the other 69.5 per cent is free float, of which 59.3 per cent is held by institutional investors and 10.2 per cent by private investors. Deutsche Post DHL offers integrated services and tailored, customer-focused solutions for managing and transporting letters, goods and information. The group is divided into four corporate divisions, namely; mail, express, global forwarding and freight and supply chain.

In the Mail division, Deutsche Post delivers mail and parcels in Germany. The business units of this division are mail communication, dialogue marketing, parcel Germany, global mail and press services. It is an expert provider of dialogue marketing, press distribution services as well as corporate communication solutions. They operate a nationwide transport and delivery network in Germany. They also deliver mail across borders, serving the domestic markets of countries outside of Germany and also provide other special services beyond mail transport. They serve business customers in key domestic mail markets, including the US, the Netherlands, the UK and Spain. This division has 82 mail centres and 33 parcels centres. They also have 20,000 retail outlets and points of sale, 2,500 Packstations and 1,000 Paketboxes to collect and send parcels and small packages in Germany.

The express division, transports, time-sensitive documents and goods reliably from door-to-door via fixed routes and using standardised workflows. Their network spans more than 220 countries and territories in which more than 100,000 employees serve over 2.5 million customers. Their three product lines are DHL Time Definite, DHL Same Day and DHL Day Definite, which offer customers courier and express services in each of the three standard time segments. Special express business services such as customs brokerage, medical services and repair and return complement their portfolio. They are also the first express service providers to offer Go Green climate-neutral shipping products in around 30 countries. Outside of Germany, they maintain more than 22,000 service points. Their cargo carrier AeroLogic consists of seven new Boeing aircraft and they plan to add another 11 aircraft by 2012. DHL express is the international express market leader in all regions outside of North America.

With its global forwarding and freight division, DHL is the world's largest provider of air and ocean freight services and one of the leading over-land freight forwarders in Europe and the Middle East. They develop global and individual transport solutions for their customers, provide capacity and coordinate the dispatch of goods and information in more than 150 countries. They also secure cargo space and charter capacity from other airlines, shipping companies and freight carriers at competitive prices. Their range of services includes handling customs formalities and providing insurance. DHL is also one of the leading providers of trade fair, exhibition and event logistics.

Their supply chain division provides many industry sectors with customer-focused solutions that span the entire supply chain. By offering warehousing, distribution, managed transport and value-added services, they ensure that products and information reach markets faster and more efficiently. They serve customers in more than 60 countries, providing support for complex business transformations as well as providing sector-specific supply-chain solutions. Their other business unit within this division is the Williams Lea business unit, an expert on outsourcing corporate information management. The solutions include office document and marketing solutions and customer correspondence management.

Driven by the company's goal of 'Becoming the Logistics Company for the World', the recent global campaign is designed to address first and foremost, the decision-makers in today's business world.

They also sponsor various sports and cultural events around the globe. In the area of corporate responsibility, they make a positive contribution to society through their programs in the areas of disaster management, education and through many of their local initiatives, in addition to being committed to increasing their resource efficiency and reducing their carbon footprint. (www.dp-dhl.com)

Deutsche Telekom

Deutsche Telekom AG is one of the world's leading telecommunications and information technology service companies. They have around 200 million customers worldwide and are represented in approximately 50 countries.

The present headquarters are located in Bonn. As of fiscal year 2011, the group generated global net revenue of €58.7 billion. They have over 236,000 employees worldwide as of December 2011. The current CEO and Chairman of the Board of Management is René Obermann, and Ulrich Lehner is the Chairman of the Supervisory Board. Deutsche Telekom AG was founded in 1995, when the second phase of the German national postal and telecommunications reform took place. It marks the transition from Deutsche Bundespost Telekom to the initially state-owned stock company, Deutsche Telekom AG. In November 1996, the company launched the T-Share on the stock market in Germany. The initial public offering, the largest ever seen in Europe then, using the abbreviation DT1, released more than 713 million initial shares. In Germany, these shares known as T-Shares became the first widely bought 'peoples share'. Further share releases occurred in 1999 (286 million shares) and in 2000 (200 million shares). As of 31 March 2012, the shareholder structure consists of 68.01 per cent free float, 14.96 per cent owned by the German Federal government and 17.02 per cent by the KfW banking group. The company is listed on all German stock exchanges and in the NYSE and Tokyo exchanges.

Deutsche Telekom offers broadband and fixed network services in several European countries, called T-Home. The second line of business is Deutsche Telekom's mobile communications outside of Germany, represented by the well-known T-Mobile brand which is available across Europe and in the US. The third line of business covers business customers, where T-Systems offer a one-stop for ICT solutions for large and medium-sized businesses worldwide.

T-Home gives the experience of community at home by providing communication solutions and entertainment services by way of Internet, IPTV and phone for work, information or leisure. For TV, they provide all the popular channels, access to a video library and cable TV services too. For the Internet, broadband services with several types of packages are offered, which are combined with telephone services as well.

Since April 2010, Deutsche Telekom has provided customers in the domestic German market with product and service offerings tailored to their requirements and the best network quality from a single source. For this reason, the company consolidated its previously independent business units for fixed-network (T-Home) and mobile (T-Mobile) communications and offered different package offerings for its customers. The 'T' is the group's corporate umbrella brand emblem and it stands for innovation, competence and simplicity.

T-Systems, Deutsche Telekom's corporate customers arm is focused on business, involving network-centric ICT solutions – with offers, combining IT and telecommunication services. T-Systems offers global companies the solutions they need from a single source. In addition, it is increasingly focusing on services such as cloud computing and IT solutions for the energy, healthcare, media distribution and automotive sectors which are in the process of undergoing radical changes.

Deutsche Telekom focuses on major technical and social trends and plays a key role in shaping them. From the increasing digitisation of the many spheres of life, the personalisation of products and services leads to increased mobility and globalisation.

They have stayed abreast of the growing convergence of technologies with an increasingly integrated product portfolio, where personal data such as music, videos and addresses can be accessed through any and all terminal equipment. The latest of these is the launch of Entertain Sat, a TV service from Deutsche Telekom available throughout the whole of Germany. They have also introduced LTE (Long Term Evolution) the latest standard for rapid transmission including UMTS. From now on, business clients as well as private customers will also benefit from the advantages of cloud services.

With its marketing of the Apple iPhone, of which several million devices have been sold, as well as the launch of the GI 'Internet Cell Phone', Deutsche Telekom provided crucial momentum for increased use of the mobile Internet. This trend is showing no signs of stopping and is set to grow further. The company is meeting rising demand for mobile bandwidth by investing in the latest mobile communications technologies such as HSPE (high-speed packet access) and LTE. Deutsche Telekom is thus endeavouring to obtain additional, mobile communications spectrum as part of the regulatory authority's bidding process.

With its strategy of 'Compete-Transform-Innovate', the group is trying to lead the competition and maintain and win market share by transforming itself through innovation, the objective being to transform its business and aim for a broader revenue mix. The group is also targeting new pockets of growth to account for a significant per cent of future revenues.

Deutsche Telekom is one of the largest sponsors of sports and culture in Germany, the goal, being to increase awareness of the company, the brands and individual products for customer retention, acquisition of new customers and for socially responsible reasons. The corporate slogan for Deutsche Telekom is, 'Life is for Sharing', which is Telekom's brand promise to its customers.

Another noteworthy effort was the establishment of the T-City, which was a joint venture with the city of Friedrichshafen. It was a sort of futuristic lab for Deutsche Telekom and the city of Friedrichshafen which is located on Lake Constance. Up until 2012, T-City Friedrichshafen was a showcase for modern information and communications technology, demonstrating how it improves the quality of life of the community. Ordinary citizens, companies, schools, scientists, the medical community and the city administration collaborated with innovative applications for day-to-day use in and around the city. The group has also made broadband access free to 12 million schoolchildren in Germany.

As well as driving down its own electricity consumption, Deutsche Telekom also devises innovative solutions to help customers worldwide to save energy. In Germany, the group meets 100% of its electricity requirements from renewable energies. Smart metering and home management also let customers monitor their electricity usage patterns at any time, and this helps in taking effective steps to reduce energy consumption at home from individual appliances. They are busy forging connections between the worlds of life and work. (www.telekom.com)

Deutsche Bank

Deutsche Bank was founded in Berlin in 1870 to support the internationalisation of business, and to promote and facilitate trade relations between Germany, other European countries and overseas markets. Two years later, in 1872 the first international branches opened, in Yokohama and Shanghai, and trade relations began with the Americas. In the following year the first London branch opened.

In 1926, Deutsche Bank arranged the merger of Daimler and Benz, took on advisory roles for BP in a major UK deal and advised on and financed the £2.6 billion financing of the London Underground. In the 1970s, globalisation of Deutsche Bank continued: Deutsche Bank Luxembourg S.A. was founded and offices opened in Moscow, Tokyo, Paris and New York. Furthermore, Deutsche Bank's 'diagonal in the square' logo was developed by Germany's design pioneer Anton Stankowski and first introduced to the public in 1974.

In 1989, Deutsche Bank took over UK merchant bank Morgan Grenfell – a milestone in its presence in the City and since 3 October 2001, Deutsche Bank is listed on the New York Stock Exchange. In 2010, Deutsche Bank announced the successful conclusion of the Deutsche Postbank takeover offer. Two years later in 2012, Jürgen Fitschen and Anshu Jain became Co-Chairmen of the Management Board and the Group Executive Committee. Since May 2012, Paul Achleitner is the Chairman of the Supervisory Board of Deutsche Bank AG. Group net income in 2011 was €4.3 billion, up from €2.3 billion in 2010, on pre-tax profits of €5.4 billion, up from €4.0 billion in the prior year.

As a leader in Germany and Europe, the bank is continuously growing in North America, Asia and key emerging markets. With more than 100,000 employees in more than 70 countries, Deutsche Bank offers unparalleled financial services throughout the world. The bank aspires to be the leading client-centric global universal bank. It serves shareholders best, by putting their clients first and by building a global network of balanced businesses, underpinned by strong capital and liquidity.

Deutsche Bank values its German roots and remains dedicated to their global presence. Deutsche Bank commits to a culture that aligns risks and rewards, attracts and develops talented individuals, fosters teamwork and partnership and is sensitive to the society in which it operates.

Deutsche Bank is comprised of four business divisions: Private and Business Clients (PBC), Asset and Wealth Management (AWM), Corporate Banking & Securities (CB&S) and Global Transaction Banking (GTB). The management board of Deutsche Bank AG has as its prime responsibility, the group's strategic management, resource allocation, financial accounting and controls, capital and risk management, as well as internal controls.

PRIVATE AND BUSINESS CLIENTS

Deutsche Bank's Private and Business Clients Corporate Division (PBC), provides branch banking and financial services to private customers, self-employed clients as well as small and medium-sized businesses.

ASSET & WEALTH MANAGEMENT

Asset & Wealth Management (AWM) helps individuals and institutions worldwide to protect and grow their wealth, offering traditional and alternative investments across all major asset classes.

CORPORATE BANKING & SECURITIES

Corporate Banking & Securities (CB&S) is comprised of two businesses: corporate finance and markets and includes regional coverage in the bank's key growth areas.

GLOBAL TRANSACTION BANKING

This division is a provider of cash management, trade finance and trust and securities services for corporate clients and financial institutions.

Deutsche Bank continues to win accolades for its performance across all product disciplines and regions. In the Euromoney Awards for Excellence 2011, Deutsche Bank was named Best Global Bank and received a host of other awards including Best Global Debt House and Best Global Flow House. Deutsche Bank achieved further success in The Banker's Investment Banking Awards 2011 when it was named the Most Innovative Investment Bank of the Year.

Deutsche Bank has always stood for ground-breaking social commitment. Its goal as a responsible corporate citizen is to build social capital – wherever it does business. With a total investment of more than €80 million per year, Deutsche Bank and its foundations are among the world's most committed corporate citizens. And roughly 20,000 employees support nearly 3,000 non-profit organisations as corporate volunteers each year.

Deutsche Bank's claim – 'Passion to Perform' – has always been much more than a marketing slogan or advertising tag line: it's the way the bank does business. Through consistent delivery of the claim and the Deutsche Bank brand personality, the bank aims to live its brand promise of excellence, relevant client solutions and responsibility to all stakeholders. (www.db.com)

Bertelsmann

Bertelsmann SE & Co. KGaA is an international media company, which was founded in 1835 in Gütersloh, a town in the state of North Rhine-Westphalia. It was on 1 July 1835, that the printer, Carl Bertelsmann founded the C. Bertelsmann Verlag (Publisher) in Gütersloh. He had already operated a lithographic printing shop there since 1824. His first publishing effort was a compilation of Christian Songs and Hymns. 2010 was an important anniversary year for the Bertelsmann Group, which celebrated 175 years of its existence.

The Bertelsmann Group, produces, serves and markets media in over 50 countries worldwide. Their content is contributed by the RTL Group, the number one European television and radio broadcaster, Random House, the world's largest book publishing group, and Gruner+Jahr, Europe's biggest magazine publisher. Their other division Arvato provides media and communication services.

Bertelsmann is a privately held stock corporation. The shareholders, the Bertelsmann Stiftung (Foundation), Reinhard Mohn Stiftung and the BVG Stiftung own 80.9 per cent and the Mohn Family 19.1 per cent of the capital shares, held via intermediate companies. The present Chairman and CEO of Bertelsmann SE & Co. KGaA is Thomas Rabe, while Gunter Thielen is the Chairman of the Supervisory Board.

Together with its four major divisions, the Bertelsmann group holds assets in more than 200 companies worldwide. The joint venture with Sony BMG was given up in 2008. Today, their employees number over 104,000 worldwide. For fiscal year 2011, the group generated total worldwide revenues to the tune of around €15.3 billion. They occupy a position of worldwide leadership in most of their business ventures, ranging from television, radio, books and magazines to various media and communication services.

Former CEO Mr. Hartmut Ostrowski said, 'A company that strives for peak performance must be able to rely on its clients and fully unleash its energies. Here we are guided by Bertelsmann's corporate culture as shaped by Reinhard Mohn. It is a culture based on the essential values of partnership, entrepreneurship, creativity and citizenship – and it is the culture that made Bertelsmann, unique and successful for decades'.

As per their mission statement, Bertelsmann is an international media corporation that provides information, entertainment and media services to inspire people's daily lives. They aspire to make a valuable contribution to society, striving to be leaders in their markets with a focus on creative content and consistent customer relations. Their new corporate slogan is 'Creativity meets Entrepreneurship'.

The RTL Group is Europe's leading entertainment group with more than 170 million viewers. They have holdings in 42 TV channels and 32 radio stations in 10 countries as well as in production companies around the world. The TV channels owned by Europe's biggest broadcaster includes the families of channels clustered around RTL television in Germany, M6 in France, Five in the UK, the RTL channels in the Benelux region, in Croatia and in Hungary. In Russia they have their own Ren-TV and Antenna 3 in Spain. Its flagship radio station is RTL in France. RTL Group's content production arm, Fremantle Media produces more than 10,000 hours of programming every year.

Random House is the world's largest trade book publishing group, and the only one that publishes original adult and children's fiction and non-fiction hardcovers, paperbacks and audio books in English, German, Spanish, Japanese and Korean. Its portfolio is comprised of more than 120 editorially independent imprints. Random House sells more than

500 million books annually. Each year, some 11,000 new books enhance an active catalogue of over 60,000 titles worldwide. With authors such as Dan Brown, John Grisham, Toni Morrison and John Updike, no other trade publisher tops the national bestseller lists more often. It also publishes the works of more than 50 Nobel Prize laureates. Random House has its world headquarters in New York and is a wholly-owned division of Bertelsmann.

Gruner+Jahr are another division of Bertelsmann which is Europe's biggest magazine publisher. The media company publishes over 285 magazines, newspapers and websites, in more than 20 countries. G+J publications includes Stern, Brigitte, Geo, Capital, Gala, Eltern, Auto Motor und Sport, Financial Times Deutschland, Essen & Trinken, News, Femme Actuelle and many more of which many are in several different country editions. Its portfolio of titles is constantly being expanded with innovative new launches and line extensions. Gruner+Jahr stands for quality journalism in the best possible sense – thoroughly researched, informative, inspiring and entertaining. A total of 74.9 per cent of the Hamburg-based company is owned by Bertelsmann SE & Co. KGaA, while the Jahr publishing family owns 25.1 per cent.

Arvato AG is one of the world's largest internationally networked media and communication services providers. They have around 270 subsidiaries operating in around 30 countries. The Arvato Group is comprised of Arvato Services, Arvato Print, Arvato Digital Services and Arvato Systems. Their operations run the gamut from gravure and offset print operations to call and service centres, customer loyalty programs and logistics services. The portfolio of services offered also includes supply chain management, optical storage media production, IT services, address and database management, mobile services and knowledge management. Arvato AG has its headquarters in Gütersloh and is a wholly-owned division of Bertelsmann SE & Co. KGaA.

Bertelsmann's core businesses are focused on media content and media-related services and production activities. While developing existing businesses further, Bertelsmann is focusing on moving into new growth markets. They see their core markets in Western Europe and in the US where the focus of their future investments are. Although over the medium to the long term, they are working to expand their presence into major growth markets such as China. Most of their current businesses hold leading market positions in attractive, developed markets.

Bertelsmann SE & Co. KGaA, sees protecting the environment as part of its corporate responsibility. In the fall of 2004, the executive board adopted guidelines for responsible treatment of natural resources, as part of an environmental policy for all of Bertelsmann. The group, its divisions and companies emphatically support efforts to ensure that no wood from primary forests or other forests in need of protection are used in producing the papers procured or used by Bertelsmann. They support environmentally friendly pulp and paper production that meets high ecological standards. Using chlorine free paper and recycling waste paper.

They are also aware of the special responsibility incumbent on them as a media company. Their core principles or mandate in this regard states: 'We promote artistic freedom and freedom of thought, the protection of democracy and human rights and the respect of traditions and cultural values. Consequently, the content we provide reflects a wide range of viewpoints and opinions'. (www.bertelsmann.com)

4 *The Star Brands*

The companies and brands that I have selected in this section constitute the shining stars of the German and European industrial landscape. A large number of them are listed companies in the German, European and World exchanges. Most of them are highly visible, professionally managed and have reasonable advertising and promotional expenditures to advertise and promote their products and services. They are among the most successful companies at the national and international arenas in their respective categories.

These leading reputed brands are fairly visible to competitors, investors, consumers and the general public at large. Several of them are traditional, family-owned, well-known brands and they cover a wide spectrum of industries and categories. Although their primary markets are European, most of them operate globally and are amongst the market leaders.

The criteria for selecting them are current turnover, profitability and market success; other factors are visibility, listing on the stock exchange (not all), traditionally well known, and size and reputation of the companies and brands. It is fair to say that they are among the leading German brands and companies in their respective businesses and product/service categories, especially in the large- to medium-sized enterprises, in addition to, of course, the Superstar brands.

The selected brands and companies cover a wide range of industries from consumer goods, industrial goods, retail and wholesale trade, a health insurance company, a bank and a stock exchange, chemical companies, energy companies, healthcare and pharmaceutical, food and drink, confectionery, lifestyle products, perfumes, fashion products, jewellery, construction services, tyres, aerospace, engines and other engineering components, precious metals and metal technology, facilities, logistics, passenger and mobility, media, ophthalmic, agri-goods, speciality chemicals, copper, semiconductors, real estate, fertilizers, salt, sugar, domestic appliances, travel and tourism, hotels and several others.

I have selected 45 of the best such large and medium-sized enterprises which I call the Stars of the German industrial landscape. (It must also be mentioned here, that there were some companies in the initial list that did not wish to be included in this illustrious list as they are apparently, publicity shy.)

The majority of the companies included here are public limited companies and are listed on the various indices of the German stock exchanges: the Xetra DAX 30 and the MDAX indices. There are also a fair number of family-owned enterprises, private limited companies, cooperative organisations and state-owned enterprises. Although most of them operate globally, their primary area of activity is Germany and Europe, from where they derive most of their sales revenue.

I have listed them in a random order and they do not follow any particular order of size or importance. So, the top large to medium-sized, Star brands are as follows: RWE, METRO Group, E.on, Tui, MAN, Evonik, Continental, Linde, Henkel, Fresenius, Merck, Fielmann, Schaeffler, Miele, K+S, Infineon, Commerzbank, Wacker, Douglas Holding, HARIBO, HUGO BOSS, GEA, BARMER GEK, HOCHTIEF, Tengelmann, Aurubis, REWE, Deutsche Boerse (Xtra Dax), Lanxess, Baywa, Otto-Fuchs, Bilfinger, Deutsche Bahn (DB), Suedzucker, Boehringer Ingelheim, EDEKA, Haniel, Heraeus, MTU Aero Engines, Voith, ZF, MAHLE, Fraport, Würth and Axel Springer. Brief descriptions about the company and its brands, its profile and other relevant aspects follow.

RWE

RWE AG is a German electric power and natural gas public utility company with headquarters in Essen. The company was founded in 1898 in Essen, with the purpose of supplying the city of Essen with the still new energy form of electricity. RWE started as the Rheinisch Westfälisches Elektrizitätswerk. Today, it is Germany's largest energy producer.

RWE is one of Europe's five leading electricity and gas companies. It is active in the generation, trading, transmission and supply of electricity and gas. More than 72,000 employees supply over 17 million customers with electricity and approximately 8 million customers with gas. In fiscal year 2011, RWE recorded sales revenue of around €52 billion.

RWE is the leading energy producer in Germany, second in the Netherlands and third in the UK. Their market position in central and southeastern Europe is growing continuously. Through RWE Dea, the group is successfully active in the gas and oil production business in Europe, northern Africa and the Caspian region. RWE Supply and Trading is one of Europe's leading energy trading companies. They generated a total of 205.7 TWh^2 of electricity through various means, i.e. lignite, hard coal, gas, nuclear power, renewables and others.

Peter Terium is the CEO of the Executive Board of RWE, and Manfred Schneider is the Chairman of the Supervisory Board. The RWE Group has earmarked several billion Euros in annual investments in environmentally friendly and flexible generation capacity; this includes power plants, grids and open-cast mines. A billion Euros will go towards renewables, mainly wind energy and bio-mass energy. Their present corporate slogan is 'The Energy to Lead'.

The RWE Group has over the years offered its customers, new electricity, gas and energy efficiency products for homes, commercial establishments and the industry. Today, climate protection and energy efficiency are increasingly important, one reason, for its effort into electric cars. The company's declared aim is to expand the electricity and gas business while reducing its own CO_2 emissions.

It intends to grow by way of organic growth, mergers and acquisitions (M&A) and through innovative technologies, business models and products. According to Leonhard Birnbaum, Board Member of RWE AG, Group Strategy and Business Development, 'RWE is becoming greener, more robust and more international. We intend to develop competition in new markets and plan to be a Europe-wide energy provider. Therewith, RWE will be better positioned for the future than ever'.

RWE offers the right sales and services in electricity, gas and water for each customer group in Germany and many parts of continental Europe as well as in the UK. The group structure of RWE AG includes RWE Power, RWE Deutschland, RWE Service, RWE Consulting, RWE Technology and others. The value chain is as follows: power generation, gas and oil exploration, energy trading, power and gas grid, power and gas sales and energy efficiency.

In Germany, the group activities include power generation, distribution networks, retail/sales, energy efficiency and its generating companies. In the Netherlands and Belgium the company is represented by Essent and in Great Britain by RWE npower. In Central and Eastern Europe the company is represented by RWE Hungaria, RWE Polska, VSE (Slowakia), RWE Transgas (The Czech Republic), Net4Gas and RWE Turkey. Renewable energy is handled by RWE Innogy and upstream gas and oil by RWE Dea. Trading/gas upstream is handled by RWE Supply and Trading.

Among the many research-related activities of the RWE Group is its effort in the area of renewables. For instance, RWE with 12 other international companies and the Desertec Foundation are investigating how Europe could be supplied with environmentally friendly solar and wind power from North Africa and the Middle East. They hope to meet 15 per cent of Europe's energy needs by 2050. The world's most progressive algae growing plant for CO_2 conversion was commissioned on 6 November 2008 at Niederraussem in Germany. The goal is to optimise the entire process chain from seaweed production to the final product. In a trial plant measuring some 600 square metres, the seaweed is fed with flue gas from the power plant and the resulting algae bio-mass is to be possibly used as a bio-fuel.

The big step toward a completely new power plant technology is being taken by RWE with its planned IGCC station for a climate friendly, coal-based power plant. Here the gasification of coal is combined with the capture of CO_2 and electricity is produced in downstream, gas and steam turbines. The capture of CO_2 is also known as CO_2 scrubbing and it is a process that will help lower emissions from existing power plants in the course of retrofit measures. Safe and long-term CO_2 storage in deep rock layers is another component of their research work.

Another of their important research projects called ADELE or Adiabatic compressed-air energy storage (CAES) for electricity supply aims to compress air at times of high electricity availability, to place the resulting heat in an interim heat-storage device and to inject the air into subterranean caverns. When electricity demand rises, this compressed air can be used to generate power in a turbine – while recovering the heat.

RWE is also making e-mobility suitable for daily use; that is for electric cars. They are testing customer acceptance and the systems used for billing, network of charging points and their control in pilot projects.

The RWE Energy Home of the Future is a demonstration of how they can slash their customer's energy bills with no loss of comfort, while helping the environment with reduced CO_2 emissions. Innovative measures include 'Smart Metering', air technology, home ventilation, intelligent home control systems, etc. Other efforts include developing an e-energy marketplace of the future and distributed generation using micro-combined heat and power, distributed combined cycle plants, bio-mass gasification and organic fluids. (www.rwe.com)

METRO GROUP

The METRO GROUP is a diversified retail and wholesale business group with headquarters in Düsseldorf. Otto Beisheim is the founder of METRO. The first METRO self-service wholesale store opened in 1964 in the town of Mühlheim/Ruhr. In July 1996, METRO AG was formed through a merger of the retail companies Asko Deutsche Kaufhaus AG, Kaufhof Holding AG and Deutsche SB–Kauf AG. Its shares were listed for the first time on the DAX, German Stock Index, the very same year, with a market capitalisation of 12.07 billion German Marks.

Today, the METRO Group is the world's fourth-largest wholesale and retail group in terms of total group sales. More than 280,000 employees from 180 nations work at over 2,200 outlets in 32 countries in Europe, Africa and Asia. The corporate slogan of the group is 'Made to Trade'. Operational responsibility lies with the sales divisions of METRO Cash & Carry (wholesale), Real (hypermarkets), Media Markt and Saturn (consumer electronics retailing) and Galeria Kaufhof (premium department stores). The group's real estate business is managed by METRO Properties. Olaf Koch is the current Chairman of the Management Board of METRO AG, and Franz Haniel is the Chairman of the Supervisory Board. For fiscal year 2011, total sales revenue for the group was €66.7 billion.

The METRO GROUP offers both private and commercial customers a broad array of services in wholesale and in retail. The group's sales brands have become strong individual retail brands in many ways. They have continuously fine-tuned their sales concept with the aim of convincing customers of the value of their service offerings and as a result have helped strengthen the foundation of their business success.

The five main sales divisions or brands under the umbrella METRO GROUP are as follows: METRO Cash & Carry, Real, Media Markt, Saturn and Galeria Kaufhof.

METRO Cash & Carry is the leading international player in self-service wholesale, i.e. customer-focused, international and innovative. The concept is oriented towards helping customers to successfully run their own business. This brand has over 750 locations in 29 countries. They offer up to 20,000 different food items and 30,000 non-food items, catering to the specific needs of national and local customers. Their concept is based on retailers selecting their own purchases directly at a store and taking those goods with them. This saves the retailer or business the time and money in placing orders with multiple vendors and waiting for their delivery. Today, the company has grown to become the leading international player in self-service wholesale. METRO Cash & Carry's product range and services extend from ready-made business solutions to delivery. Their diversity and quality are excellent with a very profitable price-benefit ratio. Up to 90 per cent of METRO Cash & Carry's goods are purchased from local producers and suppliers. Close cooperation with them builds trust and increases the level of acceptance that this brand enjoys at each of its locations. They have superior expertise in providing fresh food products.

The sales division Real started in 1992 and was created from a merger of 13 hypermarket operators with different sales concepts. In 2006, it also acquired all of Walmart's hypermarkets in Germany. Real now operates in 425 locations in six countries. They have up to 80,000 articles in their product offerings. The brand 'Real' stands for a multifaceted range of food products, offering a great price-performance ratio with a large share of fresh produce completed by an attractive non-food assortment. Branded articles and strong private labels, guarantee a high-quality product line in both the food and non-food segment. They place a high priority on quality and freshness in the food segment, which accounts for the bulk of sales. Made from 100 per cent organic produce, the Real BIO products meet the stringent EU ecological guidelines. In addition to its attractive pricing, Real's market success can be attributed to a sophisticated logistics system that facilitates on-time store deliveries.

The sales brands Media Markt and Saturn are managed by the holding company Media-Saturn, which is the German and European market leader in customer electronics retailing. Media Markt and Saturn together have over 900 store locations in 15 countries. The first Media Markt opened in an industrial park in Munich in 1979. This brand is synonymous for a comprehensive assortment in the fields of consumer electronics, telecommunications, photography, entertainment, computers, software and household appliances. With reasonable prices, an extensive assortment and network, a wide range of services including individual customer service, characterise this brand. Usually located close to the city with comfortable parking, Media Markt offers brand products at fairly low prices. They undertake fairly extensive advertising campaigns in promoting the brand.

The sales brand Saturn represents consumer electronics stores mostly in central, downtown locations, offering up to 100,000 products. The Saturn quality characteristics are the competent customer advice provided by qualified expert staff and a comprehensive range of services. The first Saturn consumer electronics store opened in Cologne in 1961. Saturn's claim is to take the pole position in the respective area among all potential suppliers and always offer its customer the latest product innovations.

Lastly is Galeria Kaufhof, with its lifestyle and event-oriented Galeria concept. The brand is an innovation leader among German department stores. Galeria Kaufhof is a synonym for a comprehensive range of premium products, international brands, a matching product presentation and service personnel who are eager to serve their customers. The company began in 1879 in a town called Stralsund. Today this brand has 137 store locations and operates in Germany and in Belgium, where they are known as Galeria Inno. They have positioned themselves as a 'House of Brands', with fashionable, ultra-modern, national and international brands. Galeria Kaufhof is a modern lifestyle provider, a trend-setter offering a unique ambience of quality. (www.metro.de)

E.ON

E.ON AG, with headquarters in Düsseldorf, is one of the world's largest investor-owned power and gas companies. E.ON was formed in June 2000 by the merger of VEBA and VIAG, two of Germany's largest industrial groups.

Today the group has more than 79,000 employees on its rolls. They generated total sales revenue of around €113 billion for financial year 2011; with leading market positions in power and gas they have around 26 million customers and operate in more than 30 countries. They have over 1,300 subsidiary companies and holdings worldwide.

Their integrated business model in power and gas extends from power generation and gas production to distribution and sales. They have one of the broadest geographic footprints in the industry plus one of the most balanced fuel mixes in power and gas. In addition to their activities in Europe and Russia, they also operate renewable generation assets in North America. They pursue a value-oriented management approach aimed at enhancing their competitiveness and delivering profitable growth, committed to providing cleaner and better energy. In order to further diversify their geographic footprint, E.ON has identified Brazil and Turkey as target regions for its business outside of Europe.

E.ON's business is segmented into five global units that are responsible for generation, renewables, optimisation and trading, new building and technology and exploration and production. Eleven regional units manage their operational business in their respective target markets. The lead company of each market unit is responsible for coordinating operations in individual countries or regions and is the first point of contact for customers, communities and government agencies. They have a combination of geographically and functionally segmented market units to leverage synergies and pool expertise. Johannes Teyssen is the CEO and Chairman of the Board of Management, and Werner Wenning is the Chairman of the Supervisory Board of E.ON AG.

Today, E.ON has an installed power-plant capacity of 69 GW at their disposal. They are one of the world's most geographically diversified power producers with major asset positions in Germany, Great Britain, Sweden, Russia, the US, Italy, Spain, France and in the Benelux countries. In addition, they possess one of the most diverse and well-balanced generation portfolios in their sector. As of year-end 2011, they had a generation capacity of 32 GW in gas and oil-fired energy, 19 GW in coal-fired, 8 GW in nuclear, 6 GW in hydro and another 5 GW in wind, solar and renewables. By 2030 they plan to reduce CO_2 emissions by at least 50 per cent compared to 1990 levels. E.ON is following a double strategy to reduce the CO_2 emissions of its coal power plants by means of an efficiency enhancement of the 700 degree technology and by using CCS (carbon capture storage) technology.

Natural gas can be cooled to minus 161.5°C, thus reducing its volume considerably and making it easier to transport it in large quantities. The cooling process in fact transforms 600 m^3 of gas into 1 m^3 of liquefied gas. The technology for liquefying gas in so-called LNG trains and ships in the producer countries and re-gasifying it at the port of destination is now developed to such a level that every year nearly 180 billion m^3 of gas are now transported in this way throughout the world. It is a reasonably priced alternative to pipelines gas. This is particularly true for supply regions which are not yet connected to the pipeline system or where connections make no sense.

'Smart Grids' have been so named because they are fitted with innovative information technology. They can already be found in the high-voltage transmission grids at E.ON. Management takes place automatically and the remote operation of large power plants has now become common practice.

These systems now need to be made workable for low- and medium-voltage distribution networks. E.ON is already taking up this challenge by researching many aspects of the use of the Smart-Grid technology in over 110 individual projects. These focus on findings regarding power flow and its dependence on wind, sun, customer behaviour, batteries (as in electric cars) and the integration of these elements into the existing system landscape of network control systems; this, so as to identify suitable components for communication technology in transformer substations, electrical substations and network control stations. This will harmonise the supply and demand of energy that gets that much more complex and lays the foundation for the future of the Smart Grid.

Another important step towards the future and a cornerstone for the efficient use of electricity and gas is the 'Smart Meter'. They offer a wealth of possibilities to provide information about current energy usage so as to identify concrete ways to save energy.

E.ON will soon install 1.8 million Smart Meters across Europe. As of now, a million Smart Meters are already in use in Sweden.

In 2010, E.ON invested around €93 million in the research and implementation of innovative technical solutions. E.ON is addressing the challenges of climate change, with research and development into key technologies that offer solutions for a sustainable energy future. In conventional production, it is looking at 700° technology in coal and CCS technologies, use of H-class turbines and flexible generation in natural gas, and in renewable energies, the focus is on wind, bio-energy, solar and marine power by way of wave and tidal power. Other projects include modern infrastructure and energy-efficient applications, from the Smart Grid, E-Mobility and Fuel Cell to Load Control.

The main focus of E.ON's investments is on enlarging their renewable capacity, mainly in wind power. Within the last five years (2007 to 2011), E.ON has invested about €7 billion in renewables and will be investing the same amount in this business within the next five years from 2012 to 2016.

The group is already the top 10 wind operators in the world. In Europe and in the US, they operate onshore plants with an installed capacity of over 3,200 MW and their offshore wind farm at Scroby Sands of the English coast can supply up to 33,000 households with energy from its 30 wind turbines. In Germany they are developing one of the first wind farms in the open sea, 45 kilometres from the coast off the island of Borkum in waters 30 metres deep. They intend to expand onshore and offshore installed capacity to about 4,000 MW. In Lockerbie, Scotland, they operate one of the largest bio-mass power plants with an installed capacity of 44 MW, while Germany has bio-mass plants with an electricity output of 30 MW. Several have been planned for the near future in the UK and Germany.

The global carbon market has witnessed sharp growth in recent years and was worth €105 billion in 2009, representing an attractive market for E.ON to be involved in. The E.ON Carbon Sourcing Unit buys carbon certificates (CERs/ERUs) directly from owners of certified emission reduction projects on a non-guaranteed basis. The E.ON Energy Trading Unit is responsible for trading European Emission Allowances (EUAs) as part of the emissions trading scheme and wholesale trading of CERs and ERUs on the secondary market as well as trading in electricity, natural gas, coal, oil, freight and bio-mass. E.ON energy trading is one of Europe's leading energy trading houses.

For many years, E.ON has been supporting several sports and sporting events all over Europe. Among these efforts are being a partner for FC Bayern Munich, the FA Cup in the UK, the Gothia Cup for football in Sweden, promoting football in the Czech Republic and being a diamond partner for the Hungarian Olympic swimming team. (www.eon.com)

TUI

TUI AG is one of the world's largest travel and tourism companies. It began as an industrial and transportation company named Preussag AG in Berlin in 1923. After the Second World War the company moved to the city of Hannover where TUI AG's present headquarters are located. It was in 1968 in Hannover that Touristik Union International (TUI) was formed through a merger between several travel companies of the time. In 1997, Preussag redefined itself and moved into services, focusing on the travel industry. The company acquired Hapag Lloyd AG, a global player in transport and tourism of which TUI was a part. Finally on 1 January 2001 Preussag AG had 100 per cent control of TUI AG, and on July 2002 the new company name TUI AG was accepted by a majority of the shareholders at their annual general meeting. Preussag AG had been on the stock market for decades and the AGM voted for a name change. By March 2009, TUI sells the majority of the container shipping company Hapag Lloyd AG to Albert Ballin Holding GmbH AG & KG for €4.45 billion. With this move TUI becomes an exclusive travel and tourism group, having divested itself of the container shipping business, although they still hold a 22 per cent stake in Hapag Lloyd AG.

Today, TUI AG is Europe's leading travel and tourism group from retail shops and tour operators to airlines, hotels and cruise ships all the way to services at the respective holiday destinations. The brands and companies of the world of TUI offer the complete range of services associated with one's travel and holidays.

Currently, with 248 hotels and a capacity of around 157,000 beds in 30 countries, TUI Hotels and Resorts is Europe's largest holiday hotelier. With over 140 aircraft, TUI Travel has one of the largest and most modern holiday aircraft fleet in Europe.

Over 30 million customers entrust TUI with organising their holidays every year. TUI AG employs more than 73,000 employees worldwide to create unforgettable holiday experiences. In the financial year of 2010/11 the turnover of the TUI Group was €17.5 billion. The present CEO of TUI AG is Friedrich Joussen and Klaus Mangold is the Chairman of the Supervisory Board.

TUI AG combines the three sectors – TUI Travel with its tour operators, on and offline distribution, airlines and incoming services – and there is also TUI Hotels and Resorts followed by the Cruise sector which is comprised of the two brands Hapag-Lloyd Kreuzfahrten and TUI Cruises.

The stated mission of TUI AG is 'Putting a smile on people's faces', with values of opening doors, creating value, enjoying life and going beyond.

Balancing economic goals with social, public and ecological concerns forms one of the reasons for sustainable economic success. Responsibility towards society, employees and the environment is therefore an important yardstick for entrepreneurial activity in the TUI Group.

TUI Travel was created in 2007 by the merger of TUI Group's retail section, tour operating business, airlines and incoming activities with the British company First Choice Holidays Plc. The new company is listed on the London stock Exchange. TUI AG has a majority shareholding in TUI Travel and is represented in 27 markets around the globe, serving more than 30 million customers. Its business is divided into the four sectors: mainstream, specialist and emerging markets, activity and accommodation and destinations. TUI Travel offers a broad choice of leisure travel, ranging from package tours to individual niche products.

TUI Hotel & Resorts is the largest holiday hotel company in Europe and is responsible for managing the hotel subsidiaries of the group. The TUI Hotels & Resorts portfolio consists of 248 hotels in 30 countries around the world and includes such famous hotel brands such as Riu, Grecotel, Grupotel, Iberotel, Dorfhotel, Robinson and Magic Life. The hotels of the various brands are situated at prime locations in attractive holiday regions of the world. They offer guests a diverse range of hotel concepts with the highest level of service and quality, meeting high environmental standards.

TUI Cruises was formed as a joint venture between Royal Caribbean Cruises Ltd. and TUI AG. They began operations in the spring of 2009, catering to the premium cruises segment with the liner Mein Schiff – 'My Ship' in German. TUI Cruises primarily targets couples and families who appreciate ample space, quality and generous personal service. Hapag Lloyd Kreuzfahrten is the other brand in this business sector which offers a broad range of cruise experiences, hundreds of destinations and excursions and short cruises to recharge the battery, cruises for bon vivants and connoisseurs. The fleet includes the cruise ships, MS Europa, MS Hanseatic, MS Bremen and MS Columbus. They are the leading expedition and luxury cruise operator in the German-speaking region.

The TUI Eco Resort is the group's internal seal of quality that has been created to honour the TUI Hotels & Resorts that fulfil recognised national and international standards on environmental management systems, such as ISO 14001.

The TUI AG headquarters in Hannover as well as the tour operator TUI Deutschland have been certified as per ISO 14001, as have several hotels in the group. (www.tui-group.com)

MAN

MAN SE or the MAN Group is one of Europe's leading manufacturers of commercial vehicles, engines and mechanical engineering equipment with annual sales of around €16.5 billion in financial year 2011. They employ over 52,500 employees worldwide, with headquarters in Munich. MAN supplies trucks, buses, diesel engines as well as turbo-machinery and special gear units and holds leading market positions in all its business areas. Georg Pachta-Reyhofen is the present CEO of the Executive Board of MAN SE, and Ferdinand K. Piëch is the Chairman of the Supervisory Board.

The MAN Group's roots reach back 250 years into the past. The first visible result of its pioneering efforts was in 1758, with the opening of the St. Antony Iron Mill in Oberhausen, the first heavy industrial operations in Germany's Ruhr area. In 1782, the Gute Hoffnung or 'Good Hope' iron mill followed. It was in 1897, that Rudolf Diesel built the world's first functioning diesel engine at what was then known as the Maschinen-Fabrik Augsburg AG. This company merged in 1898 with the Maschinenbau AG Nürnberg to become the Vereinigte Maschinenfabrik Augsburg and Machinenbaugesellschaft Marber AG. In 1908, this conglomerate was renamed MAN from the Maschinenfabrik Augsburg-Nürnberg AG. This was the first time the name MAN was officially used. Finally, in 1921, the majority of MAN was taken over by the GHH Germany, which was founded in 1873. MAN has existed in its current form as a contractual group since 1986. In that year, the MAN Group merged with GHH and its headquarters were transferred to Munich. In May 2009, the group incorporated itself as a European corporation, MAN SE. Today, Volkswagen AG, Wolfsburg holds 75 per cent of MAN SEs shares/voting rights.

The Companies and products of the MAN Group have ideally positioned themselves in the market. MAN Truck & Bus, based in Munich, is one of Europe's leading commercial vehicle manufacturers. They produce trucks from 7.5 to 50 tons gross weight for any application as well as buses and coaches to order, engines for vehicles, boats and power generation and an international sales and service network with extensive services connected with commercial vehicles like the MAN service card, MAN Repair Card and Comfort Service System. They also have MAN Fleet Services and MAN Telematics & Communications; this sub-group also has MAN Top Used, the international label for used vehicles. MAN Finance International provides a portfolio of services for financing solutions for trucks and buses from MAN.

MAN Diesel & Turbo is a world leader in large diesel ship engines and stationary engines. They also offer the largest turbo-machinery product range in the world. This sub-group based in Augsburg, designs two- and four-stroke large-bore diesel engines that are manufactured both by the company and by its licensees. They also design and manufacture gas and steam turbines. Their product range is rounded off by turbo chargers, CP propellers, gas engines and chemical reactors. They also include complete marine propulsion systems, turbo-machinery for the oil and gas and process industries as well as turnkey power plants.

MAN Latin America has a leading position in heavy trucks in Brazil. They have been manufacturing trucks and buses in Resende, in Brazil since 1996. The vehicles are primarily sold in Latin America and Africa. They have a total production capacity of 80,000 vehicles per year. The Resende plant has one of the most modern truck production facilities for trucks and buses in Latin America. They offer over 40 models, marketed in 30 countries of Latin America, Africa and the Middle East under both the VW and MAN brands.

Another sub-group is the Augsburg based, Renk. They are acknowledged as one of the world's highest quality manufacturers of special gears, components of propulsion technology and test systems. They produce high-value products for power transmission engineering.

The MAN Group's strategy aims to create sustainable value in commercial vehicles and power engineering – its fast-growing business areas. The group is highly diverse and multifaceted and expresses the many nuances of their corporate values, such as reliability, innovation, dynamic strength and openness. Their present corporate slogan is 'Engineering the Future – Since 1758'.

Cutting-edge technology provides top-level performance and environmental compatibility. Since 1988, the particle emissions from trucks have been reduced by 97 per cent, while over the same period, nitric oxide emissions declined by 86 per cent. The CO_2 output by passenger cars dropped by merely 0.5 per cent between 2001 and 2005, while that of buses fell by 30 per cent.

MAN has equipped its Lions City Hybrid Bus with serial hybrid drive systems and super condensers for energy storage. In regular service, this saves about 25 per cent in fuel consumption, in some cases even up to 30 per cent. In Brazil, MAN Latin America's trucks already rely on a mixture containing up to 20 per cent bio-diesel, and the company is currently experimenting with pure bio-diesel as a fuel.

Both the high- and low-pressure turbines for use in the Andasol 3 solar-energy power plant are built at MAN Diesel & Turbo in Oberhausen. Andasol 3 is a Spanish solar project which will supply up to 200,000 people with solar energy. Engineers from the same sub-group are transforming the container ship Alexander Maersk into the Green Ship of the Future by installing an exhaust gas recirculation system which will drastically reduce nitric-oxide by up to 80 per cent and lower fuel consumption. Almost two thirds of the merchant fleet operating on the seas owe their drive to a MAN engine.

Another interesting project of theirs is the one to extract energy from waste material in the Alps, at a place called Fritzens. These and several other efforts are helping them to be at the cutting edge of new, environmentally friendly technology.

The group has won many awards for its products, in particular 'Truck of the Year' award for 2006 and 2008 and the 'Bus of the Year' award for 2006.

MAN Diesel has also won the German 'Business Innovation Prize' in the major enterprises category in 2008. The innovation being the 32/40 PGI (performance gas engine) that uses no spark plugs yet has the efficiency of a diesel engine with extremely low nitric oxide emissions. (www.man.eu)

Evonik

Evonik Industries AG is a modern industrial group with headquarters in the city of Essen, which is in the centre of the Ruhr area in the state of North-Rhine Westphalia. For the year 2010, Essen was the 'European Capital of Culture' on behalf of the whole Ruhr area.

Evonik is one of the world's leading speciality chemical companies, especially in the areas of consumer products, health, nutrition, resource efficiency and speciality materials. They also have investments in the energy and real estate sectors.

Their speciality chemicals operations are grouped into six business units. They have administrative units that provide infrastructure services for the group's 11 largest chemical sites in Europe. With a separate procurement unit, they make sure they have a strong market orientation with the goal to create value within Evonik.

In 2011, the Evonik Group had around 33,000 employees with a total sales turnover of about €14.5 billion. A total of 60 per cent of the sales revenue was generated outside Germany. They have production plants in 28 countries and sales and other activities all around the world. Their R&D expenditure for 2011 was €365 million. They have over 2,400 R&D staff at more than 35 locations around the world and 300 partnerships with universities and other institutions worldwide. The group has more than 24,000 existing patents and several pending as well, in addition to 7,500 registered trademarks and several applied for.

The company was officially founded on 12 September 2007 as Evonik Industries AG, however its core business, chemicals, as well as its investments, in the energy and real estate sectors, have a long and chequered history of ownership and growth. The chemical business started in 1873 in Frankfurt as the Deutsche Gold und Silber Scheide-Anstalt. The company officially became Degussa AG in 1980. After a couple of mergers with other companies, the Essen based RAG AG acquired 46.48 per cent of Degussa shares in February 2003. By September 2006, RAG AG had acquired all of Degussa's shares. Finally on 12 September 2007, Degussa became the chemical business arm of the new group known as Evonik Industries AG. The origins of investment into the energy sector began with the establishment of the Stein Kohlen-Elektrizität AG or (STEAG) in the 1930s. While real estate investments were established in 1993, the large and highly diverse real estate holdings of the company date back to the nineteenth century and have their roots in the workers housing development in the Ruhr valley and other mining regions.

Klaus Engel is the present CEO and Chairman of the Executive Board of Management of Evonik Industries AG, while Werner Müller is the Chairman of the Supervisory Board.

Evonik Industries focuses on speciality chemicals that find applications in the most diverse products and industries, from automotive to pharmaceuticals; working closely with their customers, they develop innovative custom designed products and solutions and in doing so shape people's everyday lives. They develop various substances, formulations and technologies that create added value and a competitive advantage for their customers. Their most famous product is PLEXIGLAS® the versatile plastic that recently turned 75 years old and will continue to help shape modern living. Other popular products are polyurethane rigid foam panels for thermal insulation, nicotine patches and methacrylate resins to give plastic coatings superior properties of functionality and aesthetics, used mainly in electronic appliances. Also in their product line is SIRIDON®, an ultra-pure glass made from chlorosilane, which is used for making fibre optic cables. They are the market leader in the production of this speciality chemical. Other popular products include mineral UV filters for sunscreen lotions, amino acids for animal nutrition and ROHACELL®, a high-performance rigid foam that is lightweight and highly stress resistant used in helicopter rotor-blades for high mountainous terrain and reliable lift-off and many more such innovative product applications.

Evonik is also a leading global supplier of catalytic system solutions. It offers an extensive range of catalysts from a single source as well as integrated services for customers in the life-sciences, fine-chemical, industrial chemical, chemical intermediate, petrochemical and polymer industries.

Using nanotechnology, Evonik has developed SEPARION®, a novel separator membrane for safer lithium ion batteries which supports more widespread use of fuel-saving hybrid vehicles.

Among the future areas of growth they are working on are the Biotechnology Science-to-Business Center with research on 'white biotechnology', i.e. sustainable industrial production processes based on renewable raw materials.

Another area being developed is flexible, thin-film solar cells for harvesting solar energy more economically, an area with enormous growth potential. Evonik Industries now also offers primary and secondary solar-lenses for concentrating photovoltaics (CPV), for converting solar energy into electricity with greater efficiency.

Evonik Industries see themselves as a creative industrial group, whose performance is shaped by creativity, specialisation, continuous self-renewal and reliability. They mastermind innovative products and solutions tailored to their customers' needs. (www.corporate.evonik.com)

Continental

With sales of €30.5 billion in 2011, Continental is among the leading automotive suppliers worldwide. As a supplier of brake systems, systems and components for powertrains and chassis, instrumentation, infotainment solutions, vehicle electronics, tires and technical elastomers, Continental contributes to enhanced driving safety and global climate protection.

Continental is also an expert partner in networked automobile communication. Continental currently has approximately 169,000 employees in 46 countries. Elmar Degenhart is the Chairman of the Executive Board and Wolfgang Reitzle is the Chairman of the Supervisory Board.

Continental-Caoutchouc und Gutta-Percha Compagnie was founded in Hannover, on 8 October 1871 as a joint stock company. Manufacturing, at the main factory, included soft rubber products, rubberised fabrics and solid tires for carriages and bicycles.

Today, Continental is divided into five divisions: chassis and safety, powertrain, interior, tires for passenger and light truck tires and commercial vehicle tires and finally ContiTech.

The Chassis and Safety division combines core competencies in the areas of networked driving safety, brakes, driver assistance, chassis, active and passive safety and sensor technology for the avoidance of accidents and injury. The Powertrain division is responsible for innovative and efficient powertrain system solutions to make drive concepts easier on the environment in future. The Interior division bundles all activities relating to information, communication and networking solutions, their presentation and operability in vehicles – including vehicles with alternative drives. The interior division also includes the commercial vehicle and retail activities of the automotive group. Passenger and Light Truck Tires develops and produces tires for compact, mid-range and luxury segment vehicles, SUVs, vans, motorcycles and bicycles. Commercial Vehicle Tires offer a wide range of truck, bus, industrial and off-the-road tires for a variety of uses and application requirements. ContiTech develops and manufactures functional parts, components and systems for the automotive industry and almost all key industries and is one of the world's biggest specialists for rubber and plastics technology.

Chassis and Safety creates systems for an automotive future in which life is protected and injuries are prevented. All expertise is bundled in the areas of driving safety and driving dynamics. Thanks to more than a century of experience in the automotive industry, Continental is capable of integrating active safety such as braking and driver assistance systems, sensors, driving stability and chassis components as well as passive safety such as airbag electronics that, from individual components to networked systems, only serve one purpose – to increase driving safety.

Active safety systems, like electronic braking and driver assistance systems, warn of imminent dangers and intervene to assist with steering, braking and suspension control. Passive safety systems, such as airbags and pedestrian protection, provide the best possible protection in the event of an accident.

The vision is a networked vehicle that acts and reacts to relieve the driver and alleviate critical traffic situations. Together, Continental calls this innovative and integrated safety concept that combines active and passive lifesaving driving safety elements ContiGuard. Chassis and Safety maintains a presence at 66 locations in 19 countries.

The products of the Powertrain division not only make driving more environmentally compatible and affordable, they also enhance comfort and driving pleasure. Starting with the concept of clean power, Continental offers its customers a comprehensive portfolio of gasoline and diesel systems including sensors, actuators and tailor-made electronics, through to fuel supply systems, engine management and transmission control units, down to systems and components for hybrid and electric drives. The modular approach includes solutions to enhance energy efficiency for all kinds of drives in all vehicle categories. The powertrain division has 64 locations in 21 countries.

The Interior division optimises the use of information in vehicles. In an age in which people are increasingly networked with each other, solutions have to be found that facilitate safe networking even when driving. This means that information has to be filtered, prioritised, further processed and presented in a comprehensible manner. A crucial factor for using this information is the interface between the vehicle and people. The aim is to make all the necessary information available to the driver at the right time and to present it in such a way that it can be comprehended quickly, thus enabling the driver to adapt optimally to current driving demands. The solutions of interior are therefore developed around people and their needs in order to network drivers and passengers with their own and other vehicles, the environment and mobile devices. The vision is 'Always On', which means that they see the networked vehicle of the future as a partner that assists drivers and passengers. Interior has production facilities at 93 locations in 25 countries.

The Passenger and Light Truck Tires division has been developing and producing tires for cars since 1898. Continental tires stand for excellent transmission of forces and exceptionally reliable tracking in all weather conditions as they offer an outstanding connection between the vehicle and the road in all kinds of weather. The division maintains a presence at 54 locations in 35 countries. The passenger and light truck tires division's range is comprised of tires for compact, mid-range and luxury segment vehicles, SUVs, vans, light trucks and RVs. The division produces tires under the brand names of Continental, Uniroyal (except in NAFTA, Colombia and Peru), Semperit, General Tire, Viking, Gislaved, Euzkadi, Sime Tyres, Barum, Mabor and Matador.

The Commercial Vehicle Tires division stands for economic mobility in the fields of goods, people, construction and services. The division operates at 44 sites in 33 countries and provides its customers with high-mileage tires, a reliable transmission of forces and low fuel consumption. This is because, as a global partner to the transport and logistics industry, Continental is equally well acquainted with the world's markets and its roads. The division offers truck, bus and industrial tires for various applications and service requirements. Continental premium brand tires are marketed worldwide. The range is supplemented by the Barum, Semperit, Uniroyal and Matador brands in Europe, the General Tire and Ameri*Steel brands in America and the Euzkadi brand in Mexico. In Asia, the product portfolio includes Sime Tyres brand tires. To supplement Continental's new tire range, they have therefore also included a hot-retreaded and a cold-retreaded line of tires under the ContiRe and ContiTread brand names. The industrial tires unit develops and produces tires of the Continental, Barum, Simex, General Tire, Ameri*Steel and Novum brands.

Engineering green value technologies – at ContiTech, this basic idea underlies a strong corporate commitment and technological expertise in the development and use of innovative products. The division maintains a presence at 78 locations in 24 countries. With its high-tech products and systems, ContiTech is a global development partner and original equipment supplier to the automotive industry, the printing, mining and commercial vehicle industries, as well as the machinery and plant construction, aviation and aerospace and railway engineering industries. The products have many uses – they are flexible and thermally stable, formable, abrasion resistant, reversible and eco-friendly. They lend themselves well to combinations with other materials such as glass, metal and ceramics. (www.conti-online.com)

Linde

Linde is a world-leading gases and engineering company with around 62,000 employees working in more than 100 countries worldwide. As of financial year 2011, Linde generated total revenue of €13.787 billion. The Linde Group has its headquarters in Munich. They are geared towards sustainable earnings based growth and focused on the expansion of its international business with forward-looking products and services. The Linde Group is divided into three divisions: gases, engineering and Gist, a provider of logistics solutions. Their stated vision is 'To be the leading global gases and engineering group admired for their people, who provide innovative solutions that makes a difference to the world'.

The group was founded in 1879 in Wiesbaden by Carl Van Linde and is named after him. His engineering company, the Gesellschaft fur Linde's Eismaschinen helped create a new industry within just a few decades, that of refrigeration, from air liquefaction to air separation. The mid-1970s to the start of the new millennium saw a lot of organic expansion, as well as acquisitions. For example, the former British Oxygen Company (BOC) became a part of the Linde Group in 2006.

Wolfgang Reitzle is the CEO of Linde AG, while Manfred Schneider is the Chairman of the Supervisory Board.

Their Linde Gases Division includes two global business units (GBUs); healthcare (medical gases) and tonnage (on-site) and the two business areas (BAs); merchant and packaged gases (liquefied and cylinder gases) and electronics (electronic gases). They are a world leader in the industrial gases market. They offer a wide range of compressed and liquefied gases as well as chemicals and are an important and reliable partner for a huge variety of industries. Their gases are used in the energy sector, in steel production, chemical processing, environmental protection, welding, food processing, glass production and electronics; they range from hydrogen, acetylene, carbon monoxide, CO_2 to shielding gases for welding applications, noble gases, calibration gas mixtures to high-purity gases within their HiQ® program for speciality gases. Beyond industrial gases, they also supply hardware, safety products and other services.

Linde Healthcare is dedicated to providing pharmaceutical and medical gas products and services that enable healthcare professionals to provide optimal therapy for their patients in hospitals, clinics, intermediate care centres, emergency centres and patient homes. In addition to oxygen therapy, aerosol therapy and anaesthesia, they also provide medical gas solutions for other specialised needs and treatments.

Their second core division is the Linde Engineering Division which is a leading technology partner for plant engineering and construction worldwide. Their global success is built on their extensive process engineering expertise in the planning, project development and construction of turnkey industrial plants. They focus on market segments, such as, plants for the production of hydrogen and synthesis gas, air gases, olefins as well as plants for natural gas treatment. With more than 1,000 process engineering patents and 4,000 completed plants projects, Linde ranks among the leading international plant contractors, especially to petrochemical, chemical and pharmaceutical industries. Customers all around the globe trust Linde's unparalleled reliability, efficiency and competence in project scheduling. They also provide for after sales service, maintenance and spare parts.

Their third and final division is called Gist, a leading provider of logistics and supply chain solutions. Gist operates in a wide range of commercial and industrial sectors, including grocery, retail, electronics and gas. The company employs about 5,000 people in 40 locations, serving customers like, Marks and Spencer, British Airways, Carlsberg, Bakkavör, Uniq and Dairy Crest.

As the world's largest hydrogen plant manufacturer and leading gas company in Europe, Linde has delivered hydrogen for a number of applications since 1910, for example, in the chemical, petrochemical and food industries.

In hydrogen technology, Linde acts as a supplier and developer of a new, reproductive future energy source. Linde traditionally maintains close cooperation with the scientific research establishment and industry. This enables continuous advancement and creation of new, innovative applications. Besides developing new hydrogen technologies, they develop innovative tank systems and collaborate with leading car manufacturers, from production, liquefaction and on-site supply to hydrogen storage and filling stations.

Increasingly, strategic lines of business for their engineering division includes the latest process technologies to efficiently produce bio-fuels from bio-mass and hydrogen from regenerative energy sources. They also deliver products and processes that make renewable energies cost effective, dramatically cut consumption of natural resources and help reduce or even eliminate harmful emissions.

Linde's activities also involve innovative solutions to replace harmful gases with climate-neutral ones and enable further expansion of the eco-friendly, solar cell industry. High-purity gases from Linde are also often an environmentally friendly alternative to conventional materials used in the manufacture of electronic components. Their electronics business area is a trusted partner and supplier in this field. (www.linde.com)

Henkel

Henkel is an international company which holds leading market positions, globally, both in the consumer and industrial businesses, with well-known brands such as Persil, Schwarzkopf and Loctite. In 1876, Fritz Henkel and two of his partners founded the company Henkel and Cie in Aachen, and marketed their first product, a universal detergent based on silicate. Over the years, this German family of entrepreneurs, together with thousands of its employees, has built Henkel, expanding and transforming it into a global company. Today, Henkel's headquarters are located in Düsseldorf. The company employs about 47,000 people worldwide and counts among the most internationally aligned German-based companies in the global market place. People all over the world trust and rely on Henkel's brands and technologies. Henkel's current corporate slogan is 'Excellence is our Passion'.

Henkel has subsidiaries in more than 70 countries worldwide. In fiscal year 2011, the company generated total sales revenue of €15.605 billion. Kasper Rorsted is the Chairman of the Management Board, and Simone Bagel-Trah is the Chairwoman of the Stakeholders' Committee and the Supervisory Board.

Henkel is organised into three operating business units globally: laundry and home care, beauty care and adhesive technologies.

Laundry and Home Care has always played an important role for Henkel. In fact the company's success story started with a product from this business division. Some brand names from this business sector have become an integral part of the daily lives of consumers in many different countries. This sector enjoys leading positions in the laundry care and household cleaner segments on a worldwide scale.

Henkel has been setting standards with its brands for several decades now. Persil is Germany's number one detergent which offers premium quality and ultimate care for laundry. Some other popular brands from this sector are: Mir, a special detergent for wool and silk, Perwoll; Purex, a detergent for delicate fabrics which gives clothes a thorough cleaning; Sil, the stain remover; Spee, the heavy-duty laundry detergent which offers outstanding cleanliness at an affordable price and Vernel, the leading fabric softener which comes in various fragrances that cares for fibres.

While Pril is a leading brand with more than five decades of hand dishwashing experience, Somat offers automatic dishwashing systems for outstanding results. Bref the powerful, universal, cleaner from Henkel ensures effortless deep-cleaning efficacy combined with surface safety.

Henkel's Beauty Care business unit develops, produces and sells numerous, successful high-quality products worldwide for cosmetics and body care in the following categories: hair, body, skin and mouth.

In the hair category, Henkel offers salon-exclusive brands as well as retail hair products for consumers. Schwarzkopf Professional, Indola and Clynol are some of the popular salon-exclusive brands. In the retail category, Henkel has won the trust of its consumers thanks to some of its popular brands such as Palette, Brilliance, Gliss Kur, Schauma, Syoss, got2b and 3 Wetter Taft.

In the body and fragrances category, Henkel offers high-quality bath and shower products, deodorants, soaps, body lotions and fragrances under the following brands: bac, Barnängen, Coast, Dial, Dry Idea, Fa, La Toja, Mont St. Michel, Neutromed, Right Guard, Soft and Dri and Tone.

Henkel's skin care brands AOK and Diadermine provide product lines specifically formulated for the needs of the skin. They are high-performance skin-care brands developed by dermatologists.

Finally, in the oral care category, Henkel offers a wide assortment of high-quality products for oral hygiene. Its popular brands in this category are; Antica Erboristeria, Denivit, Licor del Polo, Theramed and Vademecum their only toothpaste brands. Many of its brands are only locally available in certain geographical markets.

Adhesives, sealants and surface treatments from Henkel's adhesive technologies business unit serve the transportation, electronics, aerospace, metal, durable and consumer goods, maintenance, repair and packaging industries. This unit also offers a broad range of products for the craftsman and the consumer. It is subdivided into four main categories: industrial; home, school and office; do-it-yourself and craftsmen and construction.

In the industrial category, Henkel supplies many different manufacturing industries with advanced products and systems solutions. The areas of application include: abrasives, adhesives, cleaners, coatings, equipment, gasketing, lubricants, micro-spheres, moulding, mould releases, repairing, sealants, solders, for potting and encapsulating, surface treatments as well as thread-sealing and thread-locking. Ranked among the best in their respective applications, the leading and trusted brands are Bonderite, Liofol, Loctite, technomelt and Teroson.

Its leading brands in the home, school and office are used for gluing, correction and as humidity absorbers, super glues and tapes. These brands include: Pritt, Sellotape, Ariasana, Loctite and Pattex. Meanwhile in the do-it-yourself (DIY) category, the brands are used for renovation and decoration, strong bonding and as sealants and PU (polyurethane) foams and tapes. The leading brands are Metylan, Pattex, Ponal, Rubson, Sista, Ceresit, Lepage, Loctite, Solvite and UniBond.

In the craftsmen and construction category, its brands are used for chemical anchoring, flooring, tiling, wall-papering, water-proofing, pipe-installation and fire protection, as construction adhesives and for external thermal insulation composite systems (ETICS).

Some popular brands from this category are, Ceresit, Elch Pro, Fester, Metylan, Pattex, Ponal, Sista, Tangit, Teroson, Thomsit andUniBond.

About 2,700 employees work in the company's research and development (R&D) departments worldwide. Henkel's technologies worldwide are protected by more than 8,000 patents, and there are around 5,000 patent applications pending. Henkel also has about 2,000 registered designs protecting its intellectual property rights.

To ensure excellent quality and product safety, Henkel verifies, during the R&D process, that there will be no risks associated with its products during their manufacture, use and disposal and that they comply with all statutory regulations. By the end of 2011, about 70 per cent of the production output was generated by factories certified according to the international standard for environmental management systems, ISO 14001.

Henkel's excellent performance in the field of sustainable development has been regularly recognised by numerous national and international ranking agencies: Henkel has been listed in the international FTSE4Good index for 11 consecutive years. And the company is also included in the Ethibel PIONEER and Ethibel EXCELLENCE investment registers. At the last World Economic Forum in Davos, Henkel was ranked seventeenth in the Global 100 Most Sustainable Corporations in the World. It was also included in the list of the Ethisphere Institute's World's Most Ethical Companies for the fifth year in a row. In September 2012, Henkel was listed in both the World and the Europe Indexes of the Dow Jones Sustainability Index, for the sixth consecutive time, as the sustainability leader in the nondurable household products sector. (www.henkel.com)

Fresenius

Fresenius is a global healthcare group with products and services for dialysis, hospitals and medical care for patients at home. The group's present headquarters are in the town of Bad Homburg in the state of Hessen. The company was founded in 1912 in Frankfurt am Main, when the pharmacist and proprietor of the Hirsch Pharmacy, Eduard Fresenius, started a chemical–pharmaceutical company as his namesake. He expanded the pharma lab into a small manufacturing operation with pharmaceutical specialties such as infusion solutions, serological reagents and a nasal ointment.

Today, the Fresenius Group consists of four business segments, each of which is responsible for its own worldwide business operations. They are Fresenius Medical Care, Fresenius Kabi, Fresenius Helios and Fresenius Vamed. Fresenius holds approximately 31 per cent of Fresenius Medical Care, (Fresenius became a European company, or SE, in 2007, then converted into a SE & Co. KGaA in 2011).

The group has over 160,000 employees dedicated to the service of health in about 100 countries worldwide. Total group sales for fiscal year 2011 were €16.522 billion. Ulf Mark Schneider is the CEO and Chairman of the Management Board, and Gerd Krick is the Chairman of the Supervisory Board. Fresenius garnered its highest sales from Europe and North America, followed by Asia-Pacific, Latin America and Africa.

Fresenius Medical Care is the world's leading provider of products and services for individuals undergoing dialysis because of chronic kidney failure, a condition that affects more than 1.89 million patients worldwide. Through its network of 3,135 dialysis clinics, Fresenius Medical Care provides dialysis treatment to 256,521 patients worldwide. The company also provides a wide range of products for hemodialysis, acute dialysis, peritoneal dialysis care, liver support therapy and for therapeutic apheresis. They provide hemodialysis machines, dialyzers and related disposable products. As a vertically integrated company, they offer products and services for the entire dialysis value chain.

Fresenius Kabi is the market leader in infusion therapy and clinical nutrition in Europe and holds leading positions in the company's most important countries of Latin America and the Asia-Pacific region. In the field of intravenously administered generic drugs (IV drugs), Fresenius Kabi ranks among the leading global suppliers. The company is focused on the therapy and care of critically and chronically ill patients both in the hospital and home care environments. Fresenius Kabi's portfolio is comprised of a wide range of infusion solutions, blood-volume replacement products, IV drugs as well as parenteral and enteral nutrition products. To administer these products, Fresenius Kabi also offers related medical devices. In addition, the company provides transfusion technology products for blood banks and blood donor centres.

While Fresenius Helios, specialises in hospital management with a focus on acute treatment and subsequent medical rehabilitation, and owns 72 hospitals with a total of more than 23,000 beds. Among 50 acute care hospitals six are maximum care hospitals, in Berlin-Buch, Erfurt, Krefeld, Schwerin, Duisburg and Wuppertal; the HELIOS group also includes 22 rehabilitation clinics. Fresenius Helios thus holds a leading position in the German hospital market with regard to private clinics. They also rank among the largest providers of in-patient and out-patient healthcare in Germany. The goal is to provide high-quality, state-of-the-art medical care in all areas and at all care levels. More than 42,000 employees treat over 2.7 million patients annually, more than 750,000 of them in-patients, at its hospitals.

Finally, Fresenius Vamed is a leading international provider of services in planning, contracting and managing healthcare facilities. It offers hospitals a complete value chain to achieve and maintain efficiency at every stage, from project development, planning and turnkey construction to facility and total operational management. With, headquarters in Vienna, Austria, VAMED AG boasts a track record of approximately 600 completed healthcare projects in more than 60 countries over the past three decades. The approach of 'everything from one source' has formed the cornerstone of Fresenius Vamed's reputation as a reliable partner in the healthcare industry.

The Fresenius Group has firmly integrated environmental protection targets into their organisation. Certifications in accordance with ISO 14001 at various plants of the Fresenius Group prove that they take environmental protection seriously. A focus in 2006 was on reducing energy consumption at a number of their production sites. In St. Wendel, one of their largest European production sites, they achieved a significant reduction in their consumption of steam through the use of heat recovery systems, and lowered their annual consumption of natural gas by 4 per cent. They have also increased the production of PVC-free infusion bags at their infusion-solution production facilities. (www.fresenius.com)

Merck

Merck KGaA is a global pharmaceutical, chemical and life science company with around 40,000 employees in 67 countries. Merck is the world's oldest pharmaceutical and chemical company, whose roots date back to 1668. In 1917, the US subsidiary Merck & Co. was expropriated and it has been an independent company ever since. Merck & Co. holds the rights to the name within North America, while outside the region the US Company operates as Merck, Sharp & Dohme or MSD. Merck KGaA has the rights to the name elsewhere in the world, while in North America it operates under the umbrella brand name EMD, made from the first letters of Emanuel Merck, Darmstadt.

The company's beginnings can be traced back to 1668, when Friedrich Jacob Merck acquired the Angel Pharmacy in Darmstadt. Later, in 1827, Heinrich Emmanuel Merck began industrial-scale production of alkaloids, plant extracts and other chemicals.

At present, the operational business is managed under the umbrella of Merck KGaA with headquarters in Darmstadt. Around 30 per cent of the company's total capital is publicly traded, while the Merck family owns an interest of about 70 per cent via the general partner E. Merck KG.

Karl-Ludwig Kley is the Chairman of the Executive Board of Merck and Rolf Krebs is the Chairman of the Supervisory Board. For fiscal year 2011, the group had total sales revenue of €10.276 billion.

The pharmaceutical business division is comprised of innovative prescription drugs as well as over-the-counter products. The chemicals business division offers speciality products for electronics, printing, coatings, cosmetics, food, pharma and bio-tech industries. The pharmaceuticals business division is comprised of Merck Serono and the Consumer Health division.

At Merck Serono they specialise in the treatment of cancer, neuro-degenerative diseases, infertility, endocrine and metabolic disorders, cardiovascular diseases and other conditions with unmet medical needs. They are internationally recognised as a biotechnology leader with innovative and successful products such as antibodies and interferons along with a well-stocked and promising developmental pipeline. Specialised know-how in research and production ensures high-quality manufacturing. They devote 22 per cent of their earnings to the pursuit of innovative new therapies through their own R&D as also with other strategic alliances and agreements. They are mainly into new chemical entities (NCEs) and new biological entities (NBEs). Their popular, innovative technology brands are Erbitux®, GONAL-F®, Serostim®, Rebif® and Saizen®. At the Medical Design Excellence Awards (MDEA) ceremony, Merck Serono's easypod®, their first electronic growth hormone injection device, received a gold medal for its innovative design and use.

The Consumer Health division consists of over-the-counter products for cough and cold, supplements for mobility, everyday health protection and women's and children's health products. Their popular and well-known brands are the Nasivin® range of products, an effective cold remedy. The main healthcare companies are Seven Seas and Lamberts Health Care in the UK, Merck Médication Famíliale in France, Merck Selbstmedikation in Germany and Merck Consumer Health in Shanghai. The Seven Seas® and Flexagil® range is for mobility and flexibility. Bion®, Bion3®, Cebion® and Diabion® are pro-biotic based food supplements. The Femibion® and Kidabion®/Haliborang® range of products is for women's health and growing children supplements.

Their second important business sector is the Chemicals division where they offer speciality products for the electronics, printing, coatings, cosmetics, food, pharmaceutical and bio-tech industries.

Merck Millipore: The portfolio of Merck Millipore is comprised of products for life science research such as assays, biomarkers and target solutions, as well as bio-processing, lab water purification and filtration. Additionally, the division supplies speciality chemicals mainly to regulated markets, for example, the pharmaceutical, cosmetics and food industries. Analytical and scientific laboratories use the reagents and test kits supplied by the division.

Merck Millipore is comprised of three business units. Bio Science sells products used by life science laboratories in academia and industry. Lab Solutions supplies general lab products and equipment for applications in both life sciences and industrial markets and process solutions markets products used in the production of chemical and bio-pharmaceutical drugs.

The Performance Materials division manufactures liquid crystals which are used around the world in LCD televisions, monitors, tablet PCs, notebooks, mobile phones and digital cameras. Besides high-tech chemicals and materials for liquid crystal displays, this division also offers new display technologies such as OLEDs as well as innovative effect pigments for the plastics, printing and coatings industries. Their pigments are also used for example, in skin care and colour cosmetics. In view of climate change and high energy prices, they are also active in the growth markets of renewable energy sources. They are working to utilise solar energy more efficiently and to develop innovative technologies for energy saving LEDs.

Merck manufactures more than 50,000 different products and has a presence in more than 150 locations in 67 countries. Merck strives to continually improve its performance and uses energy, water and materials economically and efficiently. Merck is doing this to reduce its impact on the environment, but also to achieve cost savings derived from efficiency. Merck is currently focusing on climate protection. By 2020, Merck aims to reduce its total direct and indirect greenhouse gas emissions by 20 per cent – measured on the basis of 2006 levels. In 2009, 54 production sites were certified for the first time in accordance with ISO 14001:2004, the international environmental management standard. Merck's spending on environmental protection, health and safety totalled €140 million in 2010. (www.merckgroup.com)

Fielmann

Fielmann AG is a German ophthalmic company that retails eye-wear of all sorts, from prescription to sunglasses. Fielmann is a market leader in Germany and Europe's largest optician. Today, a total of 23 million Germans wear Fielmann spectacles. Every second pair sold in Germany is a Fielmann. Their strategy has been one of affordable eye-wear fashion. Their slogan 'You are the Customer' forms the basis of their corporate philosophy.

The company was founded in 1972 by the present CEO, Günther Fielmann, in Cuxhaven, a town in the northern state of Lower Saxony. He started off as an ophthalmic specialist (being a state approved master optometrist) who later saw and developed the niche for low-cost or affordable spectacles with a wide variety of models to choose from. By the 1980s he started to grow at a fast pace and by 1994 he was listed in the stock index. Today, Fielmann's stock index has advanced from the SDAX to the MDAX, a sign that the market has recognised the company's success and further growth potential.

The company's present headquarters are in Hamburg. Günther Fielmann is the CEO and Chairman of the Management Board and Mark K. Binz is the Chairman of the Supervisory Board.

As of fiscal year 2011, total sales revenue was €1.053 billion. They have a total of 663 branches covering Germany, Austria, Switzerland, Poland, Luxembourg and the Netherlands, with around 14,000 employees of which around 2,500 are trainees.

Fielmann is firmly rooted in the industry and is active at every level of the value-added chain in the optical industry. They are manufacturers, agents and opticians. The company has shaped the optical industry, especially in Germany and parts of Europe.

It was Fielmann that made health service spectacles attractive and socially acceptable and thus democratised eye-wear fashion. The basis for their success has been customer-friendly services, an extensive selection of models at prices that are reasonable, the best technical equipment and a high level of professional competence.

Every branch of Fielmann stocks over 2,000 pairs of spectacles from big-name brands as well as international couturiers. Fielmann offers a wide selection of modern, metal and plastic frames, all at a guaranteed, low Fielmann price. The company has a ladies' and men's collection in a wide variety of frames as well as prescription sunglasses with optimum UV protection and a three year guarantee at fair prices. Fielmann also stocks a broad range of contact lenses, of all optical strengths and for all types of wear.

At Fielmann you can still get trendy spectacles at no extra charge with the zero-cost insurance. For example, with the Hanse Merkur insurance policy you are entitled to a pair of trendy metal or plastic framed spectacles from their zero-cost collection, plus a three-year guarantee. Other innovative schemes include zero-cost spectacles for children and young people under 18, complete with lenses by Carl Zeiss Vision. All you have to do is present your prescription or medical insurance card. Competent opticians also test your eyesight for free, using state-of-the-art technology. If customers are not satisfied with their glasses, they can exchange or return them with a full refund, even after six weeks.

Fielmann makes sure that what you get is certified quality. All the frames in the Fielmann Collection have passed the EN ISO 12870 utility test, done in their labs. This test is in accordance with the German Commodities Ordinance which makes sure that the frames are corrosion-proof, non-fading and do not release any nickel.

Their retail shops or branches are larger than the average optician's shop. They are usually located in premier city locations alongside other premium brands from other industries. Fielmann's shops have high-quality furnishing and fittings with attractive product displays, eyesight testing rooms and workshops.

With its advertising campaigns, Fielmann has made eye-wear or spectacles into a fashionable item, like a fashion accessory, which is also affordable.

Industrial production, logistics and the service division are located in Rathenow in Brandenburg. The branches are connected to the logistics centre online and spectacles ordered are delivered overnight. With its own production facilities, Fielmann can control the flow of goods along the entire output chain.

They prepare mineral and plastic lenses to order and then fit them into the frames in their grinding plant. In a two-shift operation they produce more than 14,000 lenses a day, on average. In 2010, they produced more than 3 million lenses of all levels of finish and supplied over 6.5 million frames.

Another significant achievement is the setting up of the Fielmann Academy, a non-profit, public educational institution for the optical industry. The new training centre for the entire optical industry in Germany and Europe is located at Plön Castle, a renovated heritage site in Schleswig-Holstein. The next generation of professional opticians is trained here, and it is also open to external students and qualifies 6,000 opticians annually.

In addition to sales growth in the optical sector, they also expect additional growth from the continued expansion of their hearing-aid implements.

In the area of social responsibility, Fielmann plants a tree each year for each employee and to date have planted more than one million trees. They also fund long-term monitoring programmes in ecological agriculture, conservation and medicine, in addition to promoting monument protection, teaching and research. (www.fielmann.de)

Schaeffler

Schaeffler with its brands INA, FAG and LUK is a leading manufacturer of rolling bearings and linear products as well as a renowned supplier to the automotive industry for high precision products and systems for engines, transmissions and chassis applications. Schaeffler is one of the largest German and European industrial companies in family ownership.

The brothers Wilhelm Schaeffler and Georg Schaeffler started their business with a great deal of courage, creativity and vision. They created a global company along with their employees from very humble beginnings in Herzogenaurach in 1946. FAG, which has been under Schaeffler ownership since 2001, was founded in 1883 when Friedrich Fischer invented the ball-grinding machine in Schweinfurt, and thus laid the foundation for the entire rolling-bearing industry. FAG stands for 'Fischers Aktien Gesellschaft'. LUK was also founded by the brothers, in 1965.

Today, Schaeffler develops and manufactures high precision products for everything that moves from machines, equipment and vehicles to aviation and aerospace applications. The group headquarters are based in the town of Herzogenaurach in Bavaria. They employ around 76,000 employees at 180 plants and sales offices in more than 50 countries. For fiscal year 2011, total group sales was around €10.7 billion, of which around two-thirds was earned by the automotive division and the rest by the industrial division. The group is owned by Maria-Elisabeth Schaeffler, the widow of the late Georg Schaeffler, and their son Georg FW. Schaeffler, who is also the Chairman of the Supervisory Board. Jürgen M. Geißinger, is the PCEO of Schaeffler AG and is responsible for the operational business and the strategic focus of the group companies.

Around, 6,000 employees work on new products and technologies in more than 40 R&D centres all over the world. They own the rights to more than 18,000 patents, while around 1,800 inventions are filed for patent applications every year.

All production locations of the Schaeffler Group have been certified worldwide according to international standards, i.e. DIN ISO 9001:2008, ISO TS 16949: 2009, AS 9100, AS 9120 and have been audited according to ISO 14001, (EC) 761/2001 EMAS with regard to environmental management and according to OHSAS 18001 with regard to occupational safety.

With their three strong brands INA, FAG and LUK, Schaeffler is active with its automotive and industrial divisions.

The Automotive Division caters to the automotive industry and contributes to 60 per cent of group sales. Their products contribute significantly to environmentally friendly mobility. As an engineering partner and supplier for almost all automobile manufacturers, they develop and manufacture the latest products and system solutions for engines, transmissions and chassis. They use their Advance Development and Product Innovation

Process to work on requirements and solutions for the future. They manufacture components and systems for valve trains, primary drives, accessory drives and camshaft phasing units for customers worldwide. INA and FAG products also provide state-of-the-art innovative bearing solutions in chassis applications for use in brake systems, steering columns and suspension struts.

The Industrial Division has a product range consisting of around 40,000 catalogue products as well as numerous special designs. Their spectrum of bearing solutions ranges from rotary and linear bearings including tribology to the integration of sensors, drives and controls. Customers from around 60 different industrial sectors rely on rolling and plain bearings, linear guides and direct drives from the INA and FAG brands. With customer-oriented applications such as linear technology, wind power, production machinery and aerospace and sector managements such as heavy industries, power transmission, power generation, railways, consumer products/medical equipment, motorcycles and small combustion engines, fluid and pneumatics, they offer products for high machine availability and to reduce the overall weight with compact system designs.

FAG and Barden brands stand for the development and manufacture of special bearings for aviation and aerospace applications. Nearly all modern aeroplanes use FAG's bearing technology. FAG Aerospace also took part in the development of bearings and other precision components used in the engine of the new wide-body A380 Airbus and the Boeing B787 Dreamliner.

In addition, FAG is a developmental partner and supplier for leading manufacturers of helicopters worldwide. International space travel consortia rely on the quality, reliability and efficiency of their aviation even under extreme temperatures and speeds. The group products have also been used in the Space Shuttle and the European launch vehicle Ariane, where they have proven to be reliable.

Applications of these highly reliable bearings can also be found in sectors such as nuclear and medical technology, for example, the low-noise, thin-section bearing systems for computer tomography.

LUK also is comprised of the automotive after-market business and offers replacement parts and services for distributors and repair shops worldwide, as well as maintain a top position in clutches and systems for transmissions.

'Zero Defects' in all processes and products is the declared quality objective of Schaeffler, where quality is not limited to only detecting and removing defective products, but to a quality mindset that is geared towards preventing defects from occurring in the first place.

A consistent and strong quality management system through all phases from design to manufacturing ensures the highest product safety possible. State-of-the-art manufacturing technology makes a significant contribution to 'zero defect manufacturing' for high precision products. Schaeffler is among the world's technological leaders in the fields of cold forming technology, forging technology, machining and assembly.

All Schaeffler sites worldwide are certified in accordance with ISO 14001 and the more stringent EMAS directive. This leading role in implementing excellent environmental management systems is verified by the numerous international awards its sites have received. (www.schaefflergroup.com)

Miele

Miele is a manufacturer of premium-quality domestic appliances, commercial equipment and appliances for the kitchen, laundry room and even the broom closet. It has been a family-owned and run company with headquarters in Gütersloh a town in the state of North-Rhine Westphalia.

It was founded in 1899 by Carl Miele and Reinhard Zinkann, who started a production facility in the Westphalian town of Herzebrock, to make cream separators. The Miele trademark or logo was used very early on and appeared consistently in all machines, nameplates, printed materials and advertising produced by the company. From the mid-1920s, importance was attached to using a sloping dash as the dot on the 'í' in Miele, giving the brand a high recall and recognition amongst their target audience.

Today, the company has over 16,600 employees in 12 production facilities including Austria, the Czech Republic and China as well as sales representation in nearly 100 countries. Total sales turnover was over €3 billion per their latest business report. The proprietors are the Miele and Zinkann families of which there are at present 60 family shareholders.

Markus Miele and Reinhard Zinkann are the Managing Directors and Co-Proprietors of the company.

Miele sees itself as a German brand for which 'Made in Germany' is a very important international hallmark of quality, although they are now expanding into new countries with their subsidiaries and sales and service presence in China and India also. Their aim is the same everywhere: Miele appliances must be the best. As a premium appliance brand represented on all continents, Miele is steadfastly committed to the highest quality, performance and environmental standards. The company's innovative heritage, state-of-the-art design and engineering aesthetic have inspired comparison with the best of other brands.

Miele's range of exceptional consumer appliances includes vacuum cleaners; laundry systems; rotary irons; dishwashers; built-in-convection, speed and steam ovens; cook-tops; ventilation hoods; refrigeration; wine storage and coffee systems. A recent addition has been the kitchen designed by Porsche Design and Poggenpohl with Miele appliances, the ultra-modern P'7340 kitchen specially designed for men. This kitchen will exclusively feature Miele built-in appliances.

In their Miele Professional range, they offer products like dishwashers, washing machines, tumble dryers and rotary irons for commercial use as well as washer-disinfectors for medical, dental and laboratory needs.

In the words of their founding fathers, Carl Miele and Richard Zinkann, 'Success is only possible in the long term if one is totally and utterly convinced of the quality of one's products'. It is thanks to this enduring philosophy that focuses on the dynamic development of quality that the Miele brand is identified with unsurpassed product quality.

Their basic slogan has always been, 'Forever Better' or 'Immer Besser' in German. While in some other places and ads, the tagline has been, 'Anything else is a compromise'. Over the years, Miele as a company and brand has earned great trust and confidence to a degree unparalleled by other manufacturers of domestic appliances.

Quality, durability, innovative power and tradition, these are all strong arguments in favour of Miele, but the other reason for their success is Miele generates a 'feel-good' factor while using Míele appliances, whether cooking, washing, cleaning or drinking an espresso prepared with a Míele coffee machine. They appeal to the senses in a special way that leaves the customer truly satisfied. It is a coveted brand that is loved and revered in many places and is considered the first choice when it comes to high-quality residences, hotels and even offices.

Their quality and technological leadership have not come by chance – their investment in R&D has been around 7 per cent of annual turnover, which comes to about €150 million a year.

From 2001 to 2005, Míele registered a record 350 inventions with the German patent office, as well as filing 112 European and 62 US patents. At Míele they manufacture the great majority of their product components themselves in their state-of-the-art production facilities, which guarantees the quality for which Míele is a byword. The average lifespan of Míele appliances is said to be around 20 years, sometimes even longer.

Among the many innovations that have given Míele the quality and technological edge are the patented Honeycomb Drum, the innovative Steam Cooker, smart Supertronic Sensor-Touch Controls, the Miele@home system, the S6 compact Vacuum Cleaner and the new S8, completely new ranges of laundry-care appliances, dishwashers and refrigeration appliances with LED lighting.

Míele appliances are also very user-friendly, have high energy efficiency and are very good in terms of their capacity to be recycled. All Míele washing machines and dishwashers across the globe have the energy-efficiency category A. In the case of domestic washing machines, the water consumption has been reduced by 42.4 per cent since 1990 and electricity consumption by 29.2 per cent. In its consumer information campaign 'Eco–Top Ten', released in 2006, the Öko-Institute e.v. stated that, Míele appliances are particularly economical and environmentally friendly.

In 2008, Míele and Cie.KG was certified in accordance with ISO 9001 and ISO 14001 quality and environmental standards of production. In the same year, the locations in Germany, Austria and the Czech Republic were certified in accordance with the SA 8000 social standards, while, in 2010, the company was certified in accordance with DIN EN ISO13485 (quality management for medical products). The company achieves and manages sustainability targets through its 'Integrated Míele Management System'.

Among the several awards Míele has received over the years has been, as a 'Top Employer' and 'Fair Company'. In 2008, the Míele company brand was also awarded three honours: amongst 'The Best Brands', a 'Super Brand' and as the 'Most Trusted Brand'. (www.miele.com)

K+S

The K+S AG, is one of the world's leading suppliers of standard and speciality fertilizers as well as being the world's leading producer in the salt business, in terms of production capacity.

The roots of the K+S Group go back to the middle of the nineteenth century when the first fertilizer factories were established in Germany, mainly producing phosphate and super-phosphate. In 1889, a joint stock company for mining and deep drilling was established in a place called Goslar, which later became Salzdetfurth AG, the oldest forerunner of today's K+S AG. Over the years, they have been mining and processing raw materials and the depth of their value added has grown. Through acquisitions in the fertilizer and salt business, K+S as a group have changed fundamentally over the past few decades. The K+S name came about after a merger between Salzdetfurth AG and Wintershall AG to form a new company called Kali and Salz Gmbh which later became Kali and Salz AG. So the K+S name was first used to denote that merger and has since been their group logo to this day. In 2008, K+S got included in the DAX index, the only commodities stock in the DAX index.

In 2011, they sold their plant care and fertilizer business operations with COMPO to the private equity investor Triton and in 2012, the nitrogen business (K+S Nitrogen) to Euro Chem.

Today, the K+S Group employ more than 14,000 people and achieved total sales revenue of around €5.2 billion in fiscal year 2011. Norbert Steiner is the Chairman of the Board of Executive Directors and Ralf Bethke is the Chairman of the Supervisory Board. Their present headquarters are in Kassel, a town in the state of Hessen. Their corporate slogan is 'Experience growth'.

K+S offer a comprehensive range of goods and services for agriculture, industry and private consumers by way of various potash and magnesium products and salt.

The potash and magnesium products business division extracts potash and magnesium crude salts at six mines in Germany. They process the raw materials to arrive at the vital minerals of potassium, magnesium and sulphur that are converted into high-quality fertilizers as well as intermediate products for the manufacture of industrial products, food and pharmaceuticals. K+S KALI GmbH is the fifth largest producer in the world and the leading supplier in Europe for potash and magnesium products, providing a range of products more diverse than that offered by any other potash producer in the world. They continue to develop their specialisation strategy which is focused on higher value addition and differentiation. To expand their potash production capacities, they recently took over the Canadian company Potash One in early 2011. This company holds a number of potash exploration licences in the province of Saskatchewan.

Their other core business sector of salt consists of the European producer ESCO, the South American supplier Sociedad Punta des Lobos (SPL) and Morton Salt. As a result of the Morton Salt acquisition in 2009, K+S has become the largest salt producer in the world. ESCO operates three rock salt mines, brine plants as well as several evaporated salt facilities and is the largest supplier of salt in Europe. Their salt is of 99 per cent purity and is well sought after in Europe.

The South American supplier, Sociedad Punta des Lobos (SPL) extracts rock salt through cost-effective, open-cast mining in the Chilean desert. The excellent quality of the crude salt allows it to be processed into special products for a large number of applications. It is said that the salt reserves in these deposits are sufficient to supply the world's population with salt for several centuries.

Morton Salt has a large number of production sites in the US and in Canada. They have six rock salt mines, seven solar plants and ten evaporated salt facilities. Morton Salt is one of the leading producers of consumer, industrial and de-icing salts in North America. The production capacity of Morton Salt is about 13 million tons of crystallised salt per annum.

The main application areas of the above mined salts are for use in households, in the food processing industry, for water softening, as feed, for preserving fish, in tanneries, in infusions and dialysis solutions, in medicines, in the chemical industry, in drilling fluids, dying works, in leather treatment, pottery and for winter road maintenance and public road authorities. K+S have several brands specially catering to the said applications.

Among the other complimentary businesses of K+S are logistics by way of their company K+S Transport and its subsidiaries in Hamburg and through the Chilean Empremar. They handle one of Europe's largest trans-shipment facilities for export of bulk goods.

At their Salzdetfurth site, they also granulate animal hygiene products, CATSAN and Thomas for the Mars Company. They also have a waste management and recycling unit that uses their underground caverns for the long-range disposal of waste and for waste recycling using the latest solutions in the said areas.

Finally, their subsidiary Chemische Fabrik Kalk (CFK) trades in various basic chemicals, including among others, calcium chloride, sodium carbonate (soda), caustic soda and sodium sulphate.

Among the innovative products that are said to be in the pipeline are potash fertilizers that increase the efficiency of plants to utilise water, liquid fertilizers to enable the supply of nutrients despite dry soils and sulphate-based fertilizers to combat further soil salinisation.

At K+S, the majority of the energy required for production processes are currently provided by natural gas and efficiency levels in their power stations are said to exceed 90 per cent.

They also intend to further reduce and avoid production of residues, have implemented measures to improve the quality of the water of the Werra and Weser rivers and improve their environs. As of now, they will be investing a total of up to €360 million in environmental protection measures. (www.k-plus-s.com)

Infineon

Infineon Technologies AG focuses on the three central challenges facing modern society: energy efficiency, mobility and security. The company offers semiconductors and system solutions for automotive and industrial electronics and chip card and security applications. Infineon's products stand out for their reliability, their quality excellence and their innovative and leading-edge technology in analogue and mixed signal, RF and power as well as embedded control. The company was founded in 1999 with headquarters located in Neubiberg, near the city of Munich.

With a global presence, Infineon operates through its subsidiaries in the US from Milpitas, California, in the Asia-Pacific region from Singapore, and in Japan from Tokyo. Infineon has several facilities in Europe that include one each in Germany, Austria, Hungary and Italy. It also runs R&D centres in France, Singapore, Romania, Taiwan and India, with fabrication units in Germany, Austria, Hungary, US, Singapore, Malaysia, Indonesia and China.

In the 2012 fiscal year (ending 30 September), the Company reported sales of €3.9 billion with close to 26,700 employees worldwide. Infineon is listed on the Frankfurt Stock Exchange (DAX Index) and in the US on the over-the-counter market OTCQX International Premier. Reinhard Ploss is the CEO and Chairman of the Management Board, while Wolfgang Mayrhuber is the Chairman of the Supervisory Board.

Among the wide range of product categories they manufacture today are automotive ICs, chip card and security ICs, discrete and standard products, ESD and EMI protection devices and filters, interface devices, lighting ICs and LED drivers, micro-controllers, power management ICs, power modules and discs, RF, sensors and wireless control, silicon carbide power products and wireless communication products.

Their application areas include automotive, consumer, security, industry, lighting, motor control and drives, power management and renewable energy areas. Infineon's products stand out for their reliability, their excellent quality, innovation and leading-edge technology in analogue and mixed signal, RF and power as well as embedded control.

Infineon is the world's second largest chip supplier to the automotive industry. The sustained success in automotive electronics is attributed to a consistent focus on automotive applications and their requirements, a profound understanding of the automotive system based on more than 40 years of experience and a broad innovative product portfolio of outstanding quality. Infineon serves automotive applications such as the car's power train (comprising engine and transmission control for optimised fuel consumption and to meet government emission regulations addressing chips for emerging technologies, such as hybrids, starter alternators and electromechanical valve-trains), body and convenience (including light control; heating, ventilation and air-conditioning HVAC; comfort locking; power windows; seat memory and keyless entry), safety management (e.g. electronic power steering, collision avoidance, anti-lock brake system, airbag, stability control, tire pressure monitoring) and infotainment (including e-call and information access). The automotive division supplies the automotive industry with sensors, microcontrollers, power semiconductors and power modules that contribute to a more sustainable mobility in terms of reduced fuel consumption and emissions, improved safety and affordability.

The industrial power control division concentrates on electrical drives and renewables. This primarily encompasses components for drives in industrial applications, such as machines or locomotives, and energy generation components in solar or wind power plants.

The power management and multimarket division focuses on components for efficient power management or high-frequency applications. The components are mainly used in computing (server, notebooks, PC) lighting and metering products, solar inverters, gaming and mobile devices as well as in wireless base stations.

Infineon provides security components for passports, identity cards and contactless payment cards and is the leading supplier of chips for credit cards, access cards and trusted computing solutions worldwide. The company has been the world market leader in chips for card applications for 14 years in a row and continues to pioneer new technologies in the field of chip-based security. The focus on security-critical fields allows Infineon to make the most of its expertise in high-security applications as security requirements become more stringent. The chip card and security division is helping to improve data security in today's information society. As users become ever more mobile, advanced security solutions are very much in demand. Consistent deployment of security products has the potential to act as a pacesetter for cutting-edge applications in transport and IT infrastructure. Infineon has the industry's largest portfolio of chips and interfaces to meet the relevant security requirements in these areas.

Infineon also offers their customers a variety of design tools, which support them in finding an appropriate product solution for their application design based on their specific requirements. Their design tools include, LED Driver Selection Tool, Design and Simulation Tool for Low and High Voltage MOSFET's, Simulation Program for power modules or disk drives and Micro-controller Development Tools.

In 2000, Infineon initiated the project called 'Green Product' in order to meet legal as well as even more stringent quality requirements by modifying soldering processes. Infineon Green Products are in compliance with the European RoHS (Restriction of Hazardous Substances) Directive (2011/65/EU) which restricts the use of hazardous substances in electrical and electronic equipment as well as in compliance with the European End-of-Life Vehicle Directive (2000/53/EG). In April 2009, the DA5 consortium, which is led by Infineon, was formed in order to address and mutually define the direction of Pb-free solder die attach-technology development. For Infineon, the main reason to join the consortium was the identification of sustainable, enduring, standardised, reliable and dependable solutions for their customers.

As a global company and a participant of the UN Global Compact initiative, Infineon voluntarily takes responsibility towards the international community. The company takes social responsibility and environmental protection very seriously and both are part of its overall corporate strategy. This voluntary commitment reflects its fundamental values. Infineon has defined the necessary structures, processes and guidelines internally on the basis of the UN Global Compact principles. The involvement with the UN's Global Compact initiative, to which the company signed up in 2004, is proof of Infineon acting as a conscientious and responsible enterprise.

Infineon is a key enabler of sustainable society; with its products the company enables a net ecological benefit of more than 3.6 million tons of CO_2 emission reduction per year.

In 2010, Infineon entered the *Sustainability Yearbook 2011*, which lists 15 per cent of the world's best performers in terms of corporate sustainability between 2,500 participating companies. This study includes companies that are better equipped to identify and respond to emerging opportunities and risks presented by global trends.

IMPRES, the Infineon Integrated Management Program for Environment, Safety and Health, formulates objectives, standards and policy for the entire company in the fields of occupational safety, environmental protection and health. IMPRES was implemented worldwide in 2005 and Infineon received the multi-site certification according to the international ISO 14001 and OHSAS 18001 standards the very same year. (www.infineon.com)

Commerzbank

Commerzbank AG is the second largest bank in Germany. It was founded in 1870, when a number of merchants, merchant bankers and private bankers founded the Commerz und Disconto Bank in Hamburg. As of around 1900, its business focussed increasingly on Berlin. It became one of the country's leading big banks with an extensive branch network.

From 1970 onwards the bank's administrative activities were shifted to Frankfurt am Main, which has been its domicile since. In May 2009, the merging of Dresdner Bank into Commerzbank sees the union of two major banks to form one leading bank. This merger made Commerzbank one of the leading banks for private and corporate customers in Germany.

Commerzbank is a leading bank in Germany and Poland. It is also present worldwide in all markets for its customers as a partner to the business world.

Commerzbank has one of the densest branch networks among German private banks. In total, the Commerzbank group boasts nearly 15 million private customers, as well as 1 million business and corporate clients. In 2011, it generated revenues of just under €10 billion with some 58,000 employees. In Germany, Commerzbank has some 1,200 branches. Outside Germany, the bank is represented through 24 branches, 35 representative offices and seven major subsidiaries in 53 countries on all continents. Their market capitalisation is at €8.1 billion as of September 30, 2012. Commerzbank features among the 30 stocks in the German stock market index Dax and is represented in the Euro Stoxx Banks.

Martin Blessing is the present CEO and Chairman of the Executive Board and Klaus-Peter Müller is the Chairman of the Supervisory Board of Commerzbank AG.

'Commerzbank. The bank at your side' is their new brand promise. They aim to provide products and services that benefit their customers and satisfy their needs. The campaign will portray Commerzbank as a reliable, fair and competent partner.

With the segments areas of private customers, Mittelstandsbank, corporate customers and markets and Central and Eastern Europe, it offers its private and corporate clients as well as institutional investors the banking and capital market services they need.

In their private customers segment, Commerzbank's more than 11 million private and business customers in Germany are advised by some 10,000 consultants in around 1,200 branches.

Their Mittelstandbank has approximately 150 locations in Germany and some 60 locations abroad service more than 100,000 small- and medium-sized corporate customers.

They are Germany's leading bank for private and corporate customers in Central and Eastern Europe with over 4 million customers in the region.

For their corporate customers and markets they offer customer-centred investment banking and are leading in German equities, DCM products and in the delivery of international risk management solutions and investment products.

Their non-core assets segment is comprised of the business areas of commercial real estate, public finance and Deutsche Schiffsbank.

Since 1951, approximately 4,000 international bankers from all parts of the world have participated in Commerzbank's specially structured training course and on-the-job training as well.

As one of the leading private-sector banks in Germany, Commerzbank takes its business responsibility for climate protection very seriously. They intend to reduce their greenhouse gas emissions and to gradually make Commerzbank climate neutral. They actively support renewable energies and other climate friendly products and services. (www.commerzbank.de)

Wacker

Wacker Chemie AG is a market leader in the chemical and semiconductor sectors, pushing ahead with technical innovations and the development of new products for the world's key industries. The company was formed on 13 October 1914 by Alexander Wacker, who set up the Wacker Chemie Gmbh at Burghausen, in Bayern, to produce acetaldehyde, acetic acid and acetone.

Today, they are a globally operating chemical company with business divisions in silicones and polymers, bio solutions and polysilicon. For fiscal year 2011, total group sales were €4.91 billion with around 17,200 employees worldwide. Wacker has a global network of production sites spanning all key regions. Their corporate slogan is 'Creating Tomorrow's Solutions'.

Rudolf Staudigl is the present President and CEO of the Executive Board of Wacker Chemie AG, and Peter-Alexander Wacker is the Chairman of the Supervisory Board. In 2000, The Wacker family gained the majority share of 51 per cent of Wacker Chemie AG and by 2005 they became a stock corporation, Wacker Chemie AG. Their present headquarters are in Munich. The Wacker Group is divided into five divisions: Wacker Silicones, Wacker Polymers, Wacker Bio-solutions, Wacker Polysilicon and Siltronic.

Wacker Silicones is one of the world's leading silane and silicone producers. It offers complete and customised solutions in a broad range of industries. With a range of 3,000 silicone products, their application experts develop and optimise customer formulations according to the latest technological advances, ensuring the best of service quality. Their product portfolio ranges from silanes through silicone fluids, emulsions, elastomers, sealants and resins to pyrogenic silicas. Thanks to their highly diverse properties, silicones offer virtually unlimited potential for intelligent customised solutions in numerous sectors. Key application areas include engineering, electronics, chemicals, cosmetics, textile and paper. They also develop new products and innovative production processes to help their customers cut costs and optimise their business.

Wacker Polymers are global market leaders in binders and polymer additives, which are underpinned by the excellent services and product expertise, provided by Wacker's technical and sales centres. Cutting-edge products include dispersions, polymer powders, polyvinyl acetates, surface coating resins and polyvinyl alcohol solutions. They are used in a wide variety of industrial applications and as base chemicals. VINNAPAS®, VINNOL® and POLYVIOL® rank among their high-tech brands. Key application areas includes, automotive engineering, construction chemicals, paper, adhesives as well as printing inks and surface coatings.

Wacker Bio-solutions, with its innovative product portfolio and long standing expertise in biotechnology, organic syntheses and silane chemistry makes it a preferred partner for customers in the life sciences and consumer care industries – especially for highly challenging bio-tech, custom-manufactured products. Their extensive product range includes pharmaceutical proteins, fermentation-grade cysteine and biotech-based cyclodextrins. Among, their top quality products are those marketed under the CAVASOL® and CAVAMAX® brands. Polyvinyl acetate solid resins, fine chemicals and complex organic building blocks for synthesis supplement their offering. They also offer complete, customised solutions for this product portfolio. Application areas range from food products, pharmaceuticals and agrochemicals through cosmetics, personal care and household to industrial and speciality chemicals.

In their Wacker Polysilicon division, an extensive portfolio of hyper-pure silicon, chlorosilanes and pyrogenic silicas for semiconductor and photovoltaic applications makes Wacker among the world's leading polysilicon manufacturers. Their products result from ground-breaking research and then undergo advanced technical development to fulfil high-end requirements in semiconductor and photovoltaic applications.

This division's highly integrated production system not only maximises synergy effects but also optimises all technical and business interfaces and processes.

Their Siltronic division is one of the world's top manufacturers of hyper-pure silicon wafers and supplier to many leading chip manufacturers. Their production facilities in Europe, Asia and the US develop and manufacture wafers with diameters of up to 300 mm. They are made in several diameter sizes and thicknesses with various additives and surface finishes. Siltronic's silicon wafers are at the heart of today's microelectronics and we can find them in computers, cell phones, flat-screen displays, navigation systems and several other applications.

Wacker ranks among the 10 most research-intensive chemical companies in the world with an annual R&D expenditure of about 3.5 per cent of sales. Wacker's corporate research centre, The Consortium, ensures continuous innovation. It has built up an impressive record of some 800 patents over the decades. Their research labs in Munich are the birthplace of tomorrow's product developments and customised solutions.

The Wacker Academy, with headquarters in Burghausen, where their largest production facilities are located, is a completely new type of international training centre that has attracted enormous interest from customers and business partners since its inception in 2007.

The company ensures that all their products, if used properly, pose no risk to humans or the environment. Only some 40 per cent of Wacker products require material safety data sheets by law. Nevertheless, they provide data sheets for all their products to ensure they are used safely. In total, over 40,000 material safety data sheets are available from Wacker in up to 30 languages. Environmental protection, just like safety and health protection, is a core component of all processes at Wacker. The Burghausen site has also been certified with ISO 14001 standards. (www.wacker.com)

Douglas Holding

Douglas Holding AG is a top-quality, lifestyle retail organisation with retail divisions in perfumes, books, jewellery, fashion and confectionery. The group was founded in 1821 by a Scotsman by the name of J.S. Douglas, who established a perfumery and soap factory in Hamburg, writing the first chapter in a fascinating success story in European retail. With the success of its perfumes and soaps, the group expanded into retail and over the years by acquisitions and organic growth diversified into other product categories as well. In 1989, the group officially got its name Douglas Holding AG. They also have other service companies which are into real estate, IT, leasing, insurance and trading.

Today, the Douglas Group is an essentially European retail organisation with around 2,000 speciality stores spanning 17 countries. In fiscal year 2010/11 they posted sales of €3.378 billion with a roster of over 25,000 employees. The group has its headquarters in Hagen a city in the state of North-Rhine Westphalia. The holding organisation, Douglas Holding AG, is responsible for investments and management. It also performs key leadership and service functions for the Douglas Group subsidiaries. Henning Kreke is the President and CEO of the group, and H.C. Jörn Kreke is the Chairman of the Supervisory Board. The Douglas Group stands for 'Retail with heart and mind'. They are committed to their lifestyle philosophy of offering their customers outstanding service, first-class product ranges at a fair price and a stimulating shopping ambience with the industry's friendliest employees. 'Excellence in Retailing', is their current operative slogan.

The Douglas Group is divided into five divisions with their Douglas perfumeries, Christ jewellery stores, Thalia bookshops, Appelrath Cüpper fashion stores and Hussel confectioneries. They are among the market leaders and trend-setters in their respective segments.

The Douglas Perfumeries division is currently represented in 17 countries. As a market leader in Europe, Douglas stands for competence in the areas of fragrances, cosmetics and body care. This division has a total of 1,184 stores of which two-thirds are in Germany. They had total sales of €1.878 billion. This division's slogan is 'Douglas makes life more beautiful', and they offer the world's top brands in perfumes and aftershaves, hair care, make-up, body care, accessories, men's watches, gift items and natural cosmetics for both men and women. Needless to say they put great emphasis on service in their offline and online stores. For regular customers, there are always attractive promotions as well as expert advice. They also have a Douglas card service, which makes it easier for their regular customers with the added benefit of availing of benefits and promotions, events and workshops and several such offers and services, one of the many reasons why it was awarded the 'Most Popular Retailer' in Germany for 2009.

The Thalia division is named after the Greek muse of the same name; she is the muse of comedy and serene poetry. At Thalia, they offer a wide assortment of books, audio books, CDs, DVDs and stationery. It is the very special combination of product and friendly service that makes a visit to Thalia a special experience. Sales at the 295 venues in Germany, Austria and Switzerland rose to around €934.5 million. The Internet platform of the Thalia Group serves as the basis for implementing its multi-channel strategy. They also have a dominant stake (60.2 per cent) of Germany's second largest online bookseller, www.buch.de. Today, customers can buy e-books and download content from the online stores, Thalia.de, .at and .ch for Germany, Austria and Switzerland, respectively. They are also assimilating e-books into the industry.

In the Christ jewellery stores division, there are 207 stores which posted sales of more than €340.4 million in Germany. The systematic development of the product range also served to boost its market position. The company has a brilliant tradition, whose roots date back to 1863. The first jewellery and chronometer shop was set up in Frankfurt am Main by the Master watchmaker William Alexander Christ. Today few other jewellers offer its customers such a large, international selection of fine jewellery and fine watches in an impressive ambience. They also have an in-house jewellery and watch line that matches with international trends and classics and an exclusive, quality brand by Christ. Among the brands doing well are the Jette brand, a Hamburg based jewellery and fashion designer. Trend brands like Pandora with its famous charm bracelets captured the consumer mood and sold well, as did chic and fashionable labels like Guess and Skagen and established brands like Longines and Tissot. In the wedding ring sector, Christ built a platform for renewed growth by developing its new 'Wedding Ring Configurator' and by creating locally based wedding-ring lounges.

The Appelrath Cüpper fashion division consists of 13 stores, with the three top-selling flagship stores in Hamburg, Cologne and Frankfurt that offer their customers a state-of-the-art shopping ambience. They had total sales of €124.5 million. They stock some of the best, up market brands, from Armani, Polo, BOSS to Lacoste and Ralph Lauren. The store is also known as AC, in short. They recently relaunched the AC emblem with the goal of progressively establishing it as a synonym for fashion and brand expertise, backed by service excellence. In its Exquisit segment AC has enhanced its merchandising proficiency with the successful brands Marccain, HUGO BOSS and Burberry. In its trend ranges, the Napapijiri and Desigual labels proved top sellers.

The Hussel Confectionery division succeeded in extending its leadership in the specialist confectionery segment. They have a total of 245 shops in Germany and in Austria with sales of €98.1 million.

In range, Hussel underscored its innovation and its quality with the new Organic Chocolate and Top Chocolatiers in the World. The Hussel name has now completed over 60 years of very successful business. Among their top favourites are Soul food, the Desert Truffles and Gran Cru Chocolates, Hussel is known for its impeccable quality in final products and processed raw materials as well. They also offer varied types of biscuits, sweets and sweet greetings as gift ideas. (www.douglas-holding.de)

HARIBO

HARIBO Gmbh and Co. KG is a family business with headquarters in Bonn. They are specialised in non-chocolate confectionery manufacturing, the market leader for fruit gums and liquorice products worldwide.

The company was founded in 1920 by Hans Riegel, when he set up a shop in a courtyard kitchen, thus starting the company's first production facility. The name HARIBO comes from the first two letters of the founder's first and last names as well as the first two letters from the name of the city Bonn. In 1922, Hans Riegel came up with the idea that would become HARIBO's flagship product; the Dancing Bear (today's Golden Bear) made of fruit gum. In the 1930s, the company came up with the slogan, 'HARIBO makes children happy' which is used till today. Over the years the company grew by leaps and bounds and today they manufacture their products at five factories in Germany and 10 production facilities all over Europe. They also have sales offices in almost every European country, in Australia and the US. HARIBO products are sold in over 105 countries worldwide, with Germany accounting for 40 per cent of total sales revenue. Today, in addition to the famous 'Bear' fruit gum, the company produces over 150 other chewy sweets, including fruit gum products, liquorice, marshmallow candies, jellies, chewing gum and other variations of chewy candy. Besides HARIBO the company also markets the brand MAOAM, Vademecum, and the former DULCIA which is now known as HARIBO Chamallows (this made a uniform global marketing approach to HARIBO marshmallow products possible.)

The new holding company of the HARIBO Group is the HARIBO-Holding GmbH and Co.KG. The management of the holding company consists of Managing Directors: Hans Riegel, who is responsible for marketing, sales and finance and Hans-Guido Riegel the son of the late Paul Riegel, who is responsible for production and technology. The Chairman of the Supervisory Board is Hans-Arndt Riegel the youngest son of Paul Riegel. The company has over 6,100 employees working for them of which 3,000 are in Germany. Given the private nature of the firm, company details like total sales figures are said to be confidential. Nevertheless, some market analysts put the annual sales figures in a couple of billion Euros, for the group as a whole, given worldwide operations and sales.

The group has over the decades been increasing its market standing and expanding its product range through the purchase of top-quality brands both in and outside Germany. Every year, 10 to 15 new HARIBO products are launched into the market. An additional component that may help to explain the extraordinary success that HARIBO has enjoyed around the world is the development of several sweet treats, which seem to match perfectly to a variety of country-specific tastes. The HARIBO range of products differs from country to country. The French for example clearly prefer marshmallow products such as Tagada or Chamallows and sugar-coated candies like Dragibus. While, in England Star Mix is the number one seller among young and old alike. In the Scandinavian countries a clear preference is Matador Mix a mixture of fruit-flavoured gum drops and liquorice. Whereas, the Golden Bears have become a continual international best-seller. The small fruit-flavoured gum drops are cherished by their fans from around the world. The Americans love their Gold Bears, people in Spain their Ositos de Oro and in Poland their Zlote Misie, to mention a few examples. In 2003, the Golden Bears were chosen as the most trustworthy confectionery brand in Germany, by the largest European consumer poll, conducted by Readers Digest and given the Pegasus Award.

The main ingredient of the fruit gums is glycose syrup. Fruit gums consist of gelatine, which contains neither fat nor carbohydrates and is low in calories as well. Scientific studies have shown that gelatine can prevent lasting joint damage and if taken regularly, strengthens the skin and connective tissue. The vegetarian, kosher and Halal versions of the product are made with the aid of starch or agar-agar a type of tropical algae. Liquorice products contain glycyrrhizin acid which is said to calm the stomach lining and the bronchial tubes and is useful for colds, stomach complaints and some virus infections.

HARIBO is very particular about the ingredients of its products and only the best, quality raw materials are used in HARIBO's production processes. It is no surprise therefore that many products produced by HARIBO carry the Gold Quality Award of the CMA (The Central Marketing Organisation for the German Agricultural Industries). They have 15 production facilities in 10 European countries and five of them in German locations. All HARIBO production sites in Germany have been certified as attaining the 'higher level' by the IFS (International Food Standard) for safety and quality. The company produces around 100 million Golden Bears in a day, in production runs worldwide!

HARIBO's advertising campaigns over the years have seen spectacular success, with high recall and recognition of the brand in over 98 per cent of kids and grown-ups alike. They also have a Guinness Book of World Records record for having the longest serving spokesperson advertising a brand. Thomas Gottschalk, the German television star and celebrity has been the face of HARIBO in Germany for over 21 years. In 1998, the HARIBO homepage was set up as the Planet HARIBO site which has been a game, entertainment and information site. The HARIBO homepage was fully relaunched in 2010. Other innovative advertisement efforts, have been the painting of two TUI fly airlines Boeing 737 with the HARIBO logo and Golden Bear painted all over the plane, since then, this plane has become the flying ambassador of the HARIBO brand. They also have a truck painted in the same fashion that visits large superstores and self-service supermarkets in Germany. Then they have a HARIBO Touring show that has become a cult brand event with their Golden Bear.

In 2004, the marketing research firm GfK undertook an assessment of the 'Best Brands' in Germany for the first time, where HARIBO took, first place in the 'Most Dynamic Brand' category. Additionally, a variety of HARIBO and MAOAM products were selected for the highly-coveted DLG Gold Medals in connection with the DLG Quality Competition. (www.haribo.com)

HUGO BOSS

HUGO BOSS AG is a premium, German lifestyle and fashion company with headquarters in a town called Metzingen in the state of Baden-Württemberg, south of Stuttgart. It was founded in 1924 by Hugo Ferdinand Boss who started a clothing company there. In 1985, the company was floated on the stock exchange and is now listed on the MDAX list of companies, for medium-sized stocks.

For fiscal year 2011, the total sales revenue was around €2.1 billion. Claus Dietrich Lahrs is the Chairman of the Managing Board and CEO of HUGO BOSS AG, while Helmut Albrecht is the Chairman of the Supervisory Board. They have just over 11,000 employees worldwide.

The success of the HUGO BOSS Group is based upon their coordinated integration of its divisions which are part of the value chain. HUGO BOSS has a global and exclusive sales network with excellent market knowledge, automated logistics processes with their state-of-the-art, new logistics centre at Metzingen, reliable purchasing structures, outstanding product expertise and high-quality fashion form the basis of its relationship with its international customers.

Intensive marketing activities, such as, involvement in the sponsorship of sports and cultural events and design of their own retail stores, enhances the worldwide recognition and image of the HUGO BOSS brands. The company also sets the standard with high-profile fashion events in the world's fashion capitals further highlighting the appeal and acceptance of the group's brands for its key target groups, imbuing the HUGO BOSS brand with passion The company has succeeded in positioning itself as a trend-setter and in generating maximum publicity and media attention for the BOSS and HUGO brands.

The company has seen high demand for luxury goods, especially in Asia and Eastern Europe. HUGO BOSS products can now be purchased in 124 countries and at some 6,300 points of sale. The worldwide presence of their own retail stores was expanded in the past year to bring the number of stores to around 700. Taking into account the more than 1,000 franchise stores and shops, the HUGO BOSS Group has at present over 1,600 mono-brand or exclusive stores.

The brand world of HUGO BOSS at present consists of various collections of the core brand BOSS and the trendy HUGO brand. These brand collections and their fashion lines are aimed at various target groups, creating a brand world of extraordinary fashion diversity at a constantly high level of quality. All HUGO BOSS brands are accompanied by accessory collections.

The women's and menswear collection in the BOSS Black line offers versatile fashion ranges with a rich array of elegant 'modern classics' in business, leisure and formal wear, perfect looks that satisfy the most demanding tastes and accentuate the wearer's personality.

Positioned in the upper market segment, the luxurious BOSS Selection menswear line represents the premium world in the BOSS brand universe. The interplay of sophisticated design, exclusive materials and beautiful tailoring, guarantees clothing of the highest standard for customers of distinction.

The BOSS Orange collection offers leisurewear for both men and women who enjoy dressing in style and sporting surprising looks. Unconventional material mixes, a playful approach to proportions and contrasting colours and patterns appeal to a savvy clientele that delights in experimentation.

BOSS Green presents golf and sportswear for men who combine classic cuts with refreshing designs in brand new constellations. This line successfully bridges the gap between regular sports apparel and sportswear fashion.

Their HUGO line delivers unconventional looks for men and women, clothes that are progressive yet never overstated. The collection features architectonic lines and new takes on classic shapes. By offering trend-setting design and superior quality, HUGO satisfies the high expectations of its fashion-conscious customers.

Licensed products such as fragrances, cosmetics, shoes, accessories, watches and eyewear complete the HUGO BOSS product range. Since the end of 2008, HUGO BOSS in cooperation with Samsung Electronics have made available a HUGO BOSS range of cell phones and matching accessories.

HUGO BOSS also added a children's fashion collection that is produced and sold by a licensed partner.

The company sponsors several sports and sportsmen, among them are the Formula 1 Racing Championship with Lewis Hamilton and Jenson Button of the McLaren-Mercedes Team. In addition to this they also sponsor sailing, golf, tennis and football stars and tournaments. The company also has a lifestyle magazine, several arts sponsorships/awards and some of the well-known fashion shows and tracks that are made exclusively for HUGO BOSS, as well as an online store. (www.group.hugoboss.com)

GEA Group

GEA Group AG is one of the largest system providers for food and energy processes. The group has roots going back to 1881, when it was established as a metals trading company called Metallgesellschaft AG or (MG). In 1920, the Gesellschaft für Entstaubungsanlagen or (GEA) was founded, a company producing de-dusting equipment. In 1989, GEA went public and by 1999 Metallgesellschaft AG acquired GEA AG. Finally in 2005, the company name changed from MG technologies AG to GEA Group AG.

Today, as an internationally operating technology group, the company focuses on process technology and components for demanding production processes in various end-user markets. The group generates about 70 per cent of its revenue from the growing food and energy industries.

With headquarters in Duesseldorf, the GEA Group AG is present and active in more than 50 countries worldwide and is said to be active in all growth regions. At present, the group generates around 80 per cent of its revenue outside of Germany. For fiscal year 2011, they generated total sales revenue of about €5.4 billion. The company's workforce is comprised of over 24,000 employees worldwide as of 31 March 2012. The GEA Group is a market and technology leader in its respective business areas and the company is listed on the MDAX Index in Germany. Jürg Oleas is the present CEO and Chairman of the Executive Board, and Jürgen Heraeus is the Chairman of the Supervisory Board. Their new corporate slogan is 'Engineering for a Better World'.

On 1 January 2010, the group was reorganised into five segments or divisions without altering the overall portfolio of the group. The five divisions are GEA Farm Technologies, GEA Heat Exchangers, GEA Mechanical Equipment, GEA Process Engineering and GEA Refrigeration Technologies. In March 2011, GEA successfully concluded the takeover of Convenience Food Systems (CFS) based in Bakel, the Netherlands. This acquisition has added a sixth segment to the GEA Group: GEA Food Solutions.

The GEA Food Solutions division is a leading manufacturer of machines for the preparation, marinating, processing, slicing and packaging of meat, poultry, fish, cheese and other food products. This segment specialises in performance focused solutions for the food industry from a single machine to a complete production line. This makes GEA Food Solutions one of the most multifaceted suppliers of food processing and packaging machinery.

GEA Farm Technologies is one of the world's leading manufacturers of technical innovations, integrated product solutions and effective animal hygiene products for cost-efficient milk production, while professional manure technology and barn equipment round up the segment's profile as a systems provider for all sizes. Their products are used as milking equipment, for parlour and herd management systems, milk cooling systems, hygiene for animal equipment and farm, barn equipment, manure technology, consultancy and design and original spare parts. The company is based in Bönen, with state-of-the-art facilities alongside R&D, logistics, sales and marketing and other departments. Located in the vicinity of the Center of Excellence for Bio-Security, this division also plays a leading role in the development of new processes and systems for the safe production of food.

GEA Heat Exchangers, by focusing on all heat exchanger activities in one single segment, GEA now highlights its position as a world leader in the market for heat exchangers. GEA Heat Exchangers covers numerous application areas, from air-conditioning systems to cooling towers and therefore provides the widest portfolio for heat exchangers worldwide. They have finned-tube heat exchangers, single-tube heat exchangers, Heller systems, air-cooled condensers, wet-cooling towers, plate heat exchangers, HVAC systems and all kinds of shell and tube heat exchangers. The new GEA division for heat exchangers offers a one-stop source for the best possible solutions. They also support planning efforts in all areas of heat transfer, from design and production up to delivery and service. They particularly focus on the markets for food and the energy industry as well as for climate and environmental technology. A total of 90 individual companies at 96 locations belong to the seven new business units of the GEA Heat Exchanger's segment.

In the GEA Mechanical Equipment division, high-quality process engineering components like separators, decanters, valves, pumps and homogenisers ensures smooth processes and cost-optimised production flows in virtually all important industrial sectors. Their wide range of products and services provides solutions for the most varied tasks and challenges in a whole range of branches around the globe. Whether for food processing, chemicals, the pharma industry, biotechnology, the marine sector, mineral oil, energy recovery or environmental technology – the components from GEA Mechanical Equipment are always the first choice. Their liquids handling forms the basis for high value added, at the same time, they help cut production costs and significantly and sustainably reduce the impact on the environment.

GEA Process Engineering is a business division in the GEA Group with headquarters in Copenhagen, Denmark, with representation in around 50 countries around the globe.

This division specialises in the design and development of process solutions for the dairy, brewery, food, pharmaceutical and chemical industries. They specialise in liquid processing, concentration, drying, powder processing and handling, emission control and solid dosage forms and sterile products. They are widely recognised as market leaders in these specialised areas.

Finally, in the GEA Refrigeration Technologies division, the companies are active in the fields of solutions and services, manufacturing and freezing. The solution and services companies offer design, engineering installation and service and maintenance for refrigeration solutions for various industries from food processing to the power and process industries. They have an extensive network with 24/7 service stations. In manufacturing, the companies offer reciprocating compressors and packages, screw compressors and packages, chillers for HVAC applications and industrial processes, heat pumps, ice-makers and valves and other fittings. While in freezing, the concerned companies offer state-of-the art freezers for the chilled and frozen food sectors.

The GEA magazine *GENERATE* is a bridge between the technologies of GEA and its applications in everyday life. An interesting environmental fact about GEA is that more than 3,000 fixed and mobile GEA systems are used worldwide in the treatment of industrial and municipal waste water. GEA also uses natural refrigerants in industrial refrigeration, the power-alcohol plant and the facilities of GEA for flue gas treatment as well as for the GEA systems for industrial air-cooling. (www.gea.com)

BARMER GEK

BARMER GEK is a statutory health insurance company, a public corporation that is self-governed. It was established on 1 January 2010 from the voluntary union of the October 1884 established BARMER Ersatzkasse and the May 1878 founded Gmünder Ersatzkasse (GEK).

Today, BARMER GEK is the largest provider of health insurance in Germany and Europe as well. The name BARMER is derived from a town by that name that existed then, until it merged with Wuppertal in 1929 as a district. This was where the Health Insurance for Business Employees in Barmen e.h (registered relief fund) was established in 1904, from the earlier Mercantile Association for Clerks in Barmen set up in 1884. The headquarters moved to Berlin later and after the war to Wuppertal once again. Today the legal seat of BARMER GEK is in Berlin. Although the central offices of the prior insurance companies in Wuppertal and in Schwabisch Gmünd still remain, even after the merger. There are more than 800 offices, nationwide with regional offices catering to institutions, political bodies and associations on regional issues of healthcare. Their corporate slogan is 'The Health Experts'.

As of today, BARMER GEK caters to around 8.7 million people or policy holders who are insured with it. They have around 15,000 employees nationwide with a financial volume of around €25 billion with a premium of around 15.5 per cent and a total reserve of €900 million, as of June 2012. The insured select a 30-member volunteer board of directors, who in turn choose the executive board and CEO/Chairman for BARMER GEK.

Christoph Straub is the CEO and Chairman of the Board of BARMER GEK, and Rolf-Ulrich Schlenker is the Deputy-Chairman. The third member of the executive board is Jürgen Rothmaier, while, Holger Langkutsch is the Chairman of the Management Advisory Board.

The BARMER GEK knows no waiting and no exclusion of pre-existing conditions. The members and their family members are insured from the first day of membership and entitled to full benefits. From the doctors and medicines, in the hospital, regular dental care, protection when on holidays, prevention and early detection with timely check-ups, even a free skin check-up, nursing care as and when needed, post-operative, at home, etc.

Together, with their partner HUK COBURG they also offer tailor-made, supplementary insurance for every situation, from global health insurance abroad, outpatient treatment at naturopaths, optimal dental treatment, etc. For older insured and self-employed individuals they also have reasonable rates and services.

BARMER have an 'Advice and Contact' department, a service for their customers, so as to make their lives as easy and pleasant as possible with lots of practical ideas and features. They have a call-back service, an e-mail service and search offices and counselling with health experts to help with problems, diagnosis or medical errors. Other services include a tele-doctor, online forums, doctor/hospital and pharmacy search, as well as brochures, newsletters and a member's magazine.

Forms and certificates have also become user-friendly with the ability to fill out forms online and download them at convenience, whether communicating changes, downloading applications or requesting and printing out insurance certificates, things have been made easier and simpler for the BARMER customer. Their customers can also avail of a bonus program and print out a personal bonus card as well.

BARMER helps prevent and treat diseases by providing useful tips on how to stay healthy and fit. Their customers learn interesting facts about the family and everyday life with children, from family planning, development, nutrition, vaccinations and so on. Their encyclopaedia provides comprehensive information on the cause and treatment of various diseases as well as information about medicines and home remedies, from generics to prescribed medicines, their risks and side effects. They also provide guides for tips for vitality and well-being like stress reduction, UV protection, a healthy back, dental health and the immune system. Further information by way of common diagnostic and treatment methods and procedures are also provided.

BARMER also has a special section on sports and nutrition with calorie tables, diets, losing weight with exercise, an interactive fitness program and various events and activities like health courses and lectures. 'Germany is Moving' is the best known and largest health initiative in Germany. Since 2003, it has been motivating people to engage in regular exercise and a healthier diet. Many campaign partners support the initiative with annual promotion days. From May to October, young and old can participate in a 'Cities Tour' programme.

Several prominent athletes and sportsmen are ambassadors representing and promoting the Germany is Moving initiative by acting as role models and actively bringing millions of people in Germany to stay active and physically fit. This initiative has also developed fitness tests developed by sport scientists to determine each person's personal fitness levels and suitability for various sports and other physical activities.

BARMER has been the only public health insurance brand to have been selected for the 'Super brands' award for Germany in 2005, 2007 and 2009. Recently, BARMER

GEK also received in 2012, the award of 'Brand of the Century', given by a German publisher. (www.barmer-gek.de)

HOCHTIEF

HOCHTIEF AG is the seventh largest provider of construction-related services in the world and the market leader in Germany. With more than 75,000 employees and a sales volume of €23.28 billion in fiscal year 2011, the company is represented in all the world's major markets. A total of 92 per cent of this output was generated abroad. HOCHTIEF was founded by two brothers, Balthasar and Philipp Helfmann in Frankfurt am Main in 1873. They started off as building contractors under the name Helfmann Brothers. In 1896, it became a publicly quoted corporation and a few years later the discovery of reinforced concrete, revolutionised construction technology and the industry in general. In 1922, the head office moved to the city of Essen in the state of North-Rhine Westphalia and officially took on the name HOCHTIEF in 1923. They still have their headquarters there.

The products and services that HOCHTIEF offers their national and international clients are comprised of three closely interrelated modules: development, construction and operations. HOCHTIEF oversees the complete life cycle of projects and continually enhances value for clients and shareholders alike.

Marcelino Fernández Verdes is the Chairman of the Executive Board and Thomas Eichelmann is the Chairman of the Supervisory Board.

HOCHTIEF is composed of a strategic management holding and three corporate divisions HOCHTIEF Americas, Asia-Pacific and Europe.

The HOCHTIEF Americas division coordinates the activities of the HOCHTIEF companies in the US. Via its subsidiary Turner, HOCHTIEF is a leading player in general building in the US, the world's biggest construction market. Turner has long been number one in the high-growth market segments of educational, healthcare and commercial real estate plus the area of sustainable building also known as Green Building. Turner Logistics, their US subsidiary, delivers complex procurement services for both Turner projects and other external customers.

Since 2007 the civil engineering company Flatiron has been rounding out HOCHTIEF's presence in North America, with regional presence in the US and Canada and is among the top 10 suppliers in the US transportation infrastructure construction sector.

With the acquisition of E.E. Cruz and Company, HOCHTIEF has expanded its position in the growing market for US infrastructure projects in 2010. The New York region-based company specialises in civil construction.

HOCHTIEF is also a market leader in Australia via its majority shareholding in the Leighton Group. Its services encompass building and infrastructure construction, raw materials extraction (mining) and concessions, project development, plus maintenance and services. With its seven operating units, Leighton spans the full value chain of construction. Leighton is also intensifying its activities in selected Asian countries and in the Gulf region.

The HOCHTIEF Europe division under the management of HOCHTIEF Solutions AG consolidates their core business. This covers building construction and civil and structural engineering projects in Europe and selected countries all over the world. They plan, develop, implement, operate and manage real estate and infrastructure facilities, also as concessions or operator projects in public-private-partnerships (PPP). The company focuses on lucrative growth markets and delivers sophisticated one-stop solutions. Their expertise is in the areas of design and construction, development and services is linked according to the customers' requirements to produce strong synergies.

These divisions are comprised of HOCHTIEF's operational units. They represent the service portfolio and reflect the company's global presence.

The company HOCHTIEF Insurance Broking and Risk Management Solutions is a level below the management holding company. This company is available to all group units as a service provider. It offers insurance services covering the entire life cycle of infrastructure projects, real estate and facilities. It also insures construction projects and facility management services. Reinsurance services are provided via their subsidiaries.

HOCHTIEF is one of the founding members of the German Green Building Council. Since January 2009, this organisation has been awarded the 'Quality Seal' for sustainable building projects. In the US, Turner Construction has already been a pioneer in Green Building for some years now. The company has realised a large number of projects that have been LEED (Leadership in Energy and Environmental Design) certified, which, is a standard awarded by the US Green Building Council. Other corporate responsibility initiatives and sustainable practices undertaken by HOCHTIEF are in the areas of renewable energies, energy management, environmental protection, biodiversity, water supply, construction materials and recycling. HOCHTIEF is also a member of the Dow Jones Sustainability Index. (www.hochtief.com)

Tengelmann

The Tengelmann Warenhandelsgesellschaft KG is a family-owned retail corporation that owns several retail chains that consist of grocery stores, home improvement and DIY stores, discount stores, apparel and accessories and lots more. The group was founded in 1867 by Willhelm Schmitz-Scholl in a place called Mülheim an der Ruhr.

Today, the group has locations in 15 countries with 4,256 stores/branches and around 83,437 employees worldwide. Annual group Sales for fiscal year 2011 was around €10.78 billion, making the Tengelmann Group a leading business enterprise with an international outlook. The holding company is located in Mülheim an der Ruhr. The operational management of the group is now in the hands of the fifth generation of the family, headed by Karl-Erivan W. Haub who is the present CEO and Managing Partner.

Its brands and business units include Kaiser's Tengelmann supermarkets, the OBI DIY stores, the textiles and non-food discounter Kik, TREI Real Estate and Tengelmann E-Commerce. There are a number of other, smaller production companies, participating interests and service providers that round off the Tengelmann Group portfolio.

Kaiser's Tengelmann, is a wholly-owned subsidiary of the Tengelmann Group, based in Mülheim an der Ruhr. Kaiser's Kaffee Geschäft AG, which was originally founded in 1880, was taken over by the group in 1971. As a food retailing concern, they are represented by 17,975 employees in 530 stores in the three regions of North-Rhine, Berlin and Munich/OberBayern. They pride themselves on being a top supplier of high-quality products in the German food-stuffs market. They make it a priority to have freshness, service, range, quality and price in a class of their own. They also make their own brands: A&P, Naturkind bio-quality, Birkenhof and Star Marke, which are available exclusively at their markets. Since 1997, they have been running a delivery service in Berlin and Munich, enabling their customers to order their requirements by Internet, fax or telephone and have them delivered to their doors. By virtue of their uncompromising product standards, Kaiser's Tengelmann has steadily built a reputation as a merchant of top-quality, fresh and packaged products. In 2011, they generated sales of €2.34 billion.

Plus Eastern Europe Gmbh is an amalgamation of the foreign subsidiaries in Austria, Romania and Bulgaria. The German and other European national companies and stores were merged with the EDEKA subsidiary, Netto Marken Discount, and other competitors. The Tengelmann Group therefore retains an active presence in the discount segment of the attractive growth market of Eastern Europe. Since May 2008, Plus Online Gmbh has been integrated into the Tengelmann Group as a separate, wholly-owned subsidiary. The product portfolio is comprised of non-food items in various segments, including household, technical and multimedia as well as fashion and other accessories.

OBI is one of the leading European DIY brands offering a wide range of home improvement and gardening products. Currently, the company operates in 12 Central and Eastern European countries with more than 561 stores, of which around two-thirds are in Germany. OBI generated total sales of €6.4 billion in fiscal year 2011, employing more than 40,610 employees. The OBI store network is managed by the OBI Group holding company. Privately owned by the Tengelmann Group, OBI was founded in 1970. As the undisputed market leader in the German DIY retail industry, OBI is the driving force which propels the entire trade. OBI stores offer a broad and comprehensive product range, which on an average, includes 40,000 to 60,000 articles per store.

The competent product range covers gardening, building materials and elements, tools, sanitary fittings and interior decoration products, targeting primarily private individuals and families, do-it-yourselfers and semi-professionals. Since 1993, the company has used its powerful position within the national market to press ahead with its expansion internationally.

The KiK Textilen & Non-Food Gmbh is a retail chain founded in 1994, offering clothing items and other non-food products at comparatively low prices. The KiK T-shirt mascot is used extensively in their advertising as is statements like, 'The clever choice in clothing', 'From top to toe for less than 30 Euros' or 'Good Quality at Reasonable Prices'. With an average of 200 new store openings across Europe every year, KiK is growing rapidly in Germany, Austria, the Czech Republic, Slovenia, Hungary and Slovakia. Textile discounter KiK offers its customers a broad range of ladies', men's and children's wear as well household linens, hosiery and other non-food items. They last had a total of 3,025 stores/branches while employing around 20,009 people and generating sales of around €1.66 billion.

Other non-retail divisions of the Tengelmann Group consist of TREI Real Estate GmbH which is engaged in letting branch and warehouse premises elsewhere in Europe and the Tengelmann Energie Gmbh (TEG) which is an independent consultant and supplier, specialising in the optimised supply, procurement and billing of eco-friendly energy for commercial customers. Grün Hans Energie, another of their joint ventures, has been offering a green electricity tariff for domestic households and small businesses since January 2009. It is part of the Tengelmann Climate Initiative set up in 2007, under the auspices of the Climate Initiative. The environmental department of TEG supports and implements projects ranging from the first Tengelmann climate-friendly store to annually updated emissions balance sheets. They also have their Tengelmann's own, 'Frog & Turtle' environmental seal. (www.tengelmann.de)

Aurubis

Aurubis AG is the largest copper producer in Europe and the world leader in copper recycling. Their core business is the production of marketable copper cathodes from copper concentrates, copper scrap and other recycled materials. These are processed within the group into continuous cast wire rods, shapes, rolled products as well as special wire made of copper and copper alloys. Then they have precious metals and a number of other products such as sulphuric acid and iron silicate which rounds off their product portfolio.

The roots of the company go back to 1770, when Markus Salomon Beit obtained permission to construct a silver separation and smelting facility in Hamburg. Its recent previous incarnation was as the Norddeutsche Affinerie AG which was renamed as Aurubis AG on 1 April 2009. The name Aurubis is derived from the Latin word for 'red gold' – copper, the red gold.

Today, with headquarters in Hamburg, the group produces some 1.1 million tons of copper cathodes each year and from them a variety of other products as well. They have 16 production sites in 11 European countries and in the US with about 6,300 employees. Group revenues for fiscal year 2010/11 were in the region of €13.336 billion. Peter Willbrandt is the new CEO of Aurubis AG, while Heinz Jörg Fuhrmann is the Chairman of the Supervisory Board.

The business units (BU) are categorised into three segments from an organisational viewpoint – the BU Primary Copper, BU Recycling/Precious Metals and BU Copper Products.

Aurubis Group's customers include companies in the copper semis industry, the electronics and chemical industries as well as suppliers to the construction and automobile industries. Aurubis shares are part of the Prime Standard Segment of the Deutsche Börse and are listed on the MDAX, the European Stoxx 600 and in the Global Challenges Index (GCX).

All activities are included in the Primary Copper BU that concerns itself with the production of quality copper in the form of marketable copper cathodes made from the primary raw material, copper concentrates. This also covers the smelting and refining activities at the production sites in Hamburg, Olen (Belgium) and Pirdop (Bulgaria) and the marketing of the co-product sulphuric acid. The subsidiaries Peute Baustoff Gmbh and Retorte Gmbh Selenium Chemicals & Metals, which produce speciality products, are also part of this BU.

The core activities in the Recycling/Precious Metals BU is the production of copper cathodes from a very wide range of recycling raw materials. Recycling activities are performed at various locations in the group; the recycling centre is situated in Westphalian Lunen. Copper scrap and increasingly recycling raw materials, such as electronic scrap, are processed here, using environmentally friendly and innovative technology. In the Recycling/Precious Metals BU, they produce precious metals and other by-metals and co-products contained in the copper raw materials. These include, in particular, nickel, bismuth, tin, antimony, zinc, selenium and tellurium products and compounds. Other subsidiaries and affiliated companies are active in raw-material trading and treatment such as Elektro Recycling Nord Gmbh (ERN) and Cablo Metal-Recycling & Handel Gmbh.

The processing of copper cathodes is performed in the Copper Products BU. The most important copper product is electrolytic copper wire rods for the cable and wire industry. In addition, they produce continuous cast shapes for the market and for internal processing as well as pre-rolled strips, rolled and speciality products. End-users of copper, the material of the future, include the electrical and mechanical engineering, automotive, telecommunications and construction industries. The main production sites are in Hamburg, Emmerich and Avellino, Italy, as well as the affiliated company Schwermetall Halbzeugwerk Gmbh & Co. KG and the subsidiary Prymetall Gmbh and Co. KG, in Stolberg. Slitting centres in Dolny Kubin (Slovakia) and Smethwick (UK) complement their service range and supply strips in the required dimensions. Complex speciality profiles are produced at the Swiss Advanced Materials (SAM) in Switzerland.

Other administration and service groups have been set up as corporate functions, which include for instance R&D, human resources, accounting, IT as well as material procurement.

The R&D sector, located in Hamburg, makes a group-wide contribution, to enhancing performance in the production sectors, increasing technical competence, developing new products, improving processes, using modern cutting-edge technologies and recognising new trends.

Aurubis is one of the most environmentally friendly copper smelters in the world. Efficient new process technology and innovative techniques to protect the environment are used. Their management systems are certified in accordance with recognised international standards of quality and environmental protection: ISO 9001, 14001 and EMAS. Since 2000, Aurubis has invested more than €400 million into environmental protection measures. (www.aurubis.com)

REWE

The REWE Group is one of the leading retail, trading and travel and tourism cooperatives in Europe. The group is based in Germany with headquarters in Cologne. It was founded in 1927 as REWE-Zentrale which began its operations in Cologne and was officially entered that year into the Cooperative Registry. Seventeen purchasing cooperatives had joined forces by the end of 1926 and had agreed to found the organisation. The name REWE is derived from the German abbreviation of 'Revisionsverband der Westkauf-Genossenschaften' which in English stands for (Auditing Association of Western Purchasing Cooperatives). This truly successful cooperative group has developed over the years on the basis of sustainable and long-term growth.

Today, around 323,000 employees work in 15,700 stores, for the REWE Group in 13 European countries and have generated a turnover of around €35 billion for the year 2011. In Germany, the REWE Group employs 222,000 people who work in around 11,000 stores, from supermarkets, through to discount stores and self-service stores to specialist stores and travel agencies, generating a turnover in the region of nearly €36.5 billion. The group's strategy is based on strong organic growth, acquisitions and takeovers with viable, sustainable principles and structural changes. Alain Caparros is the present CEO of the REWE Group, while Heinz-Bert Zander is the Chairman of the Supervisory Board of REWE-Zentral Finanz eG and REWE-Zentral AG.

THE REWE Group has classified its activities into two core businesses: trading and travel and tourism. These two businesses are carried out under a variety of sales lines/ brands as per the country and area of operation.

In trading, the following are their markets and brands: the national full-range stores or store brands are REWE, Toom market, Toom Drinks market, Nahkauf, Kaufpark, akzenta and Temma. The international full-range stores are BILLA, MERKUR, ADEG and BIPA. The national and international discount stores are PENNY MARKT, PENNY MARKET and PENNY MARKET XXL. The specialist stores and cooperations are TOOM, B1 and ProMarkt. Other companies in this division are Für Sie, Kressner, Glocken Backerei, Wilhelm Brandenburg and iki.

In a recent study conducted by a Düsseldorf based management consultancy firm Batten & Company, it was found out that the Ja product range of the REWE Group at entry level price is the strongest private label brand in German food retailing.

The travel and tourism division consists of the following companies: ITS, JAHN Reisen, TJAEREBORG, ITS BILLA Reisen, ITS Travel Coop, DERTOUR, MEIER'S Weltreisen, ATLAS Reisen, DER Reisebüro, DERPART, DERPART Travel Service, FCM Travel Solutions, RSG, Holiday, Club Calimera, Prima Sol, Lti Hotels and Clever tours.com, covering the whole gamut of price-market options.

The management board of the REWE Group adopted a new business field structure in 2009. This is in contrast to the brand orientation of the sales structure. It runs parallel to the internal management structure and consequently reflects the internal organisational structure. This business field structure is based on the strategic business unit (SBU) concept, where the different companies are allocated on the basis of their business and area of operation. The full-range and the discount stores are divided into both national and international SBUs. The national specialist stores into DIY and consumer electronics SBUs and in travel and tourism, they have a travel sales, package tours and building-block tours SBUs.

All the individual stores/brands undertake their own advertising and promotional activities based on the markets they operate in. The REWE full-range store is the flagship brand/store of the REWE Group and they undertake a fair amount of advertising and other promotional activities. The REWE Group is also committed to sponsoring around 80 national and international activities. These focus on sports, healthy nutrition and supporting the aid organisation Deutsche Tafele.v whose 'Dinner Tables' provide free food for the needy. More than 6,000 supermarkets and warehouses of the REWE Group are helping over 800 local Dinner Table Chapters in Germany.

The REWE Group and its partners along the process chain cooperate in finding solutions to urgent ecological and social issues associated with the production of commercial goods and the portfolio of services. The goal is therefore to develop, produce and market sustainable products. The REWE Group's strategic approach is that it takes great care in selecting suppliers and commits them to complying with environmental and social standards, based on the Business Social Compliance Initiative or the BSCI.

Known as REWE REGIONAL, this product line, which will change according to the season, starts with about a dozen selected products of high quality in the fruit and vegetable range. In offering this supplementary range, REWE is adding to the line of local products that has already been available. REWE already markets local products from more than 1,000 local producers under the brand names Landmarkt and Aus Liebe zur Heimat. These and other product labelling activities are as per strict standards actively implemented. Among the significant ones are ProPlanet (quality, eco and social standards products), fair trade products, Blue Angel (high eco standards products), MSC (Marine Stewardship Council) eco-fish products, FSC (Forest Stewardship Council) the seal for eco-friendly wood products and the IFS (International Food Standard) label for quality food products.

The REWE Group has also set the goal of reducing its CO_2 emissions per square metre of retail space by 30 per cent by 2015 compared to the baseline year 2006. As of now, more than 6,000 stores of the group use green electricity. The REWE Group is increasing its energy efficiency through the REWE Green Buildings and the integration of a number of modules from the Green Buildings into existing stores, such as for example the lighting concept, the refrigeration appliance concept and the combined refrigeration, air conditioning and heating systems. The group is also committed to cutting CO_2 emissions in the product chain in addition to several other new measures. They are also involved in several societal contributions by way of charity and other worthwhile projects.

All of these socially responsible activities helped the REWE Group win it the 'German Sustainability Award' for 2009. They were one of the top three winners of the said award. In 2010, the Trade Association of Germany (HDE) awarded REWE the 'Green Building Award' for 'Store of the Year 2010' in the category 'Food', making it a company that sets a real benchmark in sustainability in the retail sector. The REWE Group was recently awarded the German CSR prize for their PRO PLANET label. (www.rewe-group.com)

Deutsche Börse

Deutsche Börse AG is one of the world's leading exchange organisations that provides investors, financial institutions and companies access to global capital markets. Based in Frankfurt on the river Main, their business covers the entire process chain from securities and derivatives trading, clearing, settlement and custody, through to market data and the development and operation of electronic trading systems. It is home to the famous Xetra® Trading Platform and the Frankfurt Stock Exchange. Deutsche Börse operates one of the largest, fully electronic cash markets in the world.

The roots of the Frankfurt Stock Exchange go back to the period of medieval fairs. At the beginning of the sixteenth century, Frankfurt had become prosperous due to its well-known fairs and it soon became a centre for wholesale commerce and the banking sector also became established, what with merchants from all over Europe who came to Frankfurt in order to engage in trade. To counter the deterioration of coinage and a lack of a single currency, merchants met at the fair in 1585 to establish uniform exchange rates. Today, this event is regarded as the moment of the Frankfurt Stock Exchange's birth. The German term Börse and the French 'bourse' come from the fifteenth-century Belgian city of Bruges. The word was used to describe a periodic meeting of rich Italian traders at 'ter buerse plaza' a market place that was named after the patrician family Van der Beurse who had lived there. In Latin, 'bursa' means a 'bag' or 'change purse'. The first share issue, a participating certificate of the Austrian National Bank, had been traded in Frankfurt back in 1820, while trading in government bonds had begun on the Frankfurt stock exchange in 1779.

The DAX® was introduced in 1988. Today, it is one of the world's most well-known blue-chip indices. Deutsche Börse AG was founded in 1993, and it has since been the operating body of the Frankfurt Stock Exchange. Xetra® the fully electronic trading platform began in 1997. The Deutsche Börse Group calculates and distributes more than

3,000 indices as of December 2009. They enable investors to display investment strategies in a transparent, rule-based and cost-efficient way. The subsidiaries Eurex, Clearstream and Deutsche Börse Systems drive the growth and the internationalisation process of the group. With the acquisition of ISE, the world's largest equity options exchange in December 2007, Eurex significantly expanded its liquidity network into the US and into US dollar products. With this process-oriented business model, Deutsche Börse increased the efficiency of capital markets, issuers benefit from low capital costs and investors enjoy the advantages of high liquidity and low transaction costs.

The group holds representative offices in the important financial centres of the world. This has helped it service a lot of on-site customers and maintain close contacts with the national authorities and capital market institutions.

Sales revenue for fiscal year 2011 was €2.233 billion with a net income of €848.8 million with a trading volume of €1,406.7 billion. Reto Francioni is the present CEO of Deutsche Börse AG while Joachim Faber is the Chairman of the Supervisory Board. A total of 3,300 employees from 69 nations shape the company's culture with their wide range of educational backgrounds and views. The Deutsche Börse Group has demarcated its activities into five main business areas: cash market, derivatives market, market data and analytics, banking settlement and custody and information technology services.

The cash market of Deutsche Börse is comprised of two market models for securities trading: floor trading of FWB® Frankfurter Wertpapierbörse (the Frankfurt Stock Exchange) and Xetra®, the fully electronic trading system. Both market places provide efficient trading and optimum liquidity. Stocks, exchange-traded funds, exchange-traded commodities, exchange-traded notes, actively managed funds as well as certificates, reverse convertibles, warrants and bonds are traded here. Since April 2008, Scoach the European exchange for certificates and warrants, offers trading in around 900,000 securities on Xetra.

In the derivatives market; Deutsche Börse AG operates the Eurex derivatives exchange – the market place for futures trading clearing. Eurex offers a broad range of international benchmark products and operates the most liquid, fixed income market in the world, featuring open, democratic and low-cost electronic access, with market participants connected from 700 locations worldwide. Trading volume at Eurex exceeds 2 billion contracts a year, making Eurex the market place of choice for the derivatives community worldwide. Eurex and ISE are the market leaders in individual equity and equity index derivatives worldwide. Eurex also operates the electronic trading platform Eurex Bonds as well as Eurex Repo.

In the business area of market data and analytics, they create, disseminate and market precise and reliable information on the international financial markets. The comprehensive market data and reference products document market developments and make them transparent. All information is tailored to the specific needs of customers in front, middle and back offices of banks and financial service providers responsible for trading, risk management and settlement as well as for information providers and issuers of financial products such as ETFs, futures and structured products.

Banking, settlement and custody services are in great demand on the securities markets with extremely high trading volumes. Clearstream International, a 100 per cent subsidiary of Deutsche Börse, is Europe's leading provider of these back office services for shares and bonds in national and international trading. They have more than 2,500 customers and settled more than 125 million transactions in 2011. In its custody accounts Clearstream holds shares, bonds and funds to the value of more than €11 trillion. Clearstream covers more than 50 markets in over 110 countries.

The Information Technology Services business area develops and operates trading and settlement systems for the entire Deutsche Börse Group. Furthermore, Deutsche Börse IT runs on additional 30 market places and exchanges around the world.

Today, Deutsche Börse's fully electronic trading and settlement processes perform vital functions for the company's core business and provide the basis for its excellent competitive position.

The Deutsche Börse Group had in 2010 met the corporate responsibility inclusion criteria for the FTSE4Good Index the leading global responsible investment index that measures the performance of companies that meet globally recognised corporate responsibility standards. (www.deutsche-boerse.com)

LANXESS

LANXESS AG is a global leader in speciality chemicals and is active in all the important global markets. Its core business is comprised of the development, manufacture and sale of plastics, synthetic rubber, speciality chemicals and intermediates. The company's current headquarters are in Leverkusen, in the state of North-Rhine Westphalia, although they will move to a new home in Cologne by the second half of 2013.

LANXESS grew from a strategic realignment of the Bayer Group's chemical and plastic business at the beginning of 2005. On March of 2004, the board of management announced the name LANXESS which is a word combined from the French verb 'lancer' (to thrust forward) and the English word 'success'. The slogan they decided on was; 'Energizing Chemistry'. LANXESS now operates as an independent company since 28 January 2005 and has been listed on the Frankfurt Stock Exchange since then. Following the spin-off from Bayer, every Bayer shareholder was issued a LANXESS share for every 10 Bayer shares they held. In June 2005, LANXESS was included in the German Midcap stock index (MDAX). Since 24 September 2012, LANXESS is a member of the DAX, the top 30 index of the German Stock Exchange.

In 2011, the company achieved total sales of €8.8 billion. Currently, they have 49 operational sites in 31 countries with a staff of around 16,900. Alex C. Heitmann is the Chairman of the Board of Management of LANXESS AG, while Rolf Stomberg is the Chairman of the Supervisory Board.

LANXESS focuses on synthetic rubbers, polymers, intermediate products and speciality chemicals. The 13 business units are grouped into three segments, i.e. performance polymers, advanced intermediates and performance chemicals. With its extensive portfolio, LANXESS focuses on premium business through innovative ideas, processes and products. They always try to generate added value for their customers.

All their polymer-based businesses are combined in the Performance Polymers segment, which now also includes its synthetic rubber and plastics manufacturing activities.

Here, LANXESS offers a broad portfolio of innovative products, many of which are international leaders. Their products are used in automobiles, in electronics, electrical and automotive engineering and in the dental sector. The business units that belong to this segment are butyl rubber, performance butadiene rubber, high performance materials and the technical rubber products unit.

The Advanced Intermediates segment, combines business operations in the fields of basic and fine chemicals, in fact LANXESS is one of the leading global suppliers in this area. They owe their strong presence in the global market to many years of expertise, successful branding and the intensive global isomer management in their unique aromatics network. The business units Basic Chemicals and Saltigo belong to this segment. The Advanced Industrial Intermediates or AII is one of the most important suppliers of high-quality industrial chemicals in the world. Their main products and brands include various aromatic compounds, amines, benzyl products, hydrofluoric and sulfuric acid, phthalic anhydride, malcic annhydride, hydrazine hydrate, trimethylol propane and hexanidol. Among others, these are used in the application areas of agriculture, automotive and construction industry and in the production of polymers, pigments/dyes, paints and fuels.

LANXESS' subsidiary Saltigo is dedicated to their custom synthesis and manufacturing services for small molecules and serves the needs of customers in the pharma, agro and speciality chemical industries. Their main product brands are active ingredients and intermediates for a variety of industries including Saltidin®, an insect repellent.

In the field of performance chemicals, LANXESS enjoys an excellent reputation with its colourful brands. The following business units belong to this segment: Functional Chemicals unit, Inorganic Pigments unit, Ion Exchange Resins unit, Leather unit, Material Protection Products unit, Rhein Chemie and Rubber Chemicals unit. The Functional Chemicals unit (FCC) provides plastic additives, phosphorus chemicals and speciality chemicals such as organic and inorganic colorants. These meet the needs of customers in a very wide range of industrial sectors. FCC also provides water treatment agents like Bayhibit®. Among the other popular brands are Genitron®, Macrolex® and Mersolat®.

The Inorganic Pigments unit (IPG) is one of the leading manufacturers of inorganic pigments, like iron oxide and chrome oxide pigments which are used for the coloration of paints and coatings, plastics and papers as well as for use as speciality pigments for toner and other applications. The Ion Exchange Resins (ION) business unit is a global manufacturer of ion exchange resins like Lewatit® and Ionac®. These are used in a wide range of applications from industrial waste water treatment, chemical catalysis to metal processing and sugar, starch and pharma production. With the introduction of reverse osmosis membrane technology the business unit offers end-to-end solutions for water treatment. The filter elements are marketed under the brand Lewabrane®.

LANXESS Leather (LEA) is one of the few suppliers providing the full range of chemical products necessary for the manufacture of leather, whereas the Material Protection Products (MPP) unit offers a broad range of fungicides and insecticides. It is one of the leading suppliers of biocides for protecting construction materials such as wood, plasterboard and coatings.

LANXESS's subsidiary, Rhein Chemie (RCH) offers an extensive palette of tailor-made active ingredient compounds and speciality chemicals for the rubber, lubricant and plastic industries. The Rubber Chemicals (RUC) business unit is a global leader in the manufacture and distribution of rubber chemicals and their main brands are Vulkanox®, Vulkacit®, Renacit® and Cohedur® used in the tyre industry, in rubber products for technical applications as well as in the pharma and mining industries.

LANXESS aims for the same high standards in quality, safety and environmental protection at all of its locations worldwide. The LANXESS Group's integrated quality and environmental management system is in accordance with ISO 9001 and 14001. LANXESS is also a member of the leading sustainability indices, the Dow Jones Sustainability Index (DJSI) and FTSE4Good.

LANXESS had dedicated the year 2012 to the topic of 'Green Mobility'. As a technological leader in speciality chemicals, LANXESS develops new applications that enable more environmentally friendly 'Green Mobility'. The company's synthetic rubbers extend the service life of 'Green Tyres', helping to conserve raw materials resources. Its plastic-metal hybrid technology reduces the weight of components for cars and other means of transportation. This cuts fuel consumption without compromising on safety. LANXESS products also include stabilisers to enable the use of fuels produced from renewable raw materials. (www.lanxess.com)

BayWa

The BayWa AG Group of companies operates in wholesale retail and other services in the business areas of agriculture, building materials and energy. Its present headquarters are in Munich. It was founded in 1923 during a period of severe inflation when the Bayerische Zentral–Darlehenskasse separated its merchandise business from its financial business, thus leading to the creation of BayWa. Over the years, BayWa has grown from a regional trading company to a group with international trading operations and services.

Today, the group, is established throughout Europe, the US and New Zealand and maintains global trade relations. In fiscal year 2011, the group had total sales revenues of €9.585 billion, with 16,800 employees worldwide. Its strategies are geared towards growth in Germany and other world markets as well as the development of new business lines. Klaus Josef Lutz is the present CEO, while Manfred Nüssel is the Chairman of the Supervisory Board of the BayWa Group

BayWa shares are traded on the regulated markets of the Frankfurt and Munich Stock Exchanges. In September 2009, reflecting its growing value, BayWa was admitted to the MDAX index, a stock index of 50 leading mid-sized German companies.

BayWa's business model combines trading/retail, logistics and services in the three segments of agriculture, energy and building materials. Traditionally, BayWa has its roots in the cooperative business, especially of farmer cooperatives – one reason why it has been strong in the rural areas. Customer relationships in the segments have developed over many years and often span several generations. The company's broad sales and service networks as well as its franchise operations ensure BayWa's proximity to this substantial customer base and give it a considerable competitive advantage.

The agriculture segment consists of three units: agriculture, agricultural equipment and fruit. With a share of 44 per cent, the segment is the mainstay of BayWa's business activity.

The Agriculture Business Unit operates in the traditional agri-business of trading agricultural products and equipment and providing related services. The unit's range of products includes grain and oilseed, fruit and other agricultural produce. It also provides a full range of crop protection products, fertilisers, feed-stuff and seeds. BayWa also assists farmers through hedging against price fluctuations. Business in agricultural raw materials is marked by considerable market volatility, which poses a challenge for all farmers and traders. BayWa's approach is defined by a high degree of risk awareness, its reliability, trust and transparency.

The Agricultural Equipment business unit provides farmers with technical facilities and machinery as well as repair and maintenance services. Its sales, delivery, financing and advisory services covers the whole range of technical equipment including tractors, self-propelled machinery accessories and spare parts. Through its numerous workshops and contractual partners, the unit offers quality repair and service throughout Europe. With its online shop, it also provides second-hand agricultural machinery worldwide.

The Fruit Business Unit of the BayWa Group is a leading supplier of German table fruit for food retailers and Germany's largest supplier of organically grown fruit. It owns and operates state-of-the-art facilities for storage, sorting and packaging of fruit. This unit recently has unlocked new potential in international growth markets through the majority acquisition of Turners & Growers. T&G is New Zealand's leading distributor, marketer and exporter of premium fresh produce. In addition, the company holds the exclusive brand rights for the global cultivation and sale of a number of apple and kiwi varieties which are highly sought after in the Asian market.

In its Energy segment, BayWa operates numerous petrol stations (under the BayWa and AVIA brands in Germany and through the group holding RWA under the GENOL brand in Austria). BayWa also operates several natural gas fuelling stations, while its subsidiary TESSOL provides bio-ethanol at one sale outlets. The segment's other products include over 20 biodegradable lubricants, heating and fuel oil, solid fuels such as coal and wood products as well as a large range of mineral oil equipment such as pumps and storage tanks. In 2011, the energy segment, contributed around 32.5 per cent to group revenues.

BayWa has also been consistently building up activities in the field of renewable energies under its BayWa r.e. renewable energy brand. It concentrates its activities in project management and in the building and operation of wind farms, photovoltaic and biogas plants.

The Building Materials business segment of BayWa is Germany's second largest building materials company (by turnover) and in 2011 generated 21.5 per cent of group sales. Its range of products and services includes building materials and systems for excavation, structural work, roofing, façades and interior work as well as interior components (windows, doors and stairs), garden materials, equipment and tools. The focus of the unit is on construction, modernisation and renovation. It also provides products and services in areas such as photovoltaics, solar heating and rain-water management.

Finally, BayWa´s DIY and Garden centres are a subsidiary of the group. They operate in Germany, Austria and through a franchise network as well. These centres offer customers a full range of DIY products including building materials, tools, garden products, plants, electrical goods, paint, wallpaper, wood and tiles. These centres are substantial suppliers for rural areas and range from small, compact centres to flagship stores with retail space of up to 12,000 square meters. (www.baywa.com)

Otto-Fuchs

Otto-Fuchs KG is an internationally operating group of companies that specialises in alloying, casting, extruding, forging and the manufacture of high-quality, semi-finished products, component parts and other finished products for the aerospace, automotive, construction and general engineering industries.

The company was founded in 1910, when they set up the company as a brass foundry. Today, they have plants in Germany and in locations throughout Europe and other parts of the world. Otto-Fuchs KG (a limited partnership) has its corporate headquarters in a town called Meinerzhagen in the state of North-Rhine Westphalia. Hinrich Mählmann is the current President and CEO of the company. In 2011, they generated sales of around €3 billion while employing more than 9,000 people worldwide.

Otto-Fuchs has their main plant in Meinerzhagen where they manufacture die and hand forgings from aluminium, magnesium, titanium and nickel alloys. They also produce extruded, semi-finished sections, bars and tubes made from aluminium and magnesium alloys, forged aluminium wheels and components that are ready for installation for the aerospace, automotive, construction and general industries.

Because it is the headquarters and main plant, it is also responsible for material, product and process development and testing, tool manufacture and construction of jigs and fixtures, heat treatment shop, plant engineering and maintenance and other management functions.

Otto-Fuchs manufactures components for fuselages, engines, empennages, wings, landing gear, wheel and rotor systems for the aerospace industry. Together with their American subsidiary, Weber Metals, they supply all major western aerospace companies with their specific requirements like Airbus, Boeing, Liebherr, MTU, Rolls Royce, Snecma etc., as well as the Ariane Space Industries. The variety of materials, processes and products makes Otto-Fuchs unique worldwide. More than 250 customers in 40 countries trust in their quality and reliability as they fulfil the strict requirements of the FAA (Federal Aviation Authority). They are represented in the field with over 5,000 products made from almost 100 different alloys.

Since the 1970s, Otto-Fuchs has continuously set new standards in the automotive industry and vehicle construction. Practically, all car manufacturers in Europe use component parts manufactured by Otto-Fuchs. Extrusion products, safety critical components like ABS/ESP housings or parts in specifically developed alloys with crash absorption characteristics for structural applications in space-frame structures are some of their specialities.

They are also one of the leading manufacturers of synchroniser rings for over 50 years. Their special alloys and precision forging techniques meet the highest standards for function and service life. Otto-Fuchs also manufactures forged aluminium wheels for most European car manufacturers including the legendary Porsche cars.

For years, Otto-Fuchs has been successfully supplying innovative components to the commercial vehicle industry and logistics sector. Their lightweight structural components are also used as light and sustainable truck and trailer floors and walls as well as for lift platforms, gangways and doors. Similar applications for buses, railroads, as well as for ship-building are also manufactured.

In the construction industry, their subsidiary Schüco International is Europe's number one and also a globally operating company producing architectural elements and façade systems, with partner companies in more than 70 countries. Schüco last generated sales of around €1 billion with a workforce of around 4,600 employees.

Schüco is the market leader and system supplier for windows, doors, façades, balconies and conservatories. Their products range from aluminium profile systems for avant-garde architecture, 'synergistic facades' with photovoltaic systems, conservatories and aluminium windows and door systems. Other products include burglar-proof windows and doors, fire-proofing systems, universally applicable aluminium balcony and balcony glazing systems as well as special façade structures.

The Otto-Fuchs Group also supplies a comprehensive range of rods, tubes, sections and forged parts, both as semi-finished and finished products. The high material strengths allow for intricate, delicate but safe structures which fulfil complex requirements of the industry.

The widespread application of their lightweight materials in the field of general engineering is due to their properties of dynamic strength, low-density and good corrosion resistance.

Otto-Fuchs produces profiles and forged parts according to customer specifications from aluminium, magnesium and titanium alloys. They are widely used for oscillating and rotating components in textile and packaging machines, turbines and centrifuges, while their copper and brass alloys have a wide range of applications, particularly in hydraulics and pneumatics.

The group's quality management system ensures that product characteristics conform to customer specifications and that their internal processes are as per the relevant quality systems and standards. Their quality management system is based on DIN EN ISO 9001. This is supplemented by ISO TS 16949 which is applicable to the automotive industry, while their physical and chemical laboratories have been accredited by NADCAP in accordance with ISO/IEC Guide 17025.

Certification according to DIN EN ISO 14001 confirms their environmentally compatible production methods, reduction of energy consumption, emissions and waste water as well as the efficient use of resources.

Over the years, the Otto-Fuchs Group has won several awards, a recent one being the 'MTU Aero Engines Supplier Award' given to the group for extraordinary achievements in the innovation category. (www.otto-fuchs.com)

Bilfinger

Bilfinger SE occupies a leading position in the provision of services for industrial facilities, power plants and buildings. The group's operations are comprised of the industrial services, power systems, building and facility services, construction and concessions business segments.

Bilfinger Berger AG was established in 1975 through a merger of three construction companies, each with its own long tradition. Its historical roots reach back to the year 1880, when August Bernatz completed his first large project in what was then the German province of Lorraine. In 1883, the builder settled in Mannheim and founded Grün and Bilfinger AG. The other forerunners were Julius Berger Tiefbau AG and Berlinische Boden-Gesellschaft which were both founded in 1890. These latter two companies merged in 1969 to become Julius Berger Bauboag AG. After which in 1975, Bilfinger merged with Berger to form Bilfinger + Berger Bau AG, which officially became Bilfinger Berger AG in 2001. The company was renamed Bilfinger SE in 2012.

Bilfinger SE had an output volume of €8.476 billion for fiscal year 2011. Their present headquarters are in Mannheim. As of year end 2011, they had over 59,000 employees working for them worldwide. Roland Koch is the present Chairman of the Executive Board, while Bernhard Walter is the Chairman of the Supervisory Board of Bilfinger SE.

The Industrial Services division covers the maintenance and repair of industrial plants. Bilfinger is one of the world's leading providers of industrial services with a focus on the process industry. The group provides services for the construction, maintenance and modernisation of industrial plants, primarily for industrial sectors including oil and gas, refineries, petrochemicals, chemicals and agrochemicals, pharmaceuticals, food and beverages, power generation, as well as steel and aluminium.

The Bilfinger Power Systems division is a market leader in energy technology, nuclear and environmental technologies, piping technology, machinery and apparatus engineering and in the power plant segment. The group is focused on maintenance, repair, efficiency enhancements and lifetime extensions as well as the manufacture and assembly of components, especially boiler and high-pressure piping systems for power plants.

Their Building and Facility Services division focuses on providing real estate and lifecycle services. Core competence covers, order development, design and turnkey construction through to rehabilitation and portfolio optimisation for all forms of real estate for private and public-sector clients.

Bilfinger is a market leader in facility services in Germany and is among the leading providers in Europe. As a general services provider, Bilfinger offers a broad range of technical, commercial and infrastructural real estate services in Europe, the US and MENA countries.

Bilfinger also offers a comprehensive range of services for the construction and operation of real estate properties for government agencies as well as national and international organisations in particular government agencies in the US. The services offered range from the design and execution of building and industrial construction projects, commercial, technical and infrastructural facility management through to energy management for buildings.

In the Construction division Bilfinger occupies a leading position in the design and construction of major infrastructure projects. Business activities are focused in the European markets of Germany, Austria, Switzerland, Eastern European countries, the UK and Scandinavia. The company is well positioned with highly specialised units for bridge construction, tunnelling, foundation engineering and pre-stress technology. Among its major projects have been several bridges, tunnels, subway construction projects and dams. The Sydney Opera House, stadiums like the Olympic Stadium in Munich, the new Reichstag building in Berlin, ports, highways, multi-storied skyscrapers, railways and several such projects all over the world.

In the Concessions division, Bilfinger delivers and operates transport and social infrastructure projects as a private partner to the public sector on the basis of long-term concession contracts. They focus on projects in the markets of Australia, Germany, the UK, Canada, Norway and Hungary. Actively operating across three continents, the Bilfinger Project Investments (BPI) is the Public Private Partnership (PPP) investment division of the Bilfinger Group. Among their recent projects are the East Down and Lisburn Further Education Colleges in Northern Ireland, Staffordshire Fire Stations in the UK and the British Embassy in Berlin.

Bilfinger places social and ecological aspects of sustainability at the focus of its entrepreneurial activities. The group and its employees accept responsibility for society and the environment. Their R&D activities focus on climate protection and the conservation of resources. Bilfinger also provides a full range of services for both water-supply and waste water. Safety at work, that adheres to occupational safety standards and effective measures for environmental protection play an important role in the design and execution of their work sites. (www.bilfinger.com)

Deutsche Bahn (DB)

Deutsche Bahn AG is also popularly known from its initials DB, as it is one of the world's leading passenger and logistics companies and operates in around 130 countries. The company's core business is the railway passenger transport in Germany. 2010 saw the 175th anniversary of the first steam locomotive trip in Germany. In 1835, the opening of the 6-kilometre route between Nuremberg and Fürth saw the dawn of the railway age in Germany. 1994 is the year Deutsche Bahn AG was founded. After the reunification of Germany in 1989, the merger of Bundesbahn and Reichsbahn of West and East Germany respectively saw its formation as a joint stock company operating in accordance with business principles. The German Federal Government is the majority shareholder and has the right to appoint three members to the Supervisory Board. The group's present head office is in Berlin. During the financial year of 2011 the DB Group posted revenues of about €37.9 billion. Every day about 300,000 employees worldwide, of which 195,000 are in Germany, are committed to ensuring that customers are provided with mobility and logistical services. Rüdiger Grube is the present CEO and Chairman of the Management Board of Deutsche Bahn AG and DB Mobility Logistics AG, and Utz-Hellmuth Felcht is the Chairman of the Supervisory Board.

The company caters to more than 10 million customers a day in the passenger transport segment and more than a million tons of freight is shipped by rail. More than 2 million customers travel via DB buses every day. Deutsche Bahn operates more than 27,000 passenger train runs daily on its approximately 34,000-kilometre-long, modern rail network that is open to competition as well. The DB Group has essentially three divisions: Passenger Transport Board Division, Transport and Logistics Board Division and Infrastructure and Services Board Division. These are further demarcated into several business units. They are DB Bahn Long Distance, DB Bahn Regional, DB Arriva, DB Schenker Logistics, DB Schenker Rail, DB Netze Track, DB Netze Stations, DB Netze Energy, DB Services and other affiliates.

The DB Bahn Long Distance business unit provides national and cross-border, long-distance rail services: Inter City Express (ICE), Euro City and Inter City. Regularly scheduled services by day are the key business in long-distance transport. They offer quick and comfortable connections directly into the main cities at attractive prices. DB Auto Zug also offers car transport and night-train services. They are also building on their international offerings with cooperation agreements with other rail service providers in Europe.

The DB Bahn Regional business unit provides a comprehensive regional transport network, which links semi-urban and rural areas in Europe. Regionally oriented transport operations interlock on-site, offering planning and provision of services in cooperation with local contracting agencies and transport associations. An integrated regional transport program of rail and bus are adapted to the local transport requirements. With around 756 million passengers in 2011 and 150,000 bus services daily, DB Bahn

Regional is Germany's largest provider of bus services, too. The business unit operates 22 bus companies throughout Germany and has shareholdings in a further 70 transport companies. This enables Deutsche Bahn to provide cross-carrier mobility services in the regions.

DB Regio UK operates in parts of Great Britain and DB Regio Sverige operates in parts of Sweden. They also have a cooperation agreement with the Polish PKP PR.

The DB Arriva business unit has been a part of the Passenger Transport Board Division since 2011. DB Arriva offers bus and/or train services in 12 European countries and has a workforce of more than 38,000. The company handles roughly 1.5 billion trips per annum, using more than 16,000 buses, 600 trains and 120 trams. Its business activities are divided amongst the three divisions UK Bus, UK Trains and Mainland Europe.

With nearly 59,000 employees and sales totalling €14.3 billion, the Business Unit DB Schenker Logistics is one of the world's leading service providers in this important industry. The three internal business units of DB Schenker Logistics offer European land transport, global air and ocean freight and comprehensive contract logistics solutions and global supply chain management from a single source. DB Schenker Logistics holds top positions in the automotive, high-tech and consumer products sectors and in trade fair forwarding, special transportation and services for major sporting events.

While their DB Schenker Rail business unit pools their European activities for rail freight transport. DB Schenker Rail is the leading rail freight company in Europe. Their product portfolio ranges from transport of single wagons and wagon groups through block trains as door to door solution to additional logistic services as well as holistic inter-modal transport. DB Schenker Rail operates 5,000 trains per day. With 109,000 freight cars and 3,590 locomotives, the rail freight unit of DB possesses the largest fleet in Europe. 32,500 employees in 15 countries make DB Schenker Rail the most international railway company in the world. Thanks to strong companies and joint ventures with partner railways, DB Schenker Rail offers rail freight services to most of Europe. Since, September 2011, DB Schenker Rail has operated trains from Leipzig in Germany to China. The company supplies automotive parts and components to BMW's new automobile plant in Shenyang on behalf of the car manufacturer.

The DB Netze Track business unit is the service provider for approximately 385 railway undertakings including 357 non-DB railway undertakings (RUs) all of which use the approximately 34,000-kilometre-long German rail network, the longest in Europe. They ensure non-discriminatory access and safe operation of this rail infrastructure.

Whereas, the DB Netze Stations business unit consists of the operation of the passenger stations as traffic stations as well as the development and marketing of train station areas. A total of 14 million people use their stations every day. They run more than 5,400 stations of various sizes.

The DB Netze Energy business unit is responsible for supplying energy of all kinds to Deutsche Bahn as well as other companies. They also offer technical expertise and control instruments. In addition to planning, maintenance, marketing and operations of technically complex energy networks, sustainable generation and procurement of traction and stationary energy are also included in their range of services.

The DB Services business unit covers six different sectors: DB Fahr Zeuginstandhaltung (vehicle maintenance), DB Systel (ICT), DB Services, DB FuhrPark (motor vehicle fleet) as well as DB Kommunikationstechnik (communications) and DB Sicherheit (security). The DB Group companies are the main customers of the primarily transport related infrastructure management and infrastructure services. Vehicle maintenance of trains, engines, wagons and bogies are carried out at 15 locations in Germany. For years, DB AG has been improving the ecological footprint of its trains and of the company. DB has already reduced the specific CO_2 emissions from rail transportation by a little less than 40 per cent since 1990. By 2020, it aims to reduce specific CO_2 emissions throughout the group, i.e. from rail, road, air and water transportation by a further 20 per cent over 2006 levels.

They also offer, an innovative CO_2-free train travel and freight transportation for both passengers and freight. The energy used comes exclusively from renewable sources. (www.deutschebahn.com)

Südzucker

Südzucker AG is a globally operating German food group with current headquarters in Mannheim. Mainly involved in sugar production, it is one of the largest European sugar producers today. It was formed in 1926 in Mannheim when five sugar producing companies merged to form the Süddeutsche Zucker AG.

Today, in addition to being the leading European sugar producer they also produce fruit products, fruit juices, frozen pizza, other special products and bio-ethanol.

For financial year 2011, they had annual revenues totalling €7 billion. They employ 17,500 employees worldwide. Wolfgang Heer is the *de facto* CEO and Spokesman for the Executive Board of Südzucker AG while Hans-Jörg Gebhard is the Chairman of the Supervisory Board. Südzucker AG is listed on the German MDAX index. The main shareholders are sugar beet farmers, who hold 56 per cent of the share capital via their cooperative organisation, the Süddeutsche Zuckerrüben Verwertungs-Genossenschaft e.G (SZVG), the 'South German Sugar Beet Processing Cooperative'.

Südzucker AG is Europe's leading supplier of sugar products and is well positioned in the special products, crop energies and fruit segments. They rely on their close cooperation with the agricultural industry, the basis of its raw materials, the group's in-house research expertise, its extensive manufacturing knowledge in connection with processing renewable raw materials and its marketing experience, particularly in the B2B space. They are penetrating new business fields along the value-added chain through organic growth, alliances and acquisitions.

The group has divided its activities into four divisions or segments as they call it. They are the Sugar Segment, Special Products Segment, Crop Energies Segment and the Fruit Segment.

In the Sugar Segment a total of 29 sugar factories and three refineries in Germany, Belgium, Bosnia-Herzegovina, France, Austria, Poland, Romania, Slovakia, the Czech Republic, Hungary and Moldova produced 5.4 million tons of sugar as per 2011. Their main companies in this segment are Südzucker AG, Südzucker Polska, Südzucker Moldova, Raffinerie (refinery) Tirlemontoise, Saint Louis Sucre and AGRANA. Together they produced about 24 per cent of the EU's sugar production.

Agriculture and animal feed are the two other key areas that belong to this segment. They also have four packaging plants and one cane-sugar factory in France. AGRANA Zucker Gmbh is the management company of the Austrian AGRANA sugar division that also serves as a holding company for the subsidiaries in Eastern Europe. They have a cultivated area of around 412,000 hectares. Organic farming on 1,000 hectares, organic mixed feed production as well as bio-turkey production. This segment contributed to around 60 per cent of the group turnover.

The Special Products Segment includes the activities of the Beneo Group, Freiberger, Portion Pack Europe as well as AGRANA's starch and bio-ethanol businesses. The Beneo Group (in Orafti/Remy/Palatinit) includes five production sites in Belgium, Chile, Germany and Italy. They manufacture various food products, pharma products, feed and other non-food products. They essentially produce and market functional ingredients with nutritional and technical benefits. Through a unique chain of expertise, including the BENEO Institute, they actively support industry partners in the development of a more balanced, healthy and tasty range of food products. Freiberger is the market leader for frozen and chilled pizza. They also produce frozen pasta and baguettes with production locations in Germany and UK. Their brands are Alberto, Erno's, Gourmet Royal, al Forno, Stateside, Die Dünne and Panovale. Portion Pack Europe designs, produces and sells portion packed products in the food segment consisting of sugar portions, toppings, baked and sweet products.

In the non-food segment, products like shower gels, shampoos and refreshing towels etc., are produced. They are a European market leader with eight affiliates in eight European countries. They essentially cater to other food and non-food manufacturers (contract packing), hotels, caterers, the retail and advertising and promotional markets. Finally, they have four starch factories in Austria, Hungary and Romania that make starch out of maize and potatoes for the food and beverages, paper, textiles, construction, chemicals, pharma and cosmetic industries. They also manufacture tailored solutions and apps as well as products such as wax maize and GMO-free maize.

In the Crop Energies Segment, the activities consist of bio-ethanol production in Germany, Belgium and France. They are one of the leading European producers of sustainably produced bio-ethanol for the fuel sector. They have a combined annual production capacity of over 700,000 m³ of bio-ethanol and over 500,000 tons of byproducts. Crop Energies has also put in place an efficient distribution network.

Finally, in the Fruit Segment, AGRANA indirectly owns all shares of the fruit division via AGRANA J&F Holding Gmbh. Co-ordination and operational management are carried out through the two divisional holding companies AGRANA Fruit S.A.S, Mitry-Mory France (for fruit preparations) and AGRANA Juice Holding Gmbh, Gleisdorf, Austria for fruit juice concentrates. They are a global market leader in fruit preparations and a leading producer of fruit juice concentrates in Europe. They refine raw materials to high-value intermediate products for the food industry, for the drinks, diary, pastries and ice cream industries. They have a market presence on all five continents with 37 production facilities.

Among the many sustainability measures adopted by the Südzucker Group are environmentally friendly methods in the field such as erosion protection by inter-cropping, mulch seeding, soil-preservation, optimal fertilizer quantities according to the electro-ultra filtration (EUF) method, and less use of pesticides. Other measures include effective, economical use of energy through co-generation and power-heat-coupling, utilisation of byproducts such as fertilizers and animal feed and optimised use of water by internal cycles. (www.suedzucker.de)

Boehringer Ingelheim

Boehringer Ingelheim is a global group of companies whose main business areas are human pharmaceuticals and animal health. The company was founded in 1885 by Albert Boehringer (1861–1939) in Ingelheim am Rhein a town in the state of Rhineland-Palatinate. The founder initially employed 28 people to manufacture tartaric acid salts used by pharmacies and dyeing works of the time.

Boehringer Ingelheim is a family-owned company governed by the Board of Managing Directors of which Andreas Barner is the Chairman of the Board.

Today, Boehringer Ingelheim is a group of companies dedicated to researching, developing, manufacturing and marketing novel products of high therapeutic value for human and veterinary medicine. It is among the world's 20 leading pharmaceutical companies. They have around 145 affiliated companies in 47 countries and employ around 44,000 people worldwide. For fiscal year 2011, the total sales turnover was €13.2 billion. Their corporate headquarters are still located in the town of Ingelheim am Rhein. The year 2011 saw their 125th year celebrations, 125 years of more health. Their present corporate slogan is 'Value through Innovation', with 'Lead & Learn' as the driver of their corporate culture.

The main business areas in human pharmaceuticals are prescription medicines, consumer healthcare and industrial customers, where they produce bio-pharmaceuticals, pharmaceutical production and pharma chemicals. The other major business area is animal health. In 2011, they spent 23.5 per cent of net sales on R&D for their largest business segment, prescription medicines. They have four main R&D sites and three smaller specialised sites worldwide, which focus on six major therapeutic areas: respiratory diseases, cardio-metabolic diseases, oncology, neurological diseases, immunology and infectious diseases.

In the prescription medicines business area, they manufacture medicines for effective primary and specialist care worldwide. As stated, these medicinal products require a prescription, either from primary care physicians, by specialists or form an integral part of hospital treatment. These prescription medicines which represents the bulk of their human pharmaceuticals business, account for 77 per cent of their total sales and generated €10.096 billion in 2011.

Boehringer Ingelheim's product portfolio covers the following main indications: for acute coronary diseases, their main product brands are Actilyse® (Alteplase) and Metalyse® (Tenecteplase). Benign prostate hyperplasia (BHP) is a common urinary-related medical condition in middle-aged and elderly men. Their main product brand for this condition are Flomax®, Alna®, Josir®, Pradif®, Secotex®, Urolosin®, Mecir® (tamsulosin) and OCAS.

For cardiovascular diseases and hypertension (high blood pressure) their popular brand is Micardis® (telmisartan), whereas, for chronic obstructive pulmonary disease (COPD) their product brands are Spiriva®, Atrovent®, Combivent®, Berodual®, Bronchodual®, Duovent® and their environmentally friendly hydro-fluoroalkanes (HFAs), Inhaler the Respimat® Soft Mist™ Inhaler.

They also have innovative anti-retroviral drugs to improve HIV/AIDS therapy such as Viramune® (nevirapine) and Aptivus® (tipranavir). For Parkinson's disease (PD), a degenerative disorder of the central nervous system, their product brands are Mirapex®, Mirapexin®, Sifrol® and Pexola®, as well as extended release versions of the same.

Restless legs syndrome (RLS) a neurological disorder is also treated by the prior mentioned product brands.

For strokes, the product brands are Actilyse®, Aggrenox® and Asasantin®, Retard (dipyridamole/ASA), whereas, for thrombo-embolic diseases, the product brand is Pradaxa® (dabigatran etexilate). They also have products for other indications like generalised anxiety disorder, diabetic peripheral neuropathic pain (DPNP) and for acute ischemic strokes.

The consumer healthcare business contributed some 11 per cent, i.e. €1.396 billion to Boehringer Ingelheim's total annual sales revenue in 2011. They have nine core brands that cater to various medical conditions. Antistax® is their consumer brand for the prevention and treatment of various leg health issues. Then they have Bisolvon® for the treatment of various coughs and bronchial diseases. Buscopan® is the number one global antispasmodic brand. It relieves abdominal pain caused by cramps and spasms. Dulcolax® is their leading brand for the treatment, regulation and prevention of intestinal irregularity, in other words the number one laxative in the world, marketed in over 100 countries.

Also in their product line is Mucoangin® lozenges for pain from a sore throat, also called pharyngitis. It is also known by the trade names Lizipaina® and Lizis®. Mucosolvan® is another leading cough brand that promotes mucus clearance, facilitates expectoration and eases productive cough, allowing patients to breathe freely and deeply. Their Pharmaton® range is a multivitamin and mineral supplements brand developed to enhance people's physical and mental well-being. Thomapyrin® is a popular pain reliever for headaches, migraines and other tension related headaches. Finally, they have Zantac® a heartburn brand in the US that relieves heartburn associated with acidity and indigestion.

Their third business area, Animal Health had another successful year with total sales revenue of €976 million for the year 2011, 7 per cent of total group revenues. Their product brands treat horses, cattle, pigs and other small pets like cats and dogs. Among the popular brands are Calvenza®, for virus infections, Buscopan®, for the management of abdominal pain associated with equine colic, and Equitop Gonex®, to support and stimulate the mobility and maintenance of healthy joints in horses, as well as Metacam®, Sedivet®, Sputolosin®, Ventipulmin® among others.

The Boehringer Ingelheim Group of companies also includes a contract manufacturing business as a key component of their strategy. Their contract manufacturing businesses are in the areas of bio-pharmaceuticals, offering world class expertise and a successful market introduction of 19 DNA-derived bio-pharmaceutical products.

In the small molecules, APIs and formulation business, they conduct the development, launch and post-launch as a partner for active pharma ingredients (API) and finished dosage forms (drug products).

Boehringer Ingelheim has a large and experienced global team managing and conducting clinical trials to establish the safety and efficacy of the drugs they develop. They are also actively involved in the battle against counterfeiting of medicines. Among the measures and activities they have undertaken are supply chain control and traceability, security features where appropriate, investigation and prosecution, rapid reporting and open communication and a cross-functional anti-counterfeiting team. (www.boehringer-ingelheim.com)

EDEKA

The EDEKA Group with an annual turnover of €45.6 billion as of fiscal year 2011 is Germany's leading food retailer. It was founded in 1898 when Fritz Borrmann together with 20 other merchants set up the first regional purchasing cooperative of grocers in Berlin. It was called Einkaufsgenossenschaft der kolonialwarenhändler in German or E.d.K which underwent a phonetic transformation as Edeka in 1913. The Edeka Bank was founded in 1914. In 1972, the cooperatives changed their structure and formed regional companies or cooperatives of independent supermarkets all operating under the umbrella organisation, Edeka Zentrale AG & Co. KG. All the cooperatives hold shares in EDEKA Zentrale and 50 per cent of the shares in the EDEKA regional companies.

Today, the group has about 12,000 stores and 306,000 full time employees and over 18,000 trainees. The EDEKA Zentrale is in Hamburg. Around 4,500 independent merchants shape the dynamics of the EDEKA Group. A.Scheck is the present Chairman of EDEKA AG Supervisory Board as well as that of the KG Board, while Markus Mosa is the CEO of EDEKA AG. Their subsidiary, the NETTO Marken-Discount supermarket chain, recently acquired around 2,300 Plus stores of the Tengelmann Group.

The EDEKA Group focuses on two main businesses in the retail sector: the full range of independent retailers who run the supermarkets and hypermarkets, and the discount range of retail outlets. They also have a wholesale network for fresh produce and their own production facilities for meat and sausages, pastries, wine and other food products. The market of the EDEKA Group represents a unique diversity with up to 50,000 items.

The full range of independent retailers is their core business, from the traditional supermarket to the hypermarket. The majority of the markets are run by independent retailers, while the seven regional companies or cooperatives of EDEKA own the branches. They operate a total of 1,300 branches or stores with a turnover of €8.6 billion, while the 6,300 independent retailers increased their sales to €20 billion in fiscal year 2011. They are located mainly in smaller municipalities, semi-urban areas and villages. These retailers run their companies in a traditional family way, maintain links with local producers and are characterised by a unique local customer focus. They believe in freshness of produce and a high level of service commitment, offering the best in fresh fruit and vegetables, meats, sausages, an assortment of cheeses and fresh fish, pointing to their success factors. They also have a limited non-food assortment, in their E neukauf outlets (1,000–2,500 square meters). The E center is a large business with a full range of retail from about 2,500 square meters and a full range of distinctive food supplements, non-food products and a variety of departments. The EDEKA aktiv Markt offers a full range of modern supermarket food with less retail space (400–1,000 square metres). Other retail outlets include Marktkauf with around 180 hypermarkets offering large areas with a wide variety of food products and a sophisticated non-food range on offer.

The discount priced range of stores is represented by Netto Marken-Discount. It is also well known for a well-stocked range of fresh produce, especially fruits and vegetables, dairy products, meats and sausages. They have an exceptionally broad range, with more than 3,500 articles on offer. In addition to a high proportion of branded products they also offer private labels of the company. Fiscal year 2009 through to mid-2010 saw the integration and conversion of 2,300 Plus stores into the distribution network of Netto Marken Discount. With the Plus acquisition, the Netto group has a total of around

4,000 branches in Germany with an annual sales turnover of €10.70 billion for fiscal year 2011.

In terms of wholesale, the EDEKA C+C hypermarkets, with regional and national delivery, serve large industrial customers, such as restaurants, hotels, caterers and trade, an interesting range with a focus on food. They have a comprehensive sales network in Germany with 122 locations. More than 430 delivery vehicles are on duty and ensure that all products are delivered fresh and on time. The regional distribution of warehouses provides short transport distances and optimum product freshness.

The seven regional companies of EDEKA make daily deliveries to the EDEKA retail with a comprehensive range of food produce. They pay special attention to the supply of local products as this promotes the local manufacturers and farmers who supply to EDEKA, strengthening purchasing power in the region and providing jobs. They have an efficient logistics infrastructure, which includes a dense network of 40 central and regional warehouses in Germany. Approximately 1,800 trucks comprising EDEKA's fleet are permanently on duty every day to provide the markets with fresh produce.

With their own production, the EDEKA Group is one of the leading producers of meats and sausages, as well as fresh baked goods, in Germany. They are also into the cultivation of fruit and vegetables and producing high-quality bottled wines.

For meat products they have 15 ultra-modern meat processing plants, offering their customers the best quality and safety in purchasing, as they have substantial control over their suppliers meeting their quality standards. Their extensive range of 750 different meat and sausage products also includes high-quality organic meat, the brand EDEKA Bio and the low-fat sausage Vielleicht ('Maybe').

For baked goods, the Group has 17 locations that produce fresh bread and pastries daily. Among the most popular sellers is their Schäfers Brot und Kuchen Spezialitäten GmbH (bread and cake specialities) with over 800 outlets. Their bakery K&U has around 700 outlets and is supplied by four production plants. Premium quality and a large variety has differentiated them from their competition and made them a success in processed products, convenience items and organic baked goods.

Fruits and vegetables are supplied and marketed by EDEKA Frucht Kontor as a part of EDEKA Zentrale, which purchases fruit, vegetables and flowers from more than 95 countries worldwide. They have procurement offices in several places in Germany, and one each in the Netherlands and Spain. Their popular brands are EDEKA Rio Grande for fruits, EDEKA Gärtners Beste (Gardener's Best) for vegetables and EDEKA Selection for premium fruits and vegetables. Fruits and vegetables from EDEKA stand for continuous, quality controlled integrated cultivation.

For wine, the EDEKA Weinkontor controls the supply of national and international wines and sparkling wines for the entire EDEKA Group. Germany's third largest winery the Rhineberg Winery in Bingen belongs to the Kontor. Some 480 wines and sparkling wines from 15 countries belong to the assortment, many of them created exclusively for the EDEKA Group. Several of their wines and champagnes have received the highest industry/trade ratings, supporting their corporate slogan, 'WE LOVE FOOD'.

The EDEKA Group run TV commercials and ads in other media as well. They are a service-oriented company that believes in catering to the nutritional requirements of its customers. Their website and stores help their customers with cooking tips, recipes and nutritious eating for adults and healthy eating for children, in addition to various competitions and fun events for their customers. They also have social programmes for healthy eating and encouraging the young to plant vegetables and learn gardening.

As a standard requirement for business with the EDEKA Group, they require all their business partners, whether suppliers, producers and sub-contractors to comply with given social and environmental standards. The group are also committed to reducing their CO_2 emissions and to increasingly use sustainable sources of energy. (www.edeka.de)

HANIEL

Haniel is an internationally successful, family-owned group of companies that has a diversified portfolio of companies. The holding company Franz Haniel & Cie.Gmbh is one among several companies held by the Haniel family members. It began in 1756 in a place called Ruhrort, a suburb of Duisburg in Germany today (in Prussia it was a sovereign city); the Haniel headquarters are in the exact same location where the business started in 1756, when a customs inspector by the name of Jan Willem Noot opened a packing house or trading house for groceries that were to be then sourced from the Netherlands The old Packhaus still exists and is a museum today. The leased property was owned by no less than Frederick the Great, the then King of Prussia.

Today, with group headquarters in Duisburg, in the North Rhine-Westphalia state, the group has around 57,828 employees in 500 locations and generated total sales revenue of €27.346 billion in fiscal year 2011 from its five divisions in around 30 countries worldwide. The holding company Franz Haniel & Cie.Gmbh is responsible for group-wide strategic and financial leadership as well as the development of its human resources. Stephan Gemkow has been the Chairman of the Haniel Managing Board since August 2012, while Franz M. Haniel is the Chairman of the Supervisory Board.

Their five corporate divisions are distinguished between wholly-owned investments (CWS-boco and ELG), majority investments (Celesio and TAKKT) and minority investments (METRO GROUP). CWS-boco, TAKKT, ELG and Celesio operate independently of one another in the markets. Haniel holds a share of (34.24 per cent) in the METRO Group while CWSboco and ELG are 100 per cent owned, while TAKKT is owned to 70.44 per cent and Celesio to 54.64 per cent.

The CWS-boco division is one of the leading providers of washroom hygiene, dust-control mats and textile services worldwide. CWS are the washroom experts while boco are the textile specialists. Two brands are serviced by one service partner for all around hygiene, freshness and cleanliness. CWS offers products and services for washrooms and toilets, from soap dispensers to self-cleaning toilet seats and towel rolls with antibacterial effect. Other offerings include dust control mats. This is a core company that was founded in 1899 and now has its headquarters in Duisburg. The other brand, boco, offers a rental service for working-wear for various industries. An example is the catering and hotel trade with table and bed linens, guest towels, etc., which are supplied and washed and pressed regularly.

CWS-boco claim to be the leader in its service areas in Europe. Recently they added a range of machine-cleaning clothes and oil-absorbing mats, providing an end-to-end solution for cleanliness at the workplace.

ELG, their other wholly-owned division, is a global leader in the trade and processing of raw materials for the stainless steel industry. Their product range covers stainless steel scrap and super-alloys. Linked by a global network, the company guarantees personal and quick service. ELG sets standards in global recycling and commercial business with raw materials for the stainless steel industry that meet the highest quality standards. They have now completed around 40 years in the business and also have their headquarters in Duisburg.

TAKKT is the leading B2B direct marketing specialist for business equipment in Europe and North America. The company is also fairly successful in Asia. In Europe and North America, TAKKT Europe and TAKKT America bundle the offers of hundreds of suppliers and more than 160,000 high-quality products in one place from where their customers can source all of their equipment needs for their company. TAKKT offers a comprehensive service before, during and after delivery. They also help custom build as per their customer's needs. Thanks to a sophisticated logistics system, a large portion of the product range is ready for shipment within 24 hours. They also have an on-site assembly service for office furniture. They aim to become the global market leader in B2B mail ordering for business equipment. It was founded in 1945 as Kaiser + Kraft in Stuttgart, its present headquarters.

Celesio AG is a leading international trade, logistics and service company in the pharmaceutical and healthcare sector that proactively and preventatively ensures that patients receive optimum care and support. They operate in 26 countries worldwide and employ around 45,000 people. With more than 2,200 of their own and 4,500 partner and brand partner pharmacies, they look after more than 2 million customers daily. They supply around 65,000 pharmacies and hospitals with up to 130,000 medications through their approximately 140 branches.

Finally, the METRO Group, which is among the premier international merchandisers, is headed by the METRO AG Management Holding, in which Haniel holds 34.2 per cent of the voting shares. Operative business is carried out by autonomous sales divisions. With these sales brands, the METRO Group is represented at more than 2,100 sites in 33 countries in Europe, Asia and Africa. Their present headquarters are in Düsseldorf.

One feature that distinguishes Haniel from some traditional family-owned groups is that since the twentieth century they have entrusted corporate management to external managers. Entrepreneurial decisions are thus taken independently from family commitments, so as to achieve optimal business results. The basic principle is that company interests come before individual family interests. The family members claim a maximum of 25 per cent of the group's annual net income, and they pass on Haniel shares only to each other within the family. To date there are more than 600 family members who are shareholders. The Haniel Foundation, a non-profit foundation based in Duisburg, concentrates its work on funding research and scholarships in the areas of innovative energy, commitment to achievement, social responsibility, entrepreneurial thinking and actions in line with these values as a driving force behind social development on a sustainable basis. (www.haniel.com)

Heraeus

Heraeus is an internationally active precious metals and technology group based in Hanau near Frankfurt. Heraeus focuses on precious metals, materials and technologies, sensors, bio-materials, dental and medical products as well as quartz glass and speciality light sources.

The company was founded in 1851 by Wilhelm Carl Heraeus, a pharmacist and chemist who took over his father's pharmacy in Hanau. He discovered an innovative solution to melting platinum and thus created the first German platinum melting house. He went on to create new applications for the precious metal that saw a multitude of applications in jewellery and dental factories as well as in chemical laboratories and other industries. After more than 160 years it still remains a successful, family-owned company. In 2011, Heraeus generated more than €4.8 billion in product revenue and €21.3 billion in precious metals trading revenue. As of today, they have more than 13,300 employees in over 120 subsidiaries. The company also holds more than 5,900 patents while around 25 R&D development centres around the world fuel their innovative processes. Jan Rinnert is the Chairman of the Board of Management of Heraeus Holding Gmbh and Jürgen Heraeus is the Chairman of the Supervisory Board.

Heraeus maintains a truly global production and sales presence, with more than 120 locations and 25 development centres serving every economic region. Heraeus is divided into seven business groups or divisions, consisting of precious metals, materials and technologies, sensors, bio-materials and medical products, dental, quartz glass and speciality light sources.

The Heraeus Precious Metals Group processes gold, silver, platinum group metals and special metals, essentially to produce a diversity of industrial products. The company is a world leader in industrial precious metals and special metals. A global network of companies with production facilities is utilised for all phases of precious metal production and refining. They have decades of expertise in trading industrial precious metals, providing for the lion's share of their total revenues. The business group provides professional precious metal management throughout the precious metal cycle. The principal customers of this group are from the environmental, mobility, communications and energy sectors as well as the growing healthcare industry.

Heraeus Materials Technology Group provides high-tech industrial products from precious metals such as gold, silver, the platinum group of metals as well as from high-melting-point, non-precious refractory metals. The high-quality products originating from this group can be found in many areas, including healthcare, mobility and communication, sources of energy and environmental protection.

The sensors business group, Heraeus Electro-Nite is amongst the world market leaders in sensors and measurement systems for the steel, aluminium and foundry industries. They are specialists in the measurement of molten iron, steel and aluminium. The company produces and markets high-quality sensors from global manufacturing and sales facilities worldwide. They also develop customer based product solutions that contribute significantly to greater efficiency and higher quality in production processes as well as in improving working conditions and protecting the environment.

Heraeus Dental, the dental products business group is a single-source provider of prosthetics and systems for the conservation and restoration of natural teeth. They have an extensive range of products for dental laboratories and dentists. Venus® Diamond, a universal, nano-hybrid composite that combines low shrinkage with a high degree of durability, make dental fillings stable and lustrous.

Heraeus Medical, the bio-materials and medical products business group, concentrates on medical products for orthopaedic surgery as well as traumatology and bio-surgery. An industry leader for bone cements, the company develops, produces and globally markets bio-materials used to anchor joint prostheses to bone and to stabilise spinal fractures.

In the field of bio-surgery, Heraeus Medical offers innovative antibiotic coatings for medical implants, thereby helping to prevent infections.

Their next division Heraeus Quarzglas is the technology leader and material specialist for the manufacture and processing of high-purity quartz glass. They excel in all the key processes for producing different quartz glass types for the semiconductor and telecommunications industries as well as for applications in the optical, chemical and lamp industries. From base materials to complex system components, custom-built products and solutions can be developed and produced from natural and synthetic quartz glass. Heraeus Quarzglas has the largest quartz glass smelting facility in the world and is the world's largest manufacturer of synthetic quartz glass for use in the micro-lithography and telecommunications industries, used for the production of microchips, solar cells, optical fibres and many more such products.

Heraeus Noblelight counts itself among the global market and technology leaders for special lamps with wavelengths from ultra-violet to infra-red for industrial, scientific and medical applications. With worldwide locations, the segment manufactures lamps for analytical measurement technology and the printing industry, infra-red emitters for industrial heating processes, arc and flash lamps and products for water disinfection and air treatment, as well as sun simulation and photo-chemistry with a high level of vertical integration.

Innovation at Heraeus is based on decentralised research and interdisciplinary collaboration that works in close cooperation with its customers. In 2010, Heraeus celebrated the 150th birthday of its prolific head researcher, Richard Küch (30 August 1860–3 June 1915), who made R&D a cornerstone of their corporate philosophy. Heraeus developed many inventions on his watch including his revolutionary process for the industrial manufacture of high-purity, bubble-free quartz glass by melting rock crystal at about 2,000°C using oxyhydrogen gas flames. (www.heraeus.com)

MTU Aero Engines

MTU Aero Engines AG is Germany's leading engine manufacturer and the global number one independent provider of commercial aero-engine maintenance services. It engages in the development, manufacture, marketing and support of commercial and military aircraft engines in all thrust and power categories as well as in industrial gas turbines.

The roots of the company go back to the year 1934 when the BMW Flugmotorenbau Gmbh was founded, based in Munich-Allach. It is the legal predecessor of MTU Aero Engines, with the location remaining the same to this day.

Today, the German manufacturer employs around 8,200 people worldwide and with its various affiliates has a presence in all significant regions and markets worldwide. Consolidated revenues for fiscal year 2011 were €2.932 billion. The CEO of the company is Egon W. Behle while Klaus Eberhardt is the Chairman of the Supervisory Board. MTU is a public limited company that is listed on the MDAX. A total of 97.3 per cent of the shares are in free float as defined by the German Stock Exchange.

With its technologies, MTU Aero Engines is a pace-setter for the entire aviation industry. The low-pressure and high-pressure compressors manufactured by MTU are among the most advanced in their class. MTU also has a major role in important

European technology programmes. On an international scale, it cooperates with all of the big players in the industry, a worldwide must-have partner.

MTU Aero Engines business activities are based on three primary business segments: commercial business, with the commercial OEM and spare parts business; military business, with engine manufacture; and commercial MRO that is commercial maintenance, repair and overhaul.

MTU's commercial engines are known worldwide for their quality. MTU is represented in all thrust and power categories, from the smallest propulsion system for business jets to the world's most powerful engine flying – the Boeing 777. For these engines, they develop and manufacture major subsystems and components. Their low-pressure turbines are among the best in the world. Other quality subsystems that they make are high-pressure compressors and high-pressure turbines.

Commercial engine MRO is a focal point of their strategy. In terms of sales, MTU Aero Engine's network of maintenance shops is the world's largest independent provider of commercial engine maintenance services. As an MTU Aero Engine's affiliate, the company's maintenance segment profits from its parent's years of experience in the development and production of aircraft engines.

For the mlitary, MTU Aero Engines is the German industry leader in military engine programs for practically all aircraft engines operated by the country's military. The company provides the enabling technologies, develops and manufactures engines, engine components and the required tooling as well as delivers the entire spectrum of integrated logistic support (ILS). MTU's service portfolio is comprised of the development of maintenance, facility and training concepts, continuous product monitoring and improvement, generation of technical documentation, spare parts requirements, prognostics and on-site support.

In industrial gas turbines, MTU Maintenance Berlin-Brandenburg is one of the leading maintenance providers for General Electric's LM™ series of aero-derivative industrial gas turbines (IGTs) worldwide. Their worldwide customer base is as varied as the range of applications for the products and spans the gamut from power generation companies to marine users and operators of oil rigs and compressor stations, on-shore and off-shore.

Their MTU Aero Solutions is a brand of MTU Aero Engines. They provide state-of-the art solutions in design engineering, testing, certification and production as comprehensive service packages.

While, MTU Brush Seals are innovative seals suitable for use in aircraft engines, steam and gas turbines, pumps and for a variety of other mechanical engineering applications. They are a global leader in this area. Efficient and easy to use, they reduce leakages by up to 90 per cent.

They have online services, where they have a supplier collaboration centre that enables suppliers to instantly connect with MTU Aero Engines to perform business transactions through a central portal. They also have a customer portal that enables customers to instantly connect with MTU to submit enquiries, request quotations and place or track orders online (eMRO).

The engine manufacturer complies with all statutory requirements and has obtained ISO 14001 and the European Ecology Management Audit Scheme (EMAS) certification. The company publishes regular environmental statements to inform the public on current actions, their audit status and results.

MTU Aero Engines strictly monitors compliance with its ambitious quality standards at all times and across all levels of production and personnel. Its management system ensures the company observes all applicable legal and statutory regulations and clearly defines roles and responsibilities in the company. Compliance with quality requirements are verified by government agencies and through internal and external audits.

In May 2010, readers of the *International Aircraft Technology Engineering and Maintenance* (ATE&M) magazine chose the company to be the world's 'Best Engine MRO'. (www.mtu.de)

Voith

Voith is one of the largest family-owned enterprises in Europe that has its headquarters in Heidenheim in the state of Baden-Württemberg. The roots of the company go back to 1825 when Johann Matthäus Voith took charge of his father's workshop. In 1867, the Voith company officially came into existence. Voith continues to be a family-owned enterprise, owned by the descendants of Hans Voith and the founder J.M. Voith.

Today, Voith sets the standard in paper, energy, mobility and service markets. They have a current workforce of about 40,000 people in 50 countries. Consolidated sales for the Voith Group stood at €5.6 billion for fiscal year 2010. In fiscal year 2010, Voith boosted its R&D spending by 4.6 per cent of sales to €259 million. Voith has around 10,000 active patents, with around 400 being added every year. Hubert Lienhard is the present President and CEO of the Corporate Board of Management and Manfred Bischoff is the Chairman of the Supervisory Board.

Among their Fibre Environmental Solutions, they have complete stock preparation plants and systems, components for primary fibre and recovered paper. They also produce energy from the organic waste-load-in-process water and from residual materials.

They also have forming fabrics, press fabrics, dryer fabrics and belts for paper production. They provide services for complex rolls, cylinders and components, roll covers and coatings, on site-service, measuring technology and diagnostic solutions, roll design and optimisation

The Voith Hydro division is a full-line supplier for advanced hydro-electric equipment, technology and services for the renewable energy market. For more than 140 years, more than 40,000 generators and turbines have been installed worldwide by Voith Hydro.

They provide complete equipment, installations and services for hydro-power plants, all types of turbines, standard and customised generators, excitation systems, frequency converters, protection systems, transformers and switch yards for all voltages, followed, by power plant automation and control centres, plant management and diagnostics, shut-off valves and different types of pumps, from consulting, engineering, execution and commissioning and on to the service, modernisation and rehabilitation of existing hydropower plants.

The Voith Turbo division manufactures drive systems that efficiently drive and move machinery on land and at sea – safely, reliably and comfortably propel vehicles, save energy and reduce emissions. They develop state-of-the-art drive and braking systems for the industry, rail, road and marine sectors, offering mechanical, hydrodynamic, electrical and electronic solutions.

Among their main products, for the industry, they provide hydrodynamic couplings, variable speed/mechanical/safety and highly elastic couplings, variable speed planetary gears, hydrostatic components, Hirth serrations, heavy duty Cardan shafts and control technology for steam and gas turbines.

In road transport, they manufacture automatic transmissions for buses, hydrodynamic retarders, turbochargers and torsional vibration dampers for tractors, buses, coaches and trucks.

In rail transport, they manufacture drive systems for rail vehicles, final drives, self-locking differentials, Cardan shafts, cooling systems, Scharfenberg couplers, impact protection systems as well as the diesel hydraulic locomotive families, Voith Maxima and Voith Gravita.

While in marine transport, they manufacture Voith Schneider propellers, Voith water tractors, Voith Cycloidal rudders and the Voith Turbo-fins.

Finally, the Voith Industrial Services division provides technical services for key industries worldwide, such as the automotive, energy, petrochemical and other such industries, from maintenance, shut downs and engineering to machine installations, plant engineering and facility management. All services are adapted to the individual requirements of the respective industry and locations, so that customers can receive tailor-made solutions from one single source.

Voith has undertaken the world's largest tidal current power park project called the, Sea Turtle Tidal Park, outside the coast of the South Korean Jeollanam-Do province. This is another innovative step towards tapping into the inexhaustible potential of clean, CO_2-free tidal or ocean energy for human use. (www.voith.com)

ZF

ZF Friedrichshafen AG develops, produces and services driveline and chassis technologies for the automotive industry. They are a leading worldwide supplier to the automotive and other transport industries around the world.

The origins of the ZF Group date back to 1915 when on 20 August the Zahnradfabrik was founded in Friedrichshafen in the present state of Baden-Württemberg. The object of the company then was to produce gears and transmissions for aircraft, motor vehicles and motor boats. Founding signatories are the Luftschiffbau Zeppelin Gmbh (LZ), represented by Alfred Colsman and the Max Maag Zahnräder fabrik. Count Zeppelin of the famous Zeppelin air-ship, helped found the Zeppelin Foundation that would later spawn the ZF Group.

Today, with a workforce of about 71,500 employees, the company operates 121 production companies in 27 countries, with headquarters in Friedrichshafen. ZF is among the top 10 supplier companies to the automotive companies worldwide. The ZF Group in fiscal year 2011 had total revenues of €15.5 billion. Stefan Sommer is the present CEO and Chairman of the Management Board of the ZF Group, while Giorgio Behr is the Chairman of the Supervisory Board. ZF products make a major contribution to mobility worldwide. They develop and produce transmissions, steering systems, axles and chassis components as well as complete systems for passenger cars, commercial vehicles and off-road machinery. ZF is also an important transmission specialist for rail vehicles, marine craft and helicopters. They spent around €754 million on R&D for the year.

ZF is a decentralised company with divisions and business units that operate independently and respond flexibly to the needs of their customers. However, the group sets the strategy of divisions and business units, and the group's overall interests take priority over the individual interests of the divisions and business units. The group is divided into four divisions: power line technology, chassis technology, commercial vehicle technology and industrial technology. In addition, there are the independent business units ZF Services and Die Casting Technology. In 1999, ZF Friedrichshafen AG and Robert Bosch GmbH founded the joint venture ZF Lenksysteme GmbH.

In the Powertrain Technology division, ZF pools its activities for passenger car powertrain technology. This includes development, production and sale of transmissions, axle drives, powertrain modules, as well as powertrain components. In line with reinforced customer orientation, the powertrain technology division offers complete powertrain solutions and innovative units as well as assemblies, from the engine flange to the wheel, from a single source to passenger car manufacturers.

The Chassis Technology division has the overall responsibility for complete front and rear axle systems for vehicles of up to 6 tons. The division's portfolio also includes chassis and steering components, dampers, electronic damper and chassis systems, as well as rubber-metal and plastic components for vehicles of all the renowned global manufacturers.

The Commercial Vehicle technology division is responsible for the ZF Group's international business of powertrain and chassis technology for vehicles of over 3.5 tons. The product portfolio includes automated and manual transmissions, powershift transmissions and powertrain components such as clutches and electric drives for trucks and buses. The portfolio also is comprised of complete axle systems and chassis components for vehicles of all renowned commercial vehicle manufacturers worldwide.

In the Industrial Technology division, the ZF Group pools its activities for 'off-road' applications. This includes, the development and production of transmissions and axles for agricultural and construction machinery as well as powertrain technology for forklift trucks, rail and military vehicles. The division is also responsible for the worldwide business of marine propulsion systems and aviation technology as well as the development and production of wind turbine gearboxes. In addition, the portfolio includes electronic components and switch systems as well as test systems for all applications.

ZF Services combines SACHS, LEMFÖRDER, BOGE and ZF Parts product brands as well as the global offering of the ZF group in retail, services and customer service. The business unit is currently represented by approximately 2,600 employees and aims to strengthen international customer service and to expand the after-sales business with new products and services.

As one of the world's leading automotive suppliers, ZF Friedrichshafen AG is naturally also involved in motor sports. ZF Race Engineering, a wholly-owned subsidiary of ZF Friedrichshafen AG, develops, designs, builds and markets shock absorbers and clutches especially for racing and high-performance series-production automobiles.

ZF secures the standards of tomorrow through a worldwide purchasing and product programme. The quality of ZF products is significantly influenced by the quality performance of the company's suppliers. Along with a quality management system based on ISO/TS 16949, ZF requires its suppliers to adopt effective measures to ensure the quality of all products and processes.

ZF Technology has also won various awards over the years, some of the recent ones being the 'Bus of the Year 2011' with ZF technology. It also received the 'Auto Parts Technological Innovation and Progress Award' in China for its innovative and cost-effective automatic transmission systems.

All ZF production sites operate an externally assessed environmental management system in compliance with the international environmental management standard, ISO 14001.

ZF hilft is a charitable organisation that provides humanitarian aid worldwide and helps in education, culture and sports and in other socially-responsible projects in developing countries. (www.zf.com)

MAHLE

MAHLE is a leading global development partner for the automotive and engine industry. They offer unique systems competence in the internal combustion engine and engine peripherals. The MAHLE Group ranks among the top three systems suppliers worldwide for piston systems, cylinder components, valve train, air-management and liquid-management systems. Almost all automobile and engine manufacturers around the world are customers of MAHLE.

The company was founded in 1920 as a small test workshop by the Mahle brothers, Hermann and Ernst Mahle, in Stuttgart-Canstatt.

Today, the group has grown into a global company and a technology leader. MAHLE has a local presence in all the major world markets. Around 49,000 employees work at over 100 production plants and eight R&D centres in Stuttgart, Northampton, Detroit (Farming Hills, Novi), Tokyo (Kawagoe, Okegawa), Shanghai and São Paulo (Jundiai), where around 3,000 development engineers and technicians work on innovative concepts, products and systems for the on-going development of vehicle power trains.

In fiscal year 2011, the MAHLE Group achieved Sales of €6 billion. Heinz K. Junker is the Chairman and CEO of the MAHLE Management Board. In 1964, the company founders Hermann and Ernst Mahle transferred ownership of the group to the non-profit MAHLE Foundation, which has held and administered all company shares since then in a fiduciary capacity. The corporate slogan of the MAHLE Group is 'Driven by Performance'.

MAHLE has two major business divisions: engine systems and components and filtration and engine peripherals. In the first division, they manufacture piston systems, cylinder components and valve train systems, while in the second division they manufacture air management and liquid management systems. These two divisions essentially cater to the automobile and engine manufacturers and the OEMs around the world.

The MAHLE Industry business division includes products such as large engines, industrial filtration systems as well as cooling and air-conditioning systems for railways, special vehicles, buses, ships, construction, agricultural machinery, the aerospace industry and stationary large engines for power generation. They also have an after-market business unit that offers products and spare parts for vehicle maintenance and engine repair. A small engine components business unit offers cylinder assemblies, cylinder heads, pistons and filters for small engines in hand-held power equipment, motorcycles and leisure vehicles.

The motor-sports business unit develops and produces high-quality engine components for motor sports: pistons, piston rings, piston pins, connecting rods, NIKASIL® coated cylinder surfaces, liners, bearings and bushings.

Their engineering services unit does development work that covers the full spectrum of engine design and manufacture from the initial concept to the development of complete new engines.

Finally, in the field of mechatronics, they develop and produce mechatronics systems and components for automotive applications.

MAHLE's current quality strategy is based on optimum production facilities as well as the 'Total Quality Management System' introduced in the early nineties. They have uniformly high-quality standards and a 'Zero-Error Strategy'.

Over the years, MAHLE has won several top awards for quality, best supplier and delivery from several of their blue-chip customers and several international bodies.

The MAHLE Foundation serves charitable causes by supporting healthcare, youth welfare, schooling, general adult and vocational education as well as several projects worldwide in collaboration with the UN, UNESCO, United Way and other such organisations. (www.mahle.com)

Fraport

Fraport AG, the owner and manager of Frankfurt Airport (FRA), is one of the leading companies in the international airport business. The company was founded in 1924 as the Südwest deutsche Luftverkehr AG. In June 2001, Fraport AG (a joint-stock company) – formerly Flughafen Frankfurt / Main AG – successfully completed its initial public offering with a listing on the Frankfurt Stock Exchange. Fraport's home base is Frankfurt Airport, which marked its 75th anniversary in 2011. Stefan Schulte is Executive Board Chairman (CEO) and Karlheinz Weimar holds the position of Supervisory Board Chairman. Fraport generated revenues of €2.37 billion in 2011, while employing an average of 20,595 people worldwide in 2011, including 18,391 based at FRA.

With more than 56 million passengers and 2.1 million metric tons of cargo in 2011, FRA ranks among the world's top 10 airports for passenger and cargo traffic. Frankfurt serves as the main European hub in the dense global network of the Star Alliance airlines. Frankfurt Airport not only has a reputation as a fast transfer airport but also boasts excellent intermodal connections, linking air, rail and road transportation. More than an airport, FRA is evolving into the Frankfurt Airport City, an attractive business location and globally connected urban centre, where some 75,000 people work at well over 500 different organisations.

Frankfurt Airport (FRA) is one of the busiest air transportation hubs in Europe and Europe's number two airport for cargo. Fraport is constantly expanding facilities according to demand to meet the forecast increase in worldwide passenger traffic. A new landing runway, a third passenger terminal and new A380 maintenance facilities are some of the key developments that will make it a mega hub and evolve into an airport city that sets new standards in quality and service. FRA also features a new real estate development, the Squaire complex – billed as a New Work City, a new working and living environment, with shops, offices, hotels and restaurants located on the rooftop of the long-distance train station.

The Fraport Executive Board is responsible for the company's strategic and operative business grouped into four business segments (aviation, ground handling, retail and real estate and global activities) as well as Fraport's national and international holdings. Fraport's extensive experience and know-how is increasingly in demand around the globe. The products and services offered by Fraport include airport management and consulting, traffic and terminal management, airport and aviation security, ground services, airport retailing, real estate management, parking facility management, intermodality, IT services, airport advertising and innovations. Fraport's portfolio includes a total of 13 airports on four continents worldwide. Its value-proven solutions, which stand for top quality, have been acclaimed and are in great demand globally. Fraport now operates in 13 airports worldwide and provides its expertise through numerous subsidiaries, including in Antalya (Turkey), Lima (Peru), New Delhi (India), St. Petersburg (Russia) and Xi'an in China.

A leader in sustainability initiatives, Fraport is listed regularly on the Dow Jones Sustainability Index (DJSI), thus making Fraport the only airport operator in the world to be in the DJSI. Price Waterhouse Coopers also awarded Fraport with the 'Sam Silver Class 2010' in their Sustainability Year Book of 2010. In terms of good corporate responsibility, community relations and regional support, Fraport AG is active in a variety of fields ranging from support of local school projects to being the lead sponsor of the professional Fraport Skyliners basketball team in Frankfurt as well as the Eintracht Frankfurt soccer team. Fraport also supports various arts and cultural institutions, projects and events in the Frankfurt/Rhine-Main region.

In recent years, Frankfurt Airport and Fraport AG have received numerous national and international awards, such as the 'Total E-Quality' award for equal opportunities in employment, the 'Pre-Certificate in Gold' by the German Sustainability Building Council (DGND) for its new headquarters building, the 'ACE Award for Excellence' from the *Air Cargo World* magazine for handling air freight over 1 million metric tons, the 'Baggage Improvement Program' of IATA which awarded Fraport AG as the best baggage handling airport worldwide and the UK Consulting Company Skytrax which gave FRA its Four-Star rating for passenger service satisfaction. (www.fraport.com)

Würth

The Würth Group is a world market leader in assembly and fastening products. This company was established in 1945, when Adolf Würth started a wholesale firm in Künzeslau, in the Hohenlohe region of southern Germany to supply screws, nuts and bolts.

Today, the Würth Group with headquarters in Künzeslau-Gailsbach has a stable of 400 companies spread over 80 countries. They have over 65,000 employees on their payroll, of which 32,000 are employed as sales representatives. For financial year 2011, they had a group turnover of more than €9.7 billion.

The Würth Group is a family-owned business, of which Reinhold Würth is the Chairman of the Supervisory Board of the Würth Group's family trusts. Bettina Würth is the Chairwoman of the Advisory Board and Robert Friedmann the Chairman of the Central Managing Board of the Würth Group. There are 22 members of the executive board who look after the operational management of the group and are in charge of its strategic business units.

The companies are divided into two divisions or units; companies belonging to the Würth Line and Allied Companies. The Würth Line operations focus on assembly and fastening products, supplying customers in the trades, the construction sector and industry with over 100,000 products from screws, screw accessories and anchors to tools, chemical-technical products and personal protection equipment. Internationally, the operational business units within the Würth Line is comprised of the metal, auto, wood, construction and industry divisions. The metal division includes the sub-divisions of metal, household technology and maintenance, while the auto subdivisions are car and cargo.

Allied Companies are companies that operate as a trade or production business in related business areas, as well as logistics companies and financial service providers. Their operational units are listed as, electrical wholesale, trade, the reca Group, production, tools, electronics, screws and standard parts, financial services and diversification into other areas.

As a good corporate citizen, they are involved in many initiatives supporting charitable organisations and promoting numerous projects in the fields of art and culture, research and science as well as education. They are among the major sponsors of sports such as soccer, winter sports, motor-sports and the Special Olympics. The Würth Group also has an extensive training and developmental program for their employees. In 2009, Würth was chosen for the German Logistics Award for its project, Modular Logistics: The Solution for Multi-channel Sales. (www.wuerth.com)

Axel Springer

Axel Springer AG is one of the largest multimedia companies in Europe; active in over 35 countries they offer over 230 newspapers and magazines and over 160 online offerings. They also have more than 120 apps.

Established by the publisher of the same name in Hamburg in 1946, today Axel Springer AG is Germany's largest newspaper and third-largest magazine publisher. Its broad media portfolio consists of well-established multimedia brand families such as the BILD (Picture) and DIE WELT (The World) groups.

In 2011, they had over 12,800 employees and generated total revenue of around €3.184 billion. Mathias Döpfner is the present Chairman of the Executive Board and CEO of the company, while, Giuseppe Vita is the Chairman of the Supervisory Board.

Their national media consists of a diverse range of media brands that come under the aegis of the Axel Springer umbrella. Whether print that includes the BILD and the WELT Group publications, online or audio-visual, they cover national and regional news, sports, cars and women's magazines and TV program guides. They also have computers, consumer electronics and lifestyle magazines. In addition to numerous special interest titles, online classified advertising portals such as *Step Stone* and *Immonet,* as well as online markets and general interest portals such as *autohaus24.de, buecher.de,* etc., they also publish the German version of *Rolling Stones* magazine. In television and radio they have a broad holdings portfolio. BILD their daily newspaper and flagship brand is Europe's largest circulating tabloid.

In international media they are active in practically every country in Europe and in Russia as well. They are very strong in Eastern Europe with their joint venture Ringier Axel Springer Media. In Western Europe they are strong in Switzerland, Spain and France.

Several of Axel Springer's media services are also published abroad as licensed editions. In 2010, Axel Springer also expanded its activities in India.

Axel Springer's sustainability report meets the specifications of the Global Reporting Initiative (GRI) and was given an A+. In 2008, they won the 'German Sustainability Award' in the category of 'Most Sustainable Purchasing'. Around 65 per cent of the printing paper used in the entire company contains recycled used paper. They are committed to progressively reduce their greenhouse gas emissions and to mitigate their environmental impact. Particular attention is paid to the optimisation of sustainability across the external stages of the value chain for products and services as well. Axel Springer also acknowledges and supports the United Nations, Universal Declaration of Human Rights and does not tolerate any behaviour that disregards it.

They have also contributed millions of Euros for several charitable projects including, A Heart for Children, the BILD aid organisation, among others. At Axel Springer, good corporate governance is guided by the German principles of sound corporate management laid down by the German Corporate Governance Code. (www.axelspringer.de)

CHAPTER 5

The Facilitators and Influencers

Facilitators and influencers are important elements to the 'Made in' national brand. In this chapter, I attempt to identify and describe the elements that facilitate, influence and enhance the 'Made in Germany' brand. Several of them can be called brands in themselves, on their own merits and by their performance and reputation over the years.

'National Identity plays a key role in nation branding', states Keith Dinnie in his book, *Nation Branding*, and as he elaborates, '... An awareness and understanding of the core features of national identity is a prerequisite for developing nation-branding campaigns, as the essence of any nation brand derives not only from the country's companies and brands but also from its culture in the widest sense – language, literature, music, sport, architecture and so on all embody the soul of a nation'. (Dinnie)

So to put forth an authentic understanding of a nation brand, one needs to study the social and cultural elements of a nation brand to get a glimpse into its holistic identity and all that makes for an authentic differentiator to the nation brand: the facilitators and influencers.

I would call the social and cultural elements of a nation brand the 'influencers', that is the positive, unique and differentiated images, as viewed by people from other countries and cultures. The elements that I have included concern Germany's rich literature, art and artists, music and musicians, architecture past and present, design, sports and sportsmen and a little about the media, films, food, drink and festivals. These have been included so that the reader gets a basic understanding of German society and culture in its broadest sense and the positive impact and influence they have had on its image as a nation to the rest of the world – Germany's positive contribution and enrichment to the world's knowledge and culture.

Germany, as most of you know, is called 'Deutschland' by the Germans themselves, and the German language is called 'Deutsch' by the natives. German is primarily spoken in Germany, Austria and by a large section of the populace in Switzerland. It is also spoken by the majority in Luxembourg and Liechtenstein. Like most other languages, standard German differs regionally and between German-speaking countries in vocabulary, pronunciation and even grammar. The German dialects are the traditional local variations. The earliest testimonies of the language date back to around the sixth century AD. The English language over the years has borrowed several words from the German language and in the process has enriched itself. Popular words include *uber, zeitgeist, gestalt, blitz, kindergarten, kitsch, leitmotif, wanderlust, wunderkind, rucksack, Kafkaesque, usw* which stands for *und so weiter* (and so on), etc. The German umlaut is a diacritical mark (in this case two dots ¨) that is placed over the vowels Ä, Ö and Ü in certain words and is used to signify a certain pronunciation. The German eszett ß has been made less common by the use of ss instead of ß. The German language is now one of the official and working languages in the European Union.

Another important element in this section is the introduction of the 'facilitators' to the whole process, for the 'Made in Germany' brand to manifest. I have briefly mentioned them before and here I shall endeavour to provide some more detail to them. They are the people and institutions who have to a great degree facilitated the process of the production and marketing of quality German goods and services.

Among the important facilitators that I have included here are the various research institutes and organisations that have contributed over the years to promoting scientific research in the various scientific and technological disciplines that have produced new scientific discoveries, breakthroughs, inventions and innovations.

Also discussed are the industry, trade and standards organisations that have played a crucial role in facilitating the growth of various industries and making sure the politicians and the political process are duly informed of the correct policy measures to take to encourage the respective industries/sectors. They have been the primary organisations representing the various industry groups in Germany and in facilitating an environment that has been conducive to the efficient and high-quality production of the 'Made in Germany' brands.

Standardisation is a strategic instrument for a company and a brand to succeed, as it facilitates its acceptance and market entry. Not only does it promote worldwide trade but it also encourages product/service rationalisation, quality assurance and environmental protection as well as improves on security and communication. Furthermore, it also has a positive effect on the entire product innovation process from basic research to marketing of new products.

The third important facilitator in this process is the trade fairs and exhibitions held throughout Germany that have not only boosted the German economy in real terms but also have facilitated the purpose of providing a platform to exhibit their products and services, a market place for the supply and demand in various individual business markets and sectors. Being international in nature, they have to a degree made Germany a successful exporting nation apart from enhancing and presenting the 'Made in Germany' brands in a positive light and to a global audience.

Finally, I have also included a brief description about the German political system, the main political parties and their leaders. I chose to include this section here as they constitute one of the important facilitators in the whole process of the 'Made in Germany' brands.

So, these facilitators and influencers play a major role in the making of the 'Made in Germany' brand and here's to getting to know them a little better.

Research Institutes and Organisations

The research landscape in Germany is fairly wide and varied, with a range of disciplines, research facilities and competent staff. The research locations include the usual universities, private institutes and societies, companies and federal and state-run research organisations.

There are more than 750 publicly-funded research institutions and organisations, as well as R&D centres run by industrial corporations. Together, they employ around 506,000 staff in R&D and 299,000 scientists and scholars. They have bilateral, multilateral and European cooperation with more than 40 countries and an annual research budget of around €61.5 billion!

The theory of relativity, computers, automobiles, teddy bears and aspirin are all German inventions. It is said that Germany registers an average of one patent every 22 minutes. The German government has launched a national initiative in 17 key fields, calling it 'The High-Tech Strategy for Germany'. It specifically aims to promote technologies and efforts in the selected fields, as well as cooperation with developing and other key countries in science and research, thereby contributing decisively to more international responsibility.

The significant and leading research institutes and organisations in Germany are described below.

FRAUNHOFER

The Fraunhofer-Gesellschaft (Society) conducts applied research for private as well as public enterprises and for the general benefit of the public. It has more than 80 research facilities overall, including 60 Fraunhofer institutes in Germany, and is the largest organisation for applied research in Europe. The society takes its name from Joseph von Fraunhofer (1787–1826), the illustrious German researcher, inventor and entrepreneur. One of Fraunhofer Institute's famous inventions is the MP3 which was developed in 2000. MP3, as most of you know, is the most widely adopted method for encoding and decoding digital audio. Fraunhofer is based in Munich and employs around 18,000 people, mainly scientists and engineers. They work on different areas of research such as information and communication technology, life sciences, microelectronics, surface technology, photonics, production, defence and security, materials and components. They have an annual budget of around €1.65 billion and have research centres and representative offices in the world's major economic regions.

THE HELMHOLTZ ASSOCIATION OF GERMAN RESEARCH CENTRES

The Helmholtz Association of German Research Centres is the largest scientific organisation in Germany. Its work follows the tradition of the great natural scientist Hermann von Helmholtz (1821–1894). Scientists in 17 Helmholtz Centres work on a wide range of topics ranging from space research conducted by the German Aerospace Centre (DLR) to research on the structure of matter at DESY, one of the world's leading accelerator centres. Around 30,000 people are employed by them, of which around 9,700 scientists and another 4,500 visiting scientists work in the core areas of energy, earth and environment, health, key technologies, structure of matter, aeronautics, space and transport. They have their headquarters in Bonn and an annual budget of €3.0 billion. Furthermore the association's research centres provides the most modern, scientific infrastructure, particularly large-scale facilities and instrumentation which is also used by the international scientific community.

THE LEIBNIZ ASSOCIATION

The Gottfried Wilhelm Leibniz Scientific Community (WGL), known as the Leibniz Association, is the umbrella organisation for 87 research institutions, which address scientific issues of importance to society as a whole. This association is named after the seventeenth- to eighteenth-century German mathematician and philosopher of the same name. He is known for his major contributions to physics and technology and a wide array of other subjects from biology to philosophy and philology.

Together they employ more than 16,000 people, of which 7,100 are scientists, and have an annual budget of more than €1.3 billion. The centres focus their research on humanities and social sciences, economics, spatial and life sciences, as well as on mathematics, natural sciences, engineering and environmental research. The Leibniz research institutes also performs research-based services, liaison, consultation and transfer of knowledge for public policy makers, academia and business.

THE MAX PLANCK SOCIETY

The Max Planck Society is an independent, non-profit research organisation named after the world-famous physicist Max Planck (1858–1947) who discovered quantum physics. He is said to be the founder of quantum theory, for which he received the Nobel Prize in physics in 1918.

The society is based in Munich and has 80 research institutes, of which four are abroad. They employ over 13,000 people and have an annual budget of around €1.3 billion a year. The fields of research are natural sciences, life sciences, social sciences and humanities. A total of 17 of its scientists have received the Nobel Prize since its foundation in 1948. The society is involved in numerous international cooperation projects such as institutes abroad, partner groups and multi-national research facilities. Around 5,000 foreign visiting scientists work at the Max Planck Institutes on around 2,300 ongoing international research projects.

UNIVERSITIES

Germany is home to around 400 universities providing a variety of disciplines of which over 200 are universities of applied science. They cover a broad spectrum of research activities, including basic research, applied research and development. Around 245,000 international students are enrolled at German higher educational institutions, where some 18,000 international graduate students a year are studying for their doctorates and another 26,000 foreign academics work in German higher education and research.

ACADEMIES OF SCIENCE

The key mission of the German academies of science, namely Leopoldina, acatech and Union of the German Academies of Science and Humanities, is the coordination and support of long-term research projects and the development and cultivation of interdisciplinary dialogues. They run symposia and public events, contributing to a dialogue between science, society and industry. With considered opinions, the academies support policy-makers and the public in finding suitable answers to current issues and problems.

FEDERAL INSTITUTIONS

The federal government funds 38 federal R&D institutes that the federal ministries are in charge of. This departmental research is always directly related to the activity fields of the concerned ministry. Some examples are the Robert Koch Institutes which is responsible for disease control and prevention, and the Federal Institute for Materials Research and Testing, BAM, which is responsible for the development of safety and reliability in chemistry and materials technologies.

LÄNDER INSTITUTIONS

The states (Länder) of Germany also act as research funding bodies and run several research institutions which contribute to supporting the research activities of the respective states. Today, there are more than 130 institutes/organisations covering a broad range of research areas, from engineering and natural sciences to the humanities. One example is the Centre for Solar Energy and Hydrogen Research in the State of Baden Württemberg.

COMPANIES/INDUSTRIAL RESEARCH

German companies are among the most research active in Europe. After the US and Japan, Germany registers the highest number of triadic patents worldwide. In all, 38 per cent of the research sector is represented by automotive, 19 per cent, by electronics, 14 per cent by chemical, 11 per cent by mechanical engineering and the remaining 18 per cent by other sectors. Around 322,000 people are employed in total in this area by various companies and industries, and together they spend around €46.1 billion annually on R&D.

THE GERMAN FEDERATION OF INDUSTRIAL RESEARCH ASSOCIATIONS (AIF)

The German Federation of Industrial Research Associations (AiF) was founded in 1954, as a registered non-profit association that promotes research and development in all industry sectors in favour of small and medium-sized enterprises (SMEs). There are 101 non-commercial research consortia, 46 research facilities of its own and more than 700 closely connected institutes. The AiF is organised by the industry to increase the competitive strength of SMEs by supporting usage and advancement of R&D programs.

NETWORKS AND CLUSTERS

The German federal government has initiated a series of projects aimed at the creation of networks and clusters that promote new technologies in engineering, biotechnology, energy and environment, chemistry and nanotechnology, amongst others. The German government pools both industry and academic institutions in their research and development activity. One key aim of these aggregations is to accelerate the process of making new technology products marketable.

Other research infrastructures funded by the federal government with global significance also exist in physics, earth science, climate research and the humanities. (Sources: see Note 1)

Industry and Certification Organisations

In Germany, the various industry and trade associations and certification/standardisation organisations play a crucial role in the development of various products, industries and in the growth of the economy as a whole. There are several umbrella groups and specific associations that cater to the needs of specific industry sectors. As regards certification and standards organisations, they too play a significant role in maintaining those quality norms and standards required of various products and services. They are essential to giving credibility to those products and services, so that consumers are reassured about their quality and efficacy and that they meet all the required industry and governmental standards and regulations.

In this section we shall briefly look into some of the most important organisations regarding the trade/industry and certifications/standards for Germany.

THE BDI OR FEDERATION OF GERMAN INDUSTRIES

The BDI or Federation of German Industries is the umbrella organisation of German industry; it is an association of associations, the voice of German industry. As per BDI's statues, membership is confined to 'industrial sector associations and working groups acting as umbrella organisations to represent entire industrial groups within the territory of the Federal Republic of Germany'. It speaks on behalf of 38 sector associations and represents over 100,000 large, medium-sized and small enterprises with 8 million employees.

The BDI's legal status is that of a registered society. The BDI is the umbrella organisation for industrial businesses and industry-related business service providers. As the representative of the interests of industry, the BDI coordinates the views and recommendations of its members. It also provides information concerning all fields of economic policy, thus supporting businesses in the task of staying competitive. Headquartered in Berlin, they have representations in each of the other states, offices abroad in London, Washington and Tokyo and partners in other national and international organisations.

There is a presidential board, made up of the president, who at present is Ulrich Grillo, his predecessor, the treasurer, as well as seven other representatives and 15 further elected members of the board. The competences and issues the BDI works on are as follows: SMEs and family businesses, economy, location and competition, globalisation, international markets and trade, Europe and Brussels, climate and environment, energy and resources, infrastructure and logistics, research, innovation and technology, information society and telecommunications, law and public procurement, security and defence, society, responsibility and consumers and tax and financial policy.

BDI considers itself firmly committed to a basic economic model: the social market economy founded by the late Chancellor Ludwig Erhard. This entails advocating more free entrepreneurship, unrestricted competition and social equilibrium.

THE ASSOCIATION OF GERMAN CHAMBERS OF INDUSTRY AND COMMERCE (DIHK)

The Association of German Chambers of Industry and Commerce (DIHK) is the central organisation for 80 chambers of industry and commerce in Germany. All German companies registered in Germany, with the exception of handicraft businesses, the free professions and farms are required by law to join a chamber.

Thus, the DIHK speaks for more than 3.6 million entrepreneurs. They include not only large corporations but also retailers and inn keepers. This gives the association considerable political influence. It does not represent any specific corporate group but all commercial enterprises in Germany. The DIHK's highest executive body is the General Assembly, in which all the Chambers of Industry and Commerce (IHK) are represented by their presidents and executive managers. The General Assembly elects the president and the vice presidents of the DIHK. The board of directors is provided by the chambers of industry and commerce. As a critical partner of policy-makers, they work within the municipalities and at the regional, national and European level to shape the opinions and decisions of political decision-makers. They safeguard all regulations that are binding on market participants and support companies in achieving their objectives by providing them with first-class products and services. The chambers have 16 specialist technical committees to advise the members from the business community, from foreign trade, finance and tax to research, communications and legal matters, the environment, energy and transport, to credit, budget, health and new services covering 16 important areas.

The IHK organisation works abroad through the German Chambers of Commerce Abroad (AHK) in those countries to resolve problems relating to the business locations of German firms worldwide and to promote investment in Germany.

The chambers are public corporations and responsible for their own affairs. They are business institutions and the principle representative of all commercial undertakings in their respective region(s).

GERMANY TRADE AND INVEST

With offices around the globe the GTAI is the economic development agency of the Federal Republic of Germany. Working in close cooperation with the worldwide network of German Chambers of Commerce Abroad (AHKs), they provide the latest information to German companies seeking to expand their businesses abroad and support companies looking to enter Germany with expert advice. Apart from promoting Germany as a business and technology location, the GTAI also provides market and industry reports, business and tax law information, customs and tariff conditions, international project notifications, calls for tender and business contacts as well as other practical business information.

TÜV RHEINLAND AG

TÜV Rheinland AG is based in Cologne, and is a global provider of technical, safety and certification services. It was founded in 1872, when a group of entrepreneurs started the Dampfkessel-Überwachungs-Vereine (DÜV) or the 'Steam Boiler Inspectorate' to ensure the safety of steam boilers. Today, the group employs more than 16,000 people in 500 locations in 65 countries and generated annual revenues of around €1.417 billion for 2011. They are driven by the conviction that social and industrial development can only be achieved through technological progress and the safe deployment of technical innovations, products and facilities. The group's mission is to achieve sustainable development of safety and quality in order to meet challenges arising from the interaction between man, technology and the environment. The TÜV® brand is synonymous with neutrally tested quality and safety.

Manfred Bayerlein is the present CEO of the Executive Board of TÜV Rheinland AG, while Bruno O. Braun is the Chairman of the Supervisory Board. The TÜV Rheinland Group incorporates a total of over 120 group companies. The operational holding company is TÜV Rheinland AG, of which TÜV Rheinland Berlin Brandenburg Pfalz e.V. is the sole shareholder.

The Group currently provides around 2,500 services. They pool their activities into 36 business fields that are assigned to six business streams: industrial services, mobility, products, life care, education and consulting and systems. The triangular logo of the group has inspired trust and is recognised around the world as a symbol of safety and quality tested by an independent and neutral organisation. 'Precisely Right' is their corporate slogan.

TÜV SÜD AG

TÜV SÜD AG was founded in 1866 in the German region of Bavaria. Today, with headquarters in Munich, it is the leading technical service corporation that is more than a testing and inspection organisation. TÜV SÜD's certified experts and technical consultants provide services throughout their client's entire value chains. In doing so, they focus on their core competencies of consulting, testing, certification and training. Around 17,000 employees proactively optimise technology, systems and expertise at over 800 locations in Europe, America and Asia. In 2011, they increased their sales revenue to around €1.677 billion. Axel Stepken is the present CEO of TÜV SÜD AG and Chairman of the Board of Management, while Hans-Jörg Bullinger is the Chairman of the Supervisory Board. The strategy and business segments of the group are essentially three: industry, mobility and certification. Their corporate slogan is 'Choose Certainty. Add Value'. It is owned by TÜV SÜD e.v. and the TÜV SÜD Foundation which holds, 74.9 per cent and 25.1 per cent of the shares, respectively.

DIN DEUTSCHES INSTITUT FÜR NORMUNG E.V.

DIN Deutsches Institut für Normung e.V. is the German Institute for Standardisation that offers stakeholders a platform for the development of standards as a service to the industry, the state and society. It is a registered non-profit association that has been based in Berlin since 1917.

DIN's primary task is to work closely with its stakeholders to develop consensus-based standards that meet market requirements. Around 28,000 experts contribute their skills and experience to the standardisation process. By agreement with the German Federal Government, DIN is the acknowledged national standards body that represents German interests in European and international standards organisations. At present, around 90 per cent of the standards work carried out by DIN are international in nature.

THE STIFTUNG WARENTEST (THE FOUNDATION FOR PRODUCT TESTING)

The Stiftung Warentest (The Foundation for Product Testing) is an independent foundation established under civil law in 1964 in Berlin by the federal government of Germany. The aim of the foundation is to serve the domestic consumer through comparative testing of goods and services and to offer an independent and objective analysis and report about them. They purchase goods and services anonymously and use scientific methods conducted by independent institutes in accordance with their guidelines. They evaluate the products and services tested, from 'very good' to 'poor', exclusively on the basis of their objective findings. They then publish the test ads in their journals and financial reviews and on their website. The tested products and services are permitted to print the individual test results on their packaging and promotional literature/advertising. In the 45 years since its foundation, they have conducted around 5,000 tests for around 100,000 products and over 2,000 service tests for services. The results are published each year in more than 8.5 million books. The foundation is financed by the sale of its publications, especially the test journals and financial tests, while the German government funds around 11 per cent of their annual budget. (Sources: see Note 2)

Trade Fairs and Exhibitions

As per AUMA, the Association of the German Trade Fair Industry, every year around 134 international and national trade fairs and exhibitions boost the German economic output by around €23.5 billion. These events also provide around 226,000 people with full-time jobs while generating €3.8 billion in taxes at the federal, state and municipal level. This is in addition to fulfilling the main purpose of providing a place and transparency for supply and demand in various individual sectors. In effect, they have a considerable overall economic impact when you take into consideration the amount spent by exhibitors and visitors as well. They offer a platform for well over 200,000 exhibitors and around 16 to 18 million visitors per year in addition to 9.526 million registered visitors. Furthermore, over 100,000 congresses and conferences are held annually in the business-to-business sector. The ones that accompany trade fairs attract another 400,000 visitors annually.

The key positive aspect of the German trade fairs is their internationality. More than half of the exhibitors come from abroad, of which one-third are from countries outside Europe. Of the visitors, almost one-fifth come from abroad.

To hold these trade fairs and exhibitions, around 6.2 million square meters of hall space is available at 22 German exhibition centres. Three of the five largest exhibition centres in the world are located in Germany. For German companies, trade fairs are among the most important vehicles in business-to-business communication and engagement. I will briefly describe some of the largest and most significant international trade fairs and exhibitions being conducted in Germany on a regular basis.

HANNOVER MESSE

The Hannover Messe remains the world's leading showcase for industrial technology. First started around 60 years ago in the city of Hannover in Germany, the Hannover Messe is the ideal place to obtain the latest industrial know-how. Today, it ranks as the leading international showplace for industrial technologies, materials and product ideas. Over the years, the focus has shifted from stand-alone components to end-to-end solutions. Technical innovation with a sharp focus on the creative application of existing knowledge is another. Here the visitor can experience complete value chains and swap information with experts from a complete spectrum of industry sectors.

CEBIT

CeBIT is the world's largest trade fair showcasing IT and telecommunications solutions for home and work environments. Deutsche Messe AG has organised CeBIT in Hannover each spring since 1986. The key target groups are new users from industry, the wholesale/retail sector, skilled trades, banks, the services sector, government agencies, science and all users passionate about technology. This tradeshow offers an international platform for comparing notes on current industry trends, networking and product presentations. Around 4,240 companies from 70 countries exhibited at CeBIT 2011.

THE FRANKFURT BOOK FAIR

The Frankfurt Book Fair is the largest of its kind in the world – a special event for global activities in the field of culture. It is the most important marketplace for books, media, rights and licenses worldwide. It is a meeting place for the industry's experts, be they publishers, booksellers, agents, film producers or authors. Each year in October, more than 7,400 exhibitors from over 100 countries and 300,000 visitors and over 9,000 journalists all come together and create something new. The history of the Frankfurt book fair dates back to the fifteenth century, when Johannes Gutenberg first invented the movable type or printing, in 1439, only a few kilometres from Frankfurt. This helped kick-start the Printing Revolution in Europe.

TENDENCE

Tendence is the consumer goods event with the largest international product range from arts and crafts, gift items, light industry and daily living items for the home to toys, bags, etc. Held in Frankfurt in the second half of the year, it includes exhibitors from all over the world. It's a must for buyers from all channels of distribution, because Tendence gives them the chance to order attractive products for the autumn, winter and Christmas seasons. Further, it showcases an initial preview of the trends for the coming spring and summer seasons. It stands for lifestyle and creativity in living and giving, besides providing inspiration through innovative concepts for the trade, trends and the latest design developments.

IFA

IFA is the leading tradeshow for consumer electronics and home appliances held in Berlin in September, attracting industry representatives from all over the world. This trade event serves as a global information and business platform. International experts from industry, commerce, the trades and media head to Berlin, where the leading consumer electronics and home appliances manufacturers present their latest products and innovations at IFA.

It started in 1924 in Berlin, when over 242 exhibitors came together to introduce their products at the first great 'German Radio and Phonograph Fair'.

ANUGA

As the world's most important food and beverages trade fair held in Cologne, Anuga enjoys a high regard and acceptance from exhibitors and visitors alike. Only at Anuga can you count on meeting all of the top-level national and international decision-makers from the trade, food service and catering market in one place. Anuga brings together 10 specialised trade shows under one roof. It also showcases the most important innovations and trends which generate new and dynamic momentum for the business. They also have high-quality supporting programs.

THE K FAIR

The K Fair is the largest international trade fair for plastics and rubber products held in Düsseldorf every three years. Its main product groups are raw materials, auxiliaries, semi-finished products, technical parts and reinforced plastics, machinery and equipment, as well as services for the plastics and rubber industries. No other trade fair offers such opportunities for experts in the automotive, packaging, electrical engineering, electronics and communications industries, as well as the construction, medical technology and aerospace sectors. Here they can learn about the latest developments in technical innovation in plastics and rubber applications first-hand.

DRUPA

drupa is the world's number one trade fair for the print media industry, held every four years in Düsseldorf. The next one is scheduled for 2016. It is a unique, must-see opportunity for industry experts, to see all the latest technologies and media production and processing – including 'Green Printing' live in action – for innovations, know-how and trends in the printing and paper sectors. In 2008 there were 800 exhibitors from 50 countries and visitors from around 122 countries.

INTERPACK

interpack is the world's most important trade fair for packaging and processes, offering visitors the most comprehensive range of products and innovations. Nowhere else will you find such an international, wide-ranging and innovative range of packaging machines and materials. Held every three years in Düsseldorf, the last one was in 2011. They showcase processes, machines, packaging materials, shipping materials for the packaging of food and beverages, pharmaceuticals, cosmetics, non-food consumer goods and industrial goods.

INTERNATIONAL TOY FAIR

The Spielwarenmesse or International Toy Fair, held annually in Nuremberg, is the world's leading fair for toys, hobby and leisure products. All the market leaders and top professionals from all over the world come together here. The fair, which is open exclusively to the specialist trade, provides a unique combination of a huge product range, targeted industry information and numerous networking opportunities. Around 2,700 exhibitors from 63 countries and more than 76,600 specialist visitors from over 104 countries make this annual visit. They display around 1 million products in 12 product groups with approximately 70,000 new products.

THE INTERNATIONAL HARDWARE FAIR

The International Hardware Fair is held in Cologne every two years. It last attracted around 56,500 visitors from 124 countries, with 2,686 exhibitors or suppliers from 52 countries displaying their new products and innovations in the sectors of tools, industrial supplies, fittings and fastenings, locks and fittings and home improvement. It is one of the world's leading trade platforms for the hardware sectors; indeed, suppliers and buyers from the hardware sector have been meeting in Cologne for more than 50 years. It is ideal for making contacts with various decision-makers from the hardware trade and industry.

PAPER WORLD

Paper World is the world's leading trade fair for paper, office supplies and the stationery sector. Held in Frankfurt annually, in 2012 1,800 exhibitors from all over the world presented new products and the next season's trends at Paper World. Over 49,000 visitors from around 142 countries came to visit this trade fair. The product groups here include office and school articles, writing and drawing instruments, gift articles, greeting cards/picture calendars, packaging, licences/designs and paper and film for the office and home. It is a top-order event with numerous innovations, awards ceremonies, trend shows and events apart from being one of the world's leading platforms for the presentation of new products in this industry. (Sources: see Note 3)

The Political System and Political Parties

The Federal Republic of Germany is a federal parliamentary democracy. There is a multi-party system that has been in operation since 1949. Although the President (Bundespräsident) of Germany is the head of state, it is a ceremonial role with substantial reserve powers and is a five-year term which is renewable once. Executive power is vested in the chancellor (Bundeskanzler/in) and the federal cabinet. Legislative power is vested in the Bundestag (the Parliament of Germany) and the Bundesrat which is the representative body of the 16 regional states of Germany at the federal level. The judiciary of Germany is an independent body. The Constitution or Grundgesetz (Basic Law) was formed in 1949 with minor amendments after Germany's reunification in 1990. At the state or regional level the 16 states are governed by a unicameral legislature which is usually called a Landtag (state assembly or parliament).

The present president of the Federal Republic of Germany is Joachim Gauck. He was elected by the federal convention that has been established for the sole purpose of electing the president. The chancellor of Germany is Angela Merkel, the first woman chancellor of Germany. The normal term of office is four years. She belongs to the CDU party of Germany. The previous federal government was a coalition of the CDU, CSU and the FDP parties.

The national flag of Germany is made up of three horizontal bands in black, red and golden yellow. Being a multi-party democracy, there are several types of parties spread all over the country. I will be giving brief profiles of the six main parties in terms of size and importance and a new, surprise addition to the German political spectrum.

THE CHRISTIAN DEMOCRATIC UNION (CDU)

The CDU is a Christian democratic and conservative political party that was founded in 1949. The leader of the party is Angela Merkel, the present Chancellor. It is a centre-right party that is pro-European. The CDU is a member of the European People's Party (EPP) and sits with the EPP Group in the European Parliament. The CDU is the largest party formation in the Federal Parliament (Bundestag) of Germany. This party has so far provided five German chancellors: Konrad Adenauer (1949–1963), Ludwig Erhard (1963–1966), Kurt Georg Kiesinger (1966–1969), Helmut Kohl (1982–1998) and Angela Merkel (2005–present). At present, they also have several cabinet ministers in the ruling coalition. Their official colours are black and orange and have their headquarters in Berlin. At the time of going to press, Merkel's CDU/CSU garnered the largest number of votes in the 2013 General Elections. Although short of an absolute majority, they are in talks with new coalition partners as their prior coalition partner, the FDP, fared poorly.

THE SOCIAL DEMOCRATIC PARTY (SPD)

The SPD is Germany's oldest and one of the largest parties in Germany that was first established in 1875. They are a socialist party that believes in social democracy and takes a centre-left position. At present they are the main opposition party in the Federal Parliament. The party is led by Sigmar Gabriel and Peer Steinbrück. The SPD is a full-member party of the Party of European Socialists and the Socialist International.

SPD German Chancellors after 1949 have been Willy Brandt (1969–1974), Helmut Schmidt (1974–1980) and Gerhard Schröder (1998–2005). Their official colour is red and they have their headquarters in Berlin.

THE CHRISTIAN SOCIAL UNION (CSU)

Another Christian democratic and conservative political party that operates only in the state of Bayern (Bavaria), the CSU is a sister party of the CDU, founded in 1945 with its headquarters in Munich. They also take a centre-right position. Their party leader is Horst Seehofer who serves as the Minister President of Bayern (Bavaria). The CSU is also a member of the European People's Party (EPP) and its MEPs sit with the EPP Group in the European Parliament. Their official colour is a light shade of blue.

THE FREE DEMOCRATIC PARTY (FDP)

The FDP is a centre-right, classical liberal party of Germany. It was founded in 1948 and has its headquarters in Berlin. They advocate liberalism in both the economic and social spheres. The party was led by a Vietnamese-born, medical doctor, Philipp Rösler who was the previous Vice-Chancellor and Federal Minister of Economics and Technology. The FDP was a junior coalition partner to the CDU/CSU in the federal government. A member of the European Liberal Democrat and Reform Party, they sit with the Alliance of Liberals and Democrats for Europe group in the European Parliament. Their official colours are yellow and blue.

ALLIANCE 90/THE GREENS (BÜNDNIS 90/DIE GRÜNEN)

Alliance 90/The Greens (Bündnis 90/Die Grünen) is a green political party formed from the merger of Alliance 90 and the German Green Party in 1993. Its present leaders are Claudia Roth and Cem Özdemir. The party advocates green politics, eco-socialism and green liberalism. They take a centre-left political position. The party headquarters are in Berlin while their official colour is green, of course, with a yellow sunflower.

In the 2009 federal elections, the party won 10.7 per cent of the votes and 68 out of the 622 seats in the Bundestag (Federal Parliament). In 2011, they managed to form a state coalition with the social democrats in the state of Baden-Württemberg. Their international affiliation is with the Global Greens and the European Green Party. In the European Parliament they sit with the Greens-European Free Alliance. Joschka Fischer and Petra Kelly were among their earlier important leaders.

THE LEFT (DIE LINKE)

The Left is among the most left-wing of the main German parties. They are a democratic, socialist political party who take a left-wing political position. It was founded in 2007 from a merger of two socialist parties, the PDS and the WASG. The party co-chairs are Katja Kipping and Bernd Riexinger. Their European affiliation is with the Party of the European Left and they sit with the European United Left-Nordic Green Left in the European Parliament. With headquarters in Berlin, their official colour is red, of course.

THE PIRATE PARTY OF GERMANY (PIRATEN PARTEI DEUTSCHLAND)

The Pirate Party of Germany (Piraten Partei Deutschland) is a fairly new party in Germany that is based on the model of the Swedish Piratpartiet and affiliated with Pirate Parties International. It was founded in September 2006 with headquarters in Berlin. The present party leader is Bernd Schlömer. The Pirate Party supports freedom of information, privacy, copyright and patent reform, transparency of the government, education, civil libertarianism and social liberalism. Although, they do not have any seats in the Federal Parliament, they were in the news for having won 9 per cent of the votes in the 2011 Berlin State Elections, securing 15 seats in the Landtag (State Assembly). (Source: see Note 4)

German Literature

German literature, in all its various genres and from different historical periods, has exerted an enormous influence not only on the history of Western thought, but also on the development of modern, contemporary thought in the world. The history of

German literature from the Middle Ages to the twentieth century has underscored the connections between its literature and the history of Germany as a nation. The literary and philosophical expressions of German writers were in response to the changes happening in its social, economic and political spheres. German literature has, nevertheless, left a lasting impression on the peoples of the world and has even influenced the course of modern history in many parts of the world.

I intend to very briefly cover the significant and noteworthy German writers who have helped influence the image of Germany, in more ways than one, from Goethe, Martin Luther, Karl Marx, and Sigmund Freud to Franz Kafka, Thomas Mann, Bertolt Brecht and Günter Grass.

Johann Wolfgang Von Goethe (1749–1832) was born on 28 August 1749 in Frankfurt. He is the famous German writer and polymath considered to be the most significant writer and thinker in the German language. Goethe was also a poet, novelist, playwright, philosopher, diplomat and civil servant. His works have spanned and influenced the fields of poetry, theatre, theology, philosophy, science and of course literature. His magnum opus is the two-part drama, *Faust*. Goethe's poems and novels are also very well known. A key figure of German literature, Classicism and Romanticism, he is the originator of the concept of 'Weltliteratur' or 'World Literature'. His many varied works have been a source of inspiration for many in the areas of music, drama, poetry, philosophy, and even science, where he is said to have influenced Charles Darwin! The German government's cultural institution, the Goethe-Institute, is named after him.

Martin Luther (1483–1546), the famous Christian monk, theologian and writer was born in Saxony. He started the Protestant Reformation movement in Europe when he published *The Ninety-Five Theses* in 1517. This Christian reform movement established Protestantism as a constituent branch of Christianity. His translation of the Bible into German had a major impact on the church in Germany. It also helped develop the standard version of the German language and influence the art of translation, including the later translation into English of the King James Bible. His other notable works include *Luther's Large Catechism* and *On the freedom of a Christian*. Luther was also a prolific hymn writer and it is said that his hymns influenced the development of singing in churches in Europe.

Immanuel Kant (1724–1804) was a German philosopher who was born in Königsberg, then a Prussian city, now in modern-day Russia. Kant is considered the last classical philosopher of modern Europe. He created a new perspective in philosophy which had widespread influences on various schools of philosophy and social and behavioural sciences, continuing through to the twenty-first century. His major works include *Critique of Pure Reason*, *What is Enlightenment* and *Critique of Judgement* among others. He also won the Berlin Academy Prize in 1754 for the discovery of the retardation of the rotation of the Earth!

Georg Wilhelm Friedrich Hegel (1770–1831) was born in Stuttgart and was a famous philosopher and one of the co-founders of German Idealism, also founder of Hegelianism and Historicism. He revolutionised European philosophy by establishing a comprehensive philosophical framework in an integral manner. He is said to have influenced a wide variety of prominent writers, including Marx, Nietzsche, Sartre, Russell and Heidegger among others. Hegel published only four books during his life, *The Phenomenology of Spirit*, *Science of Logic*, *Encyclopaedia of Philosophical Sciences* and *The Elements of the Philosophy of Right*.

Karl Heinrich Marx (1818–1883), born in Trier is the famous German political philosopher, historian, political economist/theorist, sociologist, communist and revolutionary, whose works *The Communist Manifesto, Das Kapital* and *Materialist Conception of History* have played a major role in the development of modern communism and socialism. If any writer has influenced the course of the history of modern mankind, then it certainly is Karl Marx and his works in class struggles and the historical process. Many see him as one of the principal architects of modern social science.

Friedrich Engels (1820–1895) was born in Barmen and was a philosopher, author, social scientist and one of the founding fathers of communist theory along with Karl Marx. He co-authored *The Communist Manifesto* with him and also edited *Das Kapital*. His other works include *The Condition of the Working Class in England, 1844, The Origin of the Family, Private Property and the State*. He also wrote articles for several prominent journals in England and elsewhere in Europe.

Friedrich Wilhelm Nietzsche (1844–1900), born in Röcken bei Lützen, is the famous German philosopher and philologist. His influence has been notable in philosophy, existentialism and post-modernism. His famous works are *Thus Spoke Zarathustra, Beyond Good and Evil, On the Genealogy of Morals* among others. The prominent ideas and concepts that he put forth include the Death of God, the 'Übermensch', eternal recurrence, herd instinct, will to power and 'der letzte mensch' (the last man).

The Brothers Grimm, Jacob Grimm (1785–1863) and Wilhelm Grimm (1786–1859), born in Hanau near Frankfurt, are among the best-known storytellers of folk tales from Europe. They were academics at the University of Göttingen who published *Grimm's Fairy Tales* and made famous such tales as 'Cinderella', 'Hansel and Gretel', 'Snow White', 'Little Red Riding Hood', 'Rumpelstiltskin', 'The Frog Prince' and 'Rapunzel'. They also did work in the field of linguistics and together wrote a German dictionary.

Martin Heidegger (1889–1976) was born in Freiburg in Breisgau. He was an influential philosopher best known for his work *Being and Time*, which explored existential questions of being. His famous concepts of 'Dasein', 'Gestell' and other Heideggerian terminology have left a profound impact on the direction of modern philosophy, in addition to other areas of literature, psychology, and even artificial intelligence.

Franz Kafka (1883–1924) was a novelist and short story writer born to German-speaking Jewish parents in Prague, then part of the Austro-Hungarian Empire, now in the Czech Republic. He's considered to be one of the most influential novelists of the twentieth century. His famous works include *The Trial, The Castle, Amerika, The Metamorphosis* among others. The term 'Kafkaesque' has even entered the English language.

Bertolt Brecht (1898–1956) was born in Augsburg and was a poet, playwright and theatre director. His famous works include *The Caucasian Chalk Circle, The Three Penny Opera, Life of Galileo, Mother Courage and Her Children* and *The Resistible Rise of Arturo Ui*, among several others. He is also known for his ground-breaking contributions to the fields of dramaturgy and theatrical production. His famous post-war theatre company, the Berliner Ensemble held internationally acclaimed productions in his prolific and brilliant career. He influenced a whole generation of writers, actors, directors and dramatists. Furthermore, Brechtian theories and techniques also exerted their influence on film theory and practice, inspiring and influencing several film-makers of his generation worldwide.

Thomas Mann (1875–1955) was born in Lübeck, and was a novelist, short story writer and essayist who was awarded the Nobel Prize for Literature in 1929. His famous works are *Budenbrooks*, *The Magic Mountain* and *Death in Venice*. He lived most of his life in exile in the US and Switzerland, although he wrote in German. He was known for a study and critique of the German and European psyche, in particular insights into the psyche of the artist and the intellectual of the time in Europe.

Hermann Hesse (1877–1962) was born in Calw, a municipality in the State of Baden-Württemberg, although he lived most of his life in Switzerland. He was a novelist, poet and painter who received the Nobel Prize in Literature in 1946. His famous works include *Siddhartha*, *Steppenwolf*, *Demian* and *The Glass Bead Game* among others. Both his parents and his grandfather served as missionaries in India. Hesse's novels have been very popular in England and in the US, having influenced several poets, writers and musicians there.

Heinrich Theodor Böll (1917–1985), born in the city of Cologne, was one of Germany's prominent post-war writers. His best-known works are *Billiards at Half-past Nine*, *Group Portrait with Lady*, *The Clown*, *The Safety Net* and *The Lost Honour of Katharina Blum* and several short stories, among others. He was awarded the Georg Büchner Prize in 1967 and the Nobel Prize in Literature in 1972. His works have been translated into more than 30 languages and he's one of Germany's most widely read authors.

Günter Wilhelm Grass, born in Danzig-Lanfuhr (now in Poland) in 1927, is the famous German novelist and playwright best known for his novel *The Tin Drum*. His other notable works include the novella *Cat and Mouse*, the novels *Dog Years* and *Crabwalk* among others. His recent works include *Peeling the Onion*, *Die Box* and *Grimms Wörter*. He was awarded the Georg Büchner Prize in 1965 and the Nobel Prize in Literature in 1999. His early books had elements of magical realism in them. He is also a trained graphic artist who also creates the cover art for his novels. In 1993, he was elected Honorary Fellow of the Royal Society of Literature. (Sources: see Note 5)

Art and Artists

Ranging from Old Masters, Impressionists and Expressionists to icons of modern and post-modern art, German art and artists play a key role in the international art market today. With over 5,000 art and exhibit houses, there is something for everyone. Berlin's Museum Island is one of the many such wonderful spots to savour arts and culture in Germany. Over the years, German art has been shaped by European and international influences and it has in no small way contributed to the art of the times. Today, the Pinakothek art galleries in Munich and the museums along the banks of the river Main in Frankfurt are worth a visit for all art lovers as are some of the world's important art fairs, namely, the Art Cologne and the Art Forum in Berlin.

Printmaking by woodcut and engraving was well developed during the fifteenth century in Germany. The brilliant and famous artist of the German Renaissance, Albrecht Dürer (1471–1528), began his career as an apprentice to a leading workshop in Nuremberg. It was here that he worked on the beautifully illustrated book of the period, the *Nuremberg Chronicle*. He soon became famous all over Europe for his brilliant and balanced woodcuts and engravings. He also did some paintings during this period. Around this time, Lucas Cranach the Elder (1472–1553) was also a famous German Renaissance painter and printmaker in woodcut and engraving who did some great work. He mostly worked on portraits of famous people and on religious and mythological themes, apart from nudes which were taken from the same themes. Cranach, together with Albrecht Dürer and Matthias Grünewald (1470–1528) are honoured with a feast day on 5 August of the Liturgical Calendar of the Episcopal Church in the US. The Lutheran Church has made him, Dürer and Burgkmair (1473–1531), another painter of the time, saints!

Albrecht Altdorfer (1480–1538) of the Danube School was one of the first Western artists to do a landscape painting in 1528. And Hans Holbein the Elder (1460–1524) was a pioneer and leader in the transformation of German art from the Gothic to the Renaissance. Mention must also be made of the brilliant sculptor and woodcarver Tilman Riemenshneider (1460–1531), whose brilliant woodcarved altars are worth viewing.

The Gothic tradition of woodcarving continued to flourish until the end of the eighteenth century. Baroque art from the period helped influence German interiors in the Baroque style, a fine example being the Wessobrunner Stucco work at Schussenried Abbey.

Also significant in German art is the development of fine porcelain work, recently commemorating 300 years of German porcelain making in 2010. Porzellanikon, in a place called Selb, is Europe's largest dedicated museum. The Meissen Porcelain factory was founded in 1710, a luxury brand that in 1722 adopted the crossed swords motif as their official trademark. It is in all likelihood, the oldest European trademark in use today. Porcelain products are amongst Germany's most exquisite and amongst the finest in the world.

Caspar David Friedrich (1774–1840) is an artist who influenced the fine arts of German Romanticism. He is particularly renowned for his sensitive depiction of atmospheric landscapes. Among his famous works is the *Wanderer above the Sea of Fog*. Another well-known painter of the nineteenth century is Carl Spitzweg (1808–1885), who depicted people in their contemporary settings, his most famous work being *The Poor Poet*.

German universities were the first to teach art history as an academic subject. It was led by Johann Joachim Winckelmann (1717–1768) whose work marked the entry of art history into the philosophical discussion on German culture. He is also considered one of the founders of scientific archaeology.

Into the twentieth century German art developed through two groups of painters who were fundamental to Expressionism. The first being Die Brücke (The Bridge), a group of German Expressionist artists who formed in the city of Dresden in 1905. They were Fritz Bleyl (1880–1966), Erich Heckel (1883–1970), Ernst Ludwig Kirchner (1880–1938), Karl Schmidt-Rottluff (1884–1976), Max Pechstein (1881–1955) and Emil Nolde (1867–1956). They were architecture students who later became painters. This group later moved to Berlin in 1911. The group believed in the medieval craft guild as a model of cooperative work that could better society. Individually, all of them went on to create endearing works of art, both paintings and prints with Ernst L. Kirchner, Max Pechstein and Emil Nolde being particularly appreciated and popular to this day.

The second seminal group of this period was called Der Blaue Reiter (The Blue Rider) and was formed in Munich in 1911, led by Wassily Kandinsky (1866–1944), Franz Marc (1880–1916), August Macke (1887–1940), Alexej von Jawlensky (1864–1941), Marianne von Werefkin (1860–1938) and some others. Paul Klee (1879–1940) was also associated with them. The name of the movement came from a painting created by Kandinsky in 1903. Although they had individual artistic approaches, as a group they shared a common desire to express spiritual truths through their art. They believed in the promotion of modern art, the connection between visual art and music, the spiritual and symbolic associations of colour as well as a spontaneous, intuitive approach to painting. Their encounters with Cubists, Fauvists and other artistic movements of the time made them move towards abstraction. Both Kandinsky and Klee taught at the Bauhaus School of Art, Design and Architecture.

Other notable artists to come forth during this period before the Second World War were artists such as Otto Dix (1891–1969), Max Beckman (1884–1950), Max Ernst (1891–1976) and Max Lieberman (1847–1935). Max Ernst, one of the main exponents of Dadaism and Surrealism, had a defining influence on twentieth-century art.

Post-war trends in Germany can be generally divided into Neo-Expressionism and Conceptualism. Notable German Expressionists of this time include Georg Baselitz, Anselm Kiefer and Jörg Immendorf (1945–2007), a student of Joseph Beuys who was one of the better known artists of his time. Gerhard Richter, Sigmar Polke (1941–2010) and Neo Rauch are representatives of the New Leipzig School, the style of which is characterised by a new realism, free of all ideology.

Joseph Beuys (1921–1986), the performance artist, sculptor, installation artist, graphic artist and art theorist, is perhaps the most influential German artist of the late twentieth century. His large body of work is grounded in concepts of humanism and social philosophy. It culminated in his extended definition of art and the idea of social sculpture as a 'Gesamtkunstwerk' (complete artwork) to include the whole of society, as expressed by his famous expression, 'Everyone is an artist'. He claimed a creative, participatory role in shaping society and politics.

Amongst other things, Beuys, helped co-found the German Green Party, Die Grünen, in 1980. He was a pacifist, vocal opponent of nuclear weapons and campaigned strenuously for environmental causes. Indeed, he was also elected a Green party candidate for the European Parliament. The only major retrospective of his work to be organised in his lifetime opened at the Guggenheim Museum in New York in 1979. (Sources: see Note 6)

Music and Musicians

Germany is known the world over as an important bastion of Western classical music, with legendary names such as composers Beethoven, Bach, Brahms, Strauss and Handel among many others. Music lovers and students from all over the world come in droves to study at its music academies and attend the numerous music festivals. There are around 80 publicly financed concert halls in Germany, the most important being in Berlin, Munich, Dresden, Frankfurt/Main, Hamburg, Leipzig and Stuttgart. The Berlin Philharmonic under the prominent British conductor Sir Simon Rattle is considered to be the foremost of around 130 symphony orchestras in Germany. The largest summer festival for classical music in Germany is the Schleswig-Holstein Music Festival. Germany also has many unique regions with their own folk traditions of music and dance. Southern German Bavarian folk music is well-known outside Germany, where yodelling and Schuhplattler dancers are among the stereotypical images of Germany. Today, you still find them during prominent festival times and catering exclusively to tourists.

German language opera appeared soon after its birth in Italy with Jacopo Peri's *Dafne* of 1598, with Heinrich Schütz providing the music translation of the same libretto in 1627. It was only with Mozart and Beethoven that German opera started getting sophisticated. Weber, Richard Wagner and Strauss established a unique German form of opera under the influence of Romanticism.

Outlined briefly are the German masters of Western classical music, and their contributions to it.

JOHANN SEBASTIAN BACH

Johann Sebastian Bach (1685–1750) was born in Eisenach, in the present state of Thuringia. He was a composer who also played the organ, harpsichord and violin. It is said that his religious and secular works for the orchestra, choir and solo instruments drew together the elements of the Baroque period and brought it to its peaking maturity. Bach's famous works include *The Brandenburg Concertos*, *The Well Tempered Clavier*, *Mass in B Minor*, *The Art of Fugue*, and *The Goldberg Variations* among several others. His works are revered for their intellectual depth, artistic beauty and technical command. Regarded as the supreme composer of the Baroque style, his 'musical science' is one of his significant contributions to western classical music.

LUDWIG VAN BEETHOVEN

Ludwig Van Beethoven (1770–1827) was born in the city of Bonn. He was a composer and pianist who progressively became deaf and yet composed, conducted and performed some brilliant symphonies. His famous works include his nine symphonies, the opera *Fidelio*, several compositions for the piano, a significant quantity of chamber music, string quartets, sonatas for solo instruments and piano variations and many more. Beethoven composed in several musical genres and for a variety of instruments. He was the central figure in the transition from eighteenth-century classicism to nineteenth-century romanticism. He remains a true legend of classical music who influenced future generations of composers.

JOHANNES BRAHMS

Johannes Brahms (1833–1897), born in Hamburg, was a composer and pianist, and the foremost musician of the Romantic period. Brahms wrote several major works for orchestra. Among his famous works are *A German Requiem*, the *Academy Festival Overture*, two serenades, four symphonies, two piano concertos, one for violin and the cello and two orchestral overtures. He was an influence on composers of both conservative and modern leanings. He created bold new approaches to harmony and melody.

GEORG FRIEDRICH HÄNDEL

Georg Friedrich Händel (1685–1759), born in Halle, a city in the German state of Saxony-Anhalt, was a Baroque composer who is famous for operas, oratorios and concertos. His famous works include *Messiah*, *Music for the Royal Fireworks* and *Water Music*, among many others. He introduced various previous uncommon musical instruments in his work, like the lute, three trombones, clarinets, the horn, double bassoon, bell chimes, the positive organ and harp. He later settled in London, where his reputation grew primarily on his English Oratorios. He is now perceived as being one of opera's greatest musical dramatists. Händel is honoured together with Bach and Henry Parcell with a feast day of the liturgical calendar of the Episcopal Church (USA) on 28 July. He is also commemorated as a musician in the calendar of Saints of the Lutheran Church on 28 July, with Bach and Heinrich Schütz.

WILHELM RICHARD WAGNER

Wilhelm Richard Wagner (1813–1883) is the German composer who was also a conductor, theatre director and essayist. He is primarily known for his operas. Although notorious for his extreme political beliefs, Wagner pioneered advances in musical language which has had a major influence in the development of European classical music. He also transformed operatic thought through his concept of the 'total work of art'. His notable works include *Der Ring des Nibelungen*, *Tristan und Isolde*, *Parsifal*, *The Flying Dutchman*, *Tannhäuser* and *Die Meister Singer von Nürnberg*.

RICHARD GEORG STRAUSS

Richard Georg Strauss (1864–1949), born in Munich, was a leading composer and conductor of the late romantic and early modern eras. He is known particularly for his operas, Lieder and tone poems. Among his prominent works are *Der Rosen Kavalier*, *Arabella*, *Ariadne auf Naxos* and *Capriccio* among many other works. He is known for his pioneering subtleties of orchestration combined with an advanced harmonic style. His music has had a profound influence on the development of Western classical music in the twentieth century.

Post-war Germany saw a lot of popular music groups and musicians coming forth in several genres but mainly limited in popularity to Germany. Nevertheless, the heavy metal/hard rock/pop rock band from Hannover, the Scorpions, were one of the first German brands to be highly successful overseas. They are said to have sold between 100 and 150 million albums worldwide. Founded in 1965, their popular numbers are 'Rock You like a Hurricane', 'Send Me an Angel', 'Still Loving You' and 'Wind of Change'.

Then there is the famous electronic band Kraftwerk, which is one of the first bands in the world to make music entirely on electronic equipment. The group was founded in Düsseldorf in 1970. They had worldwide success with their albums, 'The Man-Machine' and 'Computer World', where the single 'The Model' reached the number one position in the UK charts. Kraftwerk's music over the years has directly influenced many popular artists from diverse genres of music all over the world, from Depeche Mode, Franz Ferdinand to Jay Z and even David Bowie and Cold Play.

Kraftwerk, together with the band 'Tangerine Dream', is said to be the primary influence of the Berlin School for electronic music, which would later influence trance music. This genre began in the late 1980s and early 1990s, following the development of trance music in Germany and several other sub-genres that developed like 'anthem trance', 'progressive trance' and 'ambient trance', etc. Today, Germany has one of the largest electronic music scenes in the world, popular DJs being Paul Van Dyke, Sven Väth and Paul Kalkbrenner among several others.

In the dance music genre, the 1990s saw several worldwide hits been produced in Germany and by German record labels. In 1989, Snap!, a German euro-dance project formed by German producers Michael Münzing and Luca Anzilotti were most successful when fronted by rapper TurboB, who did the vocals on the UK number one singles

'The Power' and 'Rhythm is a Dancer'. These singles also did well in the US and in Western Europe.

Then there is Haddaway, a singer with Dutch-Trinidadian roots, who became famous in 1993 for his world-wide hit 'What is Love', made by the German label Coconut Records.

The German band Mr President produced 'Coco Jambo' in 1996, a euro-dance song that was a hit in Europe and Latin America and even reached the US Billboard Hot 100 at number 21 in 1997. Another famous German musician of Italian-Ugandan descent is Lou Bega, who is famous for the song 'Mambo No.5' which became an instant hit worldwide in 1999, charting at number one in UK, Germany and France and number three in the US. This was produced by the German Lautstark' label.

ECM (Edition of Contemporary Music) is a music label founded by Manfred Eicher in Munich in 1969. ECM has to date issued more than 1,200 albums spanning many idioms. After establishing an early reputation with standard-setting jazz recordings, it has since become a broad platform for a wide variety of composed music from the pre-Baroque era to the present day. The label is at present distributed in the US by Universal Music. ECM has been widely recognised and the label has collected many prestigious awards over the years including 'Producer of the Year' and 'Label of the Year'. The UK newspaper *The Independent* has hailed ECM 'as the most important imprint in the world for Jazz and New Music.'

German musicians of note in the other genres includes the likes of Herbert Grönmeyer, Roy Black, Nena, Udo Lindenberg, Eberhard Weber, Peter Maffay, Xavier Naidoo, Til Brönner, Sara Connor, Bushido, the teenie group sensation Tokio Hotel, the punk rock group Toten Hosen and the industrial metal band Rammstein, which are quite popular in Japan and elsewhere in Europe.

Other pop groups to do well in Europe and elsewhere include Modern Talking and, of course, the world famous disco group Boney M which was created by German record producer and writer Frank Farian in Germany in 1974, made by Hansa Records in Berlin. (Sources: see Note 7)

Architecture: Past and Present

Architecture in Germany has had a rich and diverse history, starting with the Porta Nigra, an ancient city gate in Trier, built by the Romans around 16 B.C. as well as the remains of some spas, bridges and amphitheatres. From the ninth century, Torhalle, or the gatehouse at Lorsch Abbey, is a fine survivor of the Carolingian era in the Pre-Romanesque period in Western Europe.

From the Romanesque Period (1000–1250 A.D.), the significant building of the period in Germany is the Imperial Cathedral of Speyer, which is laid out in the form of a Latin cross. Typical features are the round arched windows and Roman columns. Saxony-Anhalt is another place to see some great examples of Romanesque architecture along the thousand kilometre Romanesque Route, where one can explore over 70 castles, churches and other remains.

Next is the Gothic Period (1150–1500), a style of architecture that originated in France, its distinguishing features being the pointed arch, decorated porch with life-sized, stone sculptures, clustered columns, etc., and a front entrance with a large window in the shape of a rose. Residences during this period were mainly timber-framed buildings, many of which have survived to this day. Fine examples of Gothic architecture can be found in the Freiberger Minster, The Church of Our Lady in Munich, cities like Rostock, Greifswald and the historic old town of Lübeck, which, surrounded by water with its famous Holsten Gate, was the first old town in German to be officially declared a UNESCO World Heritage site. Of course, the most famous and wonderful example of Gothic architecture is the Cologne Cathedral with its tall twin towers, built between 1248 and 1880. When it was completed, it was the tallest building in the world, rising to a height of 157 metres. It is a landmark building in the heart of the city of Cologne.

The Renaissance Period (1420–1620) saw a revival in architecture of symmetry, proportion and regularity. Fine examples of this period include the Augsburg Town Hall, Heidelberg Castle, in Germany's oldest university town, and St. Michael's Church in Munich, which is the largest Renaissance church north of the Alps.

During the Baroque Period (1680–1780), the nobility in cities like Berlin, Munich and Dresden adopted and developed their residences and other landmarks in an elaborate style that was characterised by a conspicuous façade, magnificent staircases, opulent sculptures on the walls, beautiful frescoes on the ceilings and creative use of light and shadow. Well-known Baroque buildings include the Castle Charlottenburg in Berlin, Castle Sanssoucci and the New Palace in Potsdam, the Herrenchiemsee Palace in Munich and the Zwinger Palace in Dresden.

In the Classicism Period (1750–1840), there was an extension of the Renaissance period elements with an urge for monumentality, greatness, Greek sculpture and symmetry in the shape and form of the buildings of the time. The best examples are found in the famous Brandenburg Gate, the New Guard House and the Museum Island in Berlin. In Munich, The Royal Square is Classicism at its best.

Historicism or Eclecticism (1840–1900) was a brief period that saw a revival of the architectural styles of the past and a merger with new interpretations, when churches and Parliament buildings were built in the Neo-Gothic style, and theatres and Museums in the Neo-Renaissance with features of Neo-Baroque. Some of the best examples are The Old Masters Picture Gallery in Dresden, The Berliner Reichstag (Parliament Building) and, of course, the famous Neuschwanstein Castle which Ludwig the II commissioned in 1896 in Bavaria. It is built and set in a fairytale-like setting, a tourist hotspot.

Art Nouveau (1900–1914), also known by its German name, Jugendstil, is derived from traditional German printmaking that was characterised by precise and hard edges and is decorated with ornamentation, use of hand crafts and sculpting with an attention to interiors. Among the best examples, are the synagogue in Augsburg, residential quarters in Leipzig and Karlsruhe and the well-known Wedding Tower and the Art Nouveau Mathildenhöhe artist's colony in Darmstadt.

The twentieth century saw one of the most influential trends in modern architecture to come through in Germany with the establishment of the Bauhaus School. It was founded as a school for architecture, design, painting and the crafts in Weimar in 1919 by Walter Gropius. It was later moved to Dessau in the state of Saxony-Anhalt in 1925. The school's credo was 'that form should follow function'. So the buildings they designed were a mix of glass, steel and concrete without any elaborate ornamentation for the façade or interiors. This school has influenced the modern age of architecture like no other school or movement. Among the notable examples is the Bauhaus Dessau Building, a famous monument of classical modernism in Germany. Others include the Einstein Tower in Potsdam designed by Erich Mendelsohn, the Weissenhof Estate in Stuttgart, the Horseshoe Housing Estate in Berlin and the Zeche Zollverein (a coal mine industrial complex) in Essen.

Today, architectural construction in Germany has a varied and futuristic look to it, starting with the new glass dome designed by Sir Norman Foster for the German parliament building in Berlin. The Jewish Museum that opened in Berlin in 2001, created by the architect Daniel Liebeskind, is a striking example of modern architecture. Several measures have also been undertaken to restore and preserve the historical masterpieces in Berlin, including the wonderful Museum Island.

The Allianz Arena in Munich is the new football stadium created before the 2006 World Cup. From the outside it looks like a giant air cushion. Then there is the latest BMW building, the BMW Welt a multi-functional customer experience and exhibition facility of BMW in Munich that has a futuristic design with an 800-KW solar plant on its roof. The Munich Olympic Park and Stadium built in 1972 and designed by Günter Behnisch and the engineer Frei Otto was a landmark in architecture and engineering. Otto was a leading authority on lightweight tensile and membrane structures, and his work has inspired and influenced the likes of contemporary British architect Zaha Hadid.

The city of Frankfurt on the river Main is the only other European city with a cluster of skyscrapers in the centre. Two modern buildings worth a mention are the Messe Turm (Fair Tower) designed by Helmut Jahn and the Messe-Torhaus (Fair House-Door) designed by Oswald M. Ungers. Both were built in the post-modern architectural style. Helmut Jahn also designed the 'Sony Center' in Berlin, which displays a futuristic urban aesthetic. There are also buildings designed by the famous architect Frank Gehry with his de-constructivist, post-structural style, examples in Germany being the MARTa-Museum in Herford and his characteristic buildings situated in Media Harbour in Düsseldorf.

Other notable buildings include a pavilion called The Leonardo Glass Cube located near Bad Driburg in Germany and built by 3 Deluxe Studio. It has concrete pathways between green grass, going up to the façade of glass and concrete, all blending together for a wonderful view. An original and thoughtful design for a private house is the Dupli Casa, designed by German architect Jurgen Mayer near Ludwigsburg in Germany. It is a fine example, in pure white forms, of modernism, weaving itself with an expressive geometry of the digital era. The soon to be completed Elbe Philarmonic Hall in Hamburg is a spectacular new building with concert halls, a 250 room hotel, conference and wellness centres and exclusive apartments.

Today, Germany has a flourishing architectural scene, which includes famous names from the German and international stage as well as emerging architectural firms. They are also concerned about setting standards on green issues and on improving the environmental quality of built-up areas. Germany is considered a trail-blazer when it comes to ecological architecture. (Sources: see Note 8)

Design in Germany

The legacy of modern design in Germany goes back to the founding of an institute called Bauhaus in 1919, in the beautiful Baroque town of Weimar in the state of Thuringia, the unusual birth place for a modern aesthetic. It was here that Walter Gropius (1883–1969) founded an academy to teach the latest ideas in painting, printmaking, pottery, industrial design, interior design, typography and graphic design, weaving and textiles.

Although the institute existed for only a short 14 years from 1919 to 1933, its principles and pervasive influence changed the way the world built itself, from the sleek looking glass and steel skyscrapers to stereo components with a matte black finish, to urban kitchens, washrooms, etc., that in so many ways give us the look and feel of modern life today. In 1925, the Bauhaus moved to the city of Dessau, where the original Gropius-designed school building and a number of other buildings have been declared a UNESCO World Heritage site.

The Bauhaus style became one of the most influential schools in modern design and modernist architecture. It also had a major impact on further developments in the arts, interior and graphic design and typography. The Bauhaus School was founded at a time when the German zeitgeist had turned from an emotional expressionism to the matter-of-fact New Objectivity. Where forms were simplified and rationality and functionality were the new norm, reconciling mass production with individual artistic spirit.

Peter Behrens (1868–1940), an architect who in 1907 was appointed artistic consultant to AEG (the famous electrical engineering firm that designs and produces quality consumer electronics, now a part of Electrolux), is considered the father of German industrial product design, if not the first true practitioner of modern design. When Behrens came to AEG, he developed a powerful product design philosophy that was to be the enduring hallmark of the AEG Company and its products. His attempt was to develop electrical household appliances with an eye to both aesthetics and the specific function of the object. In his words, 'Design is not about decorating functional forms – it is about creating forms that accord with the character of the object and that showed new technologies to advantage'.

Behrens also pioneered the concept of 'corporate identity', while working for AEG he created logos, advertising material and company publications with a consistent, unified design. In other words, he was one of the first practitioners of 'branding' and brands as we know of it, by establishing the 'corporate identity' concept as the basic element of the philosophy of an industrial company and its brands. He is said to have worked closely with Walter Gropius, the founder of the Bauhaus school on several design projects.

Also important was the Ulm School of Design, a college of design founded in 1953 in Ulm in the state of Baden-Württemberg, on the Danube River. It is known in Germany as the Hochschule für Design or Hfg in short. It, too, was in operation for a short period from 1953 to 1968, nevertheless it gained in international recognition as second only to the Bauhaus as the most influential school of design. There were departments in industrial design, buildings, visual communication, information and filmmaking. It is considered to have been a progressive educational institution of design and a pioneer in the study of semiotics. The Ulm model of teaching design continues to have a major influence on design education worldwide. Among the school's successful projects was the work with Braun, the consumer products company, the corporate identity design for Lufthansa and elevated trains for the Hamburg Railroad. Among its distinguished visiting faculty were luminaries like Buckminster Füller, Walter Gropius, Charles and Ray Eames and Rayner Banham among many others.

Another German designer who emerged as one of the most influential designers of the late twentieth century is Dieter Rams, who was head of design at Braun, the consumer electronics manufacturer (now a part of P&G). His design ethos of 'less but better', design principles and his product designs have had a lasting influence on today's design landscape worldwide.

A well-known design company that has its origins in Germany is Frog Design, founded in 1969 by industrial designer Hartmut Esslinger and his partners Andreas Haug and Georg Spreng in a town called Mutlangen, as Esslinger Design. The current headquarters are in San Francisco. They now call themselves a global innovation firm that creates and brings to market products, services and experiences. Their earlier work that made them famous was the Trinitron television set for Sony in 1975 and the Apple IIc in 1984. Their present list of clients includes GE, Disney, HP, Intel, Microsoft, Siemens and several other Fortune 500 brands. It is said that many of today's design leaders got their initial start and experience at Frog Design.

While in fashion design, two German designers who have made an international name for themselves are Karl Lagerfeld and Wolfgang Joop. The fashion and lifestyle labels Tom Tailor and Gerry Weber are also fairly well-known, successful German brands, apart from the already mentioned star brand, Hugo Boss.

At the 2010 EXPO in Shanghai, the German pavilion presented German design and industrial achievements that contribute to a better life in an urban environment called Balancity; it won first prize for the best pavilion.

The spectrum of products that were selected and displayed at Balancity was quite varied. A few examples are the carbon-fibre Ultimate CF Super Record LTD bicycle frame by Canyon Bicycles GmbH to the micro-processor controlled C-Leg artificial leg by Otto Bock Health Care GmbH and the Rain shower Icon designer hand shower with a water-saving function by Grohe AG to the Yello Sparzähler Online, an intelligent electricity meter by Yello Strom GmbH. The selected, innovative design products were for the home, work, medicine, technology, entertainment and leisure sectors. They were chosen as products that make it pleasant to live in a city in equilibrium between renewal and preservation, innovation and tradition, urban and rural, community and the individual and work and leisure. (Sources: see Note 9)

Sports in Germany

Germany is a sports-loving nation and most people keep themselves physically active in one form of sporting activity or another. In Germany, group activities, team sports and competitions takes place quite frequently. In 2006, around 27.5 million people were members of more than 91,000 sports clubs in Germany.

Football is the most popular sport in Germany where most people are fairly obsessed with it, like in other parts of the world. There are around 6.6 million members who belong to around 26,000 football clubs.

The German men's national football team has so far won three FIFA World Cups, in 1954, 1974 and 1990, and the European championships three times, in 1972, 1980 and 1996.

The women's national football team won the FIFA World Cup twice, in 2003 and 2007, and they also won three Olympic bronze medals in 2000, 2004 and 2008.

Germany hosted the 1974 and 2006 men's World Cups and the European championship in 1988. In 2011, it hosted the FIFA women's World Cup.

The Dresden English football club is considered the first modern football club in Germany. It was founded in 1850 by Englishmen living and working in the city.

The German football Association (DFB) holds German league championships, the primary being the first and second division in this league called the Bundesliga.

Among the popular German teams are Bayern Munchen, Werder Bremen, FC Schalke 04, Borussia Dortmund, Hamburg SV, Bayer Leverkusen, Eintracht Frankfurt and VfB Stuttgart among several others. Bayern Munchen or Munich is the most successful German football club with 22 national championships, 15 national cups and 5 European champion titles. Germany's most famous footballer is the 'Kaiser' Franz Beckenbauer, who is one of the few men in the world to have won the World Cup, both as a coach and player.

In athletics and the Olympic Games, German athletes are among some of the best in the world, having won around 1,304 medals in the total Olympic Games medal tally. Germany ranks third in the overall country rankings. They have hosted the Summer Games twice, once in Berlin in 1936 and the other time in Munich in 1972. They are also amongst the best in the Winter Olympic Games, having won the most medals including golds at the 2006 Winter Olympic Games in Turin, Italy, especially excelling in the bobsleigh, luge and skeleton events. The German Winter Olympics team won the most medals in Turin in 2006 with 29 medals, 11 of them gold. In the 2010 Winter Olympics in Vancouver, they won 30 medals, 10 of them gold.

The annual Berlin Marathon is the largest running event in Germany with over 50,000 participants from all over the world. International marathons are also held in Hamburg, Munich, Cologne and Frankfurt.

Germany is one of the leading motor-sports countries in the world, the place where several of the cars, engines, drivers, support staff and sponsorships for Formula One and the other races have come from. They have in Michael Schumacher, the seven-time world champion in Formula One racing, a world record, while the German driver Sebastian Vettel of Red Bull racing was the 2010, 2011 and 2012 Formula One champion. The DTM is a very popular German Touring Car Masters series with rounds elsewhere in Europe. It draws huge crowds and is televised to a large audience as well. The VLN is another 10 race series held on the Nürburgring racing tracks, also known as the VLN Endurance Racing Championships, Nürburgring. It is organised by an organisation of motor-sport clubs.

In tennis, the most successful German players have been Boris Becker and Steffi Graf, who have won all the major tennis tournaments of the world during their time. Germany has also won the prestigious Davis Cup competition three times, in 1988, 1989 and 1993.

Field hockey is another team event that has seen Germany do well, having won the Hockey World Cup twice, once in 2002 in Kuala Lumpur, Malaysia and the next time in 2006 in Mönchengladbach, when they hosted it. In the 2010 Hockey World Cup held in New Delhi, India, they were runners-up to Australia. They also won the gold in the Olympics Games in 1972 (Munich), 1992 (Barcelona), 2008 in Beijing and 2012 in London. The women's team won the Olympic Gold in 2004 in Athens and the World Cup in 1976 in Berlin and 1981 in Buenos Aires.

Handball is a team sport that is popular in Germany. They hosted the men's Handball World Cup in 2007 and won it as well. They also won it in 1938 and 1978. They were Olympic champions in 1936 and runners-up in 1984 and 2004.

Ice hockey is a fairly popular sport in Germany, though not as popular as American football or ice hockey is in North America. They have the 15 team 'Deutsche Eishockey Liga'. The German Men's National Ice Hockey team features several NHL players and prospects.

For basketball in Germany, they have the Basketball Bundesliga with 18 teams playing for the German Cup. The German Men's National Basketball team have seen success as the European Champion in 1993, the Silver Medal in the 2005, European Championships and the Bronze medal in the 2002 FIBA World Championship. Germany's famous basketball export is Dirk Nowitzki, who plays power forward for the Dallas Mavericks in the US NBA league.

In boxing, the city of Frankfurt has a long tradition of holding the Heavyweight Boxing, Challenger and Title fights from the late 1920s onwards. It has seen some of the greats of boxing. In the WBO organisation, the Super Middleweight, Light Heavyweight and Cruiser-weight Division champions are the Germans Robert Stieglitz, Jürgen Brähmer and Marco Huck respectively. While in the WBC and WBA organisations, Sebastian Zbik and Felix Sturm of Germany are the Middleweight champions. They also have a women boxer who is a champion in the featherweight division, Ina Menzer.

While in golf, Germany has had Bernhard Langer, a two-time Masters champion, who was officially ranked the number one player in 1986. Then there is Martin Kaymer, who became the number one ranked golfer in the official World Golf Rankings on 27 February 2011. He had previously won the 2010 PGA championship among several other tournament wins. (Sources: see Note 10)

The German Media

Germany, like other developed countries of the world has a mature and sophisticated media infrastructure with a large readership, viewership and online presence and activity. The freedom of the press and speech is protected in the country by the Constitution as given in Article 5 of the German Basic Law.

The German newspaper market is characterised by a large number of publications catering to several regions. There are around 10 national dailies and 335 local and regional daily newspapers. Among the popular national daily newspapers are, the *Bild, Frankfurter Allgemeine Zeitung, Süddeutsche Zeitung, Die Welt, Berliner Zeitung, Berliner Morgenpost, Hamburger Abendblatt* and the *Die Tageszeitung*. Popular weekly newspapers are *Die Zeit* and *Die Woche*.

There are some 780 general interest magazines and 3,400 specialised magazines published in Germany. *Der Spiegel* is the oldest and most popular. Other popular magazines are the *Der Stern, Focus* and the German auto-club magazine 'ADAC-Motorwelt', which has a reported circulation of over 13 million.

The largest publishers of popular magazines are the Bauer Media Group, Axel Springer, Burda and Gruner+Jahr. Germany is a major book nation with around 94,000 new books and re-editions coming out each year. In addition to the regular online versions of the various print publications that have a large online audience, there is also a huge spectrum and choice of online news and blogs that keeps growing by the day.

In television, depending on the individual's technical platform, whether terrestrial, satellite, cable, mobile or broadband, one can receive hundreds of national and international TV channels in Germany. In 2012, all analogue satellite broadcast ceased in the country (with a few exceptions) as it is now only in digital transmission.

Germany has some of the largest, public broadcasters in ARD and ZDF, which, although free-to-air, are financed by nominal yearly fees. The privately owned, free-to-air stations are RTL, SAT.1, Kabel 1, n-tv, N24, Das Vierte, Tele 5, Pro Sieben, VIVA and Eurosport. The regionally produced stations that broadcast nationally are WDR, SWR, NDR, rbb, mdr, BR and hr. Other international broadcasters are Deutsche Welle or DW, the Franco-German arte and the Austro-German-Swiss cultural channel 3sat. (Sources: see Note 11)

Films and Film-Makers

The beginnings of film in Germany go back to 1895 when Max Skladanowsky and his brother Emil showcased their invention of a film projector called the Bioskop at the Wintergarten music hall in Berlin.

The first film to garner the attention of viewers and gain in popularity was Robert Wiene's *The Cabinet of Dr. Caligari* made in 1920, an expressionistic view of the hallucinations of a disturbed man. Other commendable silent works include Friedrich Wilhelm Murnau's *Nosferatu*, made in 1922, and Carl Boese and Paul Wegener's *The Golem: How he Came into the World*, made in 1920. These films had a major influence on film-making thereafter and is said to have influenced several American and European directors from Jean Cocteau to Ingmar Bergman.

The most famous film of this time, though, was the science fiction film directed by Fritz Lang, *Metropolis*, a classic made in 1927. Although much footage of this film was lost and damaged over the years, efforts to restore it proved successful recently with the use of the latest technology. In 2010, the restored film was shown publicly in New York, Berlin and Frankfurt. Lang's other non-talkie production of note was *Die Nibelungen*. Murnau made a significant film in 1925 called *The Last Laugh*.

Der Blaue Engel (*The Blue Angel*) made in 1930 by the Austrian director Josef von Sternberg was Germany's first talking film, simultaneously made in English and German. This film made an international star of the German actress Marlene Dietrich. Other early talking films that gained recognition include Lang's '*M*', Georg Wilhelm Pabst's adaptation of Bertolt Brecht's, *The Three penny Opera*, both made in 1931 and Hochbaum's *Razzia in Sankt Pauli*, made in 1932.

During the Nazi regime, several hundred actors, directors, producers and technicians migrated, mainly to Hollywood, where some of them gained in prominence. Among them were the producer Eric Pommer, actors like Marlene Dietrich and Peter Lorre and of course the director Fritz Lang.

Among the post-war German films that achieved success internationally was Bernard Wicki's Oscar-nominated film *Die Brücke* (*The Bridge*).

It was only after 28 February 1962 when a group of film-makers issued the Oberhausen Manifesto that the New German Cinema saw a renewed resurgence to make films based on artistic excellence. Among them are such luminaries like Rainer Werner Fassbinder, Werner Herzog, Wim Wenders, Volker Schlöndorff, Werner Schroeter and several others. The films, which were critically acclaimed and successful internationally, were Fassbinder's *Fear eats the Soul* (1974), *The Marriage of Maria Braun* (1979), Herzog's *Aguirre the Wrath of God* (1972) and Wender's *Paris, Texas* (1984). Gunter Grass's adaptation of the *Tin Drum* by Schlöndorff became the first German film to win the Academy Award (Oscar) for Best Foreign Language Film in 1979. The film also won the Palme dOr at the 1979 Cannes Film Festival. Schroeter's 1980 film *Palermo oder Wolfsburg* won the Golden Bear at the 30th Berlin International Film Festival.

Wim Wenders continued his success with several awards for his films, starting with the Golden Lion (Venice) in 1982 for *The State of Things*, the Golden Palm (Cannes) in 1984 for *Paris, Texas*, the Best Director Award at Cannes in 1993 for the film *Faraway, So Close!* and the Silver Bear Jury Prize in 2000 for *The Million Dollar Hotel*.

Other notable film-makers who came into the limelight during the 1980s include directors like Von Trotta, Helma Sanders-Brahms, Doris Dörrie, Loriot, Uli Edel and the late producer Bernd Eichinger.

Run Lola Run made by German director Tom Tykwer in 1998 was a critically acclaimed movie that was nominated for 41 awards; it won 26, including the BAFTA and awards at the Sundance Film Festival, Seattle International Film Festival and several at the German film awards.

In Germany today, the major film producers are Constantin Film, Studio Hamburg, Bavaria Film and the UFA or Universal Film AG founded as a government-owned film studio, which was created in Berlin in November 1917. It is today owned by the RTL Group.

Other films in the recent past to have done well include *Downfall* by Oliver Hirschbiegel, *Goodbye Lenin* by Wolfgang Becker and *Head-On* by Fatih Akin, a German film director of Turkish origin. Other notable directors working currently in Germany includes Caroline Link, whose third feature film, *Nirgendwo in Afrika* (*Nowhere in Africa*), made in 2001, won the Academy Award for Best Foreign Language Film for 2001. Prior to that Thomas Stellmach, a German producer, won the Oscar in 1997 for the short film *Quest* in the Best Animated Short Film category. Other names include Michael Verhoeven, Sönke Wortmann, Michael Herbig, Romuald Karmakar and several others.

The Berlin International Film Festival, popularly known as the 'Berlinale', is among the world's leading film festivals held in Berlin every year. It was founded in 1951 and has been celebrated annually since 1978. They award the Golden Bear and Silver Bear awards. It is a high-profile event where prominent actors, directors and other professionals of the world's film industry make an appearance. Up to 400 films are shown in several sections, and it is considered to be one of the largest publicly attended film festivals in the world with a total of around 500,000 admissions during its course. (Sources: see Note 12)

Food, Drink and Festivals

Germans are a food-loving nation who appreciate drinking all types of beers, wines and spirits and partake of its varied sausages, cheeses, breads and cakes. There are many regional specialities that are quite a culinary surprise. Over the years, they have also been influenced by the Romans, the French, the Scandinavians and other Europeans. Of late, other influences and tastes from the near and Far East have also opened up their taste buds to new culinary experiences. The Germans also love eating out with friends and family and participating in various local and regional festivals and carnivals.

In Germany, there are well over 5,000 different kinds of beer on tap and in bottles made by around 1,200 breweries spread all over the country. There are around 300 different kinds of breads from black wholemeal breads to pretzels, rolls, pastries and other baked delicacies that have made German bakers famous in most parts of the world.

Germany is the largest cheese-producing country in Europe with over 2 million metric tons being produced every year. They are also among the world's largest exporter and importer of cheese and curd.

There are over 600 different German cheese varieties. Like, with the German cuisine, the country's cheese variety also developed from other regions of Europe and as people immigrated to it. Germany produces all types of cheese, including, hard cheese, semi-hard, semi-soft, soft and fresh cheese. Around 75 per cent of the German production is produced in the state of Bavaria or Bayern, with Allgäu, the Alpine region being the largest cheese producing region, as the milk here is plentiful and of high quality. Other important cheese producing regions include the northern states of Mecklenburg-Vorpommern, Schleswig-Holstein and Saxony-Anhalt.

The country is also known for its variety and long tradition of preparing sausages or würst as they call it in German. There is bratwürst, knackwürst, bockwürst and several other varieties like the frankfurter or the hotdog as it is known in the US. The word 'frankfurter' comes from the city of Frankfurt on the river Main, where pork sausages served in a long bun similar to hotdogs originated. The famous hamburger also has its origin in Germany and has its roots in the city of Hamburg, from where it migrated to America.

The world's oldest known beer brewery, Weihenstephan, is located in a town called Freising near the city of Munich. It was started by Christian monks who started brewing beer in 1040. The Germans have all types of beer, from dark to light, extra-strong, strong to mild and even smoked beer (it has a unique ham/smoked flavour) because the malt that is used is dried over an open fire.

They also have a variety of Schnapps, a high-proof spirit that is distilled from grain and various fruits to create fine, scented spirits. Schnapps are partaken as an aperitif, an after-dinner drink or whenever one likes to. It is said that the monks first discovered that these kinds of liqueurs or bitters have medicinal properties as they add several healthy herbs to it. They are said to aid in digestion and lift the spirit.

In Germany there are around 550 natural sources of natural mineral water, where it is bottled for general consumption. Different sources have different tastes and mineral compositions. Germany's wine country has a tradition of viticulture stretching back more than 2,000 years. Its 13 picturesque wine regions attract connoisseurs from all over the world. There are around 850 wine varieties with all types of Rieslings, Chardonnays, Pinot Noirs and other varieties of wine.

Each region in Germany has its own culinary specialities apart from a large variety of traditional soups and stews, with white asparagus (Spargel) being a particular favourite of the Germans.

In Frankfurt, there are frankfurter sausages, green sauce (Grün Soße) made from seven different herbs, served with boiled eggs and baked potatoes and Apfelwein (apple wine). In Munich, you have white sausages (Weißwürste), baked pretzels, Leberknödel (bread, liver and onion soup), Schweinsbraten (pot roasted pork), Kraut (Cabbage), Obatzada, a Bavarian cheese delicacy, and of course Apfelstrudel and the Black Forest cake among several other dishes. Among the original Hamburg dishes are green runner beans cooked with pears and bacon (Bohnen, Birnen & Speck), Rote Grütze a summer pudding made from berries and served with cream, LabsKaus (a meat dish), Frikadelle a pan-fried, patty and a type of shandy called a Radler. Berlin is famous for its Curry Wurst (sausages served in a spicy sauce) of which there are several varieties now available.

Traditional meals in the Düsseldorf region are Rheinische Sauerbraten (beef marinated for a few days in vinegar and spices), Heaven and Earth (the black pudding with stewed apples and mashed potatoes), Rheinisch style mussels and steaks roasted with mustard, among several other dishes.

Today Germany also has restaurants from all over the world including nouvelle cuisine and varieties of it.

When it comes to festivals, Germany is a place that has a variety of traditional festivals and carnivals almost all year round. Being a fairly religious country, in January, there is the 'Three Hallowed Kings festivity, whereas in February the carnival month begins with colourful parades and parties that are celebrated through the streets of Germany's cities and towns. It is known as Fasching in German, a time for elaborate parades, with people in masks, attending balls and the selection of the Carnival King and Queen. The Cologne Carnival is the most famous during this season.

In March, with the beginning of spring there are many traditional festivals and events, like the one in Berlin called the Spandau Spring Festival, for the whole family.

At Easter in April there are another round of traditional festivities and parties with chocolate Easter eggs and bunnies. May is a continuation of the spring festivities with the Stuttgart Spring Festival, the Munich Spring Festival, the Dresden Classical Music Festival, the, Asparagus Festival in Darmstadt and the Bodensee Festival on Lake Constance in Friedrichshafen. The summer also sees several summer wine festivals happening all over the country.

In June, the huge, twin, Rock music event, Rock am Ring, and 'Rock am Park' which takes place in the Nürburgring racetrack and in Nuremberg respectively, attracts over 150,000 national and international visitors and some of the best rock and pop bands of the world.

In August, Wacken Open Air or WOA, held every year in a small village in the state of Schleswig-Holstein attracts over 80,000 visitors from far and near and is said to be one of the largest, open-air, Heavy Metal music festivals in the world.

Of course, Germany's most well-known festival is the Oktoberfest held each year in Munich with 6 million people attending. It is a 16-day festival from late September to early October. It is an important part of Bavarian culture, where people partake of a lot of beer with traditional Bavarian delicacies. They celebrated 200 years of this festival in 2010. The first Oktoberfest is said to have happened in Munich on 18 October 1810.

During this festival, the local Bavarians don their traditional dress with the men typically wearing green hats called Sennerhut and Lederhosen breeches made of leather that may be knee-length or shorter. The women wear the dirndl, a traditional dress consisting of a bodice, blouse, full skirt and an apron. For the festival, around 14 huge main tents are constructed, where people drink and eat, and there is lots of music and dancing. It is held on the Wiesn Fairgrounds and is opened with the traditional cry of 'O'zapft is' (the barrel is tapped).

Stuttgart also has a similar beer festival that is held every year at the end of September.

Hamburg port, built in 1189, celebrates its founding in the first week of May. Today it has become one of the largest port festivals in the world with around 1 million people attending every year.

There is also the Schützenfest fair in Hannover. It is said to be one of the world's biggest fun fairs with electrifying, thrilling rides with all the traditional fun items, food stalls, beer gardens, etc. This fair is said to have begun in the seventeenth century.

Germany is at its most colourful during the Christmas months starting in November and continuing until the New Year. Christmas markets can be found in practically every small town and city in Germany during the four weeks of Advent. It is known by several names in Germany, the WeihnachtsMarkt and the Christkindlmarkt being the popular ones. The Christmas market, first held in Dresden in 1434, is one of the oldest known of such markets. To date, it attracts between 1 million visitors every year and has over 60 market stalls. Among the popular attractions in these markets include the crib of the nativity scene, traditional Christmas delicacies such as Lebkuchen (chocolate cookies), Stollen (a type of Christmas cake), nutcrackers, gingerbread, Glühwein (hot mulled wine), Eierpunsch (an egg punch) and of course, Christmas trees, decorations, illuminations, ornaments, twinkling lights and the works, which are especially bright and colourful during the evenings. In addition to music and choir singing you can also find plays, musicals and other entertaining events during this time. Shopping and shopping centres become an exciting place with lots of opportunities to enjoy the food, lights and decorations and take in the festive atmosphere. (Sources: see Note 13)

Notes

1. www.researchingermany.de; www.fraunhofer.de; www.helmholtz.de; www.wgl.de; www.mpg.de
2. www.bdi.eu; www.dihk.de; www.gtai.de; www.tuv.com; www.tuev-sued.de; www.din.de; www.test.de
3. www.auma.com; www.hannovermesse.de; www.cebit.de; www.buchmesse.de; www.ifa-berlin.de; www.anuga.com; www.k-online.de; www.drupa.com; www.interpack.com; www.toyfair.com; www.hardwarefair.com; www.paperworld.messefrankfurt.com
4. www.wikipedia.org/wiki/Politics_of_Germany
5. Boyle; Friedenthal; Fahlbusch; Tyndale; Bainton; Inwood; Barnett; Green; Cate; Zipes; Poeggeler; Max; Walter; Garland; Beck; www.nobelprize.org; www.wikipedia.org/wiki/German_literature
6. Honour; Gene; www.wikipedia.org/wiki/German_art; www.cometogermany.com; www.tatsachen-ueber-deutschland.de
7. Boyd; Lockwood; Macdonald; Burrows; Adorno; Kennedy; www.wikipedia.org/wiki/Music_of_Germany
8. Pevsner; www.germany-tourism.co.uk; www.wikipedia.org/wiki/Architecture_of_Germany
9. Maldonado; Harper; www.aeg.com; www.frogdesign.com; www.german-design-council.de; www.designmuseum.org; www.wikipedia.org/wiki/ulm_school_of_Design/Bauhaus
10. wikipedia.org/wiki/Sport_in_Germany
11. www.tatsachen-ueber-deutschland.de/en/culture-and-media, www.pressreference.com/FaGu/Germany.html
12. www.goethe.de/kuelflm/enindex.htm; www.wikipedia.org/wiki/Cinema_of_Germany; www.berlinale.de
13. Metzger; Zug; www.wikipedia.org/wiki/German_cuisine; www.wikipedia.org/wiki/Christmas_market; www.germanfoods.org

6 *The Less-Known Champions*

Small and medium-sized businesses are the mainstay of the German economy. These SMEs account for around 70 per cent of all jobs in the country. There are approximately 3.7 million such companies in existence today. They not only form the backbone of the economy but are also responsible for bringing to the fore new innovations, technologies and patents. These have been developed by scores of technical entrepreneurs who have furthered their work into a successful, working enterprise. These enterprises constitute what in Germany is popularly known as the 'Mittelstand'. A substantial percentage of Germany's exports come from these companies.

Among the millions of such SMEs are a fairly large number of small to medium-sized firms that are very successful as exporters in international markets. Many of them are even global market leaders in their respective product categories and business sectors. These and similar such companies are, however, relatively unknown to the general public and business community as they are mainly industrial products, value-added raw materials, process technologies, etc., that facilitate the production of many consumer end-products that are well known. They essentially cater to a niche in the industry they operate in, working on their strengths, in providing innovative products and services to a global market. Adapting to consumer needs and an excellent after-sales service are some of their other differentiating factors for their ongoing success. Their service is as good as the product with on an average of a 10 per cent to 15 per cent price premium. They mainly export to EU countries, followed by the US, BRICS and other emerging economies of the world. Most of them have a minimal of advertising and promotional budget, given the nature of their products and services.

These highly successful companies were first brought to the public view in 1996, as mentioned earlier, by Hermann Simon in his insightful study of them in his book, *Hidden Champions: Lessons from 500 of the World's Best Unknown Companies* and the sequel to it in 2009 called *Hidden Champions of the 21st Century: Success Strategies of Unknown World Market Leaders.* In his earlier book Hermann Simon studied a large number of leading German-owned companies, several hundred, based on their leading market shares in their respective product/industry sectors, turnover, reputation and the level of public awareness.

I have chosen to select a large number of the best of these companies, including several of my own choices, given their success to date and how they have fared in their respective global export markets (here too some companies declined to be included as they are publicity shy and avoid the spotlight).

Further, some of them have also been included to have a diversity of industrial representation. Given that, they are some of the best in the product/service category they belong to, the best of the German-owned export enterprises that are among the market leaders in their respective product/service markets.

These 'less-known champions' as I like to call them, in contrast to the earlier-described 'hidden champions', are less hidden now after Hermann Simon's brilliant work in the area. These 'less-known champions' included here are from a wide and diverse range of industries, from cinema cameras, surgical instruments, glass showcases and hops to assembly products, consultancies, machinery and equipment for different industries and applications, writing instruments, balances and scales, chains of different types, automotive parts and systems, packaging machinery, printing presses, fragrances and flavours, optical lenses and what have you, around 80 to 90 industry/product/service categories.

They are brands that have proven to be true champions in the markets they operate in, leading in market share and the latest in technological innovations and best practices. Many of them are global market leaders and have been so for several years. Though most of them are lesser-known to the general public, they are known and respected in their respective production locations and to the niche industrial customers and suppliers that they cater to. They also provide product and service consulting, system integration and ease of use, making the entry barriers to their niche very difficult to surmount.

As with most such companies around the world, they are usually family-owned or private limited companies. They have innovation-led success, a globalised mindset and export most of their production. Relying on traditional values of hard work, common sense and loyalty, they focus on doing what they do best. I have also included quite a few that are public limited companies and are listed on the Xetra Dax indices of the Frankfurt and other German stock exchanges.

The following 100 companies – the 'less-known champions' of Germany – have been listed in alphabetical order and not in any order of merit, success or performance. They have all been chosen according to their individual merit and success in their respective product/service categories and are amongst the best in their industrial/business sectors.

ARRI

The ARRI Group is the world's largest manufacturer and distributor of motion picture cameras, digital intermediate and lighting equipment. Throughout its history, ARRI has been associated with constant innovation and revolutionary technologies, from the legendary ARRIFLEX 35 – the first movie camera with a reflex mirror shutter – to the ARRI ALEXA, the most complete digital camera system ever built. In the world of motion picture imaging, ARRI has consistently set the standard that others follow.

It was in 1917, towards the end of World War I, that the two friends and aspiring cinematographers August Arnold and Robert Richter founded ARRI in Munich, Germany. The earliest products they manufactured and sold were film printers, the first of which was assembled from parts sourced at the local flea market! The name ARRI is made up of the first two letters from their respective surnames.

Today, the ARRI Group has over 1,200 highly trained employees worldwide. Around half of them are based in Munich, at the company's headquarters. The group's offerings include cameras, location and studio lighting equipment, digital intermediate (DI) systems such as the ARRISCAN and various archive tools, as well as equipment rental and post-production services. With a strong history of film camera systems covering the 16 mm, 35 mm and 65 mm formats, ARRI now leads the field in digital motion picture cameras as well, delivering the highest quality images with minimal noise, wide dynamic range and fast, versatile workflows.

ARRI's award-winning product range is distributed to film industry centres from Hollywood to Bollywood and everywhere in between through a global network of subsidiary companies, agents and representatives. The ARRI rental division provides customers with an unrivalled range of cutting-edge products wherever they might be shooting. Facilities in America, Canada, Europe, Asia and Australia, alongside more than 40 global partners, ensure that clients are never far from world-class ARRI service and support. On the post-production side, ARRI Film & TV have a number of facilities in Germany and Switzerland that provide state-of-the-art film, lab and digital intermediate services.

Over the years ARRI's engineers and their technical innovations have been recognised with a total of 18 scientific and engineering awards from the Academy of Motion Picture Arts and Sciences. Today, as always, the ARRI brand is synonymous with the highest levels of quality and reliability; it is the first choice for film and program makers around the world, from independent production companies to major Hollywood studios. (www.arri.de)

Baader

Baader is a group of companies with headquarters in Lübeck, Germany, that manufactures machines and solutions for the food-processing industry, namely fish and poultry processing machines and systems and associated engineering. They also have belt separators and machines for the poultry processing industry.

The company was founded in 1919 as the 'Nordischer Machinenbau Rudolph Baader GmbH & Co.KG' by Rudolph M.J. Baader. Today they are among the world's leading manufacturers of machines and systems for fish and poultry processing. Since its foundation, Baader has attached much importance to the state-of-the-art production technology in order to ensure the precise manufacture of thousands of individual parts. A comprehensive quality assurance system guarantees a defined quality standard. Baader Germany is certified according to DIN EN ISO 9001:2008.

The Baader Group is family owned and employs over 1,000 people worldwide. Petra Baader is the eldest daughter of the founder, Rudolf G. Baader. She is the CEO of the Baader Group. She took over the leadership of the family enterprise in 1995. The Baader Group has production sites in Lübeck, the US, Denmark, Iceland, as well as subsidiaries and offices worldwide.

In fish processing, they have a whole range of products from fish-filleting machines to fish in-feed and mechanical grading machines. They also provide a complete line of equipment and services to poultry processors from live-bird reception, to cut up, de-boning to skinning, batching and packaging. Baader is also known as a leading manufacturer of soft separators. Baadering is a proven method for separating soft and solid food components. They offer separators in five size ranges.

Baader also plans, designs and sets up complete processing lines as well as fish-processing facilities onshore or on board shipping vessels. They also have several machines for sizing, grading and batching of products. Agencies and service stations in more than 70 locations in the world are on hand to service the machines and provide spare parts. (www.baader.com)

BAUER

BAUER AG is an international construction and machinery manufacturing group based in Schrobenhausen in the state of Bayern. The SDAX listed company BAUER AG is the parent of more than 110 subsidiary businesses in the fields of construction, equipment and resources.

The company was founded in 1790 in Schrobenhausen, when Sebastian Bauer acquired the right to set up a copper smithy there. Over the years they moved into specialist foundation construction and machinery manufacturing.

Today, BAUER AG is a leader in the execution of complex excavation pits, foundations and vertical seals as well as in the development and manufacture of related machinery for this dynamic market. The group also deploys its expertise in the exploration, mining and safeguarding of valuable mineral resources. In 2011, the companies of the BAUER Group employed some 9,700 people in some 70 countries and achieved total group revenues of €1.4 billion. Thomas Bauer is the present CEO and Chairman of the Management Board of BAUER AG while Klaus Reinhardt is the Chairman of the Supervisory Board. The Bauer family holds 48.19 per cent of the shareholding while the rest of the 51.81 per cent is in free float.

The BAUER Group has divided its activities into three business segments: construction, equipment and resources. In the construction segment, BAUER Spezialtiefbau Gmbh has been a major driving force in the development of specialist foundation engineering and carries out projects all over the world. Bauer Spezialtiefbau is organised on a regional basis in Germany and operates on all the world's continents with over 50 subsidiaries and branch offices.

The core company Bauer Spezialtiefbau Gmbh executes foundations, excavation pits, cut-off walls and ground improvements all over the world. Their main services are all kinds of bored piles, anchors, diaphragm and cut-off walls as well as injections and deep vibrations.

In the equipment business segment, BAUER Maschinen Group is the world market leader in the development and manufacture of specialist foundation engineering and mining equipment. They are also a holding company for a number of subsidiaries. The group designs and builds heavy-duty rotary drilling rigs, trench cutters, grab systems and vibrators as well as the related tooling at its plants in Schrobenhausen, Aresing and Edelshausen. The group also operates manufacturing facilities in the US, Russia, China, Malaysia, Italy and Sweden. The 'BAUER Maschinen Group' operates a global sales and service network.

In the resources segment, businesses which have grown up over a period of years or even decades in the construction and equipment sectors have been consolidated within a new organisation, beneath the umbrella of BAUER Resources Gmbh, this company coordinates activity, in the areas of water, the environment, energy and mineral deposits.

State-of-the-art technology forms the basis for all their construction engineering and equipment manufacturing processes. The success of their investment in research and development is demonstrated by around 240 current patent series, including almost 1,100 patent applications, registered patents and utility models worldwide.

The environmental management systems of their major production locations within their group are certified to ISO 14001 or EMAS. Environmental protection is a corporate goal of the BAUER Environment Group in its re-mediation of contaminated soil and ground water. The technical expertise of the BAUER companies lies in the treatment of water in a wide variety of areas such as drinking water, grey water, industrial and domestic waste water as well as in the capture, recovery and distribution of ground water, often in locations where this is particularly difficult. Their 'PURE' reed-bed sewage treatment systems can be used even in deserts. (www.bauer.de)

Barth-Haas

The Barth-Haas Group is the world's largest supplier of hops products and services. The group is family owned and has offices and operations in Germany, the US, UK, Australia and China. The brewing industry values hops as an irreplaceable ingredient in beer. Other industries value them in wide-ranging applications from environmentally friendly processing aids to health enhancing compounds.

Represented in all major hops growing areas in the world, they cater to large and small breweries around the world. The Barth-Haas Group is the world leader in hops production and cultivation, hops processing, storage and logistics services and R&D as well as application technologies for the brewing and other industries. Their corporate slogan is 'Hops are our World'.

The parent company, Joh. Barth & Sohn, was established in the city of Nuremberg in 1794 and is now managed by the eighth generation of the founding family. The company is today managed by managing partners Stephan Barth, his brother Alexander Barth and their cousin Regine Barth. They have around 600 employees worldwide of which 270 work in Germany. Group revenues as of fiscal year 2011 were €220 million.

The Barth-Haas Group consists of several companies apart from the parent company, Joh. Barth & Sohn; they include John I. Haas in the US, Hop Products of Australia, Botanix in the UK and Group Companies in China. Their plants in Germany include NATECO2 and Hopfenveredlung St. Johann, a joint venture with their minority partner HVG. Then they have Simply Hops and Barth !nnovations, two UK-based companies. The group have several trading offices and other shareholdings too.

NATECO2 is the world's biggest producer of hops, extracts and natural substances that can be obtained using CO_2 as a solvent. The Hopfenveredlung St. Johann operates not only the world's largest hops pelletisation plant, but also its own research brewery.

The Barth-Haas Group provides traditional-aroma hops products as well as several hops essential oil selections. They have the newer, more functional PHA products which add ease-of-use and flexibility for their customer's hops aroma needs. The group has established a quality management system based on ISO 9001:2000, as well as the international HACCP guidelines for quality and safety. They also have the Barth-Haas Hops Academy that offers a variety of courses in all there is to know about hops. (www.barthhaasgroup.com)

B.Braun

B.Braun supplies the global healthcare market with products for anaesthesia, intensive medicine, cardiology, extra-corporeal blood treatment and surgery as well services for hospitals, general practitioners and the home-care sector.

The company was founded in 1839 when Julius Wilhelm Braun purchased the Rosen-Apotheke, a pharmacy in Melsungen, Germany. He expanded it with a mail-order business for local herbs. His eldest son, Bernhard Braun, who had begun to produce pharma products, registered the company name in the commercial register as B.Braun in 1867. Aesculap, which is a part of B.Braun, was also founded in this year when Gottfried Jetter, a qualified knife maker, began manufacturing surgical instruments in Tuttlingen, Germany. B.Braun Melsungen AG is now a stock corporation whose corporate slogan is 'Sharing Expertise'.

Today, B.Braun is one of the world's leading healthcare suppliers with around 45,000 employees in 56 countries. B.Braun achieved a turnover in 2011 of €4.609 billion! B.Braun's corporate headquarters are located at the Pfieffewiesen site in Melsungen in the northern part of the German state of Hessen. They have over 200 subsidiaries in Germany and around the world. Heinz-Walter Große is the Chairman of the Management Board. The company is managed by a seven-member management board.

Their four divisions orient their products and services toward different medical fields, namely, hospital surgery, private practice (medical care and doctors' offices) and extra-corporeal blood treatment.

The hospital care division supplies hospitals with infusion and injection solutions as well as disposable medical products.

Their Aesculap division focuses on products and services for all of the core processes in surgery.

The outpatient market (OPM) supplies medical products, outside of the hospital market as well as for chronically ill and long-term patients.

The B.Braun Avitum division combines the supply of medical products and services, concerning extra-corporeal blood treatment.

The strengths of B.Braun lie in its know-how and perfected technologies. They create user-friendly products combining the new with the tried and tested, with safety and quality of prime importance. Four of their facilities in Germany have received both EMAS regulation and DIN EN ISO 14001 validation and certification.

The Aesculap Academy of the company contributes to the interdisciplinary communication and dialogue in medicine since 1995 through a wide range of course offerings, seminars and workshops.

Over the years, the company has won several national and international awards for their products and services, ideas, human resources and corporate social involvement. (www.bbraun.com)

Berleburger (BSW)

Berleburger or BSW is one of the leading suppliers of products made from polyurethane-bound rubber granulates. With their material Regupol®, they produce numerous elastic, protective and absorbing products for a variety of applications. Their product range focuses on the production of elastic sports floors/surfaces and insulation products. Regufoam®, their second mainstay, specializes in foams. They produce world-famous Judo mats, BSW Tatami, other sports mats and customised moulded parts in compound foams.

Recoflex® is another brand that is an innovative elastic particle board made from wood, cork, latex and polyurethane binders used in the furniture industry and also in flooring systems. Furthermore, Variofoam® is a type of foam with composites consisting of different basic materials and additives. Applications include customised products and systems components used in the auto, packaging, construction, shoes, agriculture, furniture and appliances industries.

BSW began manufacturing products from polyurethane raw material way back in 1954 in a town called Bad Berleburger. The foam products gave the company its name – Berleburger Schaumstoff Werk, which in English means the 'Berleburger Foam Factory'. The present CEOs of BSW are Ulf Pöppel and Rainer Pöppel.

Today, BSW has become a business operating on a global scale, with subsidiaries in Australia and in the US. BSW now has international sales representatives and established trading partners in over 50 countries. The Group generated an annual turnover of over €70 million with a workforce of around 360 employees. The BSW product range is comprised of several application areas, from sports floors/surfaces and regular flooring to impact protection, insulation protection, impact sound insulation, vibration technology, load securing and Judo mats.

The company, which makes their products with the highest safety and environmental standards, has been certified by TÜV Rheinland according to the DIN EN ISO 9001, DIN EN ISO 14001 and OHSAS 18001 for their award-winning manufacturing process. Usain Bolt, the Jamaican 100-metre world champion and world record holder, has recently concluded an advertising contract with BSW, having broken an amazing two world records on their blue Regupol running track. (www.berleburger.com)

Berner

Berner is one of the leading European direct sales companies in the small-parts business for professional use in the building and automobile trades as well as in other industries. The combined Berner Group is made up of Berner SE Künzelsau, Caramba and BTI in Ingelfingen.

The company was founded in 1957 by Albert Berner, who opened the business to manufacture screws in the town of Künzelsau in the state of Baden-Württemberg.

The public limited company had a sales turnover of €1billion for financial year 2011 and employs around 9,000 people worldwide, with headquarters in Künzelsau. The Berner Group and its 60 companies are located in 25 countries. Christian Berner and Lothar Aulich are the members of the Executive Board of the combined Berner Group, while the company founder Albert Berner is the Chairman of the Supervisory board. The group at present consists of Berner SE, the BTI concern and the Caramba Chemical group. Around 5,700 employees work in field sales, ensuring that customers receive professional advice and are well looked after. BTI, as one of the leading direct sellers to the building construction industry in Germany and Spain, offers an almost fully comprehensive range of products for all trades.

The Caramba Chemical Group is active in the development, manufacture and marketing of specialist technical chemicals. Their customers are supported by a sales and production network throughout Europe. Repositioning of the 100-year-old Caramba brand with its strong constituent companies Wigo, Tegee Rumler, Christian Maurer, Corra, Apex, Matecra, Ambratec and ACC was started in 2010.

The Berner Group has a product range of over 60,000 products, consisting of consumer groups, chemicals for the automotive and construction industry, tools, workshop equipment, storage systems, drilling technology, plugs and anchors, parting-off and grinding technology, DIN and standard parts, electrical components for cars, soldering and welding technology, direct assembly and several more such products. Their products essentially cater to customers in the construction and automotive sectors from the wood-working trade, water related installations, metal-working companies and industrial maintenance, from manufacturers to service and maintenance companies.

They have a total of 100,000 square metres of warehousing space in the whole of Europe. Having a high service level of 98 per cent, they deliver to the customer within 24 to 48 hours. Personalised, individual customer support has the highest priority in Berner. They also guarantee swift, process-optimised delivery of C-parts to their customer's workshop or warehouse.

Berner's corporate slogan is 'Experts with Passion'. (www.berner-group.com)

BioTest

BioTest AG is a company specialising in innovative haemotology and immunology products with the holistic approach of a global pharmaceutical group. They manufacture and sell medicinal products for the treatment of blood and immune diseases.

The company was founded in 1946 as Biotest-Serum-Institute GmbH by Carl-Adolf Schleussner and Hans Schleussner. The family enterprise initially focused on research on blood typing serology.

Sales revenue for fiscal year 2011 was in the region of €422 million. They have a total staff of around 1,700 employees worldwide. Gregor Schulz is the Chairman of the Board of Management while Alessandro Banchi is the Chairman of the Supervisory Board. Biotest AG has its headquarters in Dreieich, near Frankfurt. Their corporate slogan is 'From Nature for Life'.

Their products and services include plasma proteins and monoclonal antibodies. Biotest is one of the leading global suppliers in pharma sub-markets such as poly-specific immunoglobulins and plasma-based factor preparations.

They have subsidiaries in Germany, Europe, the US, Japan and Australia, while sales partners in 80 countries distribute their products and customers in 159 countries around the globe put their trust in Biotest's quality and safety. Biotest invests more than 10 per cent of its yearly turnover in R&D. Since the products are used in the long-term therapy of chronic diseases, in intensive care and emergency medicine, they make sure the products are of the highest quality with production processes that more than meet legally required procedures and the control and documentation requirements of government boards. Quality, user benefit, reliability and safety are their highest priorities. (www.biotest.de)

Bizerba

Bizerba is a worldwide operating technology company that has a leading market position with regard to professional system solutions in the areas of weighing, information, communication and food service technology for the retail, food and logistics industries.

The roots of the company go back to 1866, when Andreas Bizer joined the workshop of the brothers Bizer in the town of Balingen. In 1868, A. Bizer had his scales workshop entered in the trade register. The company name comes from the surname Bizer and the Ba from Balingen, the town where it was founded.

Today, Bizerba GmbH & Co.KG has around 3,000 employees and is present in over 89 countries with 41 shareholdings in 23 countries and 54 country organisations. Michael Ungethüm is the Chairman of the Supervisory Board, while Andreas Kraut is the Chairman of the Management Board.

Bizerba's headquarters are situated in Balingen, Germany. The production plants for the food-service machines are in Meßkirch and paper and labels are manufactured in Bochum, apart from other plants in Austria, Switzerland, Italy, the US and Mexico. The platforms for the Asian market are manufactured in Shanghai.

The products and services offered by Bizerba are retail scales, cash registers, food service machines, stock information systems, industrial weighing and data technology, control scales, price and goods labelling systems, logistics and shipping systems, automotive, paper and labels, service and leasing.

Bizerba believes in total quality. They have integrated management systems that are certified to ISO 9001:2000, environmental management systems certified to EN ISO 14001. Their test laboratories are accredited to EN ISO/IEC 17025, and they also have many more such certifications.

They have introduced several product innovations over the years that have helped them stay in the forefront of technology. Their corporate slogan is '... closer to your business'. Among the latest offerings, in 2010, was the K-Class Flex, a new generation of PC scales and till series, the K-Class in modular design, heralding a new age of weighing technology. (www.bizerba.com)

Böllhoff

Böllhoff is a family-run enterprise consisting of an international group of companies specialising in fastening, assembly and systems technology. They have a network of 36 companies in 21 countries with about 2,200 motivated employees. The Böllhoff Group generated a sales volume of €453 million in financial year 2011. The group completed 135 years of its existence in 2012.

The Böllhoff Group was established in 1877, when the founder, Willhelm Böllhoff, opened a wholesale hardware business in a town called Herdecke.

Wilhelm A. Böllhoff with his brother Michael W. Böllhoff took over the leadership of the company in 2004 with headquarters in Bielefeld, Germany, while Jan Rinnert is the Chairman of their Advisory board. Their corporate slogan is 'Joining Together'.

Böllhoff is a customer-oriented group divided into two business areas, namely, fastening and assembly technology and fastener service supply. Each of them offers a complete one-stop service for a particular area of technical expertise. Their team of specialists are available round the clock to provide technical support and expert advice on-site.

They are specialists in the development of innovative and high-quality advanced fastening technology. On offer are a variety of solutions for metallic and synthetic materials, including blind rivet technology, thread technology, plastic joining technology and quick-locking technologies, all in combination with a broad range of processing systems that range from single hand tools right through to full-scale robot systems.

With a view to the future, their close collaboration with customers in the aerospace and automotive sectors is helping them develop new fastening technologies for use with advanced materials and innovative assembly methods.

In addition to a broad range of fasteners they also provide numerous services designed to make things more efficient all along the customers' value-added chain. With ECOSIT®, Böllhoff provides the complete range of modern logistic services. ECOTECH application consulting service helps customers choose the right product for their applications. The ECOLINE service package provides an online platform for a continuous and fast information flow between Böllhoff and their customers. While ECOPACK service individually packs and delivers in bags to their customers. Böllhoff has its own accredited test laboratory certified to DIN EN ISO/IEC 17025. The company also has DIN EN ISO 14001 certification for environmental standards. (www.boellhoff.de)

Brähler

Brähler ICS Konferenztechnik AG develops and sells simultaneous interpreting, microphone discussion and audience response voting systems throughout the world. Brähler ICS (International Congress Service) traces its beginnings back to 1958, the year Helmut Brähler developed and built his first simultaneous interpretation systems in Bonn, Germany. Brähler ICS is regarded as one of the inventors of conference technology.

Within a few years, Brähler's, unique combination of high-quality conference technology and reliable rental service had established its market position in Europe. Through technological innovation and a high level of customer proximity, the fast-growing company set new standards in the field of consumer electronics.

Michael Brähler is the owner while Daniel Middendorf the General Manager of the Board of Management and Walter Hantzsche the Chairman of the Supervisory Board. The company headquarters are in Königswinter.

Brähler ICS also rents its conference technology systems through branches, subsidiaries and the Worldwide Brähler ICS Network, which is in more than hundred cities in 85 countries. Its rental experience flows directly into the development of new systems, whereby proximity to their clients gives the company a high degree of customer orientation. In Germany, they have branches in Berlin, Hamburg, Dresden, Königswinter, Stuttgart and Munich. Their particular strength is in providing technical support at events for seven to 20,000 participants regardless of whether it is a G8 World Economic Summit, the Olympic Games, the Berlin International Film Festival, conference centres or a confederation conference.

Brähler offers its customers complete conference systems, including the Brähler systems: CDSVAN, DIGIMIC, AUTOMIC, DIGIVOTE and INFRACOM, as well as AV systems which can be integrated with other systems. Apart from the equipment, Brähler has highly qualified staff for consultation, planning, project management, installation, as well as equipment operation. They also offer training courses for their customers and partners. Brähler ICS is ISO 9001:2000 certified for all work, including development, manufacture, sales and rental service.

Brähler has installed conference systems in some of the major international organisations, parliaments and conference centres of the world, like the European Parliament in Strasbourg, the National Conference Center in Qatar, the International Court of Justice in the Hague, the Parliament in Myanmar, the Cairo International Convention Centre, the Mannheim Congress Centre with RFID technology, The Great Peoples Hall, Beijing and the Parliament in Tunis just to mention a few.

Their rental services have been used by the WTO Conference, Hong Kong; the EU Hampton Court Meeting with 24 interpreted languages; United Nations summits such as UNEP Dubai; talks on Afghanistan in Bonn/Berlin; the Munich Conference on security policy; the annual meetings of Interpol; the Climate Change Conferences, etc.

In 2011, Brähler ICS won the iF Product design award for their new CMic Delegate Unit, which is part of the DIGIMIC classic conferencing system. (www.braehler.com)

Brainlab

Brainlab GmbH was founded in Munich in 1989 by founder, president and CEO Stefan Vilsmeier, who developed the first surgical system using menu-driven software.

Today, Brainlab is an award-winning innovator in image-guided surgery and stereoactic radio-surgery. With headquarters in Munich and regional offices across the globe, Brainlab develops, manufactures and markets software-driven medical equipment. This technology enables procedures that are more precise, less invasive and therefore less expensive than traditional treatment.

Brainlab solutions allow expansion from a single system to operating suites to digitally integrated hospitals covering all sub-specialities from neuro-surgery, orthopaedics, ENT, CMF to spine and trauma and oncology.

With more than 5,000 systems installed in over 80 countries, Brainlab is a market leader in image-guided technology. The privately held Brainlab Group employs around 1,070 people in 17 offices across Europe, Asia, Australia and the Americas. About 600 employees work in the Feldkirchen, Munich headquarters, including 280 R&D engineers, who form a major part of the product development team. English is the official language at Brainlab.

Among the core products are image-guided systems that provide highly accurate, real-time information used for navigation during surgical procedures. This utility has been further expanded to serve as a computer terminal for physicians to more effectively access and interpret diagnostic scans and other digital medical information for better informed decisions. Close cooperation with their suppliers and strong strategic relationships with industry leaders provides Brainlab with access to complimentary technologies, knowledge, distribution systems and service networks.

With 220 service engineers worldwide, Brainlab's technical support services provide the best customer service by proactively maintaining their system. They also have an academy to educate, enhance and develop user skills. The corporate values of Brainlab are, 'Simplicity, Integrity and Inspiration'. Among the many awards the founder has received are the 'Entrepreneur of the Year' awarded by Ernst & Young in 2001, 'Global Leader for Tomorrow' by the World Economic Forum and the 'Distinguished Service Medal' by the Bavarian government in 2001, while in 2012 they won the coveted Red Dot Award in product design for their feature by benefit, Curve™. (www.brainlab.com)

Brita

Brita GmbH is one of the world's leading providers in water filtration. A family-owned enterprise, it was established in 1966 by Heinz Hankammer in the town of Taunusstein. Today, the company has around 1,010 employees worldwide, with a turnover in 2011 of around €320.7 million.

The company is run by the second generation in the person of Markus Hankammer, who is the CEO of the company. They have production plants in Germany, the UK and Switzerland. Brita products are distributed worldwide in more than 60 countries on all five continents by 15 subsidiaries and numerous distribution partners. In 2000, they sold their North American business to the Clorox Company in California.

Brita is the inventor of the water filter jug for private use. Today, the company develops, manufactures and distributes innovative drinking water for the household with a wide range of jug water filters and cartridges for domestic use, from kettles to tap and fridge/freezers. Recognizing the broader applications for its innovative technology, Brita has since 1980 been manufacturing water filters for professional use in coffee and espresso machines, vending machines, steamers, conventional ovens, dishwashers and drinking water dispensers with a fixed tap connection. In doing so, they have improved the food and beverage flavour, presentation as well as the cost-efficiency.

Brita's third area of operations, Brita integrated solutions, is comprised of partnerships with international manufacturers of domestic appliances, including BSH (Bosch Siemens Haushaltsgeräte) GmbH, Cloer, Breville, Murphy Richards and Pegler, who integrate Brita's household water filter cartridges into their appliances to offer their customers the advantages of Brita filtered water.

Over the years, Brita has won several international design awards for its innovative products, apart from others for the company and its performance. Numerous national and international product patents give it a head start in the field of innovation, while product safety and quality assurance are constantly tested by independent institutes and scientists. (www.brita.net)

brose

The brose Group manufactures mechatronic systems and electric drives for around 80 automakers and more than 30 suppliers worldwide. They cater to some of the best companies of the world. The roots of the company go back to 1908 when Max Brose set up a trading company for automobile accessories in Berlin. In 1919, together with his partner Ernst Jühling, they founded the Metallwerk Max brose & Co. to include the production of automobile components as well.

Today, more than 21,000 employees work for brose at 53 locations in 23 countries in all the major automotive markets of the world. The brose Group has its present headquarters in Coburg, Germany, and is the fourth largest family-owned company among the top 100 automotive suppliers of the world. In financial year 2013, the group expects a turnover of around €4.6 billion.

Michael Stoschek, the grandson of the founder, is the present Chairman of the brose Group, while Jürgen Otto is the present CEO. Their corporate slogan is 'Technology for the Automobile'.

brose's current product portfolio includes systems for automobile doors, systems for seats, electric motors and drives and electronics for mechatronic systems in vehicles. The focus is on new products designed to cut fuel consumption. At the same time, their components and systems enable them to make automobiles safer and more comfortable to use.

Today, they annually supply more than 6.5 million seat structures, 80 million door systems and some 10 million adjuster systems to some 40 automakers and seat manufacturers. They also supply, among other things, electric motors for automobiles, of which they annually produce around 90 million.

The brose Group and several of its production locations are certified as per ISO/TS 16949:2009 in line with 9001:2008 and ISO 14001:2004. Over the years, the group, its production locations and products have won several awards, including 'Factory of the Year 2012', amongst the 'Best Employers', 'Quality Prize' and awards from several of their satisfied customers. (www.brose.com)

3B Scientific

3B Scientific is an international group of companies that specialises in the manufacture and marketing of didactic or teaching material for scientific, medical and patient education. The parent company was founded in 1948 in Hamburg by the 3Bs, namely, Paul Binhold, his wife, Hedwig Binhold, and their daughter, Marion Binhold, now Marion Kurland. The group also has subsidiaries in Hungary that began manufacturing in 1819.

Today, the brand name 3B Scientific is represented in over 100 countries in the medical and educational sector. They are the worldwide market leader in the anatomical teaching aids market. The excellent quality of 3B Scientific products manufactured by skilled and trained personnel, plus the flexibility of processing global customer requirements are the essential factors accounting for their ongoing success. 3B's corporate slogan is '... going one step further'.

They have a workforce of 600 people worldwide, of whom around 240 are placed in their headquarters in Hamburg, with a total of 350 in Germany. The company has three managing directors, Otto H. Gies, Marion Kurland and Manfred Kurland. They have subsidiaries in Germany, the UK, the US, Europe, South America and in Asia.

The 3B Scientific product line includes the following: artificial skeletons, torsos and human organ models, teaching aids and systems from the fields of physics and technology, injection training arms, patient care mannequins and medical simulators, biology, zoology and chemistry models, anatomical charts and ana(c)omical gift items, anatomical teaching and learning software and SEIRIN® acupuncture needles. They also have Pilates and fitness equipment as well as treatment furniture. Recent additions have been the Kinesiology Tape & Acu Tape, Laser Pen, Laser Shower and other therapy and fitness products.

Their customers include universities, schools, ministries of health and education, other health and education authorities, hospitals, practitioners, educational and medical distributors, students and the pharmaceutical industry. Ninety per cent of their sales are made outside of Germany.

All of their product development is carried out exclusively in Germany. The outstanding quality standards upheld in every product that carries the brand name 3B Scientific is guaranteed by their strict quality controls. 3B Scientific has been certified in accordance with DIN EN ISO 9001:2008. (www.3bscientific.com)

Claas

Claas is one of the world's leading companies in agricultural machinery with headquarters in the town of Harsewinkel in the state of North-Rhine Westphalia. They manufacture tractors, combines and forage and green harvesting machinery under the brand names Lexion in North America and Claas elsewhere. Claas is the European market leader in combine harvesters and the global market leader in its second main product group of self-propelled forage harvesters.

The company was founded in 1913 by August Claas at Clarholz, Westphalia. In 1919, they moved to Harsewinkel to manufacture straw binders.

Today, the group has 14 manufacturing operations in Germany, Europe, North America and throughout the world. They are where their customers are. Sales turnover in fiscal year 2011 was in the region of €3.304 billion with around 9,060 employees worldwide. R&D expenditure for fiscal year 2011 was around €144.3 million.

A family-owned business, Theo Freye is the Speaker of the Executive Board. Cathrina Claas-Mühlhäuser is the Chairwoman of the Claas Supervisory Board. The legal form of the company has been changed to a KGaA (a commercial partnership with limited liability).

Reliability, perseverance and innovativeness are the qualities that make Claas a strong partner to the world's agricultural industry.

Claas has recently launched a new Super Lexion, the fastest combine harvester of all time. With the new generation of the Lexion, Claas has introduced two model series, 700 and 600, that are a lot faster, much more comfortable, even more productive and economical.

Claas was one of the first to recognise the benefits that automated steering would have on operator efficiency and output and currently offers a comprehensive range of cost-effective and advanced steering systems.

Claas is bundling its electronics expertise under one name: EASY (Efficient Agriculture Systems). EASY, harnesses Claas's full spectrum of electronics expertise – from machine settings and steering systems to software solutions for a wide range of applications and working processes. For on board, on the field, on track and on the farm, their range of products and services includes combines, forage harvesters, tractors, square and round balers, forage harvesting machinery, telehandlers, agricultural management, efficient agriculture systems and original Claas parts. (www.claas.com)

Cloos

Cloos develops, manufactures and delivers innovative solutions in welding and cutting of various ferrous and non-ferrous metals. They are a pioneer in modern welding technology and an international market leader. The company was founded in 1919 by Carl Cloos who set up Carl Cloos Schweisstechnik GmbH in Siegen Weidenau, Germany, to manufacture acetylene gas generators and oxy-acetylene welding torches.

Today, with headquarters in the town of Haiger, Cloos caters to more than 40 countries worldwide, with 500 employees in their production plant in Haiger, which forms the centrepiece of their business. Their innovative and robot technology is one of their core competencies by which they accomplish the most difficult welding tasks. Ralf Pulverich and Robert Buchmann are the managing directors of the company. Their corporate slogan is 'Weld your Way'.

Their QINEO® brand is the new generation of welding machines for manual and automated applications and QIROX® the system for automated welding and cutting. Their product range covers the entire spectrum of arc-welding technology. Their product portfolio includes intelligent software, sensors and safety technology solutions – all of which are customised to meet the customer's specific needs and requirements and to achieve optimal welding results.

The QINEO® CHAMP is a quantum leap in high-tech welding. Efficient, precise and versatile, this high-tech equipment meets the highest standards in every performance and under complex performance requirements. Flexible and low cost operationally, this state-of-the-art solution is a new dimension in welding technology.

Cloos has more than 45 sales and service centres worldwide. In addition, their experienced team in Haiger are always on call for technical problems, break-downs etc. Cloos is among the pioneers of modern welding, providing added value to their customers. (www.cloos.de)

Dachser

Dachser is one of Europe's leading logistics providers. Dachser has made logistics history time and time again through its innovations in swap bodies, bar codes and the Active Report, a supply-chain event management tool, among many others.

The company was founded in 1930 by Thomas Dachser, who started a local haulage operation in Kempten, Allgäu, in southern Germany. Today, after over eight decades, this family-owned company has grown into a leading European logistics provider with worldwide operations.

Dachser employs over 21,000 employees in 315 profit centres worldwide. Annual sales as of financial year 2011 were around €4.3 billion. They have a total of around 1.63 million square metres of warehouse space and around 10,000 transport units. In 2011, they handled 49.3 million consignments, weighing a total of 37.1 million tonnes.

The present Managing Director and Management Spokesman is Bernhard Simon, who is the grandson of the company founder. Jürgen Schneider is the Chairman of the Supervisory Board. A five-member management team heads up the various business segments and divisions which consist of European logistics, food logistics and air and sea logistics. They also have specialised industry solutions: chem-logistics, DIY-logistics and contract logistics.

Dachser's corporate slogan is 'Intelligent Logistics', claiming to create the world's most intelligent combination and integration of logistic network services.

A high-capacity, pan-European network with 158 company-owned locations and 3,827 daily scheduled services makes Dachser one of Europe's leading logistics providers.

They are also one of Germany's leading specialists in temperature-controlled food logistics, maintaining top-quality standards for retailers and the industry. For its worldwide air and sea logistics, Dachser uses a network of more than 400 service stations.

In their specialised solutions, Dachser's DIY Logistics is the industry logistics solution provider for the DIY sector. Dachser has achieved an uninterrupted global value chain from the manufacturer to the point of sale and supplies 18,000 European outlets each day.

Chem-Logistics is specially tailored to chemical companies, as it fulfils the sector's strict requirements for the transport and storage of chemical products.

Dachser's IT systems that are networked, flexible and highly efficient are a key factor in their ongoing success story.

Dachser is committed to a sustainable corporate policy and are conscious of their economic, environmental and social responsibilities, an example being the use of vehicles with low-emission criteria and buildings with the latest energy-efficiency standards. (www.dachser.com)

Deichmann

The Deichmann SE Group is Europe's largest footwear retailer. It all began in 1913, when Heinrich Deichmann opened a shoemaker's shop in the Borbeck district of Essen. Six years later he began retailing factory made shoes. Deichmann have made stylish shoes affordable for everyone.

Today, Deichmann operates in 22 countries including the US. They have around 3,200 stores and 32,500 employees. In 2011, the group sold around 156 million pairs of shoes worldwide. Heinrich Otto Deichmann, the grandson of the founder, is the Chairman of the Board of Directors and of the Executive Directors of the group. The Deichmann headquarters are in Essen. Sales revenue for fiscal year 2011 was €4.13 billion.

With its range of traditional and established house brands and a wide selection of models, Deichmann is always putting something new on the shelves. Deichmann's trend scouts are active all over the world tracking down tomorrow's new styles. The company buys shoes in over 40 countries worldwide. Their employees check on production procedures and experts provide assistance and technical support to the suppliers. Every article is tested for harmful substances and the leather, sole and the sizes are carefully checked as well with constant random sampling tests. Recognised institutes and testing laboratories also ensure quality and safety standards are met. In 2010, Deichmann for the first time, brought special Elefanten and Medicus shoes to the market that have been produced under special ecological standards.

The shoes and accessories are delivered, annually to the stores from their four German distribution centres and from their Swiss, Dutch, Slovakian, British and Polish centres, to ensure the smooth supply of their merchandise. In America – Deichmann operates through their subsidiaries, Rack Room Shoes and Off Broadway, where they're quite successful. In Switzerland they sell through, Dosenbach and Ochsner, where they are the market leaders.

When sourcing shoes from Asian countries, Deichmann makes certain that a comprehensive, binding code of conduct forms an integral part of their supply contracts. Making sure of the quality and that they are ethically made. They also undertake socially responsible projects in disaster areas and other underdeveloped areas of the world. (www.deichmann.com)

Delo

Delo is a leading manufacturer of industrial adhesives and bonding systems with headquarters in Windach, a town close to Munich. The company provides tailor-made, special adhesives and equipment for applications in all lines of business: from electronics to the chip card and automotive industries as well as in glass and plastic processing.

Delo is a family-owned company managed by the two owners, a husband and wife team of Wolf-Dietrich Herold and Sabine Herold. The company was founded in 1961 in Munich to manufacture industrial adhesives. It was taken over by ESPE Dental AG in 1989 and in 1997; it became an independent company in the course of a management buy-out by the present owners.

Today, the company has around 300 employees with a turnover of around €44 million for fiscal year 2011. Fifty-seven per cent of the turnover was achieved outside Germany. They have a subsidiary in the US, distributors and representatives in Europe, the US, China, Singapore, Korea and Taiwan. Their products help make processes more efficient in a wide variety of industries which include electronics/microelectronics, smart card/smart label, automobile, mechanical engineering and plant construction, metal processing, glass and plastic processing. Delo also provides technical consulting, training and support.

Delo stands for outstanding quality and is certified to ISO 9001:2008 standards. Quality is assured by a continuous process of improvement. Furthermore, they make sure that no hazardous or toxic substances are used in the production of adhesives. Their innovative, light activated adhesives Delo-Katiobond is a world leader in their category. Delo's corporate slogan is 'Leading by intelligent bonding technology'.

They have won several awards for quality and delivery reliability. In 2009, they received the 'RadTech Award' for the development of light-curing epoxies for sealing flexible displays as well as several awards for innovation in the medium-sized businesses in Germany. They also got the seal of quality as a 'Top Employer' in 2007 for their merits in the field of human resources. (www.delo.de)

Dräger

Dräger is an international leader in medical and safety technology with headquarters in Lübeck, Germany. Founded in 1889 in Lübeck, Dräger is a fifth-generation family business that developed into a global, publicly traded company. 'Technology for Life' is the guiding philosophy of the Dräger Group and describes its mission, whether in clinical settings, industry, mining and rescue services. Dräger products protect, support and save lives.

Dräger employs around 12,000 people and operates in over 190 countries around the globe. The group operates sales and service companies in around 40 countries. They have development and production facilities in Germany, Great Britain, Sweden, South Africa, the US, Brazil, the Czech Republic and China. Group turnover for fiscal year 2011 was €2.26 billion. Stefan Dräger is the Chairman of the Executive Board of Dräger while Nikolaus Schweickart is the Chairman of the Supervisory Board.

The products and services of their medical division include medical anaesthesia workstations, ventilation equipment for intensive care and home care, emergency and mobile ventilation units, warming therapy equipment for infants, patient monitoring systems, as well as IT solutions and gas management systems.

The safety division offers its customers complete hazard management solutions with a special focus on personal safety and production protection facilities. Their current portfolio includes stationary and mobile gas detection systems, respiratory protection, fire-fighting equipment, professional diving gear and alcohol- and drug-testing instruments.

The European Society of Anesthesiology (ESA) awarded the 2012 'ESA Dräger Prize in Anesthesia and Intensive Care Medicine' for the sixth time in a row within the scope of the Euroanaesthesia Congress. Dräger donated the prize money of 10,000 euro.

They have won designer awards in the 2010 'Industry Forum of Design' Hannover, for their Evita Infinity V500 ventilator and Oxylog 3000 plus emergency and mobile ventilation equipment. Since 1998, companies at their Lübeck site have been certified in accordance with DIN EN ISO 14001 as part of a group certification. (www.draeger.com)

Dürr

The Dürr Group is one of the world's leading suppliers of products, systems and services, catering mainly to the automobile manufacturer. The company was founded in 1895 by Paul Dürr in the town of Canstatt. He started with a metal shop for roof flashing and later moved on to sheet metal processing. Although Stuttgart is the registered head office of Dürr AG, the present headquarters are in Bietigheim-Bissingen.

Today, the group has around 7,100 employees working worldwide with representation in 23 countries at various business locations. Annual sales revenue for fiscal year 2011 was in the region of €1.9 billion. Ralf Dieter is the present CEO and Chairman of the Board of Management of Dürr AG, and Heinz Dürr is the Chairman of the Supervisory Board.

The Dürr Group consists of four divisions, namely Paint and Assembly Systems, Application Technology, Measuring and Process Systems and Clean Technology Systems, under these are seven business units with an additional unit, The Schenck Technology and Industry Park.

The Paint and Assembly Systems primarily caters to systems and equipment business within the automotive industry. They are the world's leading supplier for mass production paint shops for automobile manufacturers and suppliers. The Paint and Assembly Systems division plans and carries out complete assembly lines for the final assembly of vehicles. Their range of products and services are rounded off with assembly and paint systems for aircraft construction.

Their second division, Application Technology, is a world-market and technology leader in the high-tech sector of automated paint application. Regardless of body form, paint systems or number of production units, they have well-engineered solutions and software at their disposal, for example, robots, atomisers and colour-change systems.

The Measuring and Process Systems division offers machines and systems for balancing and diagnostics as well as for industrial cleaning. Their largest group of customers are the automotive industry, where their equipment is used, for example, in the manufacture of engines and transmissions. Other major customer groups are the aerospace, engineering, electrical and power generation industries. Their range of products is rounded off with assembly, filling and test stands.

The Clean Technology Systems division was formed on 1 January 2011 and encompasses their activities in exhaust-air purification technology and energy management systems for different industries. New activities in the areas of energy efficiency have been added to this portfolio since 2011, e.g. ORC systems and microgas turbines to generate electricity from heat and waste heat.

Nearly all sites in Germany and the US implement environmental management systems certified according to ISO 14001. With Campus Energy 21 at their new headquarters in Bietigheim-Bissingen, Dürr has developed a pioneering energy supply concept, drawing on geo-thermal and heat exchangers as well as on process heat recovery. (www.durr.com)

Dussmann

The Dussmann Group is Germany's largest, private multi-services provider. Under the brand name of Dussmann Service, the Group provides facility services like catering, cleaning, security and reception services, technical services, commercial and energy management. Its second largest division, Kursana, provides nursing care to 13,600 senior citizens.

Dussmann was founded in 1963 by Peter Dussmann who began with the establishment of a home-cleaning service in Munich. Today, this multi-services provider employs around 58,000 people in 21 countries. In 2011, the Dussmann Group achieved a turnover of €1.658 billion, making it one of the largest, private, multi-services providers in the world. Several of their subsidiaries manage the work in the individual country-markets.

Dirk Brouwers is the CEO of the group while Catherine von Fürstenberg Dussmann is the Chairperson of the Board of Trustees. The Peter-Dussmann Stiftung (Foundation) manages the Dussmann Group. Client proximity, total service orientation and innovation are the characteristics which distinguish Dussmann. A growth backed by leading brands, their corporate slogan is 'Global Business, Local Service'.

The Dussmann Group is comprised of five divisions: Dussmann Service, Kursana, Dussmann das KulturKaufhaus, Dussmann Kultur Kindergarten and Dussmann Office. As mentioned earlier, Dussmann Service is the largest company division that provides comprehensive and individual services, all-in-one facility services to clients all over the world. They offer more than 70 individual facility services from catering and cleaning to security, technical, commercial and energy management, adapted according to individual client requirements.

Kursana is the leading private service provider for professional nursing and care for the elderly in Germany. The Dussmann Office division offers more than short-term, office rental services, ranging from virtual offices to offices with full service. While Dussmann Kultur Kindergarten operates in-house company child care across Germany.

Dussmann das KulturKaufhaus is one of the largest media department stores located in the heart of Berlin, right in the government district. It extends over four floors and offers a wide range of books, CDs, DVDs, audiobooks, software, gifts, fine stationery, sheet music and much more. They also host free events, featuring international celebrities from the worlds of culture, politics and business.

The Dussmann Group has a training centre in Zeuthen, where regular training of their employees ensures their long-term success. Service plus is the Dussmann service magazine for clients. The Group is committed to numerous cultural sponsorship projects in the country as part of their civic commitment. (www.dussmann.com)

Eberspaecher

The Eberspächer Group is one of the world's leading manufacturers and developers of automotive exhaust systems for the OEM industry. They also manufacture vehicle heaters and bus AC systems. The company's roots date back to 1865, when the master tinsmith Jakob Eberspächer founded a workshop in Esslingen am Neckar in Germany, which soon specialised in metal-framed roof glazing.

Today, all European, North American and several Asian vehicle manufacturers use their ground-breaking technologies and products. The Eberspächer Group is a family-owned business that employs about 6,300 people worldwide. They have more than 67 locations in 27 countries and are represented in all the key markets. Their headquarters have remained in Esslingen since the early founding days. In financial year 2011, they had a group turnover of €2.590 billion. The present management at the helm consists of Heinrich Baumann and Martin Peters, who are both Managing Partners, while the Advisory Board consists of Günter Baumann, who is the Chairman. Eberspächer's corporate slogan is 'Driving the Mobility of Tomorrow'.

Their product group consists of exhaust technology products, vehicle heaters, electrical vehicle heaters, bus AC systems, automotive electronics and automotive bus systems.

Eberspächer's technology is making an active contribution to environmentally friendly mobility, greater reliability and well-being while using the vehicle. They innovate rapidly to realise the mobility of tomorrow, today. They are able to cope with increased demands from ever more stringent emission standards placed on vehicle electronics.

Quality creates value and their objective is to reduce the defect rate at Eberspächer to zero. The group has been internationally certified, as per the quality management system ISO TS 16949 and EN ISO 9001, providing high-quality standards at each of their production locations. (www.eberspaecher.com)

ebmpapst

A worldwide innovation leader in fans and motors with over 14,500 different products, ebm-papst has the ideal solutions for virtually all air technology and drive engineering tasks. The roots of the company go back to 1963, when the Elektobau Mulfingen GmbH & Co.KG (ebm) was set up by Gerhard Sturm and Heinz Ziehl in the town of Mulfingen. They later acquired the Papst Motoren GmbH in St. Georgen, in Germany's Black Forest region and the Landshut plant from Alcatel to formally call themselves ebm-papst in 2003.

Today, the ebm-papst Group with headquarters in Mulfingen has a total turnover of €1.377 billion for fiscal year 2011. They have 17 production sites in Germany, Hungary, Slovenia, China, India and the US, employing over 10,000 employees worldwide.

Rainer Hundsdörfer is the new Chairman of the Board of Directors of the ebm-papst Group, while the co-founder, Gerhard Sturm is the Chairman of the Advisory Board.

ebm-papst has the world's widest range of fans, motors, blowers and pumps which are used in a wide variety of industries from drive technology in industries to automotive parts, in rail technology, medical and lab technology, telecommunications, computers and office technology, in household appliances, heating, ventilation, air-conditioning and refrigeration technology.

Green Tech EC technology, made by ebm-papst, is the outstanding product of a consistent efficiency strategy. With energy savings of 30 per cent, minimum noise emissions, everything included that is plug and play, they deliver comprehensive, sustainable advantages to their customers and to society. In fact, all their EC fans met the EU's energy savings targets in 2010!

Their clear philosophy based on their corporate principle states that, 'Each new product that they develop has to be better than its predecessor in terms of economy and ecology'.

Over the years they have won several national and international awards for their efforts in environmental technology, material design and technology, innovation and energy efficiency, the latest being the German CSR prize for energy efficiency and climate protection in 2012. (www.ebmpapst.com)

ElringKlinger

ElringKlinger AG is a worldwide development partner and original equipment supplier of high-performance cylinder head and speciality gaskets, plastic housing modules and thermal/acoustic shielding components, battery and fuel-cell components as well as products and services for the automotive aftermarket. The Hug Group which was acquired in 2011 has added the area of exhaust gas purification to ElringKlinger's product portfolio.

The roots of the company go back to 1879 when Paul Lechler established a merchandising business in Stuttgart for technical products and gaskets.

Today, ElringKlinger supplies the vast majority of vehicle and engine makers operating around the globe. They have some 6,200 employees at 41 locations worldwide. In financial year 2011, they had a combined group sales of €1.032 billion.

Stefan Wolf is the present Chairman of the Management Board, while Walter H. Lechler is the new Chairman of the Supervisory Board of ElringKlinger AG. Their present headquarters are in Dettingen/Erms in the state of Baden-Württemberg.

Millions of vehicles around the world are equipped with technology designed and developed by ElringKlinger: cylinder heads and speciality gaskets, housing modules, battery components and shielding systems for engines, transmissions, exhaust systems and auxiliary units. Their portfolio also includes products made of high-performance PTFE tailored to applications within the areas of medical, mechanical, chemical and aerospace engineering.

The ElringKlinger Group operates 10 divisions and is organised around the following five segments: original equipment, after-market, engineered plastics, services and industrial parks. ElringKlinger is one of the few suppliers in the world to have built up expertise in the optimisation of conventional combustion engines as well as in fuel-cell technology and battery components.

Their management system has been certified to ISO/TS 16949 since June 2000. Since 1997, it has also been certified to the environmental standard DIN EN ISO 14001. In its latest sustainability review, Oekom Research AG awarded ElringKlinger AG, the 'Prime' Seal of Quality on the basis of various social and ecological criteria. (www.elringklinger.de)

Enercon

Enercon GmbH, a wind turbine manufacturer based in Aurich, Germany, is set to be one of the largest in the world. Enercon began its road to success when a graduate engineer by the name of Aloys Wobben founded the company in 1984. He, along with a team of engineers, developed the first E-15/16 wind turbine with a rated power of 55 KW.

Today, all Enercon wind energy converters are based on a gear-less technology made in 1992, resulting in reduced mechanical stress, operating and maintenance costs. In 2004, they introduced new rotor blade geometry that significantly increases revenue, reduces noise emission and stress on the wind energy converter.

Enercon has been setting new standards for technological design for more than 25 years. As one of the world's leading companies in the wind energy sector and the long-standing market leader in the German market, Enercon directly or indirectly employs several thousand people worldwide. They have production facilities in Germany, Sweden, Brazil, Turkey, Portugal, Canada, Austria and France with international sales offices in 16 countries. To date, they have installed more than 20,000 wind turbines in over 30 countries that generate a total power of around 28 GW. Aloys Wobben, the founder, and Hans-Dieter Kettwig are the Managing Directors of the company. Their corporate slogan is 'Energy to the World'.

Their present product portfolio includes wind turbines in various models, namely E-44, E-48, E-53, E-70, E-82, E-92, E-101, E-115 and E-126. They have mobile cranes of up to 1,600 tons, hundreds of service vehicles as well as several special transporters for installing the towers and the blades.

The aim of Enercon's 2,500-strong service department is to ensure and maintain operational readiness for all Enercon wind turbines in accordance with their 'Speedy Service through Local Presence' principle, they expedite wind turbine maintenance and servicing in 300 service stations.

Service teams are also able to access all the turbine-specific documents and data using so-called Pentops (robust portable computers with a link to the service centre) ensuring that all maintenance is dealt with as quickly and efficiently as possible, making for a new standard in service management. (www.enercon.de)

EOS

EOS is the global technology and innovation leader in additive manufacturing (AM) for plastic and metal parts. The company offers design-driven, integrated e-manufacturing solutions for industrial applications. As a disruptive technology, AM paves the way for a paradigm shift in design and manufacturing. It enables the fast, flexible, cost-effective and high-quality manufacturing of components in nearly any complex form that were hardly achievable with conventional technologies. Additive Manufacturing from EOS creates products using a layering technique and requires neither tools nor moulds. It liberates designers from the limitations of conventional production technologies and offers them the greatest possible freedom.

AM accelerates product development, offers freedom of creation, optimises and makes possible lattice structures and supports functional integration. EOS provides competitive advantages to their customers and offers a complete solution portfolio, comprising systems, application know-how, software, parameters, materials and its further development apart from other services such as maintenance, application consulting and training.

Hans J. Langer, the present CEO, founded the company in 1989 and is its major shareholder, steering the strategic direction of the EOS Group. The company has its headquarters in the town of Krailling, near Munich. Their corporate slogan is 'e-Manufacturing Solutions'.

To date, EOS has sold over 1,100 systems in 32 countries with a sales turnover of €99 million for fiscal year 2010/2011. The company employs around 400 people.

EOS's product portfolio includes solutions and systems and equipment; in solutions they offer part property management and IPCM-M. PPM helps save costs and is the basis for making the manufacturing successful. This solution has constant access to standardised attribute profiles as well as to corresponding material values relevant for dimensioning. The Integrated Process Chain Management (IPCM) optimises system process flows and includes an automatic powder delivery, unpacking and sieving station with integrated power recycling as well.

In systems and equipment products, they have metal, plastic and sand laser-sintering systems. These systems distinguish themselves by ergonomic peripheral devices and a high degree of automation. Thus, they ensure maximum user-friendliness, optimal utilisation of machine capacity and excellent integration into any industrial environment.

Furthermore, EOS offers different software packages for the preparation of 3-D CAD data. They include EOSPACE, which automatically places parts in a space-saving way, in the build envelope. It is an economical production method for series production. EOS also offers a broad variety of materials for laser-sintering, tailored to the needs of specific, industry-focused applications.

E-manufacturing also makes it possible to produce customised products with highly complex shapes, which up until now would have been inconceivable using conventional series manufacturing methods. E-manufacturing target markets are in the fields of medical, tooling, aerospace, automotive, lifestyle goods and special purpose machinery manufacturing. (www.eos.info)

Faber-Castell

Faber-Castell is one of the world's largest manufacturers of high-quality products for writing, drawing and creative design. The company was founded by cabinetmaker Kaspar Faber in 1761 in Stein near Nuremberg, but it was Baron Lothar von Faber, the fourth generation of the family, who left a lasting mark on the company in the nineteenth century by modernizing operations and setting the standards for the pencils of excellent quality we know today. He marked them with the company name A.W. Faber, thus creating the first brand-name pencil in the world.

In the sixth generation, Wilhelm von Faber's eldest daughter Ottilie von Faber married Count Alexander zu Castell-Rüdenhausen in 1898, thus creating the new family name Faber-Castell. Shortly after taking over the business, Count Alexander brought out the unmistakable Castell 9000 series of pencils in 1905, the dark green colour becomes a symbol of the company, as do the advertisements depicting the 'knights of the pencil', which today make up part of the Faber-Castell logo. The year 2011 saw the 250th anniversary celebrations of this reputed company.

Today, the company employs 7,000 people in 15 production locations worldwide. They also have sales companies in 25 countries and sales agents in 120 countries. Count Anton Wolfgang von Faber-Castell is the present Chairman of the Board of Faber-Castell AG, with headquarters in the town of Stein. The Faber-Castell Group generated gross sales revenue of €570.5 million for fiscal year 2011/2012.

Faber-Castell is the world's leading manufacturer of wood-cased pencils, with a production capacity of over 2 billion graphite and colour pencils per year. The legendary Green Castell 9000 pencil has remained their flagship product. Their GRIP 2001 is another of their famous products having won several international design awards.

Among the company's notable achievements are the world's first branded writing instruments, established degrees of hardness, the hexagonal pencil, the Secural Process, use of environmentally compatible water-based coatings in production and the global Faber-Castell Social Charter (for socially responsible and ethical production norms).

They also have the Graf von Faber-Castell Kinderfonds, a foundation benefiting deprived children. The timber used for their products is to 95 per cent certified in line with the stringent requirements of the Forestry Stewardship Council (FSC) as it is sourced responsibly and replanted. The remainder is also sourced from sustainable plantations, mostly certified to the respected PEFC standard. Production facilities at Faber-Castell are certified as per ISO 9001 and ISO 14001 standards.

The core values of their brand have helped them maintain their market leadership: 'Competence and Tradition, Outstanding Quality, Innovation and Creativity and Social and Environmental Responsibility'. (www.faber-castell.de)

Festo

Festo is the world's leading supplier of automation technology and the performance leader in industrial training and education programs. The Festo Group is comprised of Festo AG & Co.KG with 59 independent national companies, Festo Didactic GmbH & Co.KG and Festo Micro-technology AG. Festo was founded in 1925 by Gottlieb Stoll and Albert Fezer. They started with the manufacture of wood cutting tools and later diversified into the automation industry. The present headquarters are in Esslingen in the state of Baden-Württemberg.

Today, the group employs around 15,500 employees globally and had a group turnover of €2.1 billion for fiscal year 2011. They have over 250 branch offices and authorised agencies in a further 39 countries. Worldwide after-sales service is available in 176 countries.

Eberhardt Veit is the Chairman of the Management Board while Joachim Milberg is the Chairman of the Supervisory Board.

The two main business sectors that they cater to are automation and didactic.

In automation, they provide pneumatic, servo-pneumatic and electric drive technology for factory and process automation for over 300,000 customers in 200 industries, from individual products to ready-to-install solutions. Regular innovations for ultimate customer productivity, a global presence and close systems partnerships with their customers are the hallmarks of Festo.

Festo Didactic is a global leader in industrial education and training as a provider of skills development for production and process automation. The services they offer range from educational equipment for training facilities to training and consulting for industrial manufacturers.

They have around 30,000 catalogue products in several hundred thousand variants. Festo invested 9 per cent of its turnover into R&D, the result being around 100 new products per year. In 2010, a team from Festo and Fraunhofer IPA were awarded the 'Deutscher Zukunfts Preis' (German Future Prize) for their Bionic Handling Assistant a high-tech helper for the industry, hospital and home. The Group has most of the required certifications for quality, environment and safety from ISO 9001 to ISO 14001 and OHSAS 18001. (www.festo.com)

flexi

The flexi retractable dog leash has made millions of dog owners around the world a happy lot with this unique innovation from Germany. They have set the standard and have established themselves as the market leader in over 90 countries. The first prototype, a serendipitous discovery, was invented in 1973 by the founder and CEO, Manfred Bogdahn; it has not changed in concept, although improvements and varied models have been introduced over the years.

The flexi-Bogdahn Group, a family-owned business, manufactures all of its high-quality products in their facility in Bargteheide, near Hamburg. From the idea in their design department to the finished product in their factory floor, all flexi leashes are manufactured under one roof with over 100 different quality tests – 'Made in Germany' at its best.

The flexi retractable dog-leash is a highly complex precision product. Although, it began with the conversion of a chainsaw mechanism, it has now grown into a patented high-tech retraction system. Quality, comfortable handling and innovative designs underline the level of perfection of their leashes. Today, they have numerous designs in several ranges, from classic, comfort and special to design, luxury and promotion.

flexi is viewed by satisfied customers as the better leash because by being retractable, it allows freedom to move for the leashed dog (up to 8 metres), control and safety, quality and their excellent service. (www.flexi.de)

Friedhelm-Loh

The Friedhelm-Loh Group of companies was founded by Rudolph Loh in 1961, when he set up a factory to manufacture electrical appliances in Ritterhausen, Germany. Today, the Group has 10 domestic subsidiaries and 63 international ones. The total group revenues for fiscal year 2011 were €2.2 billion, with over 11,500 employees worldwide. The group's present headquarters are in Haiger in the state of Hessen. Friedhelm Loh is the group's present Chairman of the Board.

The group's companies include Rittal International, ePlan, Mind 8, Stahlo, LKH and Loh Services. The Group has over 1,500 patents that they have achieved over the past 50 years.

Rittal is the largest company in the Friedhelm Loh Group and the world's leading supplier of housing and enclosure systems. Rittal's global presence spans 64 subsidiaries, 11 production sites and 40 agencies worldwide, enabling the best of local, direct contact to their customers with a unique service delivery. Rittal has six product lines: industrial enclosures, electronic packaging, system climate control, power distribution, IT Solutions and communication systems.

Their next company, ePLAN software and service, is a software supplier for global engineering solutions. Mind8 devises customer-specific, modular-based engineering processes. Furthermore Stahlo is one of the largest non–plant-dependent steel services centres in Germany. LKH develops and manufactures innovative and cost-effective plastic products for a wide range of industries from automobiles and engineering to plastic and construction. Finally, Loh Services is the central service provider of the Friedhelm Loh Group from Controlling to IT.

The Friedhelm-Loh Group has been regularly chosen as a top group to work for in Germany. The Rittal Foundation has given millions and has committed several more to supporting social, environmental and cultural issues and institutions located close to Rittal sites worldwide. (www.friedhelm-loh-group.com)

Fuchs Petrolub

Fuchs Petrolub AG, a lubricants and speciality solutions company, was founded in 1931 in Mannheim by Rudolf Fuchs. He started with his import and sales company for high-quality refinery products. Today, it is a globally operating corporation and the world's leading supplier of lubricants among the independent group of companies. Fuchs is a front runner with a complete range of lubricants. They also have customised speciality solutions for several market niches to complement its standard products as well as comprehensive consultancy and service capabilities.

They offer lubricants for hundreds of applications, including lubricants for cars, motor cycles, goods transport, passenger traffic, mining companies, the steel industry, vehicle and machinery construction, the building trade and for agricultural equipment.

The group employs more than 3,722 people worldwide at around 50 operative companies. The most important sales regions for Fuchs are Western Europe, Asia and North America. Stefan Fuchs is the present CEO and Chairman of the Executive Board of Fuchs Petrolub AG, and Jürgen Hambrecht is the Chairman of the Supervisory Board. Total sales revenue for fiscal year 2011 was €1.668 billion.

Their corporate headquarters and one of their primary production sites are located in the city of Mannheim. Among the several of Fuchs brands that are doing well are Silkolene, Titan, Fricofin, the Renocast range of concrete mould release agents, Anticorit, pre-lube oils, Renoform, process compatible deep drawing oils, Trenoil products for the hot and cold rolling of metals and other processing operations and Renoclean for industrial cleaners, the Thermisol range of products along with expert technical advice and a state-of-the-art condition monitoring service that guarantees excellent heat treatment results.

The Renolit brand with its comprehensive grease product line offers optimum solutions for a wide variety of applications. A particular focus and development in recent years has been the development of biodegradable and environmentally friendly greases, which led to the development of the Planto product range used in a wide range of applications.

Their Lowsaps engine oil for diesel engines is low in pollutants and increases the service life of particulate filters. The brand meets the stringent Euro-4 emissions standards.

CASSIDA is the name of their brand which will act as the umbrella brand under which Fuchs will integrate their internationally successful food-grade lubricants, marketed under the 'Geralyn' trademark. (www.fuchs-oil.de)

Gerresheimer

The Gerresheimer Group is a leading high-quality manufacturer of speciality products made of glass and plastic primarily for the pharma and life science industries. In addition, they make specific primary containers for a wide variety of substances and medicines, with a product and service portfolio comprising complex drug delivery systems.

The origins of the group go back to the glass factory founded by Ferdinand Heye in 1864 in the Gerresheim suburb of Düsseldorf. It was only in the last two decades that they have developed into the highly specialised, quality supplier to the pharma and life sciences industries that they are today, .

Today, Gerresheimer has a worldwide production presence in 47 locations, with headquarters in Düsseldorf. Gerresheimer employs a worldwide total of about 10,000 people. For financial year 2011, they had a sales turnover of around €1.095 billion.

The management board of Gerresheimer AG consists of four members with Uwe Röhrhoff as the CEO and Chairman of the Management Board, and Gerhard Schulze is the Chairman of the Supervisory Board. They use cutting-edge technologies, convincing innovations and targeted investments to systematically consolidate their strong market position.

They have four main business divisions: tubular glass, moulded glass, plastic systems and life science research. Their product range includes medicine vials, ampoules and special bottles, as well as complex drug-delivery systems such as pre-fillable syringes, inhalers and other system solutions for safe dosage and application of medicines. They also supply numerous product and system approaches in the field of diagnostics and medical technology, including diabetes monitoring and components for various analysis systems. They see their special strength in customised development and production, including full-service project business. Gerresheimer meets the regulatory standards imposed by the relevant supervisory authorities and collaborates closely with their customers in the drug registration process. (www.gerresheimer.com)

GELITA

GELITA is the world's leading supplier of collagen proteins for the food, health, nutrition and pharmaceutical industries and for numerous technical applications.

The holding company is GELITA AG, with more than135 years of tradition in the production of collagen proteins. The roots of the company go back to 1875 in Göppingen, Germany, where the brothers Heinrich and Paul Koepff started producing gelatine.

Today, GELITA is a world leader in the production of collagen proteins, producing nearly 80,000 tons of gelatine, collagen peptides and collagen a year, which is around 27 per cent of the total world production. Total sales turnover was more than €500 million for fiscal year 2011 while employing a total of 2,600 employees in 20 production plants and sales offices worldwide. GELITA is coordinated from the concern headquarters in Eberbach, Germany. Franz Josef Konert is the present CEO.

The product range of GELITA includes innovative, tailor-made products based on collagen proteins for the food, health and nutrition, pharmaceutical industries and for technical applications. GELITA® collagen proteins-gelatine, collagen and collagen peptides are being used in numerous areas.

Continuous investment in application technology forms the basis of the company's success. By providing high-quality technical and applications support to their customers, they are able to help their business partners develop new products. For example, GELITA is currently working on product concepts for calorie management (VITARCAL®), beauty (VERISOL®) and mobility (FORTIGEL®) and offers customers the opportunity of benefiting from the potential of the growing market in healthcare. Many of their patents have been taken out in cooperation with their customers and have resulted in mutual success.

Their corporate slogan is 'Improving Quality of Life'. In 2008, Gelita won the 'Frost & Sullivan Award' for 'European Health Ingredient of the Year', this being for their new product FORTIGEL®, honoured as an outstanding pioneer in the development of healthy joints – having excellent market applications in nutrition and medicine. (www.gelita.com)

GfK

The GfK Group is one of the world's leading market research companies, with more than 11,500 experts working to discover new insights into the way people live, think and shop in over 100 countries. Their said market position is fifth among market research organisations worldwide.

The company was founded in 1934 as a society by university professor Wilhelm Vershofen in Berlin. It was named Gesellschaft für Konsumforschung, which in German stands for 'Society for Consumer Research', the initials GfK comes from the original German name. The present headquarters are in Nuremberg, Germany.

Today, GfK is a full service institute, which regards itself as a supplier of knowledge. GfK constantly innovates, using the latest and smartest techniques and methodologies to give their clients the clearest understanding of the most important people in the world: their customers. Matthias Hartmann is the present CEO of the company, while Arno Mahlert is the Chairman of the Supervisory Board. In 2011, GfK's sales amounted to €1.37 billion. GfK delivers in all the major consumer, pharmaceutical, media and service sector market segments. Their services are divided into two business divisions or sectors, namely consumer choices and consumer experiences.

The consumer choices division focuses on market sizing, currency and convergent media as well as sales channels, delivering detailed, accurate and timely data. They investigate what's selling when and where. It is called consumer choices because the sector or division focuses on precise data, related to choices and actions consumers have made.

Their consumer experiences division explores consumers' attitudes, through creative, robust and flexible methodologies. They call it consumer experiences because this division focuses on people's perceptions of the world and the way they experience it.

Their business strategy is called 'Own the Future'. GfK is pioneering sophisticated new ways of understanding how people experience brands and services. (www.gfk.com)

Gildemeister

Gildemeister AG is the leading manufacturer of cutting machine tools worldwide and also offers innovative machine technology, services and software solutions in milling and turning technologies, for controls and services as well as for regenerative energies. The company was founded in 1870.

Gildemeister AG is a globally operating enterprise with 99 domestic and international sales and service locations in 33 countries that maintain direct contact with their customers. They have a total of 10 production plants and around 6,000 employees worldwide with headquarters in the town of Bielefeld. Total sales revenue for financial year 2011 was in the region of €1.687 billion. Rudiger Kapitza has been the Chairman of the Executive Board since April 1996, while Hans Henning Offen is the Chairman of the Supervisory Board. The Group includes the DMG, DECKEL MAHO and GILDEMEISTER brand companies. Their new corporate slogan is 'Creating the future. Forming real value'.

The business divisions include turning technology, milling technology, ultrasonic/lasertec, DMG Ecoline, DMG Automation, DMG Electronics, DMG Services and Renewable Energies.

Its products are used to machine automotive parts, aircraft engine parts, for mobile phone casings, artificial hip joints and laser micro-cavities apart from a host of other products. Their cooperation with the Japanese machine tool manufacturer Mori Seiki has strengthened their global position, while their Energy Solutions division with the Sun Carrier has developed satisfactorily.

Gildemeister is quoted in official trading at the main stock exchanges in Germany. It is listed on the MDAX and complies with the 'Prime Standard', i.e. internationally applicable transparency requirements of the German Stock Market. Despite the ongoing economic crisis, they maintained expenditure on R&D at a high level of €54.6 million for financial year 2011. Gildemeister products have set benchmarks in energy efficiency and lower energy costs. (www.gildemeister.com)

Glasbau Hahn

Glasbau Hahn is the worldwide leader in the manufacture of quality glass cabinets for display cases for museums the world over. Their display case department enjoys a worldwide reputation in constructing high-quality display cases for museums and always considers the customers needs for design, function and protection. Their corporate slogan is '… in Love with Glass'.

Glasbau Hahn was founded in 1836 in Frankfurt. From the start, this company of glaziers and tradesmen showed creativity with 'new ideas in glass'. The company has its present headquarters in the city of Frankfurt and employs a staff of around 125. A family-run concern, the present managing directors are Isabel Hahn and Tobias Hahn. They also have sales facilities in the US, China, Japan and in UK apart from numerous international sales partners worldwide.

Their product categories consists of display cases and museum technology, glass construction and louvre windows. In display cases and museum technology, Glasbau Hahn is a specialist in the construction of custom made, high-quality, freestanding, table and wall display cases; they also have a standard product called HAHN-HLS system. In order to offer their clients a full-service package, they also offer, archive storage installations, climate control technology, seismic protection and HAHN-protector picture cases.

Traditional craftsmanship combined with modern innovative manufacturing techniques supported by the experience and reliability of their personnel has been a key factor for their continued success. Their display cases can be found in famous museums and institutions around the world. They also serve the small local museums as well.

Their glass construction department offers mainly local clients every sort of glass construction for interior and exterior use.

While their louvre window department based in Stockstadt/Main offers the complete range of natural ventilation devices, including four different types of Hahn louvre windows (single and double glazed), Hahn ventilation grids and Hahn shading devices suitable for skylights and roofs and are sold worldwide. The company and its products have over the years received numerous domestic and international awards for the excellence of its products. (www.glasbau-hahn.com)

GÖTTFERT

GÖTTFERT Werkstoff-Prüfmaschinen GmbH was founded in 1962 by Otto Göttfert. GÖTTFERT GmbH is a German company associated with rheology (the study of the flow of matter, primarily in the liquid state and in soft solids). In the second generation now, the founder's son, Axel Göttfert, took over the leadership as the sole managing director.

On the world market this medium-sized organisation is well known as one of the leading companies in the niche field of rheological testing instruments, and their innovative systems are installed in laboratories as well as in production settings globally.

In order to be closer to many of its customers, they started expanding and in 1989 a subsidiary company was opened in Rock Hill, South Carolina, USA. In 2011, the GOETTFERT (China) Limited in Beijing and Gdi (GOETTFERT – Dataphysics Instruments) in Kolkata (India) started their work. GÖTTFERT runs a worldwide net of representatives in over 90 countries with a high level of technical and sales background to fulfil the near contact to interested groups.

Today, the certified and accredited company comes with a wide range of products in this field for thermoplastics, thermosets and elastomers and equipment under clean room conditions. The devices are built in modular small series to fit the different range of requirements.

GÖTTFERT presents its flexible rheological testing technology in closed product groups. The sample testing during production is covered by the ONLINE and/or AT-LINE technology as well as through film analysis. For quality control in the laboratory they deliver meltindex testing devices, and for the characterisation of new materials the capillary rheometry together with the elastomer testing systems find their place. Furthermore the pilot plant recipe development can be covered with their Extrusiometry machine range. Finally, production or testing devices with clean room requirements are part of the portfolio. All GÖTTFERT systems fulfil the highest standards on quality and innovation!

'MADE BY GOETTFERT' quality stands for taking responsibility. It also means that you cannot test 'Quality' into a product; it has to be built in, one central basic business principle, which followed from 'Technology' and 'Service' – the three fundamentals in its company philosophy.

With their philosophy of their own production, GOETTFERT consciously takes over the liability of equipment even after many years of delivery, guaranteeing support and spare parts for its customers. The reasons for their success are reliable customer service, short delivery times, comprehensive advice and partnership-based care – competencies the company demonstrates daily. Their corporate slogan is 'This is Rheology'.

The company offers workshops to get the operators familiarised with the handling of the different hardware and its accessories. They also have a well-trained, specialised service team and special remote control software that enables their service technicians to control their customer's instruments remotely. This helps in problem-solving, installing program updates and in fixing configuration problems.

Goettfert essentially caters to plastic and rubber processors, manufacturers of feedstock, universities, research institutions and laboratories worldwide. (www.goettfert. com)

Grohe

Grohe AG is Europe's largest and the world's leading single-brand manufacturer and supplier of premium quality sanitary fittings. They have around 8 per cent of the world market. As a global brand for sanitary products and systems, Grohe sets standards in quality, technology and design, while its products deliver the perfect flow of water. Grohe promises unrivalled enjoyment of water at any time. Their ambitious product philosophy, which is based on the perfect balance of quality, technology, design and sustainability, represents a guarantee that this pledge will be fulfilled. Only such products that meet this requirement can embody the Grohe brand and are brought to market; that's why their current corporate slogan is 'Enjoy Water'.

Friedrich Grohe established the company in 1936 when he took over Berkenhoff & Paschedag in Hemer, Germany. Following the take-over, Friedrich Grohe focussed on sanitary faucets only. After the first leverage buy out in 1999, the company was acquired by TPG and Credit Suisse MB, the current owner, in 2004.

Today, the company has its headquarters in Düsseldorf, employing around 8,700 people in several production plants worldwide and several sales companies and offices in all the continents. They have a presence in over 130 countries. For financial year 2011, they had a sales turnover of €1.165 billion, of which 84 per cent were exports.

David J. Haines is the present CEO of Grohe AG, while Gerhard Schmidt is the Chairman of the Supervisory Board. Their plant in the German town of Hemer has won one of the 'Top Factory' prizes, awarded by a leading German publication, while several of its products have won prestigious design awards as well, including the famous Red Dot design award. Grohe has won more than 100 awards since 2005 and in 2011, the Grohe design team was named as the Red Dot 'Design Team of the year'.

Grohe quality is one of the four mainstays of Grohe's product philosophy and is a guarantee that their products exceed the expectations of their customer by delivering a range of unique water experiences. They pride themselves on the fact that their products, materials and processes conform to the highest standards, through state-of-the-art testing. Grohe products not only comply with but frequently even exceed mandatory standards.

Grohe is a responsible company and their products combine the economic, ecological and safe use of water with excellent design. Thus, for example, the Grohe Silk Move® technology ensures precise control of water flow and temperature. All of their essential group facilities have the ISO 14001 certification standards for environmental management systems. (www.grohe.com)

Groz-Beckert

Groz-Beckert has supported the machine builders to the textile industry for more than 160 years. During this period, Groz-Beckert has evolved from being purely a manufacturer of knitting machine needles and parts into the most important system supplier of precision components in the field of textiles and beyond.

The company has branched out into the business sectors of sewing machine needles, felting and structuring needles and gauge parts tufting. This has been recently complemented by the important area of weaving machine parts, weaving preparation and knitting cylinders. Additionally, with the production of ceramic punching components

(CPC), Groz-Beckert has also become a supplier to the computer and telecommunications industry. There are currently about 70,000 different needles and precision components in their range of products.

The roots of this family-run enterprise go back to 1852 when the two companies Theodor Groz & Söhne of Ebingen, Germany and Ernst Beckert of Chemnitz were founded. This merger of two of Germany's biggest needle manufacturers happened in 1937 to form Groz-Beckert KG.

Today, the company has its headquarters in the city of Albstadt in the state of Baden-Württemberg. They have production plants in Germany, Switzerland, the Czech Republic, Portugal, North America, India, China and Vietnam with a closely knit sales network in more than 150 countries.

They employ around 7,500 people worldwide. For financial year 2011, they had a sales turnover of around €528.3 million. Thomas Lindner is the present Chairman of the Board of Groz-Beckert.

Both the company headquarters and the Groz-Beckert production plants around the world are certified to ISO 9001, in some cases since 1995. Since 2008, an integrated management system, i.e. quality, environment, occupational health and safety has been introduced and certified group-wide in compliance with ISO 9001, ISO 14001 and BS OHSAS 18001. The company was awarded the 'Kyocera Environmental Prize' in 2010 and noted as a 'Green Pioneer' at Korea EU-Awards in 2011.

Every year the company think-tank at their Technology & Development Center (TEZ) develops and designs new product types for many different areas of the textile industry. Groz-Beckert will continue to be a pioneer in the manufacture of needles and precision components. (www.groz-beckert.com)

HELLA

HELLA KGaA & Co. is a global, family-owned company with headquarters in Lippstadt, Germany, that develops and manufactures lighting and electronic components and systems for the automotive industry. It also has one of the world's largest trade organisations for automotive parts, accessories, diagnosis and services.

What began in 1899 with lamps, lanterns and blow-horns for carriages, bicycles and motor vehicles later grew into an innovative headlamp product range in 1908. This is when the product name and brand name HELLA was born, that became part of the company name in 1986.

Today, the company employs around 27,000 people at 70 locations in more than 30 countries. The HELLA Group achieved a turnover of around €4.8 billion for the financial year of 2011–2012, making it one of the top 50 automotive suppliers in the world and one of the 100 largest German industrial companies. Their corporate slogan is 'Technology with vision'

Jürgen Behrend is the Chairman and President of HELLA KGaA Hueck & Co. while Rolf Breidenbach is the CEO of the company. Michael Hoffmann-Becking is the Chairman of the Supervisory Board.

They have three main business segments: automotive, aftermarket and special applications. They have over 4,800 people working in R&D. Trends and innovations such as LED in the lighting division as well as energy management and CO_2 reduction in the electronics division have offered attractive growth opportunities worldwide.

HELLA has a balanced business model that focuses on original equipment, aftermarket and special applications under one roof. They have also ventured into new customer groups with the use of LED technology for streets, airports and internal lighting as well as a People Counter, a camera-based device for precise measurement of pedestrian flows.

Their yearly training program brings over 18,500 representatives from the wholesale trade, workshops and vocational schools up to speed with the latest technology. While their total quality management (TQM) includes and covers all the areas relating to Six Sigma, updated and upgraded since 1991. The company has ISO 9001:2008 and ISO/TS 16949:2009. (www.hella.com)

Heidelberg

Heidelberger Druckmachinen AG, or Heidelberg as it is popularly known, is with its sheet-fed offset printing machines one of the leading solution providers for the print media industry. Based in the city of Heidelberg, with development and production sites in seven countries and around 250 sales offices across the globe, the company supports around 200,000 customers in 170 countries. The Heidelberg brand name stands for reliability, production security and precision engineering.

The company was founded by Andreas Hamm in 1850, when he started a factory in the Palantine city of Frankenthal (southwest Germany) to manufacture bells, casting and forging materials, mills and steam engines. Later working with a machinist, Andreas Albert, they incorporated flat-bed cylinder presses and other machines relevant for book printing in the production plan. By the end of the nineteenth century, the firm relocated to Heidelberg where it becomes a corporation under the name Schnellpressen fabrik AG Heidelberg. In 1967, the company name was changed to Heidelberger Druckmaschinen AG.

All Heidelberg presses destined for the world market are manufactured at the Wesloch-Walldorf site in line with strict quality standards. Standardised presses in all standard format classes and folding machines for the Chinese market are produced by Heidelberg in Qingpu near Shanghai.

In fiscal year 2011/2012, Heidelberg recorded sales of €2.596 billion. As of 31 March 2012, the group had a workforce of around 15,414 employees worldwide. Gerold Linzbach is the new CEO and Chairman of Executive Board while Robert J. Koehler is the Chairman of the Supervisory Board.

The company's core business covers the entire sheetfed offset process and value chain in the format classes from 20 inches (35x50 cm) to 64 inches (120x160 cm), as well as digital printing solutions. Contract manufacturing – mainly for customers in other engineering industries and the energy sector – is also growing.

Heidelberg develops and manufactures in its equipment division precision printing presses, devices for plate imaging and postpress finishing as well as digital inkjet systems for packaging manufacturers. In addition, Heidelberg sells digital printing solutions and offers integrated offset and digital solutions.

The services division includes the company's portfolio of technical services for an absolute stable production and maximised machine availability – such as routine maintenance within the scope of service contracts, service parts supply and consumables.

They also offer further value-adding services, so-called performance services such as training at their Print Media Academy and consulting to optimize the entire range of production and management processes, the sales of used equipment as well as workflow software for integrating all processes within a printing company. With its financial services division, Heidelberg supports investments of its customers with financing concepts.

The Heidelberg sheet-fed division with its five German sites at Amstetten, Brandenburg, Heidelberg, Kiel and Wiesloch is now certified following ISO 9001 (quality management) and ISO 14001 (environmental management). (www.heidelberg.com)

Herrenknecht

Herrenknecht AG is a world market leader for tunnel-boring machines and tunnelling systems. They have the widest range of equipment and products in mechanised tunnelling technology worldwide. The Herrenknecht Group is a successful and professionally managed family enterprise that was founded in 1977 by Martin Herrenknecht.

The Herrenknecht Group with its head office in Schwanau, Germany, consists operationally of Herrenknecht AG, the parent company and 77 subsidiaries and associated companies in Germany and in other parts of the world. Martin Herrenknecht, the founder, is the present Chairman of the Board of Management, while Hans-Jörg Vetter is the Chairman of the Supervisory Board of Herrenknecht AG. The Herrenknecht Group achieved sales of €1.017 billion for 2011. They employ around 4,000 people worldwide while training around 240 young apprentices.

Herrenknecht's particular strength lies in their unequalled expertise in all tunnelling processes and technologies backed by over 35 years of experience in the field of tunnelling. They seek the best solution for each geological condition and project in order to ensure complete customer satisfaction.

The group has the widest range of equipment and products in both horizontal and vertical mechanised tunnelling technology. Including tunnel-boring machines like mixshields, earth pressure balance shields and hard rock machines or pipeline installation or shaft sinking equipment, they have both the products and systems solutions to meet their customers' specific requirements.

Wherever there are tunnels for railroads, roads, metros and the supply and disposal of utilities, Herrenknecht helps make connections all round the world. Herrenknecht tunnelling machines are currently at work on around 150 traffic tunnelling construction sites and in over 850 infrastructure projects for supply and disposal tunnels worldwide.

Herrenknecht also offers other services, like help in additional technical equipment for the jobsite and service packages upon request, e.g. in the area of technical consultancy and planning for tunnelling projects as well as personnel solutions to complement construction site crews on a temporary basis, supplying rental equipment and used tunnelling machines where required. (www.herrenknecht.com)

Herlitz

The Herlitz PBS AG is among the better-known, traditional German companies that is a leading, branded consumer goods company of paper, office supplies, stationery and papeterie in Europe. The company was founded in 1904 by Carl Herlitz, a trained book-seller, in Berlin. He then started a wholesale business dealing in paper and writing products.

Today, with strong brands like Herlitz and Susy Card, they are one of Europe's leading branded consumer goods companies of paper, office and stationery articles, greeting cards, napkins and gift wrap. They are a Europe-wide operating concern with six subsidiaries in Western and Eastern Europe. Besides a production site in Falkensee, Herlitz also produces in Poland. They employ around 1,700 people in all.

For financial year 2011, they had a sales turnover of €229 million. Herlitz also has two other concerns under its ownership: eCom Logistik that offers individual solutions across the supply chain and Mercoline that offers both consulting and software solutions with a focus on efficient customer response for the retail, consumer goods and logistics industries.

Pelikan International Corporation is the new Herlitz majority shareholder. Herlitz AG has its headquarters in Berlin and the present management board consists of Thomas Radke and Cheong Seng Ng, while Hooi Keat Loo is the Chairman of the Supervisory Board.

Herlitz stands for high-quality school and office products. They are perhaps the only company that offers around 15,000 products for the entire stationery and papeterie assortment to the European market. Recently, their new roller-ball pen, my.pen style, won the prestigious red dot design award for 2012.

In 2008, Herlitz achieved Forest Stewardship Council (FSC®) certification, as a manufacturer of paper, office and writing material produced from wood from responsibly managed forests. They also carry the German eco-label, Blue Angel, as Herlitz offers a wide range of files, folders and dividers made from 100 per cent waste paper, which are fully recyclable, saving precious natural resources. They have also implemented other measures to promote climate protection and sustainability. (www.herlitz.eu)

Hermle

Hermle AG, the mid-size machine tool manufacturing company from Gosheim, Germany, offers high-performance, highly innovative machinery centres that have given it a leading position nationally and internationally. Its corporate slogan is 'Milling at its Best'.

The company was founded in 1938 in the southwestern town of Gosheim by Berhold Hermle, a bolt and machine screw manufacturer who began production of turned parts. In 1957, they started production of milling machines.

Today, with 20,000 successfully installed machines and satisfied customers who have achieved the best results in precision and efficiency using their products, Hermle enjoys a leading position, as a partner to numerous key industries, from large complex components to the smallest components in the high-tech area. From medical technology to the optical industry, aircraft parts, automotive, tools, mould making to auto-racing, they lead the way.

Their production systems are controlled by a master computer that includes a production line arrangement of pallet stations that are highly sophisticated, highly flexible and tuned individually to their products and designed for optimum quality. They also have highly advanced robot solutions.

The proverbial Hermle precision, in combination with process consulting and project management has made them the most important machine partner in nearly all key sectors. With headquarters and main works in Gosheim, they employ some 800 people worldwide. The management of Hermle AG consists of Dietmar Hermle who is the Spokesman for the Management Board, while Wolfgang Kuhn is the Chairman of the Supervisory Board. The company has been certified according to ISO 9001:2008 quality management standards.

The service personnel of their international partner companies is available locally, guaranteeing fast supply of spare parts and maintenance contracts and response times customised to individual manufacturing processes. While their representatives are available in more than 50 countries worldwide, they also offer thorough and practical support with extensive training courses. (www.hermle.de)

Homag

The Homag Group AG's management lays claim to being the world's leading manufacturer of machines and equipment for the woodworking industry. As a global player, they are present in more than 100 countries and hold an estimated 28 per cent share of the total market.

The company was founded by Eugen Hornberger a village blacksmith, and Gerhard Schuler in 1960, in a town called Schopfloch in the Black Forest region of Germany. Two years later, the company, Hornberger Maschinenbau OHG, developed the world's first edge-banding machine to see the start of its impressive rise to become a successful, global player.

Today, in the fields of furniture manufacturing, structural elements and timber-frame house construction, they offer their customers perfectly aligned solutions, from the stand-alone machine through to complete production lines. A wide range of supporting services and specially tailored, control software make their range unique, whether, for the production of top-quality furniture, fitted kitchens, timber-frame houses, wooden flooring or staircases.

Markus Flik is the CEO of the Homag Group, while Torsten Grede is the Chairman of the Supervisory Board. They have three main divisions: machines and cells, factory installations and services. For financial year 2011, they achieved a total turnover of €798.7 million, while employing around 5,000 employees worldwide. They manufacture their product range at 17 locations in Europe, Asia and America.

The Homag Group offers a program exactly matched to their customer's requirements, for efficient and economical wood-working from panel production, sawing, drilling and mounting of fittings, sizing and edge-banding, CNC processing centres, beam processing, handling, production of structural elements, timber-frame house construction to packaging.

They have also introduced some innovative technologies and products like Lasertec, versatile glue spreader machines, high-speed vibration absorption, the latest in laminating technology and many more. Apart from a range of machines they also provide relevant software, various services and solutions for the woodworking industry. (www.homag-group.com)

Jungheinrich

Jungheinrich is a logistics service provider with manufacturing operations as well as an intra-logistics solutions provider. The Jungheinrich Group is among the world's three largest suppliers of industrial (fork-lift) vehicles/trucks, warehousing technology and materials flow technology. In Europe, Jungheinrich is the leading supplier of warehousing technology.

The company was founded in 1953 in Hamburg as the H. Jungheinrich & Co., Maschinen Fabrik by Friedrich Jungheinrich. The company introduced the first electric, four-wheel fork-lift truck/vehicle. Since then, they have been offering fork-lift-based products and services designed to get things moving for their industrial customers.

Jungheinrich offers a comprehensive product range of material handling equipment, racking systems and services for complete intra-logistics. They have a direct sales network with 17 sites in Germany and their own sales and service companies in 31 countries. Mitsubishi Caterpillar Forklift America Inc. is Jungheinrich's exclusive sales partner in America. Jungheinrich has four production plants in Germany and one in China.

Sales turnover for financial year 2011 was €2.116 billion, while employing over 10,000 people worldwide. Hans-Georg Frey is the Chairman of the Board of Management of Jungheinrich AG, with headquarters in Hamburg, while Jürgen Peddinghaus is the Chairman of the Supervisory Board. Their corporate slogan is 'Machines. Ideas. Solutions'.

Today, around 800 sales consultants as well as more than 3,400 mobile service engineers maintain a close-knit network providing competent consulting and comprehensive service all around the globe. The basis of the company's success is its broad range of products, strong direct sales and a targeted range of services. With over 600 different fork-lift vehicles to choose from, their customers are sure to find what they need for their operations, regardless of the lifting height, surface or transport distances involved. They are a one-stop shop for all customers' logistics needs.

For Jungheinrich, yellow is the new green. They think and act environmentally from the life-cycle of the vehicle to the greening of the production process (34 per cent reduction), with efficient solutions for energy consumption as well as reducing fleet energy consumption by way of developing new electric vehicles, like hybrid-drives and lithium ion battery vehicles, etc. (www.jungheinrich.com)

Kärcher

Alfred Kärcher GmbH & Co.KG, a family-owned enterprise, is the world's leading provider of cleaning technology. With pressure washers, vacuums and steam cleaners, home and garden pumps, sweepers and floor scrubbers, vehicle washes, cleaning agents, dry ice blasters, drinking and waste water treatment plants and water dispensers, it offers a range of innovative problem solutions. These include coordinated products, cleaning agents and accessories, along with advice and service. Alfred Kärcher GmbH & Co. KG with present works and headquarters in Winnenden, Germany, employs more than 9,000 people in 100 companies in 60 countries. Hartmut Jenner is the CEO and Chairman of the Management Board while Johannes Kärcher is the Chairman of the Supervisory Board.

More than 50,000 service centres in all countries ensure continuous and comprehensive supplies to customers all over the world. Innovation is the company's principal growth factor. Around 85 per cent of its products have been in existence for five years or less. More than 650 engineers and technicians are engaged in designing new problem solutions at the cleaning equipment manufacturer's development centres. Their products enable their customers to solve their cleaning tasks in an economical and environmentally friendly manner. Their corporate slogan is 'Kärcher makes a difference'.

Innovation has been a key element of the corporate culture ever since the company was set up in Stuttgart-Bad Canstatt in 1935. Alfred Kärcher, an engineer with a passion for invention, applied his inexhaustible creative drive and ingenuity to finding solutions to technical problems. Yet he never ignored his responsibility for his employees' needs and concerns. That is why the company has always seen economic success and sustainable development as going hand in hand. Kärcher invests more than the average in research and development, in modern production methods and in high-quality apprenticeships and in-service training for its employees.

Over the past 30 years Kärcher has carried out around 90 cleaning projects on historic monuments. In 1998, for instance, it cleaned the colonnades on St. Peter's Square in Rome, its biggest-ever facade-cleaning project at that time. In 2005, the cleaning of the presidents' heads on Mount Rushmore, South Dakota, attracted much attention. The company also supports various charitable, social and cultural causes in several countries. (www.karcher.com)

Karl Mayer

Karl Mayer, a family-run company, leads the world in the warp-knitting machine sector. They also set the standard in the textile world in warp-preparation equipment for warp-knitting and weaving.

The company was set up by Karl Mayer in 1937 in Oberthausen near Frankfurt, where the present headquarters are still located.

Karl Mayer supplies machines, tailor-made to very specific requirements, making them experts in the textile chain. A keen awareness of quality, expert engineering and innovative products are at the heart of Karl Mayer, which makes their customers the world over trust them completely. In 2010, they delivered their 100,000th machine. Their corporate slogan is 'We care about your future'.

They have production locations in Germany, Switzerland, Italy, the UK, Japan, China and Hong Kong, with 88 sales agencies and a total of 2,300 employees worldwide. Fritz P. Mayer is the CEO of the company.

Karl Mayer has four divisions: warp knitting, warp preparation, technical textiles and parts and components. Karl Mayer, the market leader in warp knitting machines and Raschel machines, offers machines for warp knits and specials, lace and curtain, technical textiles, specialised textiles, warp preparation for warp knitting and weaving and second-hand or pre-owned machines. They offer tailor-made solutions for garment textiles, sports textiles, home and technical textiles.

In 2003, the Textronic® Lace TL 66/1/36 and the Fascination® Lace FL 20/16 were the first machines in a new generation of lace machines to create a sensation in the market.

KAMCOS® is their system for managing all the machines computer facilities, linking the production data to the admin and control centre. The company also has a logistics centre and a customer support and development centre at their headquarters for customer service and a Karl Mayer Academy for training activities. (www.karlmayer.com)

KARL STORZ

KARL STORZ Endoskope is a global company that is highly regarded internationally in the production and marketing of endoscopes, endoscopic instruments and devices, for more than 15 medical disciplines from the head to the ankle.

The company was founded in 1945 by Karl Storz in the town of Tuttlingen. The product range initially was comprised of instruments, headlamps and binocular loupes for ear, nose and throat specialists.

KARL STORZ GmbH & Co. KG is a family-run company with headquarters in Tuttlingen. Sybill Storz, daughter of the founder, is the Managing Director of the KARL STORZ Group. The company has 43 sales and marketing offices in 38 countries as well as distribution agents all over the world. Production locations are in Germany, the US, Great Britain, Switzerland and Estonia. They employ around 5,800 people worldwide.

A modern endoscope must generate as brilliant an image as possible inside the human and animal body for proper diagnosis. The high optical power and quality of KARL STORZ endoscopes are a delight to all practitioners. Through the innovative application of state-of-the-art electronics and micro-mechanics, the therapeutic units from KARL STORZ provide a maximum of safety and operational convenience, with dedicated software to improve image quality.

Their range of endoscopic equipment for human and veterinary medicine as well as for industrial applications now encompasses over 15,000 products. The most recent innovations of KARL STORZ are in the field of digital documentation systems and the creation of comprehensive operation room (OR) solutions. These OR concepts include the integration of the varied technical equipment under medical requirements and ergonomic aspects. These developments, such as the OR1™ fully-networked Operating Room or the KARL STORZ AIDA Centralized Image and Data Management System, supplement the range and demonstrate that at KARL STORZ, the future has already become the present.

They develop sophisticated, innovative products and concepts, which, thanks to in-depth consultation with leading surgeons, university hospitals and research institutes, are closely geared to the needs of medical practice and further optimised. Since 1996 more than 1,500 national and international patents have been created and KARL STORZ sets the standard against which other companies measure themselves.

KARL STORZ also has a training and logistics centre to cater to their training needs and maintenance of instruments. Since 2011, the 'World of Endoscopy' is presented to international customers in its new visitor centre located at its headquarters in Tuttlingen.

In the recent past in 2009, KARL STORZ received a German innovation award ('Ort im Land der Ideen') for its integrated operation room concept for gentle surgery. The same innovation award was bestowed in 2012 for their MI-Report, the touchless gesture control for image and data management in the OR. On an international level KARL STORZ received in 2010, the Frost & Sullivan 'Asia-Pacific Growth Leadership Award' as well as the 2011, 'Asia-Pacific Endoscopy Company of the Year' award. (www.karlstorz.com)

Koenig & Bauer

The Koenig & Bauer Group is the second-largest manufacturer of printing presses worldwide, with the broadest product range in the industry and a key supplier to the global media industry. The company was founded in 1817 in Würzburg, Germany by Friedrich Koenig and Andreas Bauer. They established the Schnellpressenfabrik Koenig & Bauer in a secularised monastery in Oberzell near Würzburg.

Today, the parent company Koenig & Bauer AG (KBA) has six production facilities in Germany. Other subsidiaries are in Austria, the Czech Republic, Switzerland, US, China and in a few other countries as well. They have several sales and service outlets worldwide, like in Australia, Brazil, France, UK, Russia, plus a global network of dealers.

The core companies in the group with headquarters in Würzburg, employ over 6,000 people. Sales revenue for financial year 2011 was €1.167 billion. Claus Bolza-Schünemann is the President of the Executive Board of KBA, while Dieter Rampl is the Chairman of the Supervisory Board. KBA's core competence is the development and manufacture of technologically innovative yet cost-effective printing systems and peripherals. Koenig & Bauer has been listed on the Frankfurt and Munich exchanges for the last 25 years.

Their product portfolio includes, sheet-fed offset presses, web offset, newspaper and semi-commercial and digital presses, paper logistics systems, machines for special applications like money printing, metal-decorating and card presses, press consum (consumables) and industrial coding systems.

This diversity and specialisation has resulted in a unique level of know-how in many sectors of printing technology, consummate skill in translating customer's wishes into reality and extreme flexibility in meeting the technological challenges of the future. They also offer services and solutions for climate-neutral printing.

KBA has many firsts to its credit: they are a long-standing record holder for the highest number of patents registered by a press manufacturer and a global leader in security presses/money printing presses with a market share of more than 90 per cent. They are also the global market and technology leader in large-format, sheet-fed offset presses, packaging presses, newspaper presses and metal-decorating presses. (www.kba.com)

KHS

KHS is a systems provider of technologically innovative, top-quality, filling and packaging machines and other equipment for the beverages and food industries. The company was founded in 1868 in Dortmund, Germany, as Holstein & Kappert (H&K). Today, the company is a 100 per cent subsidiary of Klöckner-Werke AG.

The concern is managed centrally from Dortmund and employs around 5,000 people worldwide and realised sales of around €918 million for financial year 2011. KHS has international production facilities in the US, Mexico, Brazil, China and India. Matthias Niemeyer is the new CEO of the company, while Heinz Jörg Fuhrmann is the Chairman of the Supervisory Board.

KHS is ideally positioned in the field of holistic PET systems. Their position as an innovator in the market is continuously being consolidated thanks to new developments, such as modular packaging solutions, universal filling systems, high-performance labelling technology and modern communications and diagnostic technologies.

They are specialists for efficient technologies in the beverages, food and non-food industries, offering integrated system solutions from the processing to finished product storage. KHS gives their customer's products the right type of packaging, whether pouch, can, keg, glass or PET bottles.

They have holistic solutions and products for various types of packaging needs, solutions for PET packaging, filling, aseptic filling to keg processing, labelling, palletizing and pouching. Through their network of distributors and service points, KHS is there for their customer's needs for spare parts, technical upgrades and training offers. KHS earlier received the iF product design award for their new control panel and also received the red dot Award for its pioneering machine operating system, the Human Machine Interface or HMI. (www.khs.com)

Klais Orgelbau

Klais Orgelbau is a firm based in Bonn, Germany, that designs, builds and restores large pipe organs. The firm was founded in 1882 by Johannes Klais.

There are Klais organs on every continent. They sound in churches, cathedrals, concert halls in cities as well as in villages, from the Hedwigs Kathedrale in Berlin to the Japan Philharmonic in Kyoto. These organs are living history; they link the past with the present and the future, building history from the past 110 years with all of its changes of sound, style and function. The company's goal is to find the best solution for any organ and to realise it with the highest possible quality.

They are a family-run company that employs around 70 people. Hans Gerd Klais, the founder's grandson, has been heading the workshop since 1965; together with his son, Philip Klais, they work to further their commitment to building instruments of character and high tonal and aesthetic standards. They manage the same workshop that the founder started in 1882, on the street where Beethoven was born. They are steeped in tradition but well equipped to meet the demands of the present.

Together with a team of 65 master artisans, all musicians, each organ is painstakingly constructed by hand, custom designed for the space in which it will reside. According to Philip Klais, 'Building organs is a creative craft and requires constant consideration of all traditions'. He likes to describe his company as a 'Bonsai Global Player'.

The company has built and installed organs across Germany and the US, in St. Petersburg, Venezuela, Beijing's National Grand Theatre and for the Philharmonic Halls in Japan, Spain, Poland, Malaysia, Singapore, New Zealand and Australia.

They also carry out restorations of existing pipe organs around the world. In one case, they even incorporated sounds of Maori instruments in a new organ for the Auckland Town Hall in New Zealand. New methods appear in organ building, while Klais Orgelbau aims to strike the right note and balance. (www.klais.de)

KLS Martin

The KLS Martin Group stands for high-quality, innovative medical technology, proven and tested brands that are in high demand. As an umbrella or family brand, the KLS

Martin Group covers almost all surgical fields. The company was founded in 1923 by Rudolf Buck in Tuttlingen, Germany.

Today, some 800 people are doing their best for KLS Martin worldwide. They have partners and subsidiaries in the US, Japan, Italy, France, Russia, Netherlands and China. They also have specialised dealers in more than 140 countries around the world. Karl Leibinger and Christian Leibinger are the present Managing Directors of Gebrüder Martin GmbH & Co.KG.

In 2004, the Gebrüder Martin company and its partners established the KLS Martin Group as an umbrella organisation uniting the following companies: Rudolf Buck, Karl Leibinger Medizin technik, KLS Martin, Stuckenbrock and of course Gebrüder Martin. In the US, KLS Martin L.P. works closely with the group to cover the market there.

KLS Martin's product range includes roughly 16,000 items, plus a great number of spare parts. The group earns 75 per cent of its turnover in foreign markets with two-thirds of this generated in Europe.

Millions of physicians all over the world use and rely on the quality instruments from KLS Martin, which sets standards in surgery and dentistry. Among their many products are surgical instruments, for dental and oral surgery, Sonic Weld Rx®, MedLED Focus Headlights, Micro Stop® Sterile Containers, implant systems, laser surgery, electro surgery, operating lights, medical camera systems-surgi cam, ceiling-mounted systems and marWorld Modular Operating Rooms.

At KLS Martin, comprehensive quality management systems govern all processes from product development to customer complaints. Their systems comply with the DIN EN ISO 13485 and DIN EN ISO 9001 international standards as well as with the EU legislation relating to medical devices and now carry the CE mark. Their products have won several national and international design awards over the years. They are also a recent winner of a Green Dot award. With Go Green they are into sustainable products in medical technology that protects and conserves the environment. (www.klsmartin.com)

Knauf

Knauf is a Global Group of companies that is a manufacturer of building materials and construction systems. The company was established in 1932 in Perl an der Mosel in Saarland, Germany, by the brothers Alfons Knauf and Karl Knauf. The company Gebr. Knauf Rheinische Gipsindustrie is the nucleus of the Knauf Group, which operates globally.

Today, they operate more than 150 production sites worldwide. Originally a producer of conventional gypsum, Knauf produces construction material for dry-wall construction, Knauf plasterboards, mineral-fibre acoustic boards, dry mortar with gypsum for internal plaster and cement-based external plaster and insulating materials of glass wool and mineral wool.

Knauf has a total workforce of 24,000 employees in around 60 countries worldwide. In 2011, the group generated sales revenue amounting to €5.7 billion. The company has eight divisions: insulation materials, other building materials, pre-formed parts, interior construction, DIY, logistics, façades and mechanical engineering.

Knauf has remained a family company and is owned by the Alfons and Karl Knauf families. Knauf Gips KG is a limited commercial partnership under German law with headquarters in Iphofen. The managing partners are Manfred Grundke and Edgar Binnemann, while Alexander Knauf is the Chief Operating Officer as member of the group management Germany/Switzerland.

The quality management system, which Knauf introduced in Germany in 1994, meets the requirements of DIN EN ISO 9001:2000. Knauf is a pioneer of an all-embracing company philosophy which sets great store by intelligent, environmentally friendly and energy-conserving production processes. They have significantly reduced their CO_2 emissions and saved on energy consumption. They have also started to return the areas used for quarrying gypsum to nature by way of re-naturation of those areas. (www.knauf.com)

Knorr-Bremse

The Knorr-Bremse Group, based in Munich, is the world's leading manufacturer of braking systems for rail and commercial vehicles. Knorr-Bremse GmbH was founded in 1905 in Berlin by Georg Knorr. As a technology pioneer for over 100 years, Knorr-Bremse has been a driving force in the development, production and sale of modern braking systems in the area of rail and commercial vehicles. The company thus contributes significantly to safety on the road and on railways. More than a billion people worldwide rely daily on Knorr-Bremse braking systems.

Other lines of business include, for example, door-systems and air-conditioning systems for rail vehicles as well as torsional vibration dampers for internal combustion engines, power-train-related solutions such as the Pneumatic Booster System (PBS) and transmission control systems for enhanced efficiency and fuel economy.

They employ over 20,000 people worldwide. For financial year 2011 they had a total sales turnover of €4.241 billion.

Knorr-Bremse AG, the mother company of the group, serves as an umbrella corporation, encompassing business divisions, Rail Vehicle Systems and Commercial Vehicle Systems, as well as their regional companies. In addition to the main Knorr-Bremse brand, Knorr-Bremse Commercial Vehicle Systems sells four additional brands on the market, while Rail Vehicle Systems sells nine additional brands on the market.

The Executive Board of Knorr-Bremse AG consists of three executive directors: Klaus Deller, Dieter Wilhelm and Lorenz Zwingmann, while, Heinz Hermann Thiele is the Chairman of the Supervisory Board and the owner of the company.

Innovations are the basis of the present and further success of Knorr-Bremse, the reason why they have invested €209 million in 2011 for R&D, while employing 1,850 people. The Knorr Excellence Model (KE), introduced in 2007, describes the vision in which the company progresses from 'very good' to 'excellent' in reaching its strategic goals in all areas. This is particularly important, given that quality is the top requirement for Knorr-Bremse as a manufacturer of safety-critical-systems, from competence in product engineering to global purchasing excellence, Quality first with a zero-defect production system, given employee excellence. They have been meeting quality standards and reducing CO_2 emissions while increasing their energy efficiency for some years. (www.knorr-bremse.com)

Kolbus

Kolbus develops, manufactures and markets book-binding machinery, together with complete in-line production systems for the print-finishing industry. This medium-sized company counts among the leading manufacturers of its industry. The company's origin dates back to 1775. Since 1900, they have been manufacturing book-binding machines in Rahden, Germany, where they are based.

Today, Kolbus is an advanced engineering company, operating an ultra-modern, 87,000 square metre factory complex and employing around 1,100 people. Kai Büntemeyer is the Managing Partner of Kolbus GmbH & Co.KG.

Kolbus offers the most comprehensive product range of book-binding machines in the world. The range is comprised of more than 30 types of machines, covering all application areas for the production of bound products, starting with the folded sheet, i.e. gathering, perfect binding, sawing and trimming, case-making, embossing, book-finishing, digital print finishing, feeding, stacking, packing and conveying. Like they say in the trade, 'Print it and then Kolbus it'.

They also have the Kolbus Inline Configurations for Multi-Variable Applications and smooth production, guaranteeing maximum productivity and efficiency. While the Kolbus 360° Line Data Management System brings more transparency to the business with precise job planning and control, ideal information flows, increased quality and reduced costs.

Their sales force works within a worldwide sales network and responds to information and other requirements given the local character of the markets and the companies they manage. Kolbus also offers excellent customer service with regard to prompt problem solving, spare parts and training.

Today, there is hardly a book, brochure, catalogue, booklet, newspaper and magazine in this world which does not come into contact with Kolbus machines during its production process. The comprehensive Kolbus product range reflects customer proximity, market knowledge and intelligent engineering, accompanied by reliability and a quality orientation. (www.kolbus.de)

Krones

The Krones Group with headquarters in Neutrabling, Germany, designs develops and manufactures machines and complete lines for the fields of process technology, bottling, canning and packaging. The company was founded in 1951 by Hermann Kronseder, who started the enterprise to manufacture electric machines in Neutrabling.

Today, the group employs around 11,400 people worldwide and had a total sales turnover in financial year 2011 for around €2.480 billion. Ninety per cent of their sales come from the international export market. Volker Kronseder the son of the founder, is the Chairman of the Executive Board of Krones AG, and Ernst Baumann is the Chairman of the Supervisory Board.

Krones is the market leader in systems for filling and packaging operations in the food and beverages industry. They also cater to the chemical, pharma and cosmetics industries. Krones have five production facilities in Germany and over 80 sales and support agencies worldwide, that offer 24/7 service support. They also have a subsidiary called Kosme for machines of the low-output range.

The group's product portfolio covers the following categories: stretch blow-moulding technology, filling and closing technology, aseptic filling, labelling and dressing technology, inspection and monitoring technology, washers, rinsers and pasteurisers, packing and palletising technology, conveyor technology, systems engineering, process technology, intra-logistics and brewing technology (steinecker), information technology, PET recycling lines, factory planning and valve technology.

Krones's success is based on their specialised knowledge according to customers' sectoral needs, technical lead in its chosen fields and state-of-the-art manufacturing to stringent standards of qualitative excellence. To date, around 2,200 full and utility patents are evidence of their innovative capabilities. They continue to spend a substantial amount on R&D expenditure, while the Krones Academy is the place for basic and specialised training. In 1994, Krones received the DIN ISO 9001 certification for its plants in Neutrabling, Amberg and Nittenau. With their enviro brand Krones has taken sustainability fully on board with a concrete corporate program. (www.krones.com)

KSB

The KSB Group is one of the leading producers of pumps, valves and related systems that are setting standards worldwide. The company was founded in 1871 by Johannes Klein, who on receiving a patent on his new invention, called the Boiler Feed Apparatus set up the company, Frankenthaler Maschinen & Armatur Fabrik: Klein, Schanzlin & Becker, together with Friedrich Schanzlin and Jakob Becker to manufacture boiler feed equipment and valves. The name KSB is made up of the first letter from the surnames of the three founders.

Today, the KSB Group, with headquarters in Frankenthal a town in the southwestern state of Rhineland-Palatinate, has more than 30 manufacturing sites in 20 countries and marketing companies and service centres in more than 100 countries. They have over 16,000 employees worldwide of which around 2,600 highly-trained specialists at over 160 service centres offer their customers, global inspection, maintenance and repair of KSB products and even competitor makes.

Annual sales revenue for 2011 was around €2.091 billion. Wolfgang Schmitt is the Chairman of the Board of Management of KSB AG, while Hans-Joachim Jacob is the Chairman of the Supervisory Board.

KSB offers innovative pump and valve technology for all manner of applications, from building services to industry and water, energy and mining. Pumps and valves come in a choice of designs, sizes and materials for a whole array of applications.

KSB solutions meet the highest requirements in terms of energy efficiency, since they optimise on not only individual components but entire hydraulic systems. Customers in the municipal and industrial water and waste-water management sectors rely on KSB for engineering services and supply of the entire hydraulic and electro-technical equipment for their plants. Their scope of performance includes construction work up to the turnkey installation of pumping stations, complemented by an extensive range of services for all applications.

They have achieved worldwide implementation of quality, environmental, occupational health and safety standards as well as other management systems in line with ISO 9001, ISO 14001 and OHSAS 18001 – these, as well as a future-oriented development of their products. 'Made by KSB' is the seal that ensures high, dependable quality standards. (www.ksb.com)

KUKA

The KUKA Group is one of the world's leading suppliers of robots and automated production systems and solutions. Present headquarters are in Augsburg, Germany, where the company was founded in 1898 by Johan Josef Keller and Jakob Knappich. They started by producing acetylene for the production of cost-effective domestic and municipal lighting and later went on to include oxy-acetylene welding and then electrical resistance welding to construct the first electric spot-welding gun in Germany. The name KUKA is derived from the initial letters of the founding company name, Keller und Knappich Augsburg.

Today, KUKA, with its Robotics and Systems divisions, is one of the world's leading companies in the fields of mechanical and systems engineering. Providing cutting-edge technology to the automotive industry, they are now supplying state-of-the-art technology in other sectors as well, like medical technology, the solar and aerospace industries.

In fiscal year 2011, they had sales revenues of €1.435 billion while employing around 6,589 people worldwide. Till Reuter is the present CEO and Chairman of the Executive Board of KUKA AG, while Bernd Minning is the Chairman of the Supervisory Board.

In the Robotics division, they develop, produce and market industrial robots, robot-related services and controllers. KUKA robots offer an optimal complement to the human workforce wherever utmost quality, safety, speed and precision are required, especially in large sections of the metal-working, plastics, electrical and electronic industries; or in medicine, where image-guided, robot-supported precision radiation opens up entirely new methods of treatment.

In their Systems division, they work on custom-tailored solutions that revolve around automatic manufacturing processes. For example, in the automotive industry, they provide products and services from body production to assembly and from component development to factory operation. (www.kuka-ag.de)

Lenze

Lenze SE is a global specialist in motion-centric automation. The Lenze group offers worldwide, a complete range of products, drive solutions, complete automation systems as well as engineering services and tools from a single source. Lenze is one of the few providers in the market to support engineers in all phases of machine development – from the initial idea to aftersales. Lenze's specialised experts work with customers to develop integrated drive and automation solutions, making it easy to design, produce and service the machine.

The company was started in 1947, when the founder, Hans Lenze, took over the Stahlkontor Weser GmbH company in the town of Hamelin. In October 2009 Lenze

AG was converted into Lenze SE (Societas Europaea), a public limited company under European law.

Today, the company, with headquarters in Aerzen, Germany, employs more than 3,100 people worldwide and is represented in 60 countries with dedicated sales companies, development sites, production facilities, logistic centres as well as a network of sales and service partners. Over 330 employees work in R&D, churning out new innovations. In the financial year 2011/2012, Lenze reached a sales turnover of €567.9 million. Present Chief Executive Officer (CEO) of Lenze SE is Erhard Tellbüscher, while Jürgen Krumnow is the Chairman of the Supervisory Board.

As one of the few full range providers, Lenze offers its customers the exact, right products needed for any machine task – from controls and visualisation, to electrical drives, gears and motors right through to couplings and brakes. The extensive L-force drive and automation product portfolio, a consistent and integrated platform, is invaluable in this regard. It allows customers to quickly recognise which products represent the best solution for their specific requirements. Lenze products undergo the most stringent testing. Reliability and quality are the hallmarks of Lenze's products and services. Lenze Blue Green Solutions, furthermore, reduce energy costs by efficient and intelligent use of energy. Their drive and automation technology is used in a wide variety of industries, for example, the packaging industry, the industrial material handling sector and in automotive construction. (www.lenze.com)

Leoni

Leoni AG is a global supplier of wires, optical fibres, cables and cable systems, as well as related development services for applications in the automotive business and other industries. The company was founded in 1917 in Nürnberg as Leonische Werke Roth-Nürnberg AG. In 1999, it was renamed Leoni AG, with headquarters in Nürnberg (Nuremberg), Germany.

Today, the group of companies, which is listed on the German MDAX, employs around 63,500 people in 31 countries and generated total sales of €3.7 billion for financial year 2011. The group is among the world's largest and most successful cable manufacturers.

Klaus Probst is the Chairman of the Management Board of Leoni AG while Werner Rupp is the Chairman of the Supervisory Board. Their corporate slogan is 'Leoni – the Quality Connection'. The Leoni brand consolidates a number of activities, products and services under one umbrella brand.

The Group offers its customers – alongside customised cable solutions – complete systems in which all the components are perfectly tuned to one another – from the cable itself to the required connectors and mountings. Added to this is a product value chain, unique in the sector, which gives valuable synergistic benefits. It ranges from ultra-thin single wires, optical fibres to cables and through to complex wiring systems with integrated electronics.

Leoni focuses its efforts on the core markets: automotive, industry and healthcare, communications and infrastructure, electrical appliances as well as wires and strands. Their customer base includes blue chip clients such as ABB, BMW, Bosch, IBM, Philips, Shell, Siemens, GM, Volvo, VM and several more.

The company is already a global market leader in the supply of automotive wires, while in the field of wiring systems it is number one in Europe and comes in fourth worldwide. They have received several awards including the international 'Supplier of the Year' by Caterpillar, DAF, Peugeot-Citroën and Porsche. (www.leoni.com)

Louis Renner

Louis Renner GmbH & Co.KG is the world's premier producer of piano actions and hammerheads. Louis Renner began on a very modest level with the production of the piano mechanism in October 1882. Handcrafted production was at the heart of the company's beginnings.

The history of Renner is closely related to that of the German piano industry and their increasing demands for more specialised industrial production methods. Situated in the heart of the German Black Forest, the Renner production process combines the finest old-world craftsmanship with state-of-the-art, computer-controlled, precision tooling and machinery, in order to produce the world's finest piano actions. They use natural materials, handcrafted to the highest precision.

The Louis Renner Company is the most respected piano action maker in the world, producing the universally acclaimed Renner Action to the most demanding specifications of the world's leading piano producers.

With three factories located in central and southern Germany, Renner continues its 126 year tradition of producing the world's finest piano actions through 200 highly specialised craftsmen under the leadership of Siegfried Hoffmann. Over 3 million piano actions have left their production facilities so far, handcrafted to the highest standards of precision and the finest quality material. The production of a piano mechanism is intrinsically complicated. A total of 8,800 sections, small parts, springs and strips have to be put together for one single action.

The Renner quality story begins in Odenheim where the wood from the naturally grown hornbeam trees is carefully selected and conditioned. The wood is cut into mouldings at their Stuttgart-Gärtringen factory where hammers and the grand piano actions are also made. Mouldings and hammers are then sent to their Zeitz factory for the upright action production.

Renner is the only supplier on the European continent to have stood up to the rigorous selection process of the pianoforte industry. The have prevailed over stiff competition to produce a superior quality product. (www.louisrenner.com)

Mäurer & Wirtz

Mäurer & Wirtz are specialists for fine fragrances and luxurious body-care products. They have launched brands that have enriched the world of fragrance for generations. Fashion fragrances by Mäurer & Wirtz have set new trends while the company's luxury products play a key role in boosting the image of their international brands. The company was founded in 1845 by Michael Mäurer and his stepson Andreas August Wirtz, in a town called Stolberg in the Rhineland region of Germany. They began by setting up a soap-works enterprise there.

Today, as an independent subsidiary of the Wirtz Group, the Stolberg-based company operates in around 140 markets and is one of the world's leaders in perfumes and body-care products. They have remained a true family company and are now managed by the fifth generation. Hermann Wirtz is the Managing Partner, while Thomas Seeger-Helbach is the Managing Director. The company has three corporate divisions: Prestige, 4711 and Beauty, which successfully covers three different market and consumer segments. Their corporate slogan is 'House of Perfumes'.

The beauty unit at Mäurer & Wirtz combines the company's own classic fragrance and body-care products, such as *Tabac Original, Tosca, Nonchalance* and several others with popular licensed brands. Fashion labels like *Otto Kern, s.Oliver and Betty Barclay* tap into the potential of branded perfumes with the help of Mäurer & Wirtz. They produce fragrances for women and men and for all generations, from classic to modern, sporty to trendy. Scents, for every day and special occasions, captivating eau de toilettes, finely scented body lotions and invigorating shower gels.

The product, 4711, is the celebrated and legendary brand that is over 200 years., The rare case, where a brand has become the generic name for a product category 'eau de cologne'. The famous label with the ribbon motif has been inseparably linked to the name 4711 Original Eau de Cologne and the mysteries of its formulation. '4711' ranks among the world's most famous brands. The 4711 unit was taken over by Mäurer & Wirtz in 2006. Thanks to creative innovations such as the selective aroma therapy concept, Acqua Colonia, the product family around the heritage brand 4711 Original Eau de Cologne has a firm foot in the future.

In the Prestige unit, Mäurer & Wirtz focuses on licensed businesses in the premium and luxury segment. They have fragrances for world-famous designer, fashion and lifestyle brands, including *Strellson* and *Baldessarini*. Luxury fragrances that set fashion standards – for fashion labels and lifestyle brands with a distinctive profile, a fragrant proof of the company's perfume competence. In 2012, they acquired the Baldessarini Fragrance business from P&G. All of Baldessarini perfumes and body-care products have been integrated into their Prestige division.

Acqua Colonia which was created under the umbrella brand of 4711, won the 'Prix de Beaute' in 2010 for the best marketing strategy in the luxury category and the GALA SPA Award in 2012, while Strellson No.1 received the red dot design award for its bottle. Tabac Original and 4711 Original Eau de Cologne won the brand award, Deutsche Standards 2010 and it is now entitled to display the 'Brand of the Century' seal. (www.m-w.de)

Müller

The Müller Group is Germany's largest, privately owned dairy business with operations in several European countries and in Israel. The company was founded in 1896 by Ludwig Müller, who started with a small village dairy in the town of Aretsried, part of the Bavarian municipality of Fischach. The headquarters of the group are still based in Aretsried.

Growing from village dairy to international food company, in 1971 Theo Müller took over from his father, the dairy founded by his grandfather – with only four employees. Today, the 'Unternehmensgruppe Theo Müller' controls the dairy segment business with the stand-alone brands of Müller, Wiseman, Weihenstephan, Sachsenmilch and Käserei Loose. Private labels and commodities such as butter, UHT milk, lactose powder and milk protein complete the portfolio. In addition to the milk-processing subsidiaries, the packaging company Optipack, the company's own logistics company Culina, Fahrzeugtechnik Aretsried and Müller Naturfarm, one of the biggest fruit processing companies in Germany, also belong to the group. Under the leadership of Heiner Kamps, Stefan Müller and Henrik Bauwens, the companies of the group employ around 21,000 people and have an annual turnover of around €4.7 billion.

Since 2011, the activities of the HK Food Group, a leading food company in Germany, also have come under the umbrella of Unternehmensgruppe Theo Müller. This has extended their product range with notable brands from the chilled gourmet salad, sauce and speciality fish market segment, such as Homann, Nadler, Lisner, Hamker, Pfennigs and Hopf, plus a number of different private label products. The group also owns the licence for Livio, the traditional dressing brand.

Under the leadership of Nordsee, the group is bundling modern food concepts, serving a range of consumer groups with a variety of offerings. This is extending the rich choice of fish dishes and seafood in many Nordsee restaurants with coffee and bakery goods – in the adjoining Strandcafé, for example. Campo's and Bar di Mar have also helped to develop new food concepts, which are already on the market. The group now has a unique and innovative bakery concept in the shape of Bastian`s.

Their awareness and perception of different consumer preferences and tastes are crucial factors for their success in Europe. Being a consumer products company they conduct fairly extensive advertising campaigns in different media as per brand/country markets. (www.muellergroup.com)

NETZSCH

The NETZSCH Group is a family-owned enterprise, engaged in the manufacture of various types of machinery and instrumentation. NETZSCH was founded in 1873 by Thomas Netzsch, the great-grandfather of the late Chairman, Thomas Netzsch, and his brother Christian in the town of Selb, in Upper Franconia, Germany. Their first products were pump wagons for extinguishing fires and agricultural machines.

Today, the Group has 140 sales and production locations in 27 countries on five continents. The NETZSCH Group consists of three business divisions under the umbrella of the Erich NETZSCH GmbH & Co. Holding KG. The present Chairman of the NETZSCH Group is Dietmar Bolkart and Hanns-Peter Ohl and they still have their headquarters in Selb. As of 2012, they had over 2,700 employees worldwide and a sales turnover of €391 million. Their three business divisions are analysing and testing, grinding and dispersing and pumps and systems.

In the analysing and testing division, instruments and systems for thermal analysis are produced for the complete material characterisation of raw materials and finished products in the areas of R&D and quality assurance. These products are used primarily by the plastics, rubber, chemicals, pharma, food, paint, metallurgy, construction, and ceramics industries.

The grinding and dispersing division manufactures grinding systems for wet and dry grinding as fine as the sub-micron range. Mixing and dispersing systems for solids and suspensions and mixing systems and press-out units for highly viscous products. Application areas range from chemicals – such as paint and lacquer manufacturing to the minerals, pharma, plastic, recycling and food industries. They are technological and market leaders in their areas of expertise.

In the pumps and systems division, they produce various types of pumps, like their NEMO® progressive cavity pumps, TORNADO® brand of rotary lobe pumps, screw pumps, grinding machines, dosing systems and accessories, providing customised, sophisticated solutions for a variety of applications from food and drink, chemicals, raw materials and also for environmental protection. (www.netzsch.com)

Otto Bock

Otto Bock Health Care GmbH is a modern company with tradition. They are a global player with a strong brand worldwide, as their name stands for high quality and technologically outstanding products and services in the prostheses and orthoses product segments as well as wheelchairs and neuro-implants. They provide physically-challenged people with the highest degree of mobility and independence.

The company was founded in 1919 in Berlin by the prosthetist Otto Bock who started the Orthopädische Industrie GmbH, to supply thousands of war veterans with prostheses and other orthopaedic products. Today, Otto Bock with headquarters in Duderstadt, Germany, has 21 subsidiaries in Europe as well as several other production facilities and sales companies in North and South America, Asia, Africa and Australia. They have a total of 44 sales and service locations worldwide and exports products to 140 countries in the world. The company employs around 5,000 employees worldwide and had a sales turnover of €583 million for financial year 2011. Hans Georg Näder is the President and CEO of the company. Their corporate slogan is 'Quality for Life'.

Otto Bock provides high-quality orthotic, prosthetic and rehabilitation solutions for a wide range of clinical conditions. Their core business sectors are in what they call Orthobionic® and Bionicmobility®. The C-Leg is their most famous, innovative product. It is a computerised knee that adapts to suit different patient's walking gaits. Otto Bock Competence Centres offer state-of-the-art treatment expertise. The modern prostheses from Otto Bock make it possible to preserve or restore mobility, with wheelchairs and rehabilitation aids that are in harmony with their patient's personal lifestyle. They also have seating systems, standing devices and similar products for children.

Among their other products are support and soft orthoses for joints, ligaments and fractures as well as orthoses for paralysis patients. Their new area of expertise is neuro-stimulation, where they bring about movement in the patient using electro-stimulation after a neurological event such as a stroke or paraplegia. Otto Bock has developed the four-channel stimulator STIWELL med4 and neuro-prosthesis ActiGait®. The Dynamic Arm® is their leading product in the field of myoelectric arm prosthetics controlled by electric muscle signals.

The company spends some €30 million annually for R&D and registers over 100 product patents a year.

Otto Bock has been an official 'Worldwide Partner of the Paralympic Movement' since 2005. The cooperation agreement with the International Paralympics Committee (IPC) was renewed in 2008 during the games in Beijing, extending the partnership beyond London 2012. They also contribute to international relief efforts for disaster areas.

Otto Bock has won several awards for product design and material innovations. The iF (Gold Awards) for 2009, the red dot design award for 2009 and several more. (www. ottobock.com)

Probat

Probat, a family-owned enterprise, is a global market leader in the segment of coffee-roasting machines, equipment and plants. They also process cocoa, malt and nuts.

The company was founded in 1868 in Emmerich, Germany by Alex van Gülpen, Johann Heinrich Lensing and Theodor von Gimborn. The original name was Emmericher Maschinen Fabrik & Eisengießerei van Guelpen, Lensing & von Gimborn. Their purpose was the development of roasting technologies and the production of roasting machines for refining green coffee.

Today, with headquarters in Emmerich, Probat is represented in over 60 countries by subsidiaries and agents, while they employ over 600 people in Germany, Italy, the US, Brazil and elsewhere. Probat exports around 90 per cent of its products in Europe, North America, Central and South America.

The Probat Group has a market share of well over 50 per cent in their respective market segments, in fact, they say, every seven out of ten cups of coffee drunk worldwide are roasted with machines and equipment made by the Probat Group. To this day they have sold over 110,000 roasting machines. Wim Abbing is the Managing Director of the group.

They have essentially two divisions: roasting and plant technology and micro-roasting. In the first division, Probat continuously develops and manufactures new and innovative coffee-roasting machines and plants aimed at making the most out of each single coffee bean. Probat together with its subsidiary Bauermeister supplies whole production plants for the cocoa industry, production plants and plant components for the production of cocoa mass, starting from the intake of the cocoa-beans through to grinding and blocking-off. Their roasting machines FRD/M and Meteor are also used to roast cereals like barley, malt, green malt, maize as well as sunflower seeds and chicory. Other roasters are also used for nuts and oilseeds.

In micro-roasting, they offer speciality coffee roasters that are individually crafted, traditionally designed and industry proven brands: Probatino and Probatone. Among the components they supply are display bins, shop grinders, semi-automatic controls, de-stoner and exhaust air treatment.

Probat also has a dedicated service team that offers field service, maintenance, spare parts and customer training, apart from consulting in their areas of expertise. The Probat Group is EN 9001:2008 certified. (www.probat.com)

Roland Berger

Roland Berger Strategy Consultants is a top international strategy consultancy serving leading blue chip clients on challenging assignments in the global market. The company was founded in 1967 in Munich by Roland Berger who is the present honorary Chairman of the company.

Today, Roland Berger Strategy Consultants is an independent consultancy, wholly-owned by its 240 partners and has grown to become among the top three in Europe and among the top five in the global strategy consultancy market. The company has 51 offices in 36 countries and 2,700 professionals worldwide and advises leading international industry and service enterprises as well as public institutions and governments. The present CEO is Martin C. Wittig and the Chairman of the Supervisory Board is Burkhard Schwenker.

The three core values of Roland Berger's Strategy Consultants are excellence, entrepreneurship and partnership. Comprehensive analysis, creative strategies and reliable, pragmatic solutions are their hallmarks. A total of 76 per cent of their projects are of an international nature.

They believe in taking responsibility in order to achieve business success, in seeing their clients succeed, fostering an atmosphere of mutual trust and constructive dialog. Roland Berger Strategy Consultants also believes in being a responsible company and practice good corporate citizenship and giving back to the community through numerous projects. The Roland Berger School of Strategy and Economics (RBSE), is the new research, knowledge and teaching unit of the company. RBSE's mission is to help business leaders, master complexity and set up sustainable strategies. They build bridges between theory and practice to enable a best-in-class knowledge organisation. (www.rolandberger.com)

Roto

Roto Frank AG is another family-owned enterprise that is one of the world's leading designers and manufacturers of window and door hardware as well as suppliers of roof windows, solar roof systems and loft ladders. The company was founded in 1935 in Stuttgart by Wilhelm and Elfriede O. Frank. They started by introducing the Roto N Tilt & Turn hardware a pioneering new concept in window technology.

Today, the company has 12 production plants worldwide, a global sales network with more than 40 Roto sales subsidiaries. Net turnover for financial year 2011 was €656 million, employing around 4,100 people worldwide. They have their present headquarters in Leinfelden-Echter Dingen near the city of Stuttgart. Eckhard Keill is the present Chairman of the Executive Board while, Michael Stahl is the Chairman of the Supervisory Board of Roto Frank AG, the parent company.

They have two business divisions: window and door technology and roof windows and solar technology.

In the first division, their product range includes tilt and turn, turn-only and tilt-only hardware for inward and outward opening windows as well as sliding, tilt and slide, fold and slide and lift and slide door hardware, apart from mechanical and electro-mechanical, multi-point locking systems for main entrance doors, window-shutter hardware and electronic accessories for windows and doors.

In their second division, their product range includes roof windows, loft ladders and spiral staircases, insulated glass, roof solar systems (solar-thermal heating, photovoltaic conversion and complete roof solutions) as well as renovation of roof windows.

Their commitment to customer focus backed up by global R&D and manufacturing resources enables them to provide their customers with optimal solutions to meet their customer's specific requirements, the goal being to link security, energy management and convenience with each other.

Apart from their commitment, professional expertise and an observation for precision are the driving forces behind their work, factors responsible for Roto setting standards in the international window and door technology markets. In 1995, the company was certified in accordance with DIN EN ISO 9001 quality management standards. They also have the DIN EN ISO 14001:2005 environmental management systems. The Roto production plant in Bad Mergentheim was awarded the prize of best factory (Beste Fabrik) in Germany for 2010. (www.roto.de)

RUD

The RUD Group of companies is a family enterprise that offers chain systems and components for different applications across many industries. They are among the market leaders in industrial and snow chains. The Rud Ketten Rieger & Dietz GmbH U.Co.KG was founded in 1875 by Carl Rieger and Ferdinand Dietz in the Swabian town of Aalen.

Today, the RUD Group's main development and production facility remains at Aalen their headquarters. They have other production facilities in Germany and other parts of the world as well.

The group had an annual turnover of €170 million for 2011. At present they employ over 1,500 people in their production facilities and sales offices located in over 120 countries worldwide. The group is managed by the Rieger family, consisting of Hansjoerg Rieger, Joerg S. Rieger, Johannes W. Rieger and Benjamin T. Rieger.

They have a wide product range that includes hoist chains for hoisting, pulling, driving and conveying, lifting and lashing means, conveying systems, non-skid chains, (that offer innovative fitting systems to ensure safe driving on snow, icy roads and even on the toughest off-road terrain), tyre protection chains (that protect the tyre treads and side walls on earth-moving machines), and their newly developed barrier tech system that protects humans and their belongings against natural disasters. System solutions for the military, CRATOS/Conveyor Systems and TECDOS/Hoist chains are some of their other products. Their products have one common characteristic: progressive engineering. This comes from their many R&D alliances with research institutes, colleges and universities, suppliers and customers.

Erlau AG, a subsidiary company also located in Aalen, produces some of the above products as well as a range of outdoor furniture. With a selection of stylish designs, the range offers a complete seating solution, a range of outdoor gymnastic apparatus, suitable for the elderly or infirm, plus, the Erlau Human Care range of products that provides safety and grab-rails.

They set the latest technological standards in their product categories, especially various types of chains. Constantly innovating, the reliability and safety of their products are central to their business. Their worldwide quality commitment is reflected in their integrated QM/UM System. In 1992, they became the first chain factory to obtain ISO 9001 quality standards. Later, they also met the requirements under ISO 14001:2004 environmental quality standards.

The RUD Group is one of Germany's top 100 most innovative, mid-sized companies as recognised by the state government of Baden-Württemberg. They also received an

'Innovation Award' in 2009 for their ICE Chain System and a 'Steel Innovation Award' in 2009 for Sling and Lashing Systems. (www.rud.com)

Scheuerle

Scheuerle Fahrzeugfabrik develops and produces superlative, heavy-duty and special vehicles/transporters for applications in shipyards, plant construction, smelting and steel works, off-shore installations, air and space travel and for heavy goods freight. They are market leaders in their respective product categories. The company was founded in 1869 by Christian Scheuerle in Pfedelbach, when he started by opening a blacksmith's shop. It was only in 1937 that the founder's grandson, Willy Scheuerle, started with the development of heavy goods vehicles where he did some pioneering work. Many of their innovations, such as the Scheuerle Pendulum Axle, still form the basis of modern heavy goods transporters.

Otto Rettenmaier took over the company in 1987 and Scheuerle today is part of the TII Group, which is based in Heilbronn, Germany. Scheuerle together with its sister companies, Kamag Transport technik and Nicolas Industries, form the TII Group. The group is the global leader in developing and manufacturing top-class, heavy goods vehicles. Scheuerle Fahrzeugfabrik GmbH has its headquarters in Pfedelbach, Germany. The members of the management board consist of Andreas Kohler and Susanne Schlegel.

Their vehicles have helped move industrial plants weighing more than 16,000 tonnes. Million-pound submarines and luxury yachts, historical temples and churches, liquid ore, slag, etc. Scheuerle heavy-duty and special vehicles have changed the world. Moving enormous loads is not just a vision; with Scheuerle transporter technology, it's a daily reality.

Scheuerle's product range includes self-propelled modular transporters (SPMT), public road transporters for the shipyard, industry and off-shore installations, and plant construction for the steel industry, vehicles for the port and terminal logistics and special transporters for mining, bridge and tunnel construction as well as for the aero-space industries.

These products are sold worldwide by TII Sales GmbH & Co.KG. Their global sales team as well as numerous worldwide representatives ensures comprehensive local support for their customers. The company has quality certification according to DIN EN ISO 9001:2008, while their service department with trained technicians, specialists and engineers takes continuous care of their customers and offers maintenance/repair, consulting/training, spare parts and a help desk. Thousands of their vehicles are in operation worldwide. Over the years, they have broken several records for carrying some of the heaviest and most complex loads. (www.scheuerle.com)

Sennheiser

Sennheiser Electronic GmbH & Co.KG is an international company that manufactures top quality products for recording, transmission and reproduction of sound. The company was founded in 1945 in a town called Wennebostel near Hannover by Fritz Sennheiser.

He started a company called Labor W to manufacture voltmeters. In 1946, he started production of a microphone called DM 1.

In 2011, the turnover of the family-owned company was about €531.4 million. They employ around 2,183 employees in 90 countries around the globe. With headquarters in Wennebostel (Wedemark), Sennheiser has manufacturing plants in Germany, Ireland and the US, with sales subsidiaries and partners all around the globe.

Volker Bartels is the Speaker of the Executive Management Board, while Jörg Sennheiser is the Chairman of the Supervisory Board of the Sennheiser Group.

The world's leading manufacturer of studio microphones, Georg Neumann is part of the Sennheiser Group as is the Danish-based joint-venture company Sennheiser Communications, which develops headsets for the PC, office and call centre markets. The range of products offered by the group includes professional headphones and headsets, microphones, wireless microphones and monitoring systems, conference and information systems as well as aviation and audiology products.

A series of ground-breaking innovations over the years has given the company and their products a well-deserved global reputation. They are proud holders of numerous patents and awards. These include two prizes for innovation from the German industry, the Scientific and Engineering Award and both the Emmy and Grammy awards. Their constant development of new technology in acoustics and electronics is the key to reinforcing the strong market position held by Sennheiser. A large R&D centre in Germany and other R&D offices in California and Singapore ensure their leading position as suppliers of state-of-the-art technology.

The Sennheiser Sound Academy offers their customers tailor-made learning systems and expert knowledge on an international level. Sennheiser operates within the framework of its ISO 9001:2008 quality certification and the requirements of national and international aviation authorities. A large number of top musicians and artists from all parts of the world use Sennheiser equipment. (www.sennheiser.com)

Simon-Kucher & Partners

Simon-Kucher & Partners is a global management consulting firm with 650 employees in 25 offices worldwide. The company specialises in strategy, marketing, pricing and sales and is regarded as the world's leading pricing advisor/consultancy.

The firm was founded in 1985 in Bonn by Hermann Simon, Eckhard Kucher and Karl-Heinz Sebastian.

Today, the company is run by a team of 59 partners. The present CEOs are Georg Tacke and Klaus Hilleke; Hermann Simon now serves as the Chairman. Professor Hermann Simon is also the noted author of numerous books on pricing and two on the *Hidden Champions*, all of which have become international best-sellers.

With their 'Smart Profit Growth'℠ approach, Simon-Kucher helps clients to boost the top line instead of cutting costs. Their methods and tools have proven their value time and time again as their projects typically provide clients with a profitability improvement of 100 to 500 basis points.

Simon-Kucher is regarded as the world's leading consultancy and thought leader in pricing, with over 1,000 pricing optimisation projects conducted in the last three years alone. Clients come from all industry areas and virtually every aspect of pricing strategy and practice has been examined in detail by Simon-Kucher's experts.

According to Philip Kotler, famous author and professor of international marketing at the Kellogg School of Management, Northwestern University, 'No one knows more about pricing than Simon-Kucher'. Further, Peter Drucker the legendary management guru is reported to have said of Simon-Kucher, 'In Pricing you offer something nobody else does'.

According to a survey conducted in 2011 by manager-magazin (Germany's leading business monthly publication), top managers ranked Simon-Kucher number one in the 'Marketing and Sales' category ahead of other consulting giants. (www.simon-kucher.com)

STADA

STADA Arzneimittel AG and STADA's Group companies are active in the healthcare and pharmaceutical market and concentrate on the development and marketing of products with active ingredients – generally active pharmaceutical ingredients which are free from commercial property rights, particularly patents. STADA is an acronym for Standard Arzneimittel Deutscher Apotheker (Standard Drugs of German Pharmacists).

The company was founded in Dresden in 1895 as a pharmacists' cooperative. In 1956, they moved to their present location in Bad Vilbel close to Frankfurt a.M. By 1970 STADA became a stock corporation with registered shares exclusively for pharmacists. They have been a publicly listed company since 1997 and have been listed on the MDAX since 2001 and Euro STOXX 600 since December 2002.

Today, the STADA Group has a global network of internal and external sources for pharmaceutical production. They have grown organically and with several acquisitions all over Europe. The group is now increasingly taking advantage of production facilities required or expanded, in low-cost countries in southeast Europe, Russia and Vietnam. STADA is also represented worldwide by 53 sales companies in 33 countries. Germany is the largest national market for STADA as is Europe. Outside Europe, the group has a total of six sales companies. In financial year 2011, the Group employed over 7,800 people worldwide and had a sales turnover of €1.72 billion. Of this, most of their sales were in their generics segment.

Hartmut Retzlaff is the present CEO and Chairman of the Executive Board, while Martin Abend is the Chairman of the Supervisory Board. STADA also has an Advisory Board, whose Chairman is Frank Füßl. The corporate slogan is 'All the Best'.

Generics and branded products (OTC) are the group's two core segments. The top five generic active ingredients in products of the STADA Group in 2011 were Omeprazol (stomach medicine), Phospholipide (liver medicine), Simvastatin (for lowering cholesterol), Enalapril (ACE inhibitor) and Diclofenac (anti-rheumatic drug). Omeprazol continues to be the best-selling active pharmaceutical ingredient in both the generics segment as well as in the group, whereas, the top five branded products in the group in 2011 in order of sales were; Grippostad® (for colds), Apo-Go® (for Parkinson's disease), Ladival® (sun screen), Chondroxid® (for treatment of wear-related joint diseases) and Hirudoid® (for venous therapeutic treatment).

At numerous production sites, the group follows the good manufacturing practice (GMP) standards as also the relevant ISO standards and holds various ISO certificates, such as ISO 9001:2008, ISO 14001:2004 and ISO 13485:2007. (www.stada.de)

STIHL

The STIHL Group develops, manufactures and distributes power tools for forestry, landscape maintenance and the construction industry. The family-owned company was founded in 1926 in Waiblingen, Germany, by Andreas Stihl, who designed and hand built the first gasoline-powered chainsaw.

Today, the company is the world's best-selling chainsaw brand. For financial year 2011, the STIHL Group had a total turnover of €2.617 billion, while employing over 12,000 people worldwide. Bertram Kandziora is the Chairman of the Executive Board of STIHL AG, while Nikolas Stihl is the new Chairman of the STIHL Group's Advisory and Supervisory Boards. The STIHL Group has its headquarters and main manufacturing in Waiblingen, Germany. Since the early 1970s, STIHL has developed into an international group of companies. It manufactures chainsaws and other power tools at 10 locations in six countries: Germany, the US, Brazil, Switzerland, Austria and China. Since acquiring Zama with its plants in Japan, Hong Kong and China in 2009, the STIHL Group also develops, manufactures and distributes carburettors.

Alongside petrol and electric saws, the company's comprehensive range of products includes brushcutters, hedge trimmers, blowers and mistblowers, cut-off saws and power drills, as well as protective equipment and accessories. The product portfolio is complemented by the VIKING range of garden equipment, featuring lawnmowers, ride-on mowers, robotic mowers, garden shredders, power hoes, aerators and more.

Products made by STIHL make life easier for working people in more than 160 countries around the world. STIHL has been the world's top-selling chainsaw brand since 1971. Products are distributed exclusively through authorised dealers, including 32 marketing subsidiaries, more than 120 importers and about 40,000 dealers.

Global purchasing is equally important for the competitiveness of the STIHL Group, as is manufacture of its products close to the market. Apart from locational advantages, they also benefit from the continual innovations on the world market. STIHL guarantees success, in terms of quality, costs, innovation and service within fair, long-term customer-supplier relations. Several of their plants are ISO 9001 certified as well as ISO 14001 and BS OHSAS 18001 for occupational safety and health assurance systems.

STIHL is setting new standards for operating comfort and ergonomics, incorporating several new innovations across several product types. They have also expanded their already extensive range of emission-reduced products, like the STIHL battery hedge-trimmer which won several awards including Germany's environmental 'Blue Angel', for their low noise and emissions and a Gold Medal for Innovation.

In 2002, the Konrad Adenauer Foundation in Germany awarded the prestigious 'Social Market Economy Prize' to Eva-Mayr Stihl and her brother Hans Peter Stihl for outstanding entrepreneurial activity combined with social responsibility. (www.stihl.com)

Sartorius

The Sartorius Group is a leading international laboratory and process technology provider covering the segments of bioprocess solutions, lab products and services and industrial weighing. The Goettingen-based company was founded in 1870 by Florenz Sartorius. He set up a fine-precision machine company called Feinmechanische Werkstatt F.Sartorius and began with the production of short-beam analytical balances.

Today, the company employs more than 5,000 persons worldwide. In 2011, the technology group earned sales revenue of €733.1 million. Sartorius has its own production facilities in Europe, Asia and America as well as sales subsidiaries and local commercial agencies in more than 110 countries. Joachim Kreuzburg is the present CEO and Chairman of the Executive Board, while Arnold Picot is the Chairman of the Supervisory Board.

Sartorius helps customers all over the globe implement complex and quality-critical laboratory and production processes in a time- and cost-efficient way. The company's innovative products, solutions and services therefore focus on the key value-creating segments. Sartorius is strongly rooted in the scientific and research communities and closely allied with customers and technology partners. Their present corporate slogan is 'Turning science into solutions'.

The major areas of activity of its bioprocess solutions segment cover filtration, fluid management, fermentation, cell cultivation and purification and focus on production processes in the biopharmaceutical industry. The lab products and services segment primarily manufactures laboratory instruments and consumables, while industrial weighing concentrates on weighing, monitoring and control applications in the manufacturing processes of the food, chemical and pharma sectors.

Sartorius received the prestigious 'iF product design award for 2010' for two of their products, the first being the Cubis laboratory balance and the Arium laboratory water purification system. According to them, high-quality products are not just characterised by top quality components but also by its user-friendliness and ease of operation that incorporate the latest regulatory standards to make for customer-oriented products. (www.sartorius.com)

Schubert

The Gerhard Schubert GmbH is a medium-sized family enterprise that specialises in the supply of flexible packaging solutions. With a market share of 30 per cent, Schubert is the world's leading manufacturer of top-loading packaging machines with a special emphasis on the pick and place robot segment.

The company was founded in 1966 by Gerhard Schubert the present CEO of the company in the town of Crailsheim in the state of Baden-Württemberg, in the heart of what is known as 'Packaging Valley'. Their first product was the SKA, the first box erecting and gluing machine developed in 1966 to work with hot-melt adhesives. It was in 1985 that they developed the SNC–F2, the world's first packaging robot, which has left an enduring legacy in the field of packaging machine engineering. The Schubert Group has facilities in Germany, the US, UK and Canada. They employ around 900 people worldwide.

TLM (top-loading machine) packaging machines from Schubert are used for packaging all types of products from pharmaceutical, cosmetics, beverages to food products, frozen food, dairy and technical articles. TLM packaging machines are a pleasure to work with, highly flexible, clear and manageable, offering easy access and outstanding operating simplicity.

The TLM packaging machine system components are comprised of just seven modules – the TLM–F3 Robot, the TLM–F2 packaging Robot, the TLM F 44 – packaging Robot, a Vision System, the Transmodule, a Machine Frame and an Operator Guidance System.

They offer excellent services for their machine program encompassing the following areas: electronic service module, spare parts service, maintenance agreements, training seminars for machine operators and service personnel as well as a trouble-shooting hotline and machine conversions. Its many years of experience in the field of servo-drive engineering have made Schubert the accepted market leader in the field of digital packaging machines. Their recent development of a new TLM component under the name Transmodule will set new standards in packaging machine construction. (www.gerhard-schubert.com)

STABILO

The Schwan-STABILO Group operates worldwide and is a manufacturer of pens, pencils and other writing and colouring instruments. The company was founded in 1865 in Nuremberg, when Gustav Schwanhäußer bought the company by the name of Grossberger & Kurz which he renamed Schwan-Bleistift-Fabrik, which has since become a group that enjoys international success and has remained in the family for five generations.

Now, named Schwan-STABILO Schwanhäußer GmbH & Co.KG, the company was converted into a holding company in 1996 with headquarters in Heroldsberg, Germany. For financial year 2010, they had a group turnover of €462 million, while employing a workforce of 4,280 employees worldwide. Ulrich Griebel and Sebastian Schwanhäußer are the present Managing Directors of the Schwan-STABILO Group. They now have three divisions: the STABILO division, the cosmetics division and the outdoor division.

STABILO and the cosmetics division have subsidiaries in Germany and abroad. The cosmetics division was born in 1927, when the first eyebrow pencil was introduced, a huge success then. Today, Schwan-Cosmetics is the private-label partner for renowned cosmetics companies worldwide, from wooden eyebrow pencils to liquid eye-liners to lipstick pens and other colour cosmetics, produced exclusively for the international cosmetics industry. Their outdoor division (Deuter brand) has manufactured backpacks since the 1930s. They also have a company called STABILO Promotion Products GmbH & Co. KG that offers writing instruments for target group specific advertising with the STABILO brand quality.

The launch of the STABILO BOSS highlighter in 1971 was another of their great successes. This highlighter or 'reading pen' remains the world's best-selling highlighter to this day.

STABILO has established itself as the in-brand of choice amongst the youth in Europe; the, reasons for their success being the design trends and lifestyle that they cater to and project in their promotions. The STABILO product range extends from writing, highlighting and colouring for school and university students, for style and fashion as well as for the office. The group increasingly use FSC-certified wood in their production. They have also introduced a range of sustainable, high-quality pencils made from renewable wood. Over the years, several of their products have won prestigious design awards. (www.stabilo.com)

SGL Group

The SGL Group – the Carbon Company – is one of the world's leading manufacturers of carbon-based products, with a comprehensive graphite and carbon fibre-based product portfolio and an integrated value chain from carbon fibres to composites.

The company traces its roots back to 1878, when the company Gebruder Siemens & Co. (Gesco) in Germany started production of carbon. Over the years, it became SIGRI GmbH in 1985 and then SGL Carbon in 1992. After a merger between SIGRI Germany and Great Lakes Carbon US in 2007, it became the SGL Group – the Carbon Company, an independent and listed company.

Today, the SGL Group has a global structure with 46 production facilities throughout the world. Twenty-five of these sites are in Europe, 12 in North America and nine in Asia. The company also has a service network covering over a 100 countries.

With its head office in Wiesbaden, Germany, the publicly owned company has a broad shareholder structure and has been listed in Germany on the MDAX since 1995. For financial year 2011, the group had a sales turnover of €1.540 billion, employing over 6,500 people worldwide. Robert J. Koehler is the CEO and Chairman of the Board of Management, while Susanne Klatten is the Chairman of the Supervisory Board.

The group is organised into three business areas: performance products, graphite materials and systems and carbon fibres and composites. These are further managed by eight global business units. In the first, they have graphite and carbon electrodes and cathodes and furnace linings in the second they have graphite specialities, process technology and new markets, while in the third they have carbon fibres and composite materials, aero-structures and rotor Blades.

Carbon has unique properties, which enables the manufacture of solar-cells, LEDs and lightweight construction that reduces the weight in aeroplanes and cars. This leads to less CO_2 emissions, the reason why carbon is becoming an innovative, efficient and sustained solution for the environment and the future. Their new corporate slogan is 'Broad Base, Best Solutions'.

Accelerated innovation and substitution by carbon has resulted in alternative raw materials, energies, other materials and products. Carbon has been found to be the superior material in strength and performance. The SGL Group has a wide product portfolio, which extends from amorphous carbon to high-purity graphites and from carbon fibres to composite materials and components used in practically most industries.

The company philosophy is based on SGL Excellence that supports a culture of continuous improvement as a SIX SIGMA company with operational, commercial, innovation and people excellence. (www.sglgroup.com)

SICK

SICK AG is one of the world's leading producers of sensors and sensor solutions for industrial applications. They are a technology and market leader in factory and logistics automation as well as process automation. The company was founded in 1946, near Munich, by Erwin Sick, an inventor. In 1996, it became SICK AG a joint stock company.

Today, the company has a global presence with almost 50 subsidiaries and participations as well as numerous sales agencies. SICK currently employs around 5,800 people worldwide, and achieved sales turnover of €902.7 million for financial year 2011. SICK AG has its headquarters in Waldkirch a town in Baden-Württemberg. Robert Bauer is the Chairman of the Executive Board, while Gisela Sick is the Honorary Chairperson and Klaus M. Bukenberger the Chairman of the Supervisory board. The company invested €80.4 million in its R&D activities, while employing over 600 people for it. Their corporate slogan is 'Sensor Intelligence'.

The product portfolio consists of various types of industrial sensors, photo-electric sensors, encoders, identification solutions, opto-electronic protective devices, measuring and detection solutions, safety switches, fluid sensors, safety-control solutions, system solutions, registration sensors, analysis and gas-flow measurement, distance sensors, motor-feedback systems, automation light grids, vision sensors and software.

The diversity of its products allows SICK to offer solutions at every phase of production in a wide variety of manufacturing environments according to their customer's needs. Their solutions, increases throughput, improves safety and optimises production processes in a whole range of industries, from automotive, food and machine tools to logistics, power plants, consumer and pharma products.

Their services include analysis to the solution of customer-specific requirements, where they focus on the productivity of production with automated control concepts. They have around 400 technical service staff and also conduct various seminars and training courses as well. Since 2006, all of their German sites and manufacturing subsidiaries were certified according to DIN EN ISO 14001:2005.

The prestigious 'Vision Award' 2010, given by the British specialist magazine Imaging and Machine Vision has been awarded to SICK AG for their product, the novel Colour Ranger colour camera used for multi-aspect imaging, using one single camera. The Colour Ranger E is the world's first high-speed 3-D camera with high-quality colour capability. (www.sick.com)

Siempelkamp

The Siempelkamp Group – consisting of three business units, machinery and plant engineering, nuclear technology and foundry technology – is an international supplier of equipment to the industry. The family-owned company was established in 1883 by Gerhard Siempelkamp, who developed and built drilled hot plates and presses for the Lower Rhine textile industry. In 2008, the Group completed 125 years of productive existence.

For financial year 2011, the group had a turnover of €704.6 million, employing 3,191 people worldwide. Hans W. Fechner is the present Chairman of the Executive Board, while Dieter Siempelkamp is the Chairman of the Advisory Board of G. Siempelkamp GmbH & Co. KG, the holding company. They have their headquarters and main manufacturing plant in Krefeld, a town in the state of North-Rhine Westphalia. Moreover Siempelkamp has several subsidiaries in Germany and elsewhere around the world as well as numerous sales and service representatives spread around the globe.

The Siempelkamp machinery and plant engineering business unit has been building hydraulic presses and complete plants for more than 125 years. Their products have an excellent reputation in the wood-based panels, metal forming, rubber and composites industries.

The most successful chapter in the history of Siempelkamp has been the development of the continuous press, called Conti Roll®, used for pressing wood-based panels. It has made Siempelkamp the world market leader in this category. Among their new innovations, the modular glue blending system for fibres – the Ecoresinator – for accurate preparation and dosing of the glue mixture, is an important milestone for the industry. The company also provides energy plants by using recycled material from board production.

Siempelkamp presses for metal forming are used in the automotive, aeronautical, railway and energy markets. The hydraulic presses include cold-forming as well as hot-forming presses. From turbine disks for airplanes to pipeline pipes used in the oil and gas industries to longitudinal beams in semi-trucks, Siempelkamp provides not only the press but also the corresponding press technology. The company got the QC accreditation from ASME (American Society of Mechanical Engineers) in 2009. (www.siempelkamp.com)

Soehnle

Soehnle is one of the leading brands in the world for household and personal scales. They have, to date, sold more than 200 million scales worldwide. Soehnle is a company with a long tradition, as the first Soehnle scales were manufactured in 1868 by Wilhelm Soehnle in his workshop, in a town called Murrhardt in the state of Baden-Württemberg. In 2001, Soehnle became a part of Leifheit AG whose head office is in Nassau in the state of Rhineland-Palatinate.

In Germany, Soehnle is synonymous for scales that combine technological perfection and sophisticated design. Today, Soehnle is the market leader in many European countries such as Germany, Austria, Switzerland and the Netherlands. The brand is among the top three in other European countries like France, Italy and Spain.

Their product range includes personal scales, kitchen scales and Soehnle Relax, their modern wellness heat and massage products. In personal scales, they have various types of body analysis scales, digital personal scales, analogue personal scales and luggage scales. These innovative body analysis scales are the latest in design and functionality, welcome accessories for a modern and stylish bathroom. They are a modern partner for one's daily well-being, reliable and precise.

In kitchen scales, their state-of-the-art technology product range includes nutritional value analysis scales, digital kitchen scales, analogue kitchen scales and wall-mounted scales. Their range of products are easy to operate and chic to look at. They support both the amateur as well as professional chef equally.

While, Soehnle Relax is their new product line that includes wellness heat pillows, vario heat pillows, heated mattress covers and massagers. Excellent quality, absolute precision and an elegant lifestyle design is what makes Soehnle scales a top seller.

Based on their quality workmanship, Soehnle products are very durable and reliable. They offer a three- to five-year guarantee with the scales and a five-year guarantee with the wellness products. Soehnle's company slogan is, 'Life in Balance'. In 2012, their Page Evolution scale won the red dot design award and the iF product design award. (www.soehnle.de)

Stabilus

Stabilus is a world market leader in gas springs/struts and hydraulic vibration dampers. They have catered to over 2,400 satisfied customers in various industries, such as the automotive and office-chair manufacturing industries, in furniture making, medical technology, and several other industrial applications.

The company was founded in 1934 in the city of Koblenz. They started by manufacturing stabilizers. Today, the innovative Stabilus technology is used to provide variable motion control in a wide range of applications and to dampen unwanted vibrations. All major production technologies and machines are Stabilus's own design. They are developed and built at their headquarters in Koblenz. They have nine production sites in a total of nine countries worldwide. With an extensive sales and service network, they have established themselves as a global player with a worldwide presence.

For financial year 2011/2012, they had a sales turnover of around €443 million, while employing over 3,300 employees worldwide. In one production year, they produce around 136 million gas springs and around 7 million vibration dampers.

Stabilus offers more than 15,000 different products and product variants. A high degree of standardisation in parts, modules and production processes guarantees a high level of competitiveness.

Andi Klein is the Chairman of the Supervisory Board of Stabilus GmbH, while Dietmar Siemssen is the CEO.

Their complete product range includes non-locking gas springs, locking gas springs, swivel chairs gas springs, dampers, automatic drive systems and CAD configurators. Their services include spare parts help, CAD configurator, recycling, installation hints and tips, and other troubleshooting help.

Stabilus has consistently met all quality and environmental standards. Having received the following certificates: the DIN EN ISO 9001:2008, the DIN EN ISO TS 16949:2009, the DIN EN ISO 14001:2004 and the EMAS. (www.stabilus.com)

Staedtler

Staedtler is among the world's leading manufacturers of writing, colouring and drawing instruments as well as modelling/polymer clays. It is one of the oldest companies in Germany. The name Staedtler is closely linked with Nuremberg's pencil history. Long before J.S. Staedtler founded his pencil making factory in the city of Nuremberg, Germany, in 1835, the Staedtler family had been hand-making this well-loved writing instrument for generations. In fact, the roots can be traced back to 1662 when the first references to Friedrich Staedtler as a pencil-making craftsman were made in the city's annals!

Today, Staedtler has six manufacturing plants, of which three are in Germany, and 23 foreign sales subsidiaries. The Staedtler Group has over 2,300 employees worldwide and representatives in around 150 countries around the globe. Axel Marx is the present Managing Director of the Staedtler Group. Their corporate slogan is 'Your Inspiration'. Their products stand for perfect writing performance, high reliability and superb writing comfort.

Staedtler is, with its three production plants in the Nuremberg metropolitan region, the largest European manufacturer of graphite pencils, coloured pencils, erasers, mechanical pencil leads and modelling clays. Their product range includes wood-cased pencils, as well as the well-known graphite pencils and the coloured pencils, Lumocolor markers, highlighters, fineliners, ballpoint pens, drawing and writing accessories and the FIMO and Marsclay modelling products.

The Staedtler Group demonstrates their belief in the protection of the environment through environmentally friendly processes and a self-imposed eco-controlling. What they call 'efficient for ecology'. Use of natural materials, recycling, reduction of CO_2 emissions and certified wood for its entire range of 'Made in Germany' wood-cased pencils, in accordance with valid FSC and PEFC standards.

Over the years, the group has won several awards, the latest being the 'Design Plus' 2009, as well as the 'iF Material Award 2010' for the Staedtler innovation Wopex, a unique material mix of natural fibres, together with specially developed production technology. They also got the red dot design award in 2009 for the Staedtler triplus 776 mechanical pencils. (www.staedtler.com)

SUSPA

SUSPA is a leading manufacturer of gas springs, hydraulic dampers, vibration dampers, crash management systems, safety systems, actuators, height adjustment systems, piston rods and tubes and car adjustment systems that are used by the automotive, machine building, furniture, white goods, medical and other durable goods industries.

The company was founded in 1951 in a town called Altdorf near the city of Nuremberg. Today, apart from the holding company and headquarters in Altdorf, they have another manufacturing subsidiary in Germany, one each in the US, the Czech Republic, China and India as well as sales offices throughout the world. In many fields, SUSPA is the consistent innovator and market leader. For example, the sensor and free running shock absorbers for washing machines or the passenger and pedestrian protection system for automobiles were both introduced by SUSPA. Their corporate slogan is 'Every day is a day with SUSPA'.

The SUSPA Group manufactures around 50 million products per year in around 1,500 variations of several product lines. Gross turnover of the Group was in the region of €164 million, employing 1,600 employees worldwide. Timo Stahl, Hans Jörg Kaltenbrunner and Thomas Peuker are on the Executive Board of SUSPA GmbH.

When it comes to the large variety of applications, SUSPA products show their strengths. The reason why roughly 30 lines of businesses, with more than 1,200 applications, rely on SUSPA for gas springs, hydraulic and vibration dampers, adjustment systems, crash-management systems, automotive powered systems and other components.

High operational reliability, easy handling, comfort and safety are the focus of their solutions for the industry.

All of SUSPA's worldwide manufacturing units fulfil the quality management system requirements of ISO 9001. Manufacturing locations that deliver to automotive customers also fulfil the requirements of ISO/TS 16949. SUSPA's manufacturing locations located in Germany and US also maintain certificates, according to the ISO 14001 environmental management system. (www.suspa.com)

Symrise

Symrise is the world's fourth largest player in the flavours and fragrances market with an estimated global market share of around 11 per cent. Symrise was founded in 2003 by the merger of Haarmann & Reimer (H&R) and Dragoco, both based in Holzminden, Germany. Dragoco was founded in 1919 by Carl-Wilhelm Gerberding and his cousin August Bellmer. Whereas Haarmann & Reimer was founded in 1874 by the chemists, Ferdinand Tiemann and Wilhelm Haarmann, after they succeeded in first synthesizing vanillin from coniferin.

Today, with sites in more than 35 countries, Symrise has a global as well as regional presence in all important markets. In 2011, Symrise posted sales of €1.584 billion, employing around 5,400 people worldwide. Under the leadership of CEO and Chairman of the Executive Board, Heinz-Jürgen Bertram, their executive committee oversees the activities of their flavour and nutrition and scent and care divisions from their headquarters in Holzminden a town in the state of Lower Saxony. Each of the divisions sells over 15,000 products in around 135 countries worldwide. The Symrise corporate slogan is 'Always inspiring more'.

In the flavour and nutrition division, their product range and services includes beverages, savoury, sweet and consumer health. Their major flavour and nutrition brands are Taste for Life®, Naturally Citrus®, Brew Topia® and Simply Vanilla®. Their product range in the scent and care division includes fragrances, life essentials, aroma molecules and menthol for beauty, household and oral care applications.

They maintain a state-of-the-art edge in application technology, focusing its use on technological support and consulting for their customer's projects. R&D is central to what they do at Symrise, with highly qualified researchers working on projects in Holzminden, Singapore, Paris and the US. Since 1995, they have filed well over 430 patents.

The development of aroma chemicals made from renewable sources has long had an important role to play at Symrise. Thanks to 'white biotechnology', an even more sustainable method of manufacturing fragrances will soon be available. In 2009, select vanilla extracts received organic and fair trade certifications for the first time. Symrise has all the required, certifying quality, environment and safety standards from ISO 9001, ISO 14001 to the ECO CERT, USDA Organic, EFSA, Fair Trade, and several more. (www.symrise.com)

Tente

Tente International GmbH is a worldwide operating company that manufactures casters or wheels used for making chairs, hospital beds, trolleys and for various other institutional, medical and industrial applications. The company Tente-Rollen was founded in 1923 in the town of Wermelskirchen in the state of North-Rhine Westphalia. They started with selling ball casters and wheels for sliding cupboard doors. Eleven years later, the firm started producing their own casters. Today, Tente has gained a leading position in the world's markets with its innovative ideas, perfected products and high quality. Customers in over 100 countries treasure their robustness, reliability, durability and functional design. Their corporate slogan is 'World in Motion'.

The Tente Group manufactures at several national and international locations. They also have several sales and service subsidiaries in Europe, North America, Asia and Africa. The holding company is Tente International, situated in Cologne. The Group employs around 1,074 people worldwide. The managing directors of the group are Peter Fricke and Peter Helmert, while turnover for 2011 was in the region of €154 million.

Tente International has been the major caster manufacturer in Europe since several years with over 10,000 variations. Their product range includes chair casters, furniture casters, synthetic and apparatus casters, casters for aircraft and airport trolleys, hospital bed casters, casters for wheelchairs, shopping trolleys and transport equipment, casters for waste-disposal systems, heavy-duty casters, stainless steel casters apart from several other types and applications, where wheels, casters and mobility parts are required.

Tente has won numerous design awards over the years for several of their product category brands. Some of the recent awards are; for the Levina series, the Design Award winner, German Designer Club and Universal Design award 2009. For the Linea series, the design award winner (GDC), iF product design award and the Interzum award for intelligent material and design. The Aviana series has also won the German designer club's design award and the red dot' design award. Their other series Smiles and Decora have also won the red dot design awards. While the Integral series and 5320 and 2940 also won the iF, red dot and GDC awards, respectively. All these awards are ample tribute to the company's products for their functionality and looks. (www.tente.de)

Trumpf

The Trumpf Group is a high-tech enterprise that focuses on production and medical technology. They offer innovative and high-quality products and solutions in sheet-metal processing, laser-based production processes, high-power electronics and hospital equipment.

The family-owned company was founded in 1923 by Christian Trumpf and two other partners who acquired Julius Geiger GmbH, a machine shop in Stuttgart. They started by producing flexible shafts for dental and printing applications. Today, it has developed into one of the world's leading companies in production technology.

Trumpf is a high-tech company active in four business fields: machine tools, laser technology, electronics and medical technology. All of them are combined under the Trumpf GmbH + Co. KG holding company, based in Ditzingen near Stuttgart. They have a global network of production, sales and service companies. For financial year 2011, they had a sales turnover of €2.33 billion, while employing around 9,600 employees worldwide. Nicola Leibinger-Kammüller is the President and Chairwoman of the Management Board of Trumpf GmbH + Co.KG, while Berthold Leibinger is the Chairman of the Supervisory Board.

Their innovative product range includes products for laser processing, punching, combination processing, bending, storage systems, CO_2 lasers, solid-state lasers, marking lasers, laser systems, plasma generators, generators for induction heating, generators for CO_2 laser excitation, OR tables, surgical lights, ceiling pendants and patient transfer systems. Customers are found in almost every sector of industry, for example the automotive, steel, aerospace and medical industries. They have made production processes faster, more precise and economical.

The Trumpf Group quality has been certified according to DIN EN ISO 9001, DIN EN 13485 and QS Certificate Directive 93/94/EEC Annexe II. They also have a synchronised production system that they call SYNCHRO for short. The aim of this improvement process is to fine tune the use of manpower, material and equipment in order to achieve the best possible products with as little waste as possible, to ensure quality and sustainability for their products and services. (www.trumpf.com)

Von Ehren

Lorenz von Ehren GmbH & Co.KG is a nursery that specialises in the cultivation and sale of large specimen trees and shrubs. The nursery was founded in 1865 in Nienstedten, close to Hamburg. The founder, Johannes von Ehren, learned the gardener's craft and decided to establish his own nursery. In 1898, his son Lorenz von Ehren took over the business and soon the nursery earned an international reputation, with trees being dispatched to the royal palaces in the UK, Denmark, Prussia, as well as to the tsar in St. Petersburg.

Today, at their nursery, on a production area of more than 500 hectares, you will find areas full of trees, shrubs, conifers and specially clipped plants. Whether avenue trees or specimen trees up to 17 metres, rare and valuable specimen plants up to 60 years old, splendid evergreens up to 16 metres, hand-trimmed trees and shrubs, roses, perennials, ground cover and more, all of premium quality.

In 1994, the main nursery and the company headquarters were relocated from Nienstedten to a larger site at Hamburg-Marmstorf, south of the river Elbe. The fifth generation of the founder, in the person of Bernhard von Ehren, together with Konrad Parloh are the present managing directors of the company. They employ around 150 people. Their corporate slogan is 'We love Trees'.

Von Ehren's plant catalogue and selection consists of over 2,000 plant profiles, from the deciduous, rhododendron, roses, conifer, topiary, fruit, perennials, Mediterranean and several more. Lorenz von Ehren supplies a complete assortment and ships directly to their customer's site, anywhere in Europe, in a few days after the order is confirmed. The von Ehren plant catalogue is now available as an App in the Apple store in German and the English version will follow soon.

Family-owned Lorenz von Ehren is one of the leading producers in Europe. Their trees and plants are used throughout Europe to enhance schemes and projects on a regional scale as well as in cities, streets and gardens. Clients from all over the world recognise the high quality of their trees and shrubs and values the long-term partnerships that have resulted from a successful transaction. They also provide all the required planting tips for the trees and shrubs based on their long study and experience.

Hamburg had been named 'Green Capital Europe 2011' and the nursery Lorenz von Ehren was their official partner for the year. They gave eco-tours of their premises and displayed their trees and plants and the environmental awareness and care taken in the nursing and delivery of trees. (www.LvE.de)

Vorwerk

Vorwerk & Co.KG is a family-owned company that has developed into a highly diversified, global corporate group. The range of their products includes household appliances, high-quality cosmetics, carpets as well as Hectas facility services and the Akf Group.

The company was founded in 1883 in Wuppertal, a town in the state of North-Rhine Westphalia, by Carl and Adolf Vorwerk, who started the Barmer Teppichfabrik Vorwerk & Co. to manufacture carpets. Since 1930, Vorwerk's core business has been the direct selling of innovative, quality products.

Today, there are around 607,000 people working for Vorwerk worldwide, of whom around 34,475 are sales advisers in the business of selling household appliances. Over 556,000 people work for JAFRA Cosmetics, the rest are employees in other group companies. Vorwerk generated a business volume of €2.367 billion in 2011, while operating in more than 70 countries worldwide. Walter Muyres and Reiner Stecker are the Managing Partners of the Executive Board of Vorwerk & Co.KG, while former managing partner, Jörg Mittelsten Scheid is the Chairman of the Supervisory Board. He is the great-grandson of the company's founder, Carl Vorwerk. The Vorwerk brand is widely recognised for its legendary quality, especially regarding their household appliances.

Vorwerk employs more than 120 engineers in R&D. Production plants are in Germany, France, Italy, China, Mexico (Jafra Cosmetics) and Shanghai. The largest Vorwerk production plant is in Germany at their headquarters in Wuppertal, where they produce the vacuum cleaner line (branded as Kobold) and all of their motors that are built into their products worldwide. Their carpets are also made in Germany.

The group's product range includes Kobold, floor care systems with vacuum cleaners, electric brushes, as well as an array of accessories. Thermomix, for multi-functional kitchen appliances with cooking functions, Jafra Cosmetics for skin and body care products, decorative cosmetics, SPA products and perfumes, Lux Asia-Pacific for water purifiers and vacuum cleaners sold in the Asia-Pacific region, Vorwerk carpets for fitted carpets and carpet pieces and tiles, Hectas Facility Services for infrastructure and building services and the Akf Group for leasing and financing of investment goods and fleet management rounds of their product portfolio.

Vorwerk is unique because of their success in the direct sales method, a personal and consultative way to introduce innovative products and services and to open new markets. In addition to delighting their customers, the products have also gained recognition from design experts. Their products, the Polsterboy, the Pululux, Thermonix 31 and Tiger 260 have won the red dot design award for their quality designs. (www.vorwerk.com)

Vossloh

Vossloh AG is a leader in the rail infrastructure and rail technology markets. Their long-standing expertise, well-established, cost-efficient and eco-friendly products have made them a reliable supplier. They are seen as an innovative brand internationally. The company was founded in 1888 by Eduard Vossloh, who started the company to manufacture spring washers for rail fasteners and other hardware.

Today, the Vossloh Group with headquarters in Werdohl in the state of North-Rhine Westphalia is made of 90 companies operating in 30 countries. For fiscal year 2011, they employed a workforce of 5,000 employees and generated group sales of around €1.2 billion. Seventy per cent of this was generated in Europe outside of Germany, while the non-European share was about 30 per cent. Werner Andree is the present CEO of the company and an executive board member, while Wilfried Kaiser is the Chairman of the Supervisory Board. Their corporate slogan is 'Understanding Mobility'.

Alongside its production companies, Vossloh operates through sales companies and branches and in some instances has entered into local joint ventures and cooperation agreements with competent partners. This MDAX listed Group with its flexible mid-size structure has organised its operations into two divisions: rail infrastructure and transportation. In the first division, they specialise in products and services comprising, Vossloh fastening systems, Vossloh switch systems and all kinds of rail services, like lifecycle recycling, maintenance, etc. They are among the market leaders for switch and fastening systems.

The transportation division produces modern, diesel electric locomotives, suburban trains, bogies and electrical components for a wide variety of light rail vehicles (LRVs). It has two business units, Vossloh Transportation Systems and Vossloh Electrical Systems. Their advanced technology, diesel-hydraulic locomotives fitted with eco-friendly technology is homologated for operation in numerous European countries.

From Athens to Vancouver from Bremen to Geneva and from Philadelphia to Gdansk, you will find trams and trolley buses operating with state-of-the-art technology from Vossloh. The rail fasteners developed by Vossloh Fastening Systems ensures safe rail traffic in over 65 countries.

All the large Vossloh locations have been approved and certified according to the DIN EN ISO 14001 environmental management system. They also undergo regular audits by external, independent bodies. (www.vossloh.com)

Webasto

Webasto is a family-owned company that supplies the automotive industry with sunroof, convertible and thermo systems. The company was founded in 1901 by Wilhelm Baier in the town of Esslingen on the Neckar River. Today, with headquarters in the town of Stockdorf near Munich, Webasto has become one of the world's top 100 automotive suppliers. They are the market leaders for both roof and temperature management systems.

Since July 2012 the group has changed from Webasto AG to a European stock corporation (SE). Their earlier two divisions have become legally independent: the

Webasto Roof & Components SE for the sunroof and convertible business and the Webasto Thermo & Comfort SE for the business of heating, cooling and ventilation.

Webasto has over 50 locations worldwide, 30 of which are manufacturing plants. The name Webasto comes from the names of the founder Wilhelm Baier and the town Stockdorf. For fiscal year 2011, they had a sales turnover of €2.3 billion. The company employs around 10,000 people worldwide. Holger Engelmann is the Chairman of the Management Board while Werner Baier is the Chairman of the Supervisory Board. Their corporate slogan is 'Feel the drive'.

The core competencies of the company include the development and production of complete roof and convertible roof systems for cars as well as heating, cooling and ventilation systems for cars, commercial, special and recreational vehicles and the marine market. In addition, the company offers parking heaters and sunroofs for retrofitting by the end consumer. The know-how acquired in the automotive industry is specifically targeted to other types of vehicles. One example is the movable roof systems for the marine market segment.

They have many sales companies and partners worldwide who look after marketing, service and installation of their products in the different countries. They are a world leader in automotive products that enhance the comfort and driving experience. Ensuring quality is a primary function with Webasto. The processes and structures of the Webasto Management System are reviewed by external certification bodies on a yearly basis. Their current valid certifications are for; ISO 9001, ISO/TS 16949 and ISO 14001.

Among the notable innovations of the company are the lightweight construction for roof systems made of polycarbonate. In autumn 2012, the automotive supplier presented a highly efficient electrically powered heating system for hybrid and electric vehicles which heats the interior while driving.

Webasto was once again the best brand in the 'Conditioning/Heating' category for the seventh time in succession, as voted by the readers of ETM magazines: Fernfahrer, Lastauto Omnibus and Trans Aktuell. (www.webasto.com)

Weckerle

Weckerle is a global leader in Cosmetics Machine Manufacturing and extends to all aspects of Contract Manufacturing with full service beauty products. Weckerle GmbH was founded in 1965 by Peter Weckerle in a small garage/workshop in Peissenberg, a town in the State of Bayern. He later invented the first automatic lipstick-filling machine.

Today, they are a globally recognised specialist in the manufacture of stick and tube-filling machines. With present headquarters in Weilheim, Bayern and offices in the US, Brazil, Russia, China, France and Switzerland, the family-owned company is recognised for its state-of-the-art, automatic, high-speed filling machines for lipsticks, lip balm sticks, eyeliner pencils, eye shadow pencils and also tube-filled products for the pharmaceutical and food industries. They have two divisions: cosmetics and machines.

Since 1968, the most prestigious companies in the cosmetics industry, including L'Oreal, Christian Dior, Estée Lauder, Max Factor, Maybelline and Avon, have entrusted Weckerle to deliver precision products and services at competitive prices.

They have a global workforce of around 250, of which 100 work in their machines manufacturing plant in Weilheim. The founder's son Thomas Weckerle is the present

CEO of the company. Weckerle produces a variety of filling and processing machines not only for the cosmetic but also for the pharma and food industries.

A total of 85 per cent of all lipsticks produced worldwide are made on Weckerle machines, by more than 350 of their lipstick machines. Peter Weckerle invented Weckerle's moulding machines, the most widely used in the industry.

They deliver on all aspects of contract manufacturing with full-service beauty products for the lips, eyes, face and body, having extended their expertise to polished design and packaging services for the industry's leading cosmetic brands. Their niche is in creating customised solutions, whether it is to simply fill a formulation, to actualise a concept by providing the package, the formulation or even a new machine, they are dedicated to quality and innovation.

Other additional services that they provide are in concept creation and marketing support, formulation development, supply-chain management and design consultancy. At Weckerle, they believe that true innovation means constantly being open to new ideas and approaches in their area of expertise. (www.weckerle.com)

W.E.T.

W.E.T. Automotive Systems AG manufactures climate controlled seating for automobiles worldwide. They lead the industry with a 50 per cent market share of the global heated seating systems since several years.

The company was founded in 1968 in Munich, as the Wärme und Hygiene technik B. Ruthenberg GmbH. In 1992, they established a new headquarters in the town of Odelzhausen in the state of Bayern. By 1998, it became a public listed company. Today, they have 11 locations worldwide, of which four are production facilities. Group turnover was around €270 million, while employing around 5,500 people worldwide. Caspar Baumhauer is the present CEO of the company, while Franz Schere is the Chairman of the Supervisory Board.

Their product range includes seat climate systems, automotive seat heating, steering wheel heating, temperature controllers and automotive cable technology.

They have a subsidiary in China called Comair that manufactures fans for different industrial and commercial applications and provides blower technology and heat sinks. W.E.T. also has a R&D facility with a test lab, a prototype construction facility and an advanced engineering department to generate innovative technical concepts and to evaluate and convert them into serial products.

In close cooperation with external partners and required internal interfaces, future market trends and customer requirements for seat climate, seat comfort and linked technologies are detected and technically realised.

Some of the world's top automobile manufacturers are their customers, from Alfa Romeo, Audi and BMW to Suzuki, Toyota and Volkswagen. They cater to OEMs for passenger cars, commercial vehicles and seat manufacturers worldwide.

W.E.T.'s value creation system with continuous improvement is a central part of their business philosophy: quality first, everywhere. Strong customer focus, continuous improvement of their products and processes are preconditions for their quality, reliability and success. (www.wet-group.com)

Wirtgen

The Wirtgen Group is an international group of companies operating in the construction machinery sector. They have four traditional brands: Wirtgen, Vögele, Hamm and Kleemann. As a technological leader, they offer their customers mobile machine solutions for road construction and road rehabilitation as well as for mining and processing minerals.

Wirtgen GmbH was set up by Reinhard Wirtgen in 1961. While Vögele AG was founded in 1836 by Joseph Vögele in Mannheim, it is one of the oldest industrial companies in Germany. Hamm AG was founded by the brothers Anton and Franz in 1878 and Kleemann GmbH in Stuttgart in 1857. Together, they form the Wirtgen Group.

Today, Wirtgen Beteiligungs Gesellschaft is the holding company of the Wirtgen Group with headquarters in Windhagen a town in the state of Rhineland-Palatinate. They have four main state-of-the-art plants in Germany for the four respective brands, three other production facilities in India, China and Brazil and around 55 of their own sales and service companies located in all parts of the world. This family-owned group employees a workforce of over 5,000 people worldwide, while generating a consolidated sales turnover of €1.76 billion for financial year 2011. Their corporate slogan is 'Close to the customer'. With more than hundred selected dealers throughout the world, they aim to fulfil this promise.

The Board of Management of the Wirtgen Group consists of Jürgen Wirtgen, Stefan Wirtgen and Rainer Otto.

The Wirtgen Group offers trail-blazing solutions in two lines of business: road technologies and mineral technologies. Wirtgen GmbH specialises in machinery and processes for building new roads and rehabilitating existing ones. They are the world's market leader in the cold milling machines sector. The Joseph Vögele AG specialises in pavers and asphalt paving processes, leading the market in this segment, whereas Hamm AG specialises in rollers for soil and asphalt compaction and is the second largest manufacturer in Germany. Kleemann GmbH, their fourth brand, is a renowned specialist and market leader for mobile and stationary crushing and screening technology for processing natural stone and recycled materials for the stone and earth industries.

They provide after-sales service in terms of technical support, parts and more, information systems, training and applications consulting. A pioneer and innovator, the Wirtgen Group and its leading companies have always played a major role in the development and maintenance of traffic infrastructure on a global scale. (www.wirtgen-group.de)

Winterhalter

Winterhalter Gastronom GmbH designs and manufactures efficient ware-washing systems for the catering and hospitality industries. Commercial dish-washing systems by Winterhalter are the best available in the market. The family-owned company was founded in 1947 by Karl Winterhalter in Friedrichshafen on Lake Constance in the state of Baden-Württemberg. In 1959, they moved to the town of Meckenbeuren, close to their original site, where they also have their headquarters and a production facility. They have another production facility in Endingen, Germany and one in the Swiss Rhine Valley.

They employ over 1,000 people worldwide. There are Winterhalter sales organisations in 38 countries and qualified partners in several other countries. Most of their sales are in Europe, Asia and the Americas. The present owner and CEO of the company is Jürgen Winterhalter, the founder's son assisted by Ralph Winterhalter, the founder's grandson.

The company's product range includes under-counter ware-washers, pass-through dishwashers, utensil washers, single-tank rack conveyors, multi-tank and flight-type dishwashers, water-treatment technology, detergents and ware-washing products, rack portfolio, dosing systems, accessories as well as planning total ware-washing solutions.

Their products are made to keep water consumption as low as possible and to use phosphate substitutes and low-phosphate products for hygienic dishwashing. In January 2011, Winterhalter was awarded the comprehensive international management certification for quality, environmental protection and occupational health and safety by the Swiss Association for Quality and Management systems.

Several customer service technicians are on hand for all types of service help. They also offer training programs for their customers. Winterhalter production facilities are certified as per DIN ISO 9001 certification.

Over the years the company has won several awards for 'Product of the Year', hygiene concepts, outstanding quality, excellence and innovation, important ones being the 'Caterer and Hotel keeper, Equipment and Supplies Excellence Award 2010', for their UC Series, awarded by 'Hotelympia', London, UK. The 'Innovation Prize' 2010 once again for their UC Series, which was awarded by EUROPAIN in Paris and the 'Top 100 Innovators Award' for 2010 that celebrates innovation among Germany's mid-size enterprises. This award is based on a careful analysis, carried out by the University of Economics and Business in Vienna and then decided by an independent jury. The 'Best Brand 2011' and the 'Best of Market 2012' was recently given by a German trade journal and a trade fair in Hamburg. (www.winterhalter.de)

Zahoransky

Zahoransky AG is the world's largest supplier of brush-making machines and moulds. They manufacture machines for injection moulds, tufting and trimming through to packing machines and handling systems for the end product.

The group was founded in 1902, in a town called Todtnau in the state of Baden-Württemberg. Today, with headquarters and main production facility in Todtnau-Geschwend, they have nine other locations worldwide, of which six are production sites. The group employs a total of about 600 people worldwide. Gerhardt Enders is the Chairman of the Supervisory Board of Zahoransky AG, while Ulrich Zahoransky and Bernd Stein are Directors on the Managing Board.

Their product range includes injection moulds, automation systems, blister-packing machines, productions lines for toothbrushes, brush-making machines and mascara (cosmetic) and inter-dental brush machines.

Zahoransky is world renowned for first-class machines, mould design and construction and can draw from a comprehensive repertoire. The resulting applications of this core competence enables Zahoransky to supply key finished and fully automatic production units for injection mould construction, packaging techniques, control system techniques and palletising techniques.

From granulate to complete assembled, checked, packed and palleted products, Zahoransky supplies individual and integrated solutions for industries such as, the brush industry, medical technology, cosmetics, packaging, electro-technology, IT and many more. Some of their well-known clients include companies such as Siemens, Unilever, Colgate, IKEA, GSK, STABILO, Fischer, Oral-B and Trisa.

Their plants are fully air conditioned and have been certified as per DIN EN ISO 9001:2000 quality certification. They have a state-of-the-art R&D facility with 3-D CAD/CAM system called UNIGRAPHICS, while at their Technology Centre, sampling, optimisation, mould approval, limited lot production and training happens. Their BAT 10 blister packing unit has been distinguished with an honourable mention for the red dot design award for 2009. In 2012, Zahoransky received an award from Unilever for their Tooth-Brush Innovation Project for South-Asia. (www.zahoransky.com)

Zeiss

The Carl Zeiss Group is a global leader in the optical and opto-electronic industries. The group was founded in 1846 by Carl Zeiss in Jena, a city in the state of Thuringia. He started a precision workshop for the production of mechanical and optical components.

Today, the group is represented by over 30 production locations and by more than 50 sales companies in over 30 countries. The company's production centres are located in Europe, North and Central America and Asia. Carl Zeiss has its present headquarters in Oberkochen, in the state of Baden-Württemberg. Carl Zeiss AG is fully owned by the Carl Zeiss foundation. The foundation is also the sole shareholder of Schott AG in Mainz, Germany. Schott develops and manufactures special glass, special materials, components and systems to improve how people live and work.

The Carl Zeiss Group generated total revenues of €4.163 billion for fiscal year 2011 while employing over 24,000 people worldwide. Michael Kaschke is the current President and CEO of the Executive Board of Carl Zeiss AG, while Dieter Kurz is the Chairman of the Supervisory Board. Their corporate slogan is 'We make it Visible'.

The group has essentially divided its activities as per their markets, i.e. from medical solutions, research solutions, industrial solutions and consumer optics. They have six business divisions and 14 strategic business units. The six groups/divisions are semiconductor technology, industrial metrology, microscopy, medical systems, vision care and consumer optics/optronics. With its innovative technologies and leading-edge solutions, Carl Zeiss is a global success in the above mentioned fields.

The company develops and distributes surgical microscopes, diagnostic systems for ophthalmology, microscopes, lithography optics, industrial measuring technology, optronic products, camera, vision and cine lenses, binoculars, spotting scopes and several more. They cater to various industries and as solutions for healthcare, photography, observing, research, vision, projecting, microelectronics, analysing, measuring, semi-conductor technology and for production and services.

The Carl Zeiss business divisions hold leading positions in their respective markets. As an innovative provider of products and services in a future-oriented industry, Carl Zeiss counts among the most research-intensive, high-tech companies, having invested €390 million in 2011 on R&D alone, while employing over 2,000 people for the same. They register for several hundred patent applications every year. The Zeiss brand has stood for innovative ideas, precision and quality for more than 160 years. The group also presents the international 'Carl Zeiss Research Award' every two years to scientists for outstanding contributions in optical research.

Carl Zeiss takes a holistic approach to environmental management, which is why all of their German manufacturing sites, and several of their international sites, are certified to ISO 14001.

The company supports initiatives such as VISION 2020: The Right to Sight. It is a global initiative of the World Health Organization (WHO) and the International Agency for the Prevention of Blindness (IAPB). The goal of the initiative is to eliminate preventable blindness. Carl Zeiss has been supporting this program since 2002. (www.corporate.zeiss.com)

7   *Some Innovative and Emergent Stars*

The objective of this chapter is to highlight some of the relatively young, small to medium-sized enterprises that have been progressively innovative over the years and have garnered success and emerged as stars as a result of their innovation and entrepreneurial spirit.

Most of them, like the 'Less-Known Champions', are family-owned enterprises and have come forth as a result of the vision of that entrepreneur, scientist, researcher and pioneer all rolled into one. Several of them have had to persevere over the years through some tough, trying times as well. Nevertheless, they have come through to be successful and emergent stars in their own right.

The German industrial landscape is scattered with such fine examples of industrial entrepreneurship. I have taken the liberty to include 12 of them in this section. I could have included more but chose to limit myself to this number. These and the earlier described companies are amongst the best of the best and are representative of the over one thousand odd German enterprises that have made a mark on the global industrial arena.

The list here includes an Internet-based company, a leading development studio for interactive entertainment, an alternative energy company, a couple of organic food producers and supermarket chains, an industrial sensors manufacturer, a social media platform, a robotics company, a formwork and scaffolding technology company, a biotechnology company, a manufacturer of integrated circuits and a specialised manufacturer of innovative, professional make-up.

The basis for choosing these brands was their relative age and market success over the years, their innovative nature, reputation and the industries they come from, namely sunshine, new-tech, growth industries, as fine examples of innovative entrepreneurship.

Coincidentally, several of them have also won several awards and have over the years been chosen by Ernst & Young (Germany) for their prestigious and well-known award, 'The Entrepreneur of the Year', in several categories of industry, service, trade, information and communication, technology, media, etc. One other characteristic is that all of them were founded after the Second World War and clearly emerged and flourished in the new Germany.

The companies have been chosen on the basis of not only their impressive growth rates and market performance, but also by their willingness to take risks and come through successfully. Their ideas make them relevant for the present as well as for the future, pointing to new directions in entrepreneurial leadership. Let us also not forget that what makes them successful are primarily their innovative products and services that have kept their customers delighted and loyal to them.

Needless to say, once again, this list could have been much longer, but due to limitations of space, it has been limited to this number. The order of presentation has been random and is not in any order of importance, turnover or growth rates, etc.

So, the list in order of presentation is Alnatura, Crytek, juwi, United Internet, Xing, ISRA Vision, Kübler, tegut, ic-Haus, Kryolan, PERI and MorphoSys. All of them are worthy of being called innovative and are certainly stars that have emerged on the German industrial firmament.

Alnatura

Alnatura offers organic food and natural products produced by organic farming. They mainly sell through their own organic supermarket outlets spread across Germany. The company was established in 1984 in Fulda, a city in the state of Hessen, by Götz Rehn, who is the present CEO and director of the company. Alnatura has its present headquarters in Bickenbach, Hessen. For fiscal year 2011, they had revenues of €516 million. Their corporate slogan is 'Meaningful for People and the Earth'.

Their first store opened in Mannheim, and it was the first organic supermarket in Germany. To date, they have around 72 organic supermarket outlets in 39 cities of Germany, with new ones opening at regular intervals. Alnatura has around 1,800 employees. They also sell their products through other retail chains like DM, tegut, Budni, AEZ, Hit, Globus and Cactus, accounting for a total of 3,325 other outlets in a total of 12 countries.

Alnatura has around 1,000 organic food products in its Alnatura brand and more than 5,000 other branded products from A to Z which increase daily. They include dairy products, juices, baby and instant food, cereals, breads, other cereal products, sweet and savoury snacks, spreads, pasta, in-between meals/snacks, frozen food, etc. In addition to organic fruits and vegetables from the region, they also have natural cosmetics and children's textiles made from organic cotton. They distribute these products through regional distributors and local organic farmers and bakers.

Alnatura has more than 100 manufacturing partners from whom they source their products. Alnatura, the brand, stands for 100 per cent organic with strict quality standards. Most of the products carry the seal of a recognised association such as 'Bioland', 'Demeter' and 'NaturLand'.

At Alnatura, all their products are produced according to the EU regulation for organic farming and processing. Their products contain no artificial preservatives, colourings, sweeteners or flavourings. Furthermore, independent scientific experts regularly test their products for a variety of parameters.

Over the years, they have won several awards including the first prize for 'Sustainable SME' of 2004 awarded by the Ethik Bank, the 'Entrepreneur of the Year' (Germany) for 2005 awarded by Ernst & Young, several design awards, including the iF packaging award and the red dot design award for Alnatura Origin 2010 as well as nominations for the 'German Sustainability Award' for 2009, 2010 and 2011. (www.alnatura.de)

Crytek

Crytek Gmbh is an independent company at the forefront of the interactive entertainment industry. Its headquarters are in Frankfurt am Main, with additional studios in Kiev (Ukraine), Budapest (Hungary), Seoul (South Korea), Shanghai (China) and Nottingham (United Kingdom).

The company was founded in September 1999 in Coburg by Avni, Cevat and Faruk Yerli, three brothers of Turkish origin, who are the present managing directors of the company. Crytek relocated to Frankfurt in 2006 and employs over 700 people across its studios.

Crytek's corporate vision is 'Envision, Enable, Achieve'. Since its establishment, Crytek has built and maintained successful collaborations with world leading technology, development, tool and publishing partners with whom they collaborate on a daily basis.

Crytek is dedicated to creating exceptionally high-quality video games for the PC and next-generation consoles, powered by its cutting-edge 3D game technology CryENGINE®. The engine was awarded the 'Best Simulation in Real Time' at the IMAGINA Awards 2010, as well as the 'Most Innovative Technology' at the European Innovative Games Awards. It is not only used throughout the gaming industry, but also for several serious applications in fields such as architecture, training and simulation to learning and development. Some of the developers who use Crytek's CryENGINE® include NCSoft, Deutsche Telekom, Sohu Chang You Gaming, XL Games and Norman Foster Design.

In October 2009, Crytek launched the third version of CryENGINE® – the first game development platform for Xbox 360, Play Station® 3, MMO, and DX9/DX10/DX11 – that is truly next-gen ready. Development of the latest instalment of the multi-award winning FPS *Crysis* Series, *Crysis 3*, started in 2011.

In 2010, Crytek announced its first online free-to-play FPS *Warface*. The game is a military shooter in a near future setting and its high-quality design, constantly updated multiplayer universe and new business model mark a major milestone in the studio's history.

To further support the company's future within the free-to-play gaming model, Crytek launched an affiliate company, GFACE GmbH: a social gaming hub which serves as a platform for upcoming Crytek and third-party games. Next to its social media features, GFACE is designed to enable its users to play games together and live-share entertainment content with friends. Amongst other titles, ranging from core to casual games, *Warface* will be the first major release on GFACE.

Over the years, they have been awarded with a collection of awards for their excellent performance in several areas from 'Best Business Plan' and 'Industry Excellence Award' to the red dot design award. Critically acclaimed PC titles are Far Cry®, Crysis® (awarded 'Best PC Game' at E3 2007 and 'Best Technology' at the 2008 Game Developers Choice Awards), whilst Crysis Warhead® was awarded the 'Best Graphics Technology' at the IGN Best of 2008 awards. Crysis also won the Ernst & Young, 'International Video Game of the Year' Award in 2008. In the same year,, Crytek won the 'Develop Award for Best Independent Studio'. Among Crytek's most recent awards are six European Games Awards, including 'Best European Developer' and 'Best Action Game: Crysis 2' in 2011, in addition to the prestigious 'Deutscher Computerspielpreis' Award in 2012 for Crysis 2 (Best German Game). (www.crytek.com)

juwi

The juwi Group contributes to a power supply generated entirely from renewable sources of energy with the most modern wind turbines and photovoltaic plants, sustainable bio-energy projects and innovative technologies that increase efficiency.

The company was founded in 1996 by Matthias Willenbacher and Fred Jung. Together, they developed juwi from a two-man office to a company acting worldwide with more than 1,800 employees and a sales volume of around €1 billion. Their corporate slogan is 'Energy is here'.

Today, they construct solar, wind and bio-energy plants as well as hydro-power and geo-thermal plants. juwi has its headquarters in the town of Wörrstadt in the state of Rhineland-Palatinate. Their head office building is the world's most energy-efficient office building, for which they have received several awards as well. They have other locations in Germany, Italy, France, the US, Costa Rica, the Czech Republic, Poland, South Africa, the UK, India, Spain and Greece among others.

The juwi CEOs include Jochen Magerfleisch, Martin Winter and the founders Matthias Willenbacher and Fred Jung.

juwi not only plans and builds wind, solar, bio and geo-thermal plants, in cooperation with utilities organisations and municipalities, juwi Renewable IPP & Co. KG also operates several projects as joint ventures. The group involves all parties concerned to successfully complete its renewable energy projects. They cover the complete process chain of site selection, planning, financing, construction and operational management.

juwi's R&D department also takes part in the technical development of their products. They research new business segments, like the energy mix for a 100 per cent clean energy supply, geothermal energy and develop concepts such as E-mobility, reliable memory technologies and traffic models as well as green building and operational management.

The group has also contributed to the construction of solar power plants for social projects in Peru, Rwanda and India.

Over the years, the juwi Group has won several awards for its performance including the 'Greentech Manager Award' for 2009; 'Entrepreneur of the Year 2009' (Germany) in the 'Services' category, awarded by the auditing and consulting company, 'Ernst & Young'; the 'European Solar Award for 2007' and the 'Climate Protection Prize 2008'. They recently won the Golden Cozero Label for 2011 and the Axia Award in 2012. (www.juwi.com)

United Internet

United Internet AG is the leading European Internet services provider. They have around 11.53 million fee-based customer contracts and about 30.6 million ad-financed accounts. Ralph Dommermuth laid the foundation for today's company with the formation in 1988 of 1&1 Marketing GmbH in the town of Montabaur in the state of Rhineland-Palatinate. They originally offered systematised marketing services for smaller software companies. In 1998, they went public.

Today, the company employs around 6,110 employees and had a consolidated sales turnover of around €2.396 billion for fiscal year 2012. The founder, Ralph Dommermuth, is the CEO of the company, while Kurt Dobitsch is the Chairman of the Supervisory Board.

United Internet stands for outstanding operational excellence, with over 42 million customer accounts in 10 nations at five data centres with around 70,000 servers in Europe and the US. They have two business segments or divisions: Access – offering DSL and mobile Internet services as well as related applications for private and commercial customers.

Their applications segment targets small to mid-size companies, freelancers and private users with applications such as personal information management, web hosting, online marketing and cloud applications.

Their brands 1&1, GMX and Web.de represent United Internet's Access business. In the Applications segment, they are represented by; United Domains, Fast hosts, InterNetX, Sedo and Affilinet in addition to the other three.

Each of their brands stands for added value, enabling them to target all relevant user groups in their Access and Applications segments and to exploit existing market potential to the full. Today, they are among the largest web hosts worldwide and a leading domain registrant.

United Internet is among the leading companies in each of their current target markets of Germany, France, the UK, Spain, Austria, Poland, Switzerland and the US. In 2011, they expanded into Canada and in 2012 into Italy.

Together with UNICEF, the United Internet Foundation supports several UNICEF projects worldwide. (www.united-internet.de)

Xing

Xing AG is a social media platform where business professionals from different industries can connect, find jobs, colleagues, new assignments, cooperation partners, experts and generate business ideas. Similar to Linked In, it is very popular in the German speaking (DACH) countries and is the leading online business network for this region.

The company was founded in Hamburg in 2003 by Lars Hinrichs with the aim of providing a platform in 16 languages that enables millions of its members from various industries all over the world to network and forge contacts. As of September 2012, they had more than 12 million members worldwide, with more than 6 million in German-speaking countries alone. They also have over 50,000 specialist groups with scores of networking events. Apart from Basic free membership, they also have Premium, Sales and Recruiter membership, Partner Programs, Developers and even Xing Beta Labs. They have also expanded into e-recruiting, advertising and events markets where they have successfully established their business model.

The platform is operated by Xing AG which has been publicly listed since 2006 and was listed on the TecDAX since September 2011. In December 2010, Xing acquired 'Amiando AG', a Munich-based company and Europe's leading provider of online event management and ticketing. At the start of 2013, XING acquired 'kununu', the leading employer review platform in German-speaking countries, to reinforce its position as a social recruiting market leader. They have also expanded into the Spanish and Turkish markets with a couple of purchases of social networks there. For fiscal year 2012, they had total revenues of around €73.2 million.

Thomas Vollmoeller is the present CEO of the company, while Stefan Winners is the Chairman of the Supervisory Board. They have their headquarters in Hamburg and currently employ around 520 people from 28 different countries (December 2012). Their corporate slogan is; 'Xing – The Professional Network'. (www.xing.com)

ISRA Vision

ISRA Vision AG stands for intelligent systems robotics and automation. Their innovative core competencies lie in the development of user-specific software for sophisticated, intelligent machine systems, firmware and hardware. ISRA Vision was founded in 1985 at the Technical University in the city of Darmstadt in Germany, by Enis Ersü and other experts in robotics and image processing. Their objective was to transform scientific concepts into affordable high-tech solutions.

Today, their technological advances make them an industry leader in their respective business segments. ISRA has 25 locations worldwide, with subsidiaries in France, the US and various other international joint ventures strategically located near important production facilities of the automotive industry.

For fiscal year 2010, they had total operating revenues of €84.7 million, while employing around 438 people worldwide. The founder, Enis Ersü, is the CEO of the company, while Heribert J. Wiedenhues is the Chairman of the Supervisory Board. Their corporate slogan is 'The more you see'. ISRA's product range includes various products for robot vision, surface vision, quality inspection and in-line gauging.

BRAINWARE® is their registered brand. They, have a complete spectrum of robot vision systems that is unique throughout the world and covers all possibilities from 2D to 6D. Their fully-automated surface vision systems are designed for high-speed, in-line inspection of various complex surfaces.

Quality vision for quality control offers customer configurable solutions and vision modules that range from high-resolution, colour-line scan cameras, to PCI and PMC image processing boards and out-of-the-box software modules. These products are used by various industries, from automotive, glass, solar and photovoltaic, print, film and foils to plastics, logistics, metal, non-wovens, paper, packaging and mechanical engineering.

They enhance proven and reliable machine design and process cycles using innovative industrial image processing. This enables their customers to be more competitive and better prepared for the future. ISRA Vision AG (ISIN: DE 0005488100) is one of the global providers for industrial image processing (machine vision), a world market leader for surface inspection systems and one of the leading providers for 3D machine vision solutions.

In 2010, ISRA vision received two important awards, the first, for being a leading innovative company, the 'TOP 100' in German industry, the other, the 'MM Award' at Automatica 2010 for their Mono 3D product. They were also an Ernst & Young (Germany) finalist in 2005. In 2012, they won the Inter Solar Award for their innovative Luminescence Inspection Systems product line, the Hesse-Champions 2012 Award in the Innovation category and the Deloitte Technology Fast 50 Sustained Excellence Award. (www.isravision.com)

Kübler

The Kübler Group belongs to the leading specialists worldwide in the fields of position and motion sensors, counting and process technology as well as transmission technology. Founded in 1960 by Fritz Kübler in his hometown of Schwenningen in the state of Baden-Württemberg, the family business is now led by the next generation of the family, his sons Gebhard and Lothar Kübler. The proof of their strong international focus lies in the fact that exports currently account for over 60 per cent of turnover, with eight international group members and distributors in more than 50 countries. Their corporate slogan is '... Pulses for automation'.

Kübler has grown with vigour over the past 10 years and now boasts a turnover in excess of €45 million (2011), with many major global customers. Customer focus, flexibility as well as know-how, which have been built up over the decades, all form the basis for their broad and innovative range of products. These include individually tailored product and sector solutions, as well as solutions for functional safety. They operate with short reaction times, the overriding desire to inspire customers and a very high level of service, form additional pillars of the Kübler Group. The strict focus on quality, likewise aligned to sector requirements, ensures outstanding reliability and a long service life for all their products in the field. An additional success factor is the Kaizen culture that focuses on continual improvement.

Over 380 dedicated people worldwide, of whom 290 are in Germany, make this success possible. They ensure that customers can place their trust in their company. The Kübler Group has a clear, long-term strategy to continue as an independent, owner-managed family business. In 2010, Kübler completed 50 years of successful existence. The company won the 'Company of the Month' for their region and were an Ernst & Young finalist in 2005. (www.kuebler.com)

tegut

tegut is a supermarket chain based in the city of Fulda in the state of Hessen. The company was founded in 1947 by Theo Gutberlet, who named it Thegu, based on the first two letters of his first and surname. In 1955, it became Tegut and finally in 1998, it became the stylised tegut. Since 1982, they have been involved in the cultivation and marketing of organic food.

For fiscal year 2011, they had 312 outlets/stores that generated a turnover of €1.164 billion. The family-owned enterprise employs over 6,353 people and is managed by the late founder's grandson Thomas Gutberlet, who is the present CEO and Chairman of the Board. Their corporate slogan is 'tegut ... Good food'.

Apart from the unique range of fresh produce, they have a large selection of all that is expected in a good food market: branded goods, delicatessen, fresh fish, frozen food, magazines and personal hygiene items. They also offer a wide selection of regional specialities, such as 'Cream Cheese Hessian', local wines, breads, etc. As an organic pioneer in the classic German food retail trade, they offer over 3,000 products in their organic range. These are sourced from their own as well other producers such as Alnatura, Naturata, PuraNatura and Rhöngut.

Whether, organic meat or monastery liqueurs, beers, juices or mineral water, cheeses or fresh poultry, tegut believes in sourcing the best from the immediate region for the respective tegut stores. They have over 150 partners from the various product areas. Stringent quality assurance systems along the complete value chain, from the farms to its final display on their shelves ensures the purity pledge of tegut.

Currently there are over 785 of tegut's own branded products in many areas. They also have a premium brand range with the finest quality chocolate, premium fruit spreads and excellent cereals.

Their stores are mainly located in the states of Hessen, Thuringia, Bayern, Rhineland-Palatinate and Lower Saxony.

Over the years, tegut has won several prestigious awards for various categories – from 'Best Employer' to 'German Sustainability Award 2008' to 'Entrepreneur of the Year' for 2007 (Germany), awarded by Ernst & Young. Wolfgang Gutberlet, the late founder's son, has been inducted into the 'Hall of Fame' for being one of the world's best entrepreneurs. tegut was also one of the winners of the 'Deloitte Axia Award' for 2010, given to successful mid-size companies in the Rhine-Main region. (www.tegut.com)

iC-Haus

iC-Haus is a cutting edge, innovative market leader that develops and manufactures application-specific standard products (ASSPs), application-specific integrated circuits (ASiCs) and is a leading specialist for monolithic mixed-signal circuits and microsystems. They supply industrial, medical and automotive companies with innovative, reliable and FMEA-approved integrated circuits and microsystems for various applications.

iC-Haus was founded in 1984 by Heiner Flocke and Manfred Herz, the present leadership of the company. Their wafer backend, chip-assembly and test facilities are located in Bodenheim near Frankfurt in the centre of Europe, while their subcontracted wafer foundries and assemblers are situated all over the world and assure reliable, second-sourced products and deliveries. Quality engineering has been established in international standards, such as ISO9001.

The product groups include Driver ICs, Laser Diode and LED Drivers, I/O ICs, Power Management ICs, Sensor ICs, Linear Functions, Safety Light Curtain ICs, Encoder ICs, LEDs, tools and customer specific products.

Their range of technologies covers high voltage, linear bipolar, high density and analogue CMOS and power BCD processes. With optional opto-layers they have created OPTO-ASiCs, monolithic microsystems which have integrated sensors. Assembly is performed in standard plastic packages and for the OPTO and power ICs in the Chip-On-Board/Flex and Flip-Chip technique. The chip layout and circuit topology is tailored to customer's individual requirements, resulting in exclusive ASiCs from iC-Haus.

In 2012, iC-Haus was awarded with the Ernst & Young 'Entrepreneur of the Year' prize for Germany. They were also the winner of the AMA Innovation Award 2012 for their Energy Harvesting Encoder Chip. The same year also saw the opening of their new iC-Haus, a large, modern production and logistics facility in Bodenheim. (www.ichaus.de)

Kryolan

Kryolan Professional Make-up is a specialised manufacturer of professional make-up, serving theatre, film and television around the globe. They are also engaged in establishing their products more towards the beauty sector. The company was founded in 1945, in the French sector of the Berlin district of Reinickendorf. The present headquarters moved to Papierstrasse in Berlin in 1971.

Today, Kryolan professional make-up delivers to customers in more than 80 countries and is an acknowledged trademark for professional make-up artists. The brand Kryolan and its other trademarks stand for professional quality, exceptional diversity, flexibility and tradition. They employ over 240 employees in Berlin and Zehlendorf in Germany, as well as at their international sites in Great Britain, Poland, the US, India and South Africa. Kryolan GmbH is managed by founder and Managing Director, Arnold Langer, as well as his son Wolfram Langer.

A range of more than 16,000 items in 750 shades covers every need any professional make-up artist may have, including foundation, make-up setting, eye make-up, eyebrows and cosmetic pencils, eyelashes, blushers, lip make-up and revitalizing products, for air brushing, special effects, make-up removal and accessories like brushes, sponges, cases, sets and bags as well as books and CDs about body painting, make-up, etc. Other product lines in the portfolio of Kryolan are Dermacolor, Dermacolor light, High Definition, Private Care, Aqua Color and Supra color. Kryolan is the global brand for professional make-up.

At the company's headquarters in Berlin, qualified chemists continuously work on developing new products, looking for innovative raw materials with special skin-care properties. Kryolan has placed prime importance on assuring excellent skin compatibility from the dermatological and allergologic aspects for each and every one of its products, guaranteeing, their high quality and purity.

Some of their innovative new products are Make-up Blend, Eye Shadow Primer, HD Micro Primer, Faceliner, Eyebrow Stencils that are reusable, HD Micro-Foam Cleanser, Eye Shadow Palette with 18 colours, a Cream Liner that does not drip and is water-resistant, Living Colors, Proliner, Shimmering Vision and HD Micro Foundation Sheer Tan. (www.kryolan.com)

PERI

PERI, a global market leader in formwork and scaffolding for the construction industry, was founded in 1969 by Artur Schwörer in the town of Weissenhorn in the state of Bavaria. The company's name is taken from the Greek word 'peri' which in English means around.

PERI a family-managed company has been a competent partner to building and construction firms worldwide across the whole range of formwork and scaffolding technology, providing innovative products and cost-effective, customised solutions.

PERI with a turnover of €976 million in 2011 is one of the largest manufacturers and suppliers of formwork and scaffolding systems in the world. PERI has around 6,000 employees, 51 subsidiaries and 110 efficient storage sites worldwide. They serve their customers in more than 95 countries with innovative system equipment and a broad range of services related to formwork and scaffolding. The present managing directors are

Alexander Schwörer, Christian Schwörer and Ekkehard Gericke. Their main production plant is at their headquarters in Weissenhorn.

The PERI product portfolio consists of formwork products like girders, wall/column/slab/monolithic housing and bridge and tunnel formworks apart from climbing systems. In scaffolding, their products include working scaffolds for construction/facades and industrial uses. They have shoring and access products as well as protection scaffolds. They also provide other accessories and project-related services, especially excellent engineering solutions for project-related economic solutions. Other services are formwork assembly, project management support, repair of material and worldwide located rental parks.

In a relatively short span of 40 years they have undertaken some of the most prestigious construction/building projects in the world. Among some of the prestigious projects they are working on at present are the expansion of the Panama Canal, the Lekki-Ikoyi Bridge in Lagos, Nigeria, the Donau City Tower 1 in Vienna, Austria, plus scores of other housing developments, skyscrapers, sport stadiums, tunnels, industrial structures, water-retaining structures, power stations and multi-storey building projects.

They have an online portal called 'my Peri' through which customer-specific project data and comprehensive product information for the PERI construction site can be accessed at any time, providing additional value for the execution of construction work.

PERI was involved as a sponsor in the first International 5D Conference that took place in Constance in May 2012, as PERI considers 5D simulations to be an innovative, optimisation of construction planning and views the technology as one that provides a significant opportunity to plan and control all processes from the initial idea to the operation of buildings. (www.peri.com)

Morphosys

MorphoSys AG is located in Martinsried/Munich and is one of the world's leading biotechnology companies focussing on fully human antibodies, which are used to treat diseases such as cancer, arthritis and Alzheimer's to name a few and for research and diagnostic purposes.

The company was founded in 1992 in Martinsried near Munich by Simon E. Moroney, the present CEO of the company and Andreas Plückthun. In 1999, MorphoSys became a public limited company by floating an IPO on the German Stock Exchange and generated around €25 million. Gerald Möller is the present Chairman of the Supervisory Board.

Today, MorphoSys is a leading bio-tech company that uses its unique HuCAL technology to develop antibodies for human health care applications. They work in collaboration with renowned partners from the pharmaceutical industry such as Novartis, Pfizer, Roche, Daiichi, Sankyo, Boehringer Ingelheim, Merck & Co., and several more to develop therapeutic antibodies for more effective, safer medicines and better diagnostics. MorphoSys is one of the leading providers in Europe in the field of research antibodies and one of the top 20 worldwide.

The company is represented around the world with branches in Germany, the UK and the US. It is listed on the Prime Standard at the Deutsche Börse in Frankfurt and also in the technology index TecDAX. For fiscal year 2011, they generated revenues of €100.8

million, employing around 500 people worldwide. Their corporate slogan is 'Engineering the Medicines of Tomorrow'.

The business segments or divisions of MorphoSys AG are Partnered Discovery, Proprietary Development and Abd Serotec.

Their HuCAL technology (the human combinatorial antibody library) is comprised of several billion, different, fully-human antibodies. It is a very powerful technology which allows rapid and automated production of high-affinity antibodies. The most important feature of the library is its capability of optimizing, fully-human antibodies to meet pre-defined specifications.

MorphoSys has a partnered product pipeline comprising of over 70 antibody programs covering a range of indications and is being built with several successful partnerships. They have also developed proprietary therapeutic candidates in the areas of inflammation and oncology. These are currently in the pipeline undergoing clinical-stage programs.

The research and diagnostics segment of MorphoSys operates under the brand name AbD Serotec. They have a comprehensive catalogue comprising more than 15,000 immediately available products which are sold to life science researchers worldwide.

Over the years, MorphoSys has received several awards, some of the latest being, the 'Capital Investor Relations Award 2010' for the best company in the TecDAX index. This award is supported by Deloitte and rated by the business magazine Capital and the German Association of Financial & Asset Management. In 2009, MorphoSys was recognised as a 'Technology Pioneer' by the World Economic Forum. While in 2006, the company received Deloitte's 'Sustained Excellence Award' and the STEP Award for being an innovative growth company in the area of biotechnology. (www.morphosys.com)

Afterword

To briefly recapitulate what has been stated earlier in relation to nation branding, the nation as a brand consists of several unique, multi-dimensional elements, a collection of various sub-sets of economic, social, historical and cultural aspects that form a complex characteristic of a nation's identity, which together with the current state of its people and events, its products and services, form an image of a nation, a perception of a people.

I set forth to state that the 'Made-in-Germany' image of quality, reliability and innovativeness is a result of various factors that have combined together to produce world-class goods and services, to earn a well-deserved reputation.

The success of these German companies is assisted by what has been called the nation-brand-effect (NBE), which in turn is sustained and reinforced by those very same quality products and services to create a positively reinforced cycle.

To this discussion I have included the important aspect of the facilitators and influencers, the elements or factors that facilitate and influence the process of producing quality goods and services, which in turn enhances the nation's image.

The facilitators and influencers to the 'Made in Germany' label consist of the important governmental, trade, industry and testing institutions, the research organisations, the trade unions, the trade fairs and exhibitions. Then we have the other socio-cultural elements of literature, the arts, music, design, architecture, sports and sporting events, food and drink, festivals, current events, etc. As these elements come together, they contribute to, influence and enhance in their own unique, synergistic way the totality of a nation in terms of the image and perception it carries in the relevant audiences of the world and the quality and quantity of its output as illustrated here by the 'Champion Brands' from the 'Superstars' and 'Stars' to the 'Less-Known Champions' and to the 'Innovative and Emergent Stars'.

So, what helps make these 'Champion Brands' that are 'Made in Germany'? There are many factors that contribute, from the governmental policy of having a 'Social Market Economy', to coordinated market economy that has withstood decades of trying times, especially after the Second World War, to the will and ingenuity of its people.

All beginnings were modest, even for the large, successful global brands, the 'Superstars' and the 'Stars' of the German industrial landscape. It all starts with an entrepreneur or a technical entrepreneur who introduces an innovative product or service.

They begin in their hometown or in the immediate environs, building on their locally available strengths. Most of them start from self-financed sources and are characterised by low levels of debt financing. These pioneering entrepreneurs are motivated to build something that will be a proud legacy for their communities, children and grandchildren, believing in the long-term success of their enterprises and not by short-term gains.

For a lot of these entrepreneurs, even after they succeed, they live within modest means, without splurging on the unnecessary trappings of wealth. They know the virtues of thrift and financial prudence, without foregoing research and growth initiatives, in believing in the long-term and of delivering on quality and reliability.

The 'Mittelstand' or 'hidden' or 'less-known' champions, especially, follow the niche strategy, specializing in products and services that are innovative and that have very few competitors, as sort of oligopolies in the markets in which they operate. Niches and super-niches that attract few rivals, they constantly innovate with product, service and customised offerings that are difficult to match.

Then there are the various research institutions and organisations that help them in this research-based innovation. These successful niche players also help develop specialised industry clusters all over the country. Built by strong internal competition, they nevertheless operate in a spirit of trust and co-ordination, and produce locally made products for a global market. These stalwarts of the German economy export most of their products, which has consequently made Germany into a top export nation. The lessons that can be learnt from them are that they constantly innovate, stay close to their customer, and maintain a lean organisation where their employees are highly motivated and where they maintain long years of leadership continuity. Government policies in Germany are framed with the trade and industry associations facilitating appropriate policies to encourage the development of these companies and their respective clusters.

While the constant, growing need for skilled workers is fed by the famed German Apprenticeship System or the Vocational Training System, these systems, besides imparting professional skills and a solid knowledge foundation in their respective skill sets, also serve to instil and carry forward the solid values of hard work, discipline, efficiency and common sense, making for a well-trained, efficient and motivated workforce.

Then we have the several hundred odd, specialised trade fairs and exhibitions that help market these quality products, maintain and strengthen existing customer networks, and test and introduce new products.

The successful cooperation of labour and capital in post-Germany has been another major reason for their resounding success, where the unions have helped maintain that level of fairness and discipline in their dealings. They now even have flexible work arrangements, like work-sharing, short-shifts, other flex-time programs, etc.

The entrepreneurs for their part have been equally fair in sharing their wealth and amenities, making for loyalty and ensuring life-long employment in these champion brands. Of course, the government's welfare policies have helped shore up in those areas that needed to be.

In fact, a look at the inequality adjusted or disaggregated Human Development Index (HDI) of the UN shows that Germany and several of the other northern member states of the European Union have very high values, due in large measure to the EU state's social-market policies or welfare measures. These measures make sure that none of their citizens fall into debt when they fall sick, that education is free or at a very nominal cost, that the crime rate is much lower and life expectancy higher than other countries. All of this is also helped by the income tax the wealthy pay in these countries, which is amongst the highest tax rates in the world.

Finally, what one can say is that although general and specific principles and lessons can be learnt and are transferrable from nation to nation, in the end, each nation needs to find its own competitive advantage or niche, given its particular situation, to enable innovative and creative policies so as to solve critical problems and optimally deliver on its potential and abilities.

Nations or countries involved in nation-branding exercises need to be aware of the sum of its present image, its holistic image and the various unique, differentiating elements of a nation's identity, its authentic, positive character, so as to make it ring true to target audiences worldwide.

References

Adorno, Theodor (trans. Rodney Livingstone). (2009), *In Search of Wagner*, London: Verso Books.

Anholt, Simon. (2008), 'Practitioner Insight in the book', *Nation Branding* by Keith Dinnie, Oxford, UK: Butterworth-Heinemann, p. 23.

Askegaard, Soren and Ger, Guliz. (1998), 'Product-Country-Images: Towards a Contextualized Approach', *European Advances in Consumer Research*, Volume 3, Provo, UT: Association for Consumer Research.

Bainton, Roland. (1995), *Here I Stand: A Life of Martin Luther*, New York: Penguin.

Barnett, Vincent. (2009), *Marx*, Abingdon, UK: Routledge.

Beck, Lewis White. (1969), *Early German Philosophy, Kant and his Predecessors*, Cambridge, MA: Harvard University Press.

Benjamin, Walter. (1983), *Understanding Brecht*, London: Verso.

Booth, Hannah, 'Nations should establish a brand, says Wolff Olins', *Design Week* (2003).

Boyd, Malcolm. (2001), *Bach*, New York: Oxford University Press.

Boyle, Nicholas. (2008), *German Literature*, New York: Oxford University Press.

Burrows, Donald. (1994), *Handel*, New York: Oxford University Press.

Cate, Curtis (2005), *Friedrich Nietzsche*, Woodstock, NY: The Overlook Press.

Conard, Robert C. (1992), *Understanding Heinrich Böll*, Columbia: University of South Carolina Press.

Dinnie, Keith. (2008), *Nation Branding: Concepts, Issues, Practice*, Oxford, UK: Butterworth-Heinemann.

Doyle, Peter. (1992), *The Marketing Book*, second edition (M.J. Baker ed.), Oxford, UK: Butterworth-Heinemann.

Fahlbusch, Erwin and Bromiley, Geoffrey William. (1998), *The Encyclopaedia of Christianity*, Eerdmans Pub. Co. and Brill.

Fletcher, Banister. (1948), *A History of Architecture on the Comparative Method*, London: B.T. Batsford Ltd.

Friedenthal, Richard. (2010) *Goethe: His Life and Times*. New Brunswick, NJ: Transaction Publishers.

Garland, Henry and Garland, Mary. (1997), *The Oxford Companion to German Literature*, New York: Oxford University Press.

Gene, Ray (ed.). (2001), *Joseph Beuys: Mapping the Legacy*, New York and Sarasota: D.A.P.

Glouchevitch, Philip. (1992), 'Juggernaut', *The German Way of Business: Why It Is transforming Europe and the World*, New York: Simon & Schuster.

Green, John. (2008), *Engels: A Revolutionary Life*, London: Artery Publications.

Han, C.M. (1989), 'Country Image: Halo or Summary Construct', *Journal of Marketing Research*. Volume XXVI, May 1989.

Harper, Douglas, *Online Etymology Dictionary* [www.etymonline.com].

Hartich, Edwin. (1980), *The Fourth and Richest Reich*, New York: Macmillan.

Henderson, David. R. (2008), 'The German Economic Miracle', *The Concise Encyclopaedia of Economics*, Indianapolis, IN: Liberty Fund Inc.

Honour, Hugh and Fleming, John. (1984), *A World History of Art*, London: Macmillan.

Inwood, Michael. (1983), *Hegel*, London: Routledge & Kegan Paul.

Jaworski, S.P and Fosher, D. (2003), 'National Brand Identity & Its Effect on Corporate Brands: The Nation Brand Effect (NBE)', *Multinational Business Review*, Volume 11, Number 2.

Joseph, Warner A. (1950), *The Thomas Mann Reader*, New York: Knopf.

Kennedy, Michael. (1999), *Richard Strauss: Man, Musician, Enigma*, Cambridge: Cambridge University Press.

Lockwood, Lewis. (2005), *Beethoven: The Music and the Life*, New York: W.W. Norton.

Lynch, J and de Chernatony, L. (2004), 'The power of emotion: Brand Communication in business-to-business markets', *Journal of Brand Management*, Volume 13, Number 6.

Macdonald, Malcolm. (2001), *Brahms*, New York: Oxford University Press.

Maldonado, Tomás. (1977), 'Styling', *Industrial Design Review*, Barcelona.

Max, Brod. (1995), *Franz Kafka: A Biography*, New York: Da Capo Press.

Metzger, Christine (ed.). (2008), *Culinaria Germany*, Cambridge, Ullmann.

Nees, Greg. (2000), *Germany: Unravelling an Enigma*, Boston: Inter-Cultural Press.

O'Shaughnessy, J. and Jackson, N. (2000), 'Treating the nation as a brand: Some Neglected Issues', *Journal of Macromarketing*, Volume 20, Number 1.

Papadopoulos, Nicolas. (1993), 'What Product-Country Images Are and Are Not', Nicolas Papadopoulos and Louise Heslop (eds.) *Product-Country-Images: Impact and Role in International Marketing*, New York: International Business Press.

Pevsner, Nikolaus, Fleming, John and Honour, Hugh. (2000), *A Dictionary of Architecture and Landscape Architecture* (5th ed.), London: Penguin Books.

Poeggeler, Otto. (1987), *Martin Heidegger's Path of Thinking*, Atlantic Highlands, NJ: Humanities Press.

Porter, Michael. (1990), *The Competitive Advantage of Nations*, London: Macmillan.

Ries, Al and Ries, Laura. (2003), *The 22 Immutable Laws of Branding*, London: Profile Books.

Simon, Herrmann. (1996), *Hidden Champions: Lessons from 500 of the World's Best Unknown Companies*, Boston: Harvard Business School Press.

Simon, Herrmann. (2009), *Hidden Champions of the 21st Century: Success Strategies of Unknown Market Leaders*, New York: Springer.

Tyndale, William. (1989), *Tyndale's New Testament*, New Haven: Yale University Press.

Wallich, Henry C. (1955), *MainSprings of the German Revival*, New Haven: Yale University Press.

Zipes, Jack. (1988), *The Brothers Grimm*, London: Routledge & Kegan Paul.

Zug, J.D. (1991), *German-American Life: Recipes and Traditions*, Iowa City: Penfield Press.

Websites

[All websites were accessed in 2010, 2011 and 2012 unless otherwise noted.]

www.adidas.com
www.aeg.com (Accessed in August 2010)
www.allianz.com
www.alnatura.de (Accessed in 2011 and 2012)
www.anuga.com (Accessed in 2010 and 2012)
www.arri.de
www.audi.com
www.auma.com (Accessed in 2010 and 2012)
www.aurubis.com
www.axelspringer.de (Accessed in 2012)

www.baader.com

www.barmer-gek.de

www.barthhaasgroup.com

www.basf.com

www.bauer.de

www.bayer.com

www.baywa.com

www.bbraun.com

www.bdi.eu

www.beiersdorf.com

www.berleburger.com

www.berlinale.de (Accessed in 2010)

www.berner-group.com

www.bertelsmann.com

www.bilfinger.com

www.biotest.de

www.bizerba.com

www.boehringer-ingelheim.com

www.boellhoff.de

www.bosch.com

www.braehler.com

www.brainlab.com

www.brita.net

www.brose.com

www.bmw.com

www.3bscientific.com

www.buchmesse.de (Accessed in 2010 and 2012)

www.bvmw.de (Accessed in 2010)

www.cebit.de (Accessed in 2010 and 2012)

www.claas.com

www.cloos.de

www.cometogermany.com (Accessed in August 2010)

www.commerzbank.de

www.conti-online.com

www.corporate.evonik.com

www.corporate.zeiss.com (Accessed in 2011 and 2012)

www.crytek.com (Accessed in 2011 and 2012)

www.dachser.com

www.db.com

www.deichmann.com

www.delo.de

www.designmuseum.org (Accessed in 2010)

www.deutschebahn.com

www.deutsche-boerse.com

www.deutschland.de (Accessed in July 2010)

www.dihk.de

www.din.de

www.douglas-holding.de

www.dp-dhl.com

www.draeger.com

www.drupa.com (Accessed in 2010 and 2012)

www.durr.com

www.dussmann.com

www.dw-world.de (Accessed in May 2010)

www.eberspaecher.com

www.ebmpapst.com (Accessed in October 2012)

www.edeka.de

www.elringklinger.de

www.enercon.de

www.eon.com

www.eos.info

www.ey.com (Accessed in 2011 and 2012)

www.faber-castell.de

www.festo.com

www.fielmann.de

www.flexi.de (Accessed in October 2012)

www.fraport.com

www.fraunhofer.de

www.fresenius.com

www.friedhelm-loh-group.com

www.frogdesign.com (Accessed in 2010)

www.fuchs-oil.de

www.gea.com

www.gelita.com (Accessed in 2010)

www.german-design-council.de (Accessed in 2010)

www.germany-tourism.co.uk (Accessed in 2010)

www.gerhard-schubert.com

www.germanfoods.org

www.gerresheimer.com

www.gfk.com

www.gildemeister.com

www.glasbau-hahn.com

www.goethe.de/kuelflm/enindex.htm (Accessed in 2010)

www.goettfert.com

www.grohe.com

www.group.hugoboss.com

www.groz-beckert.com

www.gtai.de

www.haniel.com

www.hannovermesse.de (Accessed in 2010 and 2012)

www.hardwarefair.com (Accessed in 2010 and 2012)

www.haribo.com

www.heidelberg.com

www.hella.com

www.helmholtz.de
www.henkel.com
www.heraeus.com
www.herrenknecht.com
www.herlitz.eu
www.hermle.de
www.hochtief.com
www.homag-group.com
www.ichaus.de (Accessed in 2011 and 2012)
www.ifa-berlin.de (Accessed in 2010 and 2012)
www.igmetall.de (Accessed in May 2010)
www.infineon.com
www.interbrand.com (Accessed in 2010 and 2011)
www.interpack.com (Accessed in 2010 and 2012)
www.isravision.com (Accessed in 2011 and 2012)
www.jungheinrich.com
www.juwi.com (Accessed 2011 and 2012)
www.karcher.com
www.karlmayer.com
www.karlstorz.com
www.kba.com
www.khs.com
www.klais.de
www.klsmartin.com
www.knauf.com
www.knorr-bremse.com
www.kolbus.de
www.k-online.de (Accessed in 2010 and 2012)
www.k-plus-s.com
www.krones.com
www.kryolan.com (Accessed in 2011 and 2012)
www.ksb.com
www.kuebler.com (Accessed in 2011 and 2012)
www.kuka-ag.de
www.lanxess.com
www.lenze.com
www.leoni.com
www.linde.com
www.louisrenner.com
www.lufthansa.com
www.mahle.com
www.man.eu
www.merck.de
www.mercedes-benz.com / www.daimler.com
www.metrogroup.de
www.miele.com
www.morphosys.com (Accessed in 2011 and 2012)

www.mpg.de

www.mtu.de

www.m-w.de

www.muellergroup.com

www.netzsch.com

www.nivea.com

www.nobelprize.org, Herman Hesse's autobiography,

www.ottobock.com

www.otto-fuchs.com

www.ottogroup.com

www.paperworld.messefrankfurt.com (Accessed in 2010 and 2012)

www.peri.com (Accessed in 2011 and 2012)

www.porsche.com

www.pressreference.com/FaGu/Germany.html

www.probat.com

www.puma.com

www.research-in-germany.de

www.rewe-group.com

www.rolandberger.com (Accessed in September 2012)

www.roto.de

www.rud.com

www.rwe.com

www.sap.com

www.sartorius.com

www.schaefflergroup.com

www.scheuerle.com

www.sennheiser.com

www.siemens.com

www.simon-kucher.com (Accessed in September 2012)

www.stada.de

www.stihl.com

www.stabilo.com

www.sglgroup.com

www.sick.com

www.siempelkamp.com

www.soehnle.de

www.stabilus.com

www.staedtler.com

www.suedzucker.de

www.suspa.com

www.symrise.com

www.tatsachen-ueber-deutschland.de (Accessed in August 2010)

www.tatsachen-ueber-deutschland.de/en/culture-and-media

www.tegut.com (Accessed in 2011 and 2012)

www.telekom.com

www.tengelmann.de

www.tente.de

www.test.de

www.toyfair.com (Accessed in 2010 and 2012)

www.trumpf.com

www.tuev-sued.de

www.tui-group.com

www.tuv.com

www.united-internet.de (Accessed in 2011 and 2012)

www.verdi.de (Accessed in May 2010)

www.voith.com

www.volkswagen.com

www.vorwerk.com

www.vossloh.com

www.wacker.com

www.webasto.com

www.weckerle.com

www.wet-group.com (Accessed in 2011 and 2012)

www.wgl.de

www.wikipedia.org/wiki/Architecture_of_Germany (Accessed in 2010)

www.wikipedia.org/wiki/Christmas_market (Accessed in 2010)

www.wikipedia.org/wiki/Cinema_of_Germany (Accessed in 2010)

www.wikipedia.org/wiki/German_art (Accessed in August 2010)

www.wikipedia.org/wiki/German_Cuisine (Accessed in 2010)

www.wikipedia.org/wiki/German_economic_history (Accessed in July 2010)

www.wikipedia.org/wiki/German_literature (Accessed in 2010)

www.wikipedia.org/wiki/Music_of_Germany (Accessed in 2010)

www.wikipedia.org/wiki/Politics_of_Germany (Accessed in 2011)

www.wikipedia.org/wiki/Sport_in_Germany (Accessed in 2010)

www.wikipedia.org/wiki/ulm_school_of_Design/Bauhaus (Accessed in 2010)

www.wirtgen-group.de (Accessed in 2011 and 2012)

www.winterhalter.de (Accessed in 2011 and 2012)

www.wto.org (Accessed in May 2010)

www.wuerth.com

www.xing.com (Accessed in April 2012)

www.zahoransky.com (Accessed in 2011 and 2012)

www.zf.com

Index